The Unboxing of Henry Brown

By Jeffrey Ruggles

The Library of Virginia
Richmond • 2003

Library of Congress Control Number: 2003106271
Standard Book Number: 0-88490-200-5

Library of Virginia, Richmond, Virginia.
© 2003 by The Library of Virginia.
All rights reserved. First edition 2003.
Printed in the United States of America.

This book is printed on acid-free paper meeting requirements of the
American Standard for Permanence of Paper for Printed Library Materials.

Jacket illustration, **cover:** Henry Box Brown. Detail from *The Resurrection of Henry Box Brown at Philadelphia*. Peter Kramer, artist. **Back cover:** *The Resurrection of Henry Box Brown at Philadelphia*. Peter Kramer, artist. Lithograph by L. Rosenthal. Printed by Thomas Sinclair. Philadelphia, ca. 1851. Courtesy of the Library Company of Philadelphia.

Jacket design: Sara Daniels Bowersox, Graphic Designer, Library of Virginia.

The Unboxing of Henry Brown was designed by Sara Daniels Bowersox, graphic designer at the Library of Virginia. Page layout was produced by Sara Daniels Bowersox using Macintosh G4 and QuarkXpress 5.0. Text was composed in Century 731 and Franklin Gothic. Printed on acid-free, Glatfelter Natural, 55-lb. text, by Sheridan Books, Inc., Ann Arbor, Michigan.

Contents

List of Illustrations

List of Illustrations

List of Illustrations

Acknowledgments

This project began not as a book but as an inquiry, without any sense of the story as it eventually revealed itself. Over the period that the work proceeded, I operated a small restaurant called Main Street Grill in Richmond, Virginia. There the themes of the book were contemplated between orders, and patrons represented prospective readers.

At publication I am appreciative of the assistance received from many quarters, not all recognized here. Richard Blackett was generous with his findings. The staff at numerous institutions assisted my research, notably the archivists and librarians at: the American Antiquarian Society, Boston Atheneum, Boston Public Library, British Library, British Newspaper Library at Colindale, Cornell University Library, Library Company of Philadelphia, Library of Congress, Massachusetts Historical Society, New York Public Library, Bodleian Library of Commonwealth and African Studies at Rhodes House at Oxford University, Historical Society of Pennsylvania, Richmond Public Library, Alderman Library at the University of Virginia, Valentine Richmond History Center, Virginia Historical Society, Cabell Library at Virginia Commonwealth University, and Westminster Libraries and Archives in London.

Home base for the first years of the project was the Virginia State Library and Archives, a short walk up the hill from the restaurant, and it remained so when the library moved to a new building and gained a new name as the Library of Virginia. Thus it is fitting that the Library is the publisher. John Kneebone, the editor, has been the project's chief benefactor, providing facts and improving presentation. From early to end Gregg Kimball has been an advocate. Emily Salmon copyedited, fact-checked, and proofread the entire work, and Stacy Moore and Barbara Batson acquired images and assisted with editing and production. Sara Bowersox designed the book while Amy Winegardner assisted with design and supervised production and printing. All at the Library have respected my preferences; the responsibility for mistakes or misinterpretations are mine.

In long hearing of this book friends and family have been most tolerant. It is gratifying that their curiosity to see it is apparently not feigned.

JEFFREY RUGGLES
RICHMOND, VIRGINIA

Introduction

Touch this head with immortality

On the evening of 31 May 1849, Boston's Faneuil Hall was filled for the final session of the New England Anti-Slavery Convention. The people gathered to hear abolitionist oratory. The Reverend Samuel J. May was first on the platform and praised the fugitive slaves who had appeared throughout the previous days of the convention, calling them "living epistles from the South." Their escapes, he emphasized, were made "not only at the risk of a still more cruel bondage, but at the risk of their lives." He told the story of a slave shipped in a box from Virginia to Philadelphia: "never" will it "be forgotten," predicted May, that to gain his liberty the man "consented to a living entombment."[1]

That night Wendell Phillips rose last before the hall. In an era that appreciated public speaking for its arts, Phillips was one of the great orators. He, too, addressed the subject of fugitive slaves. "It is the slave, the fugitive slave from the plantation, whose tongue, inspired by oppression, speaks most forcibly to the American people," Phillips declared. "I want you to look at one man, at least. Here is a man, who has come into Boston, into Massachusetts, a fugitive."

At these words, onstage came the fugitive who had escaped in a box: a man about thirty-four years old, of average height but big, with dark skin. He was greeted with "hearty applause." Phillips continued:

> I ask you, lovers of freedom, who, in the year 1849, is the nearer child of Hancock and Adams, in venturing every thing for liberty, this man or ourselves? O, when history goes up and down this generation hereafter, to touch this and the other head with the torch of immortality, do you think our names will be remembered—we, who may have passed our lives reputably, decently, and at ease? No; when we shall rot in the common sod, the romance, the deep and thrilling interest of the coming generation, will linger about those who, alone against a whole people, have dared every thing for liberty.

Wendell Phillips and Samuel J. May were correct in their rhetorical prophecy. Henry Box Brown's escape has become a famous incident in the struggle against slavery. Pictures of his arrival in a box have been reproduced often enough to stand as an icon of abolitionism. The image of a fugitive who "dared everything for liberty" is a powerful symbol, then and now, of the resistance to the slave system by those who suffered under it. Yet it is not simply for this best-known event of Brown's life that he is worthy of remembrance. Not all fugitive slaves were comfortable in the public eye. Brown was, and he had the talent and drive to make his own way. This book is about Brown's unboxing in Philadelphia—his escape to freedom—and about how, once liberated, he seized opportunity and made much of it: the unboxing of Henry Brown.

The Unboxing of Henry Brown

The Hermitage. The main dwelling of the Louisa County, Virginia, estate was photographed for a WPA building survey in the mid-1930s.

Chapter One

Virginia

"You must be an honest boy"

Henry Brown was born about 1815. "In the midst of a country whose most honoured writings declare that all men have a right to liberty," he said in his 1851 *Narrative,* "I entered the world a slave." His birthplace and childhood home was a plantation called the Hermitage, in Louisa County, east of the Blue Ridge Mountains in the Virginia Piedmont. Located near the south fork of the Little River, the Hermitage was about two miles off the Louisa Road, ten miles away from Yanceyville, the closest settlement, and forty-five miles from Richmond.[1]

Every indication is that Henry Brown was of purely African descent. He was one of the middle children in a family that included his mother and father; sisters Jane, Martha, Mary, and Robinnet; and brothers Edward, John, and Lewis. Living at the Hermitage in 1820 were forty slaves, one free black man, and six whites. Twenty-two of the slaves were children under the age of fourteen.[2]

As a boy, Henry Brown worked in the master's household, "at intervals taking lessons in . . . the cultivation of the plantation." The Hermitage was one of the larger estates in Louisa County and mostly self-sufficient. An English traveler described Louisa farms in 1839 as producing "cotton, corn, and tobacco, in small patches of each, all growing within the limits of a few acres." Tobacco was the county's cash crop. Some tobacco was likely planted at the Hermitage, as the master had been in that business in Richmond. Perhaps for the same reason, however, the farm was diversified. An 1832 list records cows, heifers, a bull, sows and pigs, "killing hogs," a herd of sheep, and three "yoke of steers." Wheat and corn were grown for flour and meal, and the animals fed on fodder, hay, and oats. Cotton raised at the Hermitage was probably spun and woven on the farm to make bedding and to clothe the slaves. The plantation had several horses, and there were undoubtedly chickens, the master's dogs, a vegetable garden for the master's table, and possibly an orchard and grape arbor.[3]

No description exists of the dwelling where Henry Brown lived with his family. It may have resembled the Virginia type sketched by novelist John Pendleton Kennedy in 1830 as "nothing more than plain log-cabins . . . twelve feet square, and not above seven in height." The spaces between the logs were caulked with clay, and "a door swung upon wooden hinges, and a small window of two narrow panes of glass were, in general, the only openings in the front. . . . There were little garden-patches attached to each, where cymblings, cucumbers, sweet potatoes, water-melons and cabbages flourished." The slaves tended their own gardens when time permitted.[4]

The master of the Hermitage and the owner of Henry Brown was John Barret. Born at the Hermitage in 1748, Barret served in the Revolutionary War and then settled in Richmond. There he succeeded in the tobacco trade, married, built a large frame house, and raised a family. Barret conducted business with the patriot Patrick Henry, among other gentlemen, and was elected mayor of Richmond for several terms in the 1790s. Barret moved his family back to Louisa and the Hermitage about 1800. Whether either of Henry Brown's parents had lived in Richmond with Barret is not known. They might always have been attached to the plantation, which the Barret family had owned since about 1730, or one might have moved from the city with Barret and met the other at the Hermitage.[5]

"Our master was uncommonly kind, (for even a slaveholder may be kind)," Brown stated in the 1851 *Narrative*, "and as he moved about in his dignity he seemed like a god to us." The plantation was well stocked, and the slaves at the Hermitage seem to have fared better than slaves at other places. Nonetheless, Brown's mother impressed on him the insecurity of his situation. As related in Brown's 1849 *Narrative*, she took him to her knee one day in autumn and, pointing to the woods, told him, "my son, as yonder leaves are stripped off the trees of the forest, so are the children of slaves swept away from them by the hands of cruel tyrants." She wept and held him tightly. "I was young then," Brown said, "but I well recollect the sadness of her countenance, and the mournfulness of her words."[6]

His parents were church members, and his mother instructed him "not to steal, not to tell lies, and to behave myself in a becoming manner towards everybody." From the master came lessons in Christianity that emphasized the correctness of the master-slave relationship. In the remote setting of the plantation there was little to mitigate a child's impressions. Brown stated in the 1849 *Narrative* that when

John Barret, ca. 1775

he was very young, he believed John Barret was God, and Barret's son was Jesus Christ. He explained that "when it was about to thunder, my old master would approach us, if we were in the yard, and say, 'All you children run into the house now, for it is going to thunder,' and after the shower was over, we would go out again, and he would approach us smilingly, and say, 'What a fine shower we have had,' and bidding us look at the flowers in the garden, would say, 'how pretty the flowers look now.' We thought that *he* thundered, and caused the rain to fall."[7]

Brown learned better when he was eight. He overheard his mother and father talking about a woman who, wishing to join their church, was "asked by the minister if she believed 'that our Saviour came into the world, and had died for the sins of man.'" The woman replied that she "had not heard that he was dead, as she lived so far from the road, she did not learn much that was going on in the world." Brown asked his mother if "young master" had died. "She said it was not him they were talking about; it was 'our Saviour in heaven.' I then asked her if there were two Saviours." Informed that young master was not "our Saviour," he was "filled . . . with astonishment." When his mother later told his sister that to be converted she must pray to "God who dwelt in heaven," Brown realized that old master Barret was not God, which "surprised me more still."[8]

When he was a little older, Henry Brown and his brother carried grain to nearby country mills several times a year. They would wait at the mill, sometimes overnight, for the miller to grind the flour. These were Brown's first ventures off the farm. Both versions of the *Narrative* record his recognition at the mill that other slaves lived in conditions worse than his own. Once, as a group of slaves from another plantation passed by, Brown and his brother "overheard some of them say, 'Look there, and see those two colored men with shoes, vests, and hats on.'" By contrast, these slaves wore "shirts made of coarse bagging, such as coffee sacks are made from, and some kind of light substance for pantaloons, and this was all their clothing!" Other slaves Brown met were poorly fed and told him about whippings. On one trip with his brother, a young white man asked Brown if he had "ever been whipped." When he said he had not, the man said, "Well, you will neither of you be of any value, then."[9]

At first Brown and his brother went to the mill of Colonel John Ambler, the county's largest slave owner, which was some distance away, but eventually a Mr. Bullock established a mill on the North Anna River closer to the Hermitage. Bullock "was very kind to us, took us into his house and put us to bed, took charge of our horses, and carried the grain himself into the mill, and in the morning furnished us with a good breakfast." Unlike Colonel Ambler, he let them catch fish from his pond and even gave them "fishing implements." Brown's brother explained to him that the reason Bullock treated them so differently was that "this man is not a slaveholder!"[10]

When Henry Brown was about fourteen, John Barret, perhaps feeling the weight of his eighty-odd years, changed his relatively light-handed management of the slaves. He hired an overseer "whose disposition was so cruel as to make many of the slaves run away." Brown later speculated that the neighbors had complained about Barret's "mild treatment to his slaves." Regardless of the reason, "the change in our treatment," recalled Brown, was "so much for the worse."[11]

Not long after, Barret took ill, and soon his death was imminent. Brown said later that the slaves at the Hermitage remembered that Barret's son Charles "became impressed with the evils of slavery" and freed a number of his slaves and paid their way to a free state. The slaves hoped that, as he prepared to meet his Maker, John Barret might be similarly enlightened.[12]

Barret called Brown and one of his brothers to his room. "With beating hearts," the young men ran there. "Henry," Barret said, "you will make a good Plough-boy, or a good gardener; now you must be an honest boy, and never tell an untruth. I have given you to my son William, and you must obey him." The Spirit had not moved Barret on his deathbed. "We, disappointed in our expectations, were left to mourn, not so much our masters death, as our galling bondage."[13]

John Barret died on 9 June 1830, and his property was divided among his four surviving sons. In the division, the Brown family was broken up. Brown recalled it as "the most severe trial to my feelings which I had ever endured." At the parting, "my mother was separated from her youngest child," and it was not until she "begged most pitiously for its restoration, that she was allowed to give it one farewell embrace."[14]

Brown's sister Mary and her children went one way; his brother Edward another way; and John, Lewis, and Robinnet yet another. Henry, his mother, and his sisters Jane and Martha "fell into the hands of William Barret." Brown stated in the 1851 *Narrative*, without elaboration, that "William Barret took my sister Martha for his 'keep Miss.'" He did not mention his father in telling of the division of the family. Brown did report in 1851 that both his mother and father "are now enjoying such a measure of liberty, as the law affords to those who have made recompense" to their owners. One possibility is that by 1830 the senior Brown had already purchased his freedom. He may have been the free black man recorded as living at the Hermitage in the 1820 census. If in 1830 father Brown was a free man, he was nevertheless unable to preserve his family.[15]

Since Henry Brown's new master, William Barret, owned a tobacco business in

Richmond, Brown would go to the city to work in the factory. Thus did his mother's lament come to pass, for she stayed in Louisa, while her children were dispersed. Henry Brown was about fifteen years old when he departed the only home he had known.

Richmond

In 1830, Richmond was a growing city of about 16,000 people. It was the capital of an important state and a regional center for wholesale and retail trade. The city was a primary tobacco market and the falls of the James River powered flourmills and ironworks. Richmond's newspapers were the state's most influential. The city's development was uneven, however. The streets were mostly unpaved and deep with mud after rain, many residents occupied woeful dwellings, and the drinking water was brown. Of the half of Richmond's inhabitants who were African American, three-fourths were slaves.[16]

Henry Brown might have walked the Louisa Road to Richmond, or traveled there on a wagon bearing goods for market. He was likely strong from labor on the plantation and probably approaching his adult appearance as described by a friend: "the man weighs 200 lbs & is about five ft 8" in height . . . a noble looking fellow." The young man faced a challenging transition. His worldly possessions were minimal. The crowded city was a drastic change from the forests and fields of the Hermitage. In his first week in Richmond he might well have seen more people than he had ever before observed in his whole life; yet far away from his home he probably felt the most alone he had ever been. The move to Richmond made final the loss of his family and was doubtless a formative experience.[17]

His new master, William Barret, told Brown that if he would "behave well" Barret would "take good care" of him. "He furnished me with a new suit of clothes, and gave me money to buy things to send to my mother," remembered Brown. Barret put him to work in the tobacco factory, where Brown's first overseer, Wilson Gregory, was a black man. Whether Gregory was slave or free is unknown, but he took Brown under his wing and helped him adjust to his new labors. In the 1851 *Narrative* Brown recalled that Gregory "was generally considered a shrewd and sensible man, especially to be a man of colour; and, after the orders which my master gave him concerning me, he used to treat me very kindly indeed, and gave me board and lodgings in his own house. Gregory acted as book-keeper also to my master, and was much in favour with the merchants of the city and all who knew him; he instructed me how to judge of the qualities of tobacco, and with a view of making me a more proficient judge of that article, he advised me to learn to chew and to smoke which I therefore did."[18]

Brown entered work in a business that was changing. Richmond had been long established as a tobacco market, where hogsheads of leaf were auctioned for export, mostly to England. By 1830 an ever-greater portion of tobacco was shipped as a processed product, as cases of plug, twist, or snuff. Tobacco manufacturing utilized few machines, and the factories depended on slave labor. Of Richmond's black residents, both slave and free, from one-quarter to one-third, depending on the season, were employed in the tobacco industry.[19]

Henry Brown's new master was a man whose fortunes rose with the tobacco manufacturing industry. William Barret served in the War of 1812, when he was about twenty-six years old, and afterward entered business in Richmond. Barret started in tobacco in partnership with an English merchant, William Gilliat. In 1829 Barret and Gilliat had a small factory on Cary Street near Fourteenth Street. Barret must have gained the confidence of his partner, for soon afterward Gilliat returned to England. The factory subsequently operated as William Barret and Company, and the Gilliat firm in London acted as sales agent for Barret's products. This arrangement proved long-lasting and apparently mutually beneficial.[20]

Henry Brown once overheard Barret "telling the overseer that his father had raised me." Brown's relationship with his second master was never as close. William Barret's control over Brown's life came mainly through intermediaries, such as the overseer, and through the factory rules. Yet their contact was sufficient that Brown later referred to Barret as a "kind master," at least by comparison to other masters.[21]

Owners, of course, varied in the treatment of their slaves. William Barret's thoughts on the institution are unrecorded, but he did participate in an organization concerned with slavery. The American Colonization Society was formed in 1816 and drew members from the North and South. Its premise, which took for granted that blacks were inferior, was that slavery was a corrupting influence on white society and should be eliminated. The group sought government funding to compensate owners for the emancipation of slaves who would be resettled in Africa. It was largely through the society's efforts that Liberia was founded in 1822 on the west coast of Africa, as a place that "all the free persons of colour, now in the United States, and those who may be hereafter emancipated, may be transported."[22]

In 1823 the Richmond and Manchester Colonization Society was founded as an affiliate of the national society. Chief Justice John Marshall, a Richmonder, was elected president. One of the society's managers was John Tyler, later president of the United States, and another was William Barret. During the 1820s Barret actively participated in the group.[23]

Henry Brown's family had hoped for emancipation at John Barret's death. The idealism of the Revolutionary period did engender some acts of manumission on moral grounds, exemplified by George Washington's freeing his slaves in his will. The emancipation sought by the Colonization Society was less enlightened. If William Barret's views were compatible with those of the society, he saw slavery as an institution that did harm to whites and he envisioned a society cleansed of blacks. Even such a base view was better than that of most other slave owners, for implicit in it was moral uncertainty about slavery. Barret had at least thought about slavery as an institution, and his conclusions probably set a limit to harshness in policies that affected the daily life of the slaves. This was the "kind master."

The Colonization Society failed in its grand plan because it attempted to find a middle way to treat a problem for which there could be no moderate solution. Others took more extreme steps. On 12 February 1831, not long after Henry Brown arrived in Richmond, there was an eclipse of the sun. The eclipse and an outbreak of cholera not long after seemed to Brown portents that "the day of judgment was not far distant," so he decided to join the Baptist Church. In Southampton County, southeast of Richmond on the North Carolina border, a slave named Nat Turner also viewed the eclipse, and, like Brown, took it as a sign. When another solar phenomenon

William Barret as a young man

7

occurred 13 August 1831 Turner saw it as a signal for action and initiated the slave revolt known as Nat Turner's Rebellion. Though whites suppressed the uprising within three days, Turner himself evaded capture until 30 October 1831. He was hanged on 11 November.[24]

Brown remembered that "about eighteen months after I came to the city of Richmond, an extraordinary occurrence took place which caused great excitement all over the town." He asked William Barret about it but received only the vague reply "that some of the slaves had plotted to kill their owners." Brown recalled that "the whites seemed terrified beyond measure." Many of them acted irrationally and violently, and the number of slaves and free blacks killed in Virginia and North Carolina following the rebellion was far greater than the number of whites killed in the rebellion itself. Brown reported tales of slaves "cut down with the swords in the streets" and incidents of "half hanging" and other excessive punishments.[25]

The challenge of Nat Turner's Rebellion made slavery a much-discussed subject in Virginia. No doubt sensing opportunity, the Richmond Colonization Society met for the first time in three years on 15 November 1831, four days after Nat Turner was executed. It was the last meeting where William Barret is recorded in attendance. When the Virginia General Assembly convened in December 1831, the legislative session unexpectedly became a public debate on the abolition of slavery that lasted two months. On the key resolution, however, the antislavery side lost by a vote of seventy-three to fifty-eight. The legislature opted neither for abolition nor colonization, but rather for increased control over African Americans.[26]

New laws stated that slaves had to carry passes from their masters to be on the streets, and that even with passes they could not congregate in groups of more than three. Other laws prohibited possession of liquor or firearms and placed restrictions on the sale of farm products and the practice of certain trades. A primary target was black preachers. Writing shortly after Nat Turner's Rebellion, an anonymous writer charged in the *Richmond Enquirer* that black preachers were the cause of "insubordination and its horrid consequences," for they taught the slaves "that God is no respecter of persons . . . and that they are free in *Christ*—ergo that they ought to be absolutely free." One of the new laws proclaimed that "no slave, free Negro, or mulatto shall preach, or hold any meeting for religious purposes either day or night," with punishment for violators set at thirty-nine lashes. Henry Brown remembered a black preacher who "refused to obey the impious mandate" and "was severely whipped."[27]

Brown was still a newcomer to Richmond when these events occurred. For slaves, the stricter black code was a greater burden, although in practice many regulations remained unenforced until someone in authority decided there was a problem. Nonetheless, control by threat of punishment was integral to the slave system. Free blacks also felt the weight of the new regulations, which reduced the effective differences between their status and that of slaves.

The legislative debate of 1831–1832 marked the crest of Virginia-bred opposition to slavery, for in following years attitudes hardened. The field of political debate was bounded, and moral questions about slavery were excluded from Virginia discourse. A slaveholding ideology that justified a permanent slave society gained hegemony, and it became socially difficult to express opposition to slavery. William Barret may have felt the pressure of these changes, for he dropped out of the Colonization Society. Slavery was in the saddle in Virginia, and a gentleman did not question it but went about his own business.[28]

"Mr. Allen is always right"

During his first few years in Richmond, Henry Brown "very seldom heard" from his mother, he said, and "my feelings were very much tried by the separation." Brown may have had some tidings from home in 1832, when William Barret acquired from Mary Barret, his aunt, a number of slaves from the Hermitage. They included the miller Billy, his wife Jenny, and four of their children; four of Lizzy's children; and seven other slaves. If, as seems likely, Barret brought some or all of them to Richmond to work at the factory, they would have had news for Brown of his mother and the home place.[29]

Wilson Gregory, the African American overseer who advised Brown, died about two years after Brown arrived in Richmond, and Stephen Bennett, a white man with a wooden leg, succeeded him. Brown recalled in the 1851 *Narrative* that Bennett "used to creep up behind the slaves to hear what they had to talk about in his absence; but his wooden leg generally betrayed him by coming into contact with something which would make a noise." The slaves considered him "a very mean man in all his ways," and he was "very much disliked." Bennett once gave a slave named Pinkney a whipping for lacking "three pounds of his task, which was valued at six cents."[30]

Bennett's successor was Henry Bedman. "He was the best that we had," said Brown. "He neither used the whip nor cheated the hands of what little they had to receive, and I am confident that he had more work done by equal number of hands, than had been done under any overseer either before or since." Only too soon, Bedman also passed away.[31]

Henry Brown worked in Barret's tobacco factory six days a week, and went to church on the seventh. Over time Brown "formed an acquaintance" with a young woman named Nancy. "Our friendship having ripened into mutual love," he stated later, "we concluded to make application to the powers that ruled us, for *permission* to be married." This was six years or so after he came to Richmond, about 1836, when Brown was approaching twenty-one. Nancy belonged to Hancock Lee, a teller at the Farmers' Bank of Virginia. Their masters discussed the request and permitted Nancy and Henry to marry, though it was a commitment that had no legal standing. In due course Nancy gave birth to the first of their four children.[32]

At the time of their marriage, according to Brown, Lee "pretended to me, to believe it wrong to separate families." A year later "his conscientious scruples vanished," and he sold Nancy Brown. Her new master was Joseph H. Colquitt, a saddler. He was "an exceedingly cruel man, and he had a wife who was, if possible, still more cruel." In 1838 Colquitt was twenty-five years old and his wife, Mary Colquitt, was eighteen. She abused Nancy, said Brown, "not because she did not do her duty, but because . . . her manners were too refined for a slave." That Nancy Brown took time from working to care for her own infant child greatly vexed Mary Colquitt. She agitated to have her sold, and she was, to Philip M. Tabb Jr. for $450. Four months later, the Colquitts reconsidered and purchased her back for $500, but they treated Nancy Brown no better than before.[33]

⌒

By 1836 William Barret had expanded his factory to three buildings. In this era most tobacco was either chewed or taken as snuff. Barret's company made chewing tobacco from a variety of the plant known as the "yellow or Spotted Pryor," the bulk of it grown west of Richmond and brought in on the James River and Kanawha Canal. Brown described the factory in the 1849 *Narrative* as "three stories high" and reported that

"150 persons were employed, 120 of whom were slaves, and the remainder free colored people."[34]

Brown later said that the workday lasted fourteen hours in the summer and sixteen during the winter, but it is hard to imagine such hours could be sustained when working six days a week. The historian Joseph Clarke Robert stated that the "daily task took ten hours or more," certainly long enough when working six days a week. At the factory "women and boys" removed the center stem from the tobacco, and the leaf was then "moistened with a fluid made from Liquorice and Sugar." Men twisted the flavored tobacco leaf into a formed shape, a skilled task that became Brown's job, and squeezed it into lumps using a "hand-operated press of the lever-and-screw variety." The lumps went to the machine house, where at "final prizing" they were packed under "tremendous pressure" into boxes and casks. After thirty days in the "sweathouse," the chewing tobacco was ready to be shipped to market.[35]

Visitors to Richmond often toured the tobacco factories. The poet and journalist William Cullen Bryant in 1843 visited a plug tobacco factory, in one room of which "were about eighty negroes, boys they are called, from the age of twelve years up to man-

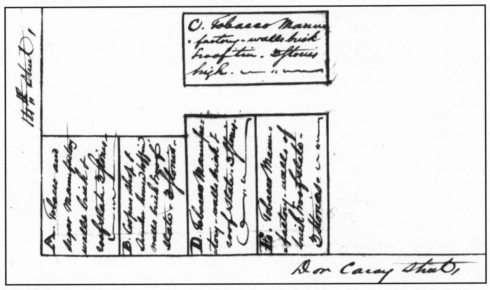

William Barret's Factory. The plat, a section of an 1844 insurance policy, shows five brick buildings of two and three stories, at the northeast corner of 14th Street and "D or Carey Street," modern-day Cary Street.

hood," who prepared the flavored tobacco for the press. Elihu Burritt, famous as the self-educated "Learned Blacksmith," toured a Richmond tobacco factory in May 1854 and reported that it had "the temperature of a bakery in July." Burritt was impressed by the high level of skill involved. "The weighing and measuring eye, and a keen sleight of hand, are requisite to a high degree in every stage of the business," he wrote, "and all these capacities seem to be readily acquired by the slaves."[36]

As tobacco manufacturing developed, the industry adopted several policies not typical of slavery on the plantation: hiring, boarding-out, and bonus pay. Rather than owning all of the slave labor force in their tobacco factories, manufacturers hired a significant proportion of it from other masters. Boarding-out was the practice of paying a stipend to slaves, whether hired or owned by the manufacturer, to rent their own housing and to purchase food and clothing. According to Brown in the 1851 *Narrative*, Barret paid a weekly allowance of seventy cents "for the hands to board themselves with."[37]

Stipends were kept low, in part, to motivate slaves to earn bonus money for overwork. A slave who surpassed an assigned quota of work could earn extra money. The slaves understood that the practice was intended, as Elihu Burritt put it, "to stimulate the slaves to an industry which no compulsion can exact," but they responded to it. "We were told that, almost without exception, every negro, young or old, was quickened to increased activity by this new impulse," Burritt reported. "Many would earn two dollars, and some *five*, a-week, by this extra work." Henry Brown was a skilled worker— by his own report, "the steadiest & swiftest hand in the factory"—and through overwork earned money to supplement his stipend.[38]

Richmond factory slaves such as Brown thus participated in the cash economy. There were merchants who catered to slaves, selling necessities such as clothing, shoes, and foodstuffs, and also merchants who sold to slaves things that were not necessities. The housing that slaves on stipends could afford was generally very poor. An English visitor to Richmond observed that "the dwellings occupied by the lower classes of coloured people are of a miserable kind, resembling the worst brick-houses in the back-lanes of English manufacturing towns." When Henry Brown first went to Richmond, he lived at the home of Wilson Gregory. Where he moved after Gregory's death is not known.[39]

William Barret's "famous" brand was "Anchor Brand." A kind of chewing tobacco known as "Negro Head," it was described in 1855 as "a very rich article put up principally by Barret of Richmond for the English & Australian markets . . . from which he has principally derived his very large fortune." Barret was indeed prosperous. In 1840 he paid taxes on forty-one slaves, and in 1843 on fifty slaves, and his worth continued to grow through the decade. In 1844, he built a fine Greek Revival house at Fifth and Cary Streets, and moved into it with his new wife, Margaret Elizabeth Williams, the widow of a minister. Because of her poor health, the Barrets often traveled overseas, which left the factory in the hands of the overseer.[40]

By the early 1840s, Barret's overseer was a white man named John F. Allen. Close in age to Henry Brown, Allen was born in Ireland and went to Richmond about 1819, when he was about four years old. Allen's father had been in the tobacco business, and after his father's death in 1841, the son, who never married, supported his mother and three sisters. Describing Allen in the 1849 *Narrative* as "a savage-looking, dare-devil sort of a man," Brown depicted Allen as petty and cruel in his dominion. When the slaves complained to Barret about Allen's unjust treatment, "his motto was 'Mr. Allen is always right.'"[41]

William Barret House. 1991. Built in 1844, the house stands at the northeast corner of Fifth and Cary Streets in Richmond.

"He understood how to turn a penny for his own advantage as well as any man," stated Brown. "No person could match him in making a bargain." John F. Allen boasted at the factory that he did not have to touch his salary to support his family. Long before sunrise he was "busily engaged in loading a wagon with coal, oil, sugar, wood, &c., &c., which always found a place of deposit at *his own door*, entirely unknown" to William Barret. Allen was a clever manager of the slaves and, according to Brown, made money on the side through their labor. Brown said Allen "excelled all I had ever seen in low mean trickery and artifice."[42]

With Allen in charge of the factory, whippings for small matters were common. One time, Brown recalled, a man "who was frequently in the habit of singing" fell sick and was not at work for three days. There was no medicine or physician sent to him. Instead, Allen directed three men to bring him to the factory. He was so feeble "that he was scarcely able to stand," but Allen had him "stripped and his hands tied behind him; he was then tied to a large post." Allen said that "his singing consumed too much time," and "he was going to give him some medicine that would cure him." According to Brown, "for no other crime than sickness," Allen lashed him until he "fainted away." The man was "sick for four weeks afterwards," and his weekly allowance was stopped. Brown stated in the 1851 *Narrative* that William Barret knew of this incident "but never interfered, nor even reproved the cruel overseer."[43]

Allen, though "very pious," was "much addicted to the habit of profane swearing," especially to denounce the slaves. Among his least offensive epithets were "'hogs,' 'dogs,' 'pigs,' &c. &c.," but neither his swearing nor his outbursts of violent punishment inhibited Allen from teaching at Sabbath school, where he was "very fervid in his exhortations to the slave children."[44]

~~~~

For many slaves church was the main event of their day off. Churchgoers arrived early to socialize and gathered again afterward. "On a Sunday afternoon . . . large numbers of them avail themselves of their leisure, and throng the sidewalks until the approach of night," noted the *Richmond Republican* in 1849. "The majority of them are generally well dressed, showing in their style an observance of the prevailing fashions." Seven years later, the northern visitor Frederick Law Olmsted saw on Sunday "many more well-dressed and highly-dressed colored people than white," a scene he compared to "the New York 'dry-goods clerks,' in their Sunday promenades, in Broadway." Some of Henry Brown's earnings from overwork probably went for the clothes that he and Nancy wore on Sunday.[45]

Brown had been required to obtain written permission from his master when he joined First Baptist Church in 1831. Most churchgoing Richmond blacks, slave and free, were affiliated with this congregation. First Baptist was the only Richmond church that allowed African Americans to attend in large numbers—they sat in a separate section from the whites—and thousands of them came. Eventually the white members of First Baptist Church, who had become a minority of the membership, decided to worship separately. In 1841 they built themselves a new church building two blocks west on Broad Street and sold the old one to the African American members. One of the rules of the whites' "splendid new church," according to Brown, was "that if any coloured person entered it, without special business, he was liable to be taken to the watch-house and to receive 39 lashes!"[46]

Brown's view, in the 1851 *Narrative*, was that the Reverend Jeremiah Bell Jeter, the pastor since 1836, had worked a calculated deception. He convinced "the negroes all around the district to believe that out of love for them, and from pure regard to their spiritual interests, it had been agreed that the old meeting house was to be given to the negroes for their own use, on their paying a small portion of the price at which it was estimated." The small portion was $3,000. Though most of the congregation at the newly formed First African Baptist Church were slaves, and earned very little, they con-

tributed their pennies each week each to pay the mortgage. The slaves "were thus provided with a strong motive for remaining where they were," said Brown, "and also by means of this pious fraud . . . they were deprived of such little sums of money as might occasionally drop into their hands."

"It is really a matter of wonder to me now," commented Brown in the 1851 *Narrative*, "considering the character of my position that I did not imbibe a strong and lasting hatred of every thing pertaining to the religion of Christ." A board of whites from First Baptist governed First African

First African Baptist Church. 1865. Built in 1802, the chamber was the city's largest and often taken over for white meetings.

Baptist and, as the law required, appointed a white preacher named Robert Ryland. As the overseer of the largest black institution in the city Ryland largely adhered to the many restrictions on its activities but did bend some rules. Henry Brown complained that the preacher's constant text was Saint Paul's admonition that servants be obedient from his Epistle to the Ephesians. Despite the prohibition on African Americans' speaking from the pulpit, Ryland allowed black assistants to lead prayers, which sometimes lengthened and took on the characteristics of a sermon. Of one prayer leader, Ryland himself admitted, "he was heard with far more interest than I was."[47]

Also apparently under black leadership was the choir. Henry Brown was "for a long while" a member of the choir at First African Baptist Church. William Cullen Bryant reported hearing during his 1843 visit to Richmond that First African had "the best choir . . . in all Richmond." It was probably among the best dressed, as well. An English visitor observed of the First African Baptist choir that the men "were dressed *en grand toilette*, handsome black coats and trowsers, white waistcoats, and white ties; the women in silks and muslins flounced *en dernière mode*, of the gayest colours, with bonnets and mantles to match." Undoubtedly Henry Brown, too, took pride in dressing well when singing for the church's large congregation.[48]

Musicologist Eileen Southern has stated that "the slaves preferred the musical activities of the religious experience above all else," and in this period music in Richmond's black churches was mainly psalmody, the singing of psalms. Over time the early New England folk style of psalmody had made its way south, and it had enough in common with African musical traditions that African Americans adopted it readily. Among other characteristics, folk psalmody favored singing by ear rather than by written notes, encouraged the addition of grace notes and embellishments, and relied on "lining-out," with "the leader reading or chanting the verses of the psalm . . . and the congregation singing them afterward." The musical form allowed room for adaptation and improvisation by the singers, and the lyrics, drawn from verses in the Book of Psalms, were acceptable to whites yet conveyed meanings to the slaves that the whites did not hear.[49]

Richmond slaves sang outside the church, too. "Many of the negroes, male and female, employed in the factories, have acquired such skill in psalmody and have generally such fine voices," wrote the Richmond chronicler Samuel Mordecai in 1856, "that it is a pleasure to listen to the sacred music with which they beguile the hours of labour." Mordecai added, "many of the slaves in Richmond have acquired some knowledge of music by note, and may be seen, even in the factories, with their books of psalmody open on the work-bench." The historian John T. O'Brien suggests "the possibility that slaves used song to determine the work pace." William Cullen Bryant wrote of his tour of a tobacco factory in 1843 that "as we entered the room we heard a murmur of psalmody running through the sable assembly." The proprietor's brother explained that singing was encouraged, for "the boys work better while singing," but that it could not be compelled. The slaves sang "wholly of their own accord," he stated, and "their tunes are all psalm tunes, and the words are from hymn-books; their taste is exclusively for sacred music; they will sing nothing else."[50]

As a singer himself Henry Brown had particularly noted that one of John F. Allen's reasons for severely punishing a slave was excessive singing. In contrast to Allen, Henry Bedman, the overseer whom Brown remembered favorably, "was very fond of sacred music, and used to ask me and some of the other slaves, who were working in the same room to sing for him—something 'smart' as he used to say, which we were generally as well pleased to do, as he was to ask us." A man who knew him later reported that Brown "has a fine voice, and understands music." Brown himself said in the 1851 *Narrative* that not only did he sing with the First African Baptist Church's choir, by all accounts a select group, but further that he was "a leading member of the choir." In a system that allowed a slave limited domain for individual accomplishments, Henry Brown's performance of music was a means of expression that probably brought him standing among his peers.[51]

Perhaps it was through music that Henry Brown met James C. A. Smith, for both sang in the church choir. James Caesar Anthony Smith was a free black who became Brown's close friend. The free blacks in Richmond, as in other southern cities, occupied an ill-defined middle position. "In all the States these people were allowed but few privileges not given to the slaves," wrote the black abolitionist William Wells Brown, "and in many their condition was thought to be even worse than that of the bondmen." The historian Ira Berlin succinctly described free blacks as "slaves without masters." In many respects they lived on the margin of society, for the occupations at which free blacks could work were limited. The situation of an urban slave like Henry Brown, who was paid a stipend, found his own lodgings, fed himself, and might even hire himself out, was hardly materially different. Many free blacks worked in the tobacco factories alongside the slaves, doing the same work.[52]

James C. A. Smith, wrote an acquaintance, was by comparison to Brown "a smaller man & by no means so dark in color." One report described him "with mustache and imperial." Smith "said that he had been a Dentist in Richmond," which explained why Brown "occasionally called him Doctor," although dentistry in this period was not the formal profession of more recent times. A Richmond newspaper described Smith as "a very 'dandyish' looking negro," who for a time "kept a cake shop and rendezvous for negroes on Broad Street" located between Third and Fourth Streets. His cake shop would have offered affordable treats for those with little money. Henry Brown and James C. A. Smith would travel a long distance together.[53]

About 1844, Joseph Colquitt, Nancy Brown's master, became very sick. According to Brown in the 1851 *Narrative*, Colquitt's minister came and his doctor came, and both prayed for him, but death seemed nigh. Colquitt sent for Brown, who came after work. "He caught hold of my hand and said;—'Henry will you pray for me and ask the Lord to spare my life?'" Colquitt was "a very cruel man, and had used my wife badly, yet I had no right to judge between him and his God." So Brown prayed for him. Then Colquitt asked Brown to gather all his slaves who belonged to the church, so they could pray for him. For three days, Brown and the other slaves prayed for Colquitt "after our work was done, and although we needed rest ourselves, yet at the earnest desire of the apparently dying man" they prayed for him long into the night.[54]

Colquitt recovered, though he spent weeks recuperating. One day when Brown was present, Colquitt's "wife appeared as if she wished to joke her husband about the coloured people praying for him when he was sick." She had been expelled from the Baptist Church, according to Brown, and professed not to believe "in God or Devil." She teased him enough that Colquitt "grew angry at last and exclaimed with an oath that it was all lies about the negroes praying for him." With his wife "still persisting," Colquitt called in his slaves one by one for questioning and then "whipped every one of them which said he had prayed as Mrs. Colquitt had stated."

Colquitt could not whip Brown because Brown did not belong to him. Instead, by Brown's account, out of spite Colquitt offered to sell Nancy Brown to Samuel Cottrell. A saddler and harness maker who was about twenty-five years old, Cottrell was looking for someone to wait on his wife and came to Brown with a proposal. Colquitt was asking $650 for Nancy Brown, and Cottrell wanted to purchase her but had only $600. If Brown gave him the remaining $50 to buy her, Cottrell "would prevent her from being sold away from me." The deal included Brown's children as well.

Since fifty dollars was a substantial sum to a slave, Brown was "a little suspicious about being fooled out of my money." He asked what "security" Cottrell could offer that he would not someday sell Nancy Brown. In his answer Cottrell "lavished" his religion, stating he "never could have the heart to do such a deed," particularly "knowing that your wife is my sister and you my brother in the Lord." Brown gave him the money, not that he had "implicit faith in his promise," but because he knew Cottrell "could purchase her if he wished whether I were to assist him or not." Brown hoped that the payment might put Cottrell "under an obligation" that would "at least be somewhat to the advantage of my wife and to me."[55]

Later that same day, Samuel Cottrell purchased Nancy Brown and the children. Immediately he returned to Brown with additional conditions. For Cottrell to let them live together, Brown "must hire a house for them and . . . furnish them with everything they wanted." Because Nancy was caring for small children and thus not able to earn much for her new master, Cottrell demanded that Brown pay fifty dollars a year for her time, and that Nancy also do his washing. "If you dont do this," Cottrell warned, "I will sell her as soon as I can get a buyer for her." Brown "was struck with astonishment to think that this man, in one day, could exhibit himself in two such different characters."[56]

Since Cottrell owned his wife and children, Brown had to accept his terms. A slave could not sign a contract to rent a house, so he turned to his friend James C. A. Smith, who made the arrangements for a house and "stood master of it." Brown's rent was six dollars per month. Nancy Brown took in washing, which, combined with Brown's stipend and overwork earnings, less the payments to Cottrell, supported the family. Nancy's master and Henry's overseer were hard-hearted men who held power over them, and Henry and Nancy were poor slaves who worked daylong. Nonetheless, they had a home and family life, and, as Brown recalled, "never had we been so pleasantly situated before."[57]

Men *"who stood high"*

A visitor said of Richmond in the 1840s "there is a high and a low town." Wealthier people lived on the hills. "If you wish to see a beautiful little city, built up of rich and tasteful villas," wrote novelist John Pendleton Kennedy, "come and look at Shockoe Hill." William Barret's house on Gamble's Hill had a choice view of the city and the river. Those with less money lived where they could, many in the "low town." Lower Richmond filled the valley of Shockoe Creek, which separated the city's eastern and western hills, and spread down to the riverfront and the docks. The location of Nancy and Henry Brown's house is not known, but because she washed clothes it may have been near a stream, perhaps Shockoe Creek or one of its tributaries.[58]

The low town was where all the strains of Richmond's population mixed. As in much of the rest of the United States in the 1840s, a significant part of the city's population was transitory. Many had recently arrived from the countryside, from elsewhere in the United States, or from Europe. The new residents brought attitudes formed in other places, which only reinforced for the Virginia elite the urgency of maintaining conformity on the issue of slavery. Early in 1830 the authorities had discovered that a Richmond free black named Thomas Lewis had been sent from Boston thirty copies of David Walker's *Appeal to the Colored Citizens of the World*, a pamphlet that called for the end of slavery in strong and impassioned language. News of the discovery had been sent right to the governor. A year later in Boston, William Lloyd Garrison founded the *Liberator*, a weekly abolitionist paper, and in 1833 he and others established the American Anti-Slavery Society. Early issues of the *Liberator* are in the papers of Governor John Floyd, sent to him by vigilant Virginians. Following Nat Turner's Rebellion in August 1831, the emergence of militant northern abolitionism intensified official intolerance for expression of antislavery sentiment in Virginia.[59]

In 1835 the American Anti-Slavery Society began to mail large numbers of antislavery tracts into the South. The tactic caused a fierce reaction in the region, with several instances of mob action to seize the tracts. In company with other southern legislatures, the Virginia General Assembly enacted in 1836 a law to suppress such "incendiary publications." It directed that they be burned, and stated further that "members or agents of anti-slavery societies who . . . advocate or advise the abolition of slavery shall be guilty of a high misdemeanor," with a penalty of up to three years in jail.[60]

Although such acts of censorship forced expression to be hidden, they did not prevent belief. Opposition to slavery was always present in Richmond. It began with the slaves themselves, prevailed among their free black comrades, and included some whites as well. The extent of slave resistance is a matter of discussion by historians. Slaves who outwardly acceded to masters such as Samuel Cottrell and overseers such as John F. Allen knew that any overt objection would bring a violent response. Inherent in the coercive nature of the system was a continual, if veiled, disquietude. A white Richmonder, writing about slaves in 1849, remarked on the mystery of "their almost invariable response to an inquiry after the state of health; for, no matter how well they feel, they almost invariably answer—'I'm only tolerable, I thank you,' or 'I'm poorly, I thank you.'"[61]

A direct way for a slave to resist was to flee. Advertisements for runaways appear in almost every issue of the newspapers published in the city in this period. Though the numbers were small relative to the total enslaved population, the disappearances were steady enough that entrepreneurs obtained from the legislature in 1835 a charter

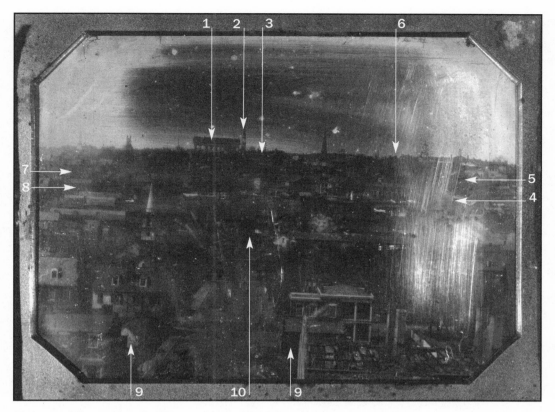

Richmond From Church Hill. ca. 1853–1854 (reversed to read correctly). The view looks west from Church Hill across Shockoe Valley to Shockoe Hill. Because of the long exposure time, neither chimney-smoke nor people appear. The large building on the horizon is the State Capitol (1). The steeple just to its right belongs to Saint Paul's Church (2), and next is the Executive Mansion (3). On the right of the image, somewhat obscured by the white scratches on the picture surface, Broad Street climbs the hill (4), and about two-thirds of the way up on the right is the First African Baptist Church (5). The Richmond, Fredericksburg, and Potomac depot (6) is on Broad Street several blocks beyond the brow of the hill. On the left side of the image is the Exchange Hotel (7), its cupola barely visible, where Adams Express received goods for shipment. Two blocks to the left of the hotel, out of the picture, was William Barret's factory. The building in the picture just below the hotel is the Odd Fellows Hall (8), a site for slave auctions; in its vicinity are other slave auction sites. The houses in the foreground have small buildings in their backyards that are probably slave quarters (9). The camera looks down Grace Street; where it stops at the bottom of the hill is Lumpkin's slave jail (10).

of incorporation for the Virginia Slave Insurance Company, "with power and authority to make insurance upon slaves absconding from their owners."[62]

For a slave to escape to freedom usually required help. The name "Underground Railroad," which was in use by the 1830s, implied a more formal structure of assistance to fugitives than actually existed. In the North there were linked organizations that helped fugitives, but in Richmond there were only informal associations between people who were, for differing reasons, willing to risk aiding in flight. The city had grown too large and diverse for the authorities to oversee all, and regard for official sovereignty was sometimes low. The *Richmond Daily Dispatch* stated as "a notorious fact" that "there are hundreds of small shops, kept ostensibly as grocery stores and cook shops by negroes and white men, who sell" liquor to slaves daily and "in defiance of all law." Such defiance of law was not limited to sales of liquor. The white observer who described the cake shop run by Henry Brown's friend, James C. A. Smith, as a "rendezvous for negroes" used a phrase pregnant with uneasiness.[63]

Court records state that on 24 June 1848, a Saturday, between noon and 2 P.M., a white man named John A. Blevins was seen "driving a wagon . . . of peculiar structure, with a high top, covering the body, deep and straight, and the covering drawn close over it." Blevins was about fifty-three years old, a native of Tennessee, and "wore a black hat invariably." Near Rocketts wharf, "in the lower part of the town," he asked for directions to Darbytown, on the eastern outskirts of the city. Later that day, probably at dusk, Blevins loaded his wagon. His cargo was four slaves: Charles Rawlings, Isaac Page, Henry Cox, and Jesse Ambler. They set out east toward New Kent County. Near midnight a white man walking the road asked Blevins for a ride. Blevins refused, saying that he had "some troublesome men" in the wagon, and that he was taking them to Williamsburg. Late in the evening of the next day, residents of a house about seven or eight miles below New Kent Court House—a location that was not on the way to Williamsburg—provided Blevins with water. The next morning, Monday, 26 June, Blevins and the four slaves went down to the shore of the York River. A small schooner, "which some days before had been partly loaded with wood in the Pamunkey river," was anchored there. "A boat put off" and "took the negroes in as quick as it could, and returned to the schooner, which immediately got under way." Blevins departed without waiting to see the ship sail off.[64]

Word of the escape was quickly spread, and police officers pursued Blevins to New Kent without finding him. A newspaper advertisement placed by the master of Henry Cox expressed what the police had already concluded: "Suspicion exists that he is aided in his escape by a white man with a covered cart." Two weeks after the escape Blevins returned to Richmond. Conclusive evidence linking him to the escape was apparently lacking, for he was not arrested, but he was suspected.

> **$100 REWARD.**—Left the tobacco factory of the subscribers, since Saturday, the 24th inst, a Negro Man named CHARLES RAWLINS. Said negro man is about 26 years old, about 6 feet high, quite black and like y. We will give the above reward of One Hundred Dollars, for his apprehension and delivery to us in this city.
> je 27—d1w   JAS H GRANT & CO.

> **50 DOLLARS REWARD!**
> HENRY, a pale-faced Mulatto, ran away between Saturday night and Monday morning, 26th June, from my Stemmery. Suspicion exists that he is aided in his escape by a white man with a covered cart.
> The above reward will be paid if he is taken out of the county; one half of it if taken within the corporation or in its vicinity, and brought to me in Richmond.
> je 28—3t   DAN'L K STEWART.

> **MISCELLANEOUS.**
> **200 Dollars Reward.**
> RAN AWAY, on Saturday, the 24th June last, a Negro Man named JESSE He is about 35 years old, 5 feet 10 inches high, strongly made, and of brown complexion. He has a large scar on his forehead. He left under the pretence of going to see his wife, at Mr. Pollard's, who resides in the neighborhood of Negrofoot, in Hanover county; but, as he has not been heard of there, it is likely he is endeavoring to escape to a free State. The above reward, if taken without the State, or $50 if within the State, will be paid, for his delivery to me, at the Enquirer Office, or to his owner, Mr. N. A. Thompson, who resides at Negrofoot.
> July 7   WM. W. DUNNAVANT.

"Suspicion Exists." The advertisements for runaways Charles Rawlings and for Henry Cox appeared in the *Richmond Whig* on 30 June 1848, and for Jesse Ambler in the *Richmond Semi-weekly Enquirer* on 14 July 1848.

Watch Captain Burrell Jenkins had noticed that "whenever Blevins and his wagon were absent from town," usually "for 10 days or a fortnight," Jenkins would "about the same time . . . hear of slaves having run off from their masters." By Blevins's own account, there were "persons sent to my house to watch my movements, and to ascertain if Negroes visited me." On 12 August 1848 two officers "saw two negroes go into Blevins' house," and as the slaves departed "Blevins gave a paper" that was taken by "John belonging to Mr. Enders." The officers arrested John, but in the struggle "he put a piece of paper in his mouth and chewed it up" and also "tore up a large paper."[65]

The torn paper was retrieved and may have been a counterfeit pass. Blevins was arrested on 14 August, "upon no specific charge," according to Blevins. Found in his possession were "some notes of a bank in Springfield, Massachusetts," dated 1 June. According to the arresting officer, Blevins "declared that he was innocent" of aiding the four slaves to escape, and then stated "that he knew all about the business; that there were men engaged in it who stood high; that he could break them up if he chose, and he pointed out the direction in which they lived." When the officer asked how he knew so much, Blevins answered with the unconvincing explanation that "he had given a negro boy twenty-five cents to steal a letter for him, which had told him all about it."[66]

Eventually three sets of charges were brought against Blevins. He faced trial at the fall term of Superior Court in November 1848 for the June escape of the four slaves. Blevins was found guilty and sentenced to the State Penitentiary, where he served until 1865.[67]

Blevins had not acted alone, as demonstrated by the coordination with the waiting schooner, but any role played by the men "who stood high" is unknown. Not clear either is the character of Blevins's motivation. He appears in 1848 tax records as the owner of one slave, a sign that he was not morally opposed to slavery. In addition, Blevins wrote of one of the slaves he was convicted of aiding to escape "that upon his first attempt to run away—about six months before this event I had him arrested." Indeed, in January 1848, when Blevins was living on Eighteenth Street in Shockoe Valley, he had provided information that led to the capture of several runaway slaves, had shared in a reward for one of them from a master, and had sought part of another reward. The particular slave for whom Blevins collected a reward was sold to a slave dealer who "sent him away to the south."[68]

According to the court records Blevins had once been a shoemaker "but for some time past he had not pursued this or any other known business." Blevins told different people that he was a trader of poultry, "bringing down butter and feathers from the mountains," or that he was "peddling in fish and oysters" between the York River and Richmond. By the evidence a significant line of commerce for Blevins was slave-related, both accepting money to transport fugitives out of Richmond and collecting rewards from masters for turning in slaves gone missing.[69]

In 1848 the Virginia House of Delegates appointed a committee to examine the laws governing the return of fugitive slaves from the North. In its report of February 1849, three months after Blevins's trial, the committee referred to "forays" by "Abolition societies." It was "notorious and undeniable that their emissaries have penetrated into the very hearts of the slaveholding states, and aided the escape of slaves whom they had seduced from the services of their owners." The Massachusetts banknotes found in Blevins's possession might have been a payment for Underground Railroad services. All in all, however, John A. Blevins seems to have been not so much an abolitionist emissary as an opportunistic peddler.[70]

Though the details of the escape of Charles Rawlings, Isaac Page, Henry Cox, and Jesse Ambler never appeared in the press, one imagines that in places like James C. A.

Smith's cake shop, and in conversations after church, the news of the escape spread through the African American community and the rest of the antislavery underground. Henry Brown surely heard about it.

"Money I will have"

One morning in August 1848, Samuel Cottrell, Nancy Brown's master, came to the Browns' house at breakfast time. He said that he needed money immediately to pay a large debt. "You know I have no money to spare," Henry Brown said to him, "because it takes nearly all that I make for myself, to pay my wife's hire, the rent of my house, my own ties to master, and to keep ourselves in meat and clothes; and if at any time, I have made any more than that, I have paid it to you in advance, and what more can I do?" Cottrell was not satisfied. "I want money," he said as he departed, "and money I will have."[71]

Nancy Brown was pregnant with their fourth child. "My poor wife burst into tears," recalled Brown, "and said perhaps he will sell one of our little children." Neither of them could eat breakfast. They embraced, and Brown went off to work at the factory.

Brown had been at work for several hours when the moment came: "I was informed that my wife and children were taken from their home, sent to the auction mart and sold." The news "burst upon me . . . so dreadful, and so sudden, that the shock well nigh overwhelmed me." His family was in the slave trader's jail and bound for the South. Cottrell had sold them for $1,050.[72]

Brown's first thought was to go to the jail. Slaves up for sale or being held for their purchaser were kept in slave jails. Richmond had several, located in the low town near the concentration of auction houses around Fifteenth and Franklin Streets, a few blocks from William Barret's tobacco factory. Brown "started for this infernal place," but a white man he knew, "a gentleman," stopped him with a warning. Cottrell had told William Barret "some falsehoods about me," and "induced him to give orders to the jailer to seize me, and confine me in prison, if I should appear there." The gentleman thought Brown "would undoubtedly be sold separate from my wife."[73] Brown convinced a young black man to carry some money to his wife and to explain why Brown did not visit her himself. As soon as the man "inquired for my wife, he was seized and put in prison." When the jailer "discovered his mistake, he was very angry, and vented his rage upon the innocent youth, by kicking him out of prison."

Brown himself went to William Barret, "my Christian master." It was a nine-block uphill walk from the factory to Barret's house. Brown begged his owner to purchase his wife and children, "but no tears of mine made the least impression upon his obdurate heart." Brown pleaded with him, reminding Barret of his faithful service and "the $5,000 I had paid him" over the years, but Barret refused to help. "He shoved me away from him as if I was not human." Brown left, but returned to appeal again to Barret later in the day. He "only answered me by telling me to go to my work and not bother him any more."[74]

When Brown returned to his home that evening, he found all the furnishings gone. Cottrell had the sheriff seize them because Brown owed him $17.21. These household possessions, Brown said, "had cost me nearly three hundred dollars." About 10 P.M., Brown went back to Barret, and told him what had happened. "I begged master to write Cottrell and make him give me up my things, but his answer was Mr. Cottrell is a gentleman I am afraid to meddle with his business."[75]

Brown returned to his empty house, missing not only his family but also "every article of furniture." He did not sleep that night. The next morning, at dawn, Brown went a fourth time to Barret. "*You can get another wife,*" said Barret. But Brown "did not want any other wife but my own lawful one, whom I loved so much." He responded to Barret with the Bible's words: "What God has joined together, let not man put asunder." At that Barret "drove me from his house, saying, he did not wish to hear that!"[76]

The sheriff had told Brown that if he paid the debt he owed Cottrell he could reclaim his possessions. He went to his friend "Doctor [James C. A.] Smith," who lent him enough to pay the debt. Later that day Brown encountered Samuel Cottrell on the street, who said he had heard Brown had been to the sheriff. "Yes," replied Brown, "I have been and got away *my things* but I could not get away *my wife and children* whom you have put beyond my power to redeem." Cottrell sent him on with "a round of abuse."[77]

In a final effort, Brown called upon two "young gentlemen of my acquaintance" and asked them to purchase his family. They told him that "they did not think it was right to hold slaves, or else they would gladly assist me." They suggested he approach William Barret again, but Brown "knew this would be useless."[78]

Cottrell had sold Nancy and the three children to a trader who was taking a slave coffle south the next day. "I received a message, that if I wished to see my wife and children, and bid them the last farewell, I could do so, by taking my stand on the street where they were all to pass." He "soon had the melancholy satisfaction" of seeing the coffle approach, "amounting to three hundred and fifty in number." Brown watched the departure with numerous others "who, like myself, were mourning the loss of friends and relations."[79]

First came five wagons of children. One child pointed to him, and he recognized his eldest. "There's my father," the child declared, "I knew he would come and bid me good-bye." Nancy Brown followed behind on foot, chained in a gang. Her expression was agonized. "I went with her for about four miles hand in hand," Brown recalled, "but both our hearts were so overpowered with feeling that we could say nothing, and when at last we were obliged to part, the look of mutual love which we exchanged was all the token which we could give each other." His tongue failed him. "I was obliged to turn away in silence."[80]

The pain of the loss affected Brown for a long time. It was a while, he said, before he "recovered my senses, so as to know how to act." He stopped attending the African Church because he associated its white authority with the people who had caused his grief. "He could not sing . . . and he refused to be comforted."[81]

Membership in the African Church was administered by the board of deacons selected from the congregation, whose periodic meetings were presided over by the church's white preacher. Church members who wished to join a new church were provided letters of dismissal that certified that they were in good standing. At the meeting of 1 October 1848, among those "dismissed by letter" was Nancy Brown. Someone undoubtedly told Henry Brown, and it was likely through this correspondence that he learned his wife and family had been sold to a Methodist preacher in North Carolina. The letter would have also provided his wife's address.[82]

According to Brown's account in the 1851 *Narrative*, he did not return to the church until December 1848, four months after the loss of his family. He began "strongly to suspect the christianity of the slave-holding church members," perhaps not least because it was a preacher who now owned his family. Nonetheless, he "yielded to the entreaties of my associates to assist at a concert of sacred music which was to be got up for the benefit of the church." His fellow choir member James C. A. Smith helped him "in selecting twenty four pieces to be sung on the occasion."[83]

The concert began at 3:30 P.M. on Christmas Day. As a benefit for the church, it is likely that whites were in attendance. While the choir sang the eleventh number of the concert, Smith, standing at Brown's right, suddenly closed his book and sank into his seat, "his eyes being at the same time filled with tears." Other choir members were "rather astonished," and "began to inquire what was the matter with him. . . . I guessed what it was." Smith's "feelings were overcome with a sense of doing wrongly in singing," for he felt "reproved by Almighty God for lending his aid to the cause of slave-holding religion." When the choir sang, "Vital spark of heavenly flame, Quit, / O! quit the mortal frame," the words struck Brown. "Stimulated by the example of Dr. Smith . . . I too made up my mind that I would be no longer guilty of assisting those bloody dealers in the bodies and souls of men." Brown did not sing in the choir again.[84]

The dramatic experience in the Christmas concert stirred in Brown the recognition that he was "weary of my bonds." He said that "thoughts of freeing myself" stayed in his mind, for "those reasons which often deter the slave from attempting to escape, no longer existed in reference to me, for my family were gone." Henry Brown emerged from his grief with a growing willingness to face the risks that escape would inevitably entail.[85]

Samuel A. Smith

If Henry Brown's thoughts of freeing himself were to be realized, he needed help. He likely confided in James C. A. Smith, whose public demonstration at the Christmas concert was an impetus to his thinking. Smith probably knew enough about a white storekeeper named Samuel A. Smith to suggest that Brown talk to him. Brown himself was "well acquainted" with the man, from whom he "used to purchase my provisions." Most important, Brown had "formed a favourable opinion of his integrity."[86]

Samuel Alexander Smith was a native of Massachusetts, about forty-two, and a shoemaker by trade. An observer described him as "5 feet 9 or 10 inches high—red face—high cheekbones—blue, dancing eyes—long nose—dark chestnut hair— . . . rather a pleasant looking man." Beginning about 1842 Smith operated a shoe store at the corner of Seventeenth and Main Streets, across from First Market in the heart of the lower city. The sign that hung outside his shop was a large red boot, and because he featured the sign in his distinctive newspaper advertisements Smith became known as the "Red Boot Man."[87]

As Henry Brown was probably aware, in his business Samuel Smith had not been averse to slavery. Tax records indicate that in 1843 Smith owned two slaves, and for the next two years Smith paid tax on four slaves, some or all probably employed mak-

TEN THOUSAND DOLLARS REWARD. — The above reward will be paid by the great Red Boot, No. 2, East Main St., opposite the end of the Old Market House, to any shoe dealer in Richmond, Egypt or Texas, who will undersell me in Boots or Shoes. My Stock is large and complete, and as I am determined to sell cheaper than any similar establishment in the above named diggings, I invite all who wish to save from 10 to 50 per cent. in their purchases, to give the Red Boot a call, where they can be supplied on the most advantageous terms. Persons wishing to shoe their servants, are particularly invited to try the Red Boot, as a very liberal discount will be made to such for cash or city acceptances. Country Dealers, too, will find it to their interest to give the Red Boot a call; in fact, it will be to the advantage of all dealers who purchase by the pair or otherwise, to call on the Red Boot.

Here let me give a partial statement of my prices, viz: Gentlemen's Boots from $1 25 to $7 50; Fine Shoes from 75 cents to $3 25; Ladies' Slippers, Ties, Springs and Turnrounds, from 37½ cents to $1 25; Servants' Shoes from 62½ cents to $1 25; Children's Shoes from 12½ to $1; Brogues from $1 12½ to $1 50; also all other kinds in proportion, it being too tedious to enumerate all my prices. Let it suffice to say, that I sell cheaper than any other house in the diggins, and I keep the cheapest store in all creation. Blacking of all the different manufacturers sold at 5 cts. per box.

☞ No Puffing. S. A. SMITH.
P. S. Don't forget that same old Red Boot.
July 9   18—wtf

"The Great Red Boot." The advertisement for Samuel Smith's shoe shop ran numerous times in the *Daily Richmond Enquirer* from September 1844 until October 1845.

ing shoes. Smith's advertisements for the Red Boot had "particularly invited" those "persons wishing to shoe their servants," and based on Brown's recollection that he "used to purchase" from Smith, some of Smith's "Servants' Shoes" were also sold directly to slaves. Samuel Smith had thus fully participated in the system of slavery.[88]

Brown likely knew too that Smith was a gambler. Samuel Smith's great passion, in company with many of his contemporaries, was for the lotteries and policy. Smith "conversed fluently," stated one account, "on various subjects, particularly that of lottery tickets." Lotteries were widespread in the United States in the early nineteenth century, most of them sponsored by local and state governments. By the 1840s abuses and anti-gambling sentiment had thinned the field to a smaller number of large lotteries. Private vendors, who collected a brokerage fee, advertised and sold tickets for the lotteries at prices ranging from $5 to $20. A related form of gambling called policy had also developed. To play policy, the bettor predicted a combination of numbers to be drawn in a designated lottery. Though it relied on their numbers, policy operated independently of the lotteries, often through citywide or regional syndicates. Samuel Smith once stated that he was connected with a large policy office in Philadelphia. The price of a policy bet was far cheaper than a lottery ticket, which made policy a way for poor people to gamble.[89]

Lottery offices "were once a great nuisance in Richmond," Samuel Mordecai stated in 1856. They were "very numerous" and patronized by all classes, including slaves. The slaves' earnings, complained Mordecai, "especially those of the hands employed in tobacco factories . . . went freely to the lottery offices, or to such of them as did not look to the color of the money or of the customers." Samuel Smith seems to have been not only in the shoe business, but also in the gambling trade; and if Smith's customers for shoes included slaves, so might have his players at chance. The "provisions" that Henry Brown purchased from Samuel Smith might have included policy bets.[90]

ALAS! ALAS! THE RED BOOT IS IN A SCRAPE!—Three Thousand Dollars Wanted, or the Red Boot, that same old Red Boot, must fall, and great would be the fall thereof. Come to the rescue, ladies and gentlemen.

I will sell from now until I raise 3,000 dollars, cheaper than any person in Richmond. My stock of Boots and Shoes is very large and complete, and, as the credit of the Red Boot must and SHALL be sustained, give me a call and I assure you the prices shall be made to suit all. Call in crowds, or dozens, or any way you please, and carry off the Boots and Shoes by dray loads, basket loads, or wheelbarrow loads, or any way you please, so you leave me the RHINO.

S. A. SMITH,
Red Boot, Main st., No. 2, Corner House.
P. S. Blacking only 5 cents per box.

"That Same Old Red Boot." Another advertisement for Samuel Smith's shoe shop that appeared regularly in the *Daily Richmond Enquirer,* October 1844–October 1845.

LOOK AT THIS! LOOK AT THIS!
Magnificent Scheme for Saturday, October 4th!
Fifty Thousand Dollars!
5 prizes of $10,000! 5 prizes of 5,000! 100 prizes of 1,000 Dollars!
GRAND CONSOLIDATED LOTTERY of Delaware and Georgia, Class No. 62, to be drawn at Wilmington, Oct. 4th, 1845:

Splendid Scheme:

1 grand prize of $50,000	100	prizes of	$1,000
5 " 10,000	50	"	600
5 " 5,000	50	"	500
3 " 3,126	150	"	300

1st and 2d, or 3d and 4th drawn nos., $200
5th and 6th, or 7th and 8th " 150
9th and 10th, or 11th and 12th " 100
12th and 13th, or 13th and 14th, " 80
Whole Tickets $20; Halves 10; Quarters 5; Eighths 2 50.

The cost of a package of 26 Whole Tickets is $460; each package must draw back in small prizes $238, therefore, on a package of Whole Tickets is only $222.

In this magnificent Scheme there are 76,076 Tickets, which comprise 2,926 packages in the whole Scheme. The adventurer, therefore, who purchases by the package has one chance in 2,927 of the Capital of $50,000; one chance in 209 of drawing either the 50,000, or a 10,000 or a 5,000, or a 3,126 Capital; and one chance in 26 of drawing either a 1,000, a 3,126, a 5,000, a 10,000, or the magnificent capital of 50,000. One package may draw the splendid amount of 80,000 dollars—consisting of the 50,000, and 3 prizes of 10,000.

Tickets in this Grand Scheme can be obtained of the All-Lucky Prize Seller, SMITH,
Sept. 25 Opposite the Old Market.

"Magnificent Scheme." The final advertisement for S. A. Smith's Prize Office appeared only once.

Over several years Samuel Smith and his wife, Mary Ann Smith, accumulated considerable personal property. Besides his slaves, Smith paid taxes one year on a gold watch, four other clocks, and a pianoforte valued at $275. That year only one other person in the city was taxed on more timepieces. Their other possessions included five featherbeds, two sideboards, three tables, thirty-six chairs, four carpets, four stools, two looking glasses, a bureau, two pair of brass andirons, plated ware, silver spoons, chinaware, and glass.[91]

Subsequent events suggest that Smith was either not managing his business well enough to afford so much personal property, or that he had suffered gambling losses. "Alas! Alas! The Red Boot Is In A Scrape," he advertised beginning in October 1844. "Three Thousand Dollars Wanted, or the Red Boot, that same old Red Boot, must fall." It may have been then that he started to go in arrears on payments for loans and shoe supplies. Yet, even as he was seeking "crowds, or dozens," to "carry off the Boots and Shoes by dray loads, basket loads, or wheelbarrow loads, or any way you please," Smith was purchasing in February 1845 a lot on Saint James Street, and then in May a second lot nearby on Duval Street, and in July a third lot on Duval.[92]

In August 1845, however, only a month after he had purchased the last lot, Smith indentured the three lots against a loan coming due. This did not solve his financial problems, but Smith still thought he could head off the reckoning. The committed gambler, no matter how far behind, knows that the next play can atone for all. In his straits Smith announced "S. A. Smith's Prize Office," and opened for business at his storefront in September 1845 as a dealer of lottery tickets. A grand prize winner was called a capital, and the "All-Lucky Prize Seller, Smith" avowed that he was "certain I have the capital now in the house." Lightning did not strike, however, and the venture quickly foundered. On 1 October Smith indentured his personal property against one debt, and soon after indentured the inventory and

Eagle Prize Office,

NO. 2, *East Main Street - Opposite the Old Market.*

LOOK AT THIS!—LOOK AT THIS!
A grand and magnificent Lottery draws Saturday, Dec. 6th—the drawing received in Richmond Dec. 8th. Grand Consolidated Lottery of Delaware and Georgia, Class 71. Grand Capitals: $40,000, 20,000, 12,000, 8,898, 4 of 5,000, 4 of 4,000, 4 of 3,000, 4 of 2,000, 100 of 1,000, &c. The lowest three-number prize is $500; and the scheme closes up with 4,158 two-number prizes, ranging from 30 to 200 dollars. 75 numbers, 12 drawn. Tickets 15.00; halves 7.50; quarters 3.75. Recollect, that the Eagle Prize Office is the place to get prizes from a thousand up to the Capital.

Come all you who never tried your luck before,
And buy in this splendid scheme, if you never
buy in any more!

Do not forget the prizes are at the Eagle Prize Office, No. 2, East Main Street, opposite the Old Market, and they must be sold.
J. MOORE & CO.

Also, Another Magnificent Lottery.
For Saturday, December 20th—Drawing received December 22d. Grand Consolidated Lottery of Delaware and Georgia, Class 73. Grand Capitals: 3 of $25,000 making 75,000, 10,000, 4,244, 3,000, 2 of 2,000, 2 of 1,750, 20 of 1,500, 20 of 1,250, 20 of 1,000, 150 of 500, (lowest three-number prize,) besides 4,356 two-number prizes, from 24 up to 150 dollars. 78 Nos., 12 drawn. Tickets only 12.00; halves 6.00; quarters 3.00.
Call at the Eagle Prize Office, and enrich yourselves. Recollect, that the Eagle is the emblem of Liberty; so, if you are in bondage, call on her at No. 2, East Main Street, and be liberated.
Dec. 5   J. MOORE & CO.

"If You Are In Bondage." In this advertisement for the Eagle Prize Office (*Richmond Enquirer*, 5 Dec. 1845), Samuel Smith's name does not appear, but the business was at his old location, selling what he had last sold, and the copy sounded like his, including the header "Look At This!—Look At This!" repeated Smith's advertisement in the same newspaper (22 Sept. 1845). The last line is rather extraordinary: "Recollect, that the Eagle is the emblem of Liberty; so, if you are in bondage, call on her at No. 2, East Main Street, and be liberated." If Smith was indeed the copywriter, he was describing himself, in one sense of the line's meaning, as a debtor beset by due bonds who hoped for liberation by means of a lucky ticket. The other sense of the line, if "bondage" referred to slavery, was probably read by many Richmonders as an ill-chosen attempt at humor. Yet it foretold Smith's role just over three years later.

accounts receivable of "the Boot and shoe business lately conducted by him" against a large bond.[93]

The terms of indenture enabled Smith to keep his possessions while he attempted to pay his debts, but his finances continued to spiral downward. On 14 October 1845 the final advertisement for the Red Boot appeared. In December a new lottery vendor, the Eagle Prize Office, opened at his former shop address. Though new proprietors signed its advertisements, the copy had the ring of Smith's, suggesting he was involved behind the scenes. This scheme also faltered, for the advertisements ceased by the end of March 1846. From November 1845 through January 1847 five judgments in court for debt went against Smith. By the start of 1847 Smith had no personal property to be taxed, and his wife was listed as the owner of a piano by herself, presumably as a separate household. In May 1847 a Richmond grand jury indicted several men on gambling charges, including Samuel Smith "for selling foreign lottery tickets without a license." When *Commonwealth* v. *Samuel A. Smith* was called in June 1847, Smith did not appear in court. Later gossip had it that he moved to Baltimore for a time, where he was "arrested for swindling, but managed to escape conviction."[94]

By 1848 Smith had returned to Richmond. How he dealt with the outstanding gambling charge against him, or with his court-certified debts, is unknown. Possibly the swindling charge that he eluded, alleged to have been in Baltimore, was the one for which he was indicted in Richmond. Certainly Smith's circumstances became more humble than those he had enjoyed a few years earlier. By April 1849 he was working in another man's shoe shop, and he may have been there several months earlier when Henry Brown approached him.[95]

There is no direct evidence that links Smith to Underground Railroad activities before 1849. By one report, however, Smith was "the comrade and next-door neighbor" of John A. Blevins, the former shoemaker convicted in 1848 of aiding slaves to escape, and another writer stated of Smith that "some years ago he was intimate with Blevins." Smith knew enough of Blevins's activities that in a letter to a northern abolitionist he identified a Richmond slave as "the person whom <u>Blevins</u> was to release." Smith himself declared several years later at a antislavery meeting that he had been involved in Underground Railroad activities since 1828. Yet it is difficult to believe that claim since Smith paid taxes on slaves as late as 1846.[96]

By the end of 1845 the legal system had become adversarial to Samuel Smith, and with the collapse of his business and the burden of his debt it is possible that he turned to less legitimate enterprise. That Smith knew of Blevins's intentions suggests that they were in communication prior to Blevins's August 1848 arrest. James C. A. Smith seems to have had more reason than mere acquaintance to refer Henry Brown to Samuel A. Smith.

Although Samuel Smith was no doubt receptive to Brown's offer to pay for his assistance, there was likely more to it. Smith later expressed higher motives that cannot be discounted simply because there was profit for him, because there was also extreme risk. Samuel Smith's involvements with gambling and the Underground Railroad were not unrelated. Each skirted the law, and in each there was not only potential profit but also the satisfaction of beating the system. When Henry Brown said that Smith had integrity, his perspective was not that of the authorities. That Smith in the eyes of the courts was near an outlaw could have stood as a credential for Brown. The purity of Smith's motives was not essential to Henry Brown. He had found an opening in slavery's fence.[97]

Chapter Two

Northbound

"Go and get a box"

Sometime after the Christmas concert, probably in January 1849, Henry Brown broached the subject of escape with Samuel Smith. "One day in the course of a little conversation with him," recalled Brown in the 1851 *Narrative,* "I said to him if I were free I would be able to do business such as he was doing." Smith responded that Brown's occupation of tobacconist was "a money-making one," and that if Brown were free he had "no need to change for another."

"As no person was near us," Brown told Smith that his wife and children had been sold away "about five months ago." Since then, he continued, "I had been meditating my escape from slavery," and he wondered if Smith might advise him how to proceed. Brown "told him I had a little money and if he would assist me I would pay him for so doing."[1]

Smith asked Brown if he "was not afraid to speak that way to him." Brown said he was not, "for I imagined he believed that every man had a right to liberty." Smith replied that Brown "was quite right, and asked me how much money I would give him if he would assist me to get away." Brown had "saved with more than a miser's eagerness every cent he could lay claim to," and told Smith he would pay him half of his money. Smith apparently assented to this amount. Accounts differ as to the agreed price but it was probably forty dollars. Smith described to him "several plans by which others had managed to effect their escape, but none of them exactly suited my taste."[2]

Brown consulted with James C. A. Smith. He, too, found the various methods of escape offered by Samuel Smith unsatisfactory. The three men mulled over possibilities. "Long did we remain together, attempting to devise ways and means to carry me away," Brown recalled, "but as often as a plan was suggested by my friend, there would appear some difficulty in the way of its accomplishment."[3]

In the face of obstacles, Brown had an inspiration. As he told it in the 1849 *Narrative,* he was at work one day, praying to God about freedom. "There darted into my mind these words, 'Go and get a box, and put yourself in it.'" His account in the 1851 *Narrative* states that he began to pray, "when the idea suddenly flashed across my mind of shutting myself *up in a box,* and getting myself conveyed as dry goods to a free state." The choice of this method of escape was undoubtedly Brown's.[4]

That his idea was feasible was due to the improvement in transportation brought by the railroad and the steamboat. Before these innovations Richmond was a long one hundred miles south of Washington by overland road, and the preferred mode of travel to the north was often the roundabout water passage via the James River to the Chesapeake Bay or the Atlantic Ocean. The Richmond, Fredericksburg, and Potomac Railroad was completed late in November 1842 and extended to Aquia Creek on the Potomac River. From there the connection to Washington was by the Washington and Fredericksburg Steamboat Company. The Washington Branch of the Baltimore and Ohio Railroad went from Washington to Baltimore, where it linked with the Philadelphia, Wilmington, and Baltimore Railroad, and that line reached Philadelphia via a railcar ferry across the Susquehanna River.[5]

By March 1849 the railroad passenger departed Richmond at 8 A.M., arrived at Washington at 4:30 P.M., at Baltimore at 7 P.M., and at Philadelphia, the first free city, "in the course of the night." The "traveler by the railroad line," boasted an advertisement, had "the advantage of being in Philadelphia in 19 hours from the time of his leaving Richmond." The northbound train that carried passengers also conveyed freight. Adams Express, a package service company, was usually able to deliver a parcel from Richmond to a Philadelphia address by noon the next day.[6]

The plan that the conspirators derived from Brown's inspiration was for him to be shipped in a box by Adams Express from Richmond to Philadelphia. The dangers involved in traveling "as dry goods to a free state" were evident. If he was detected, Brown would suffer a lashing and likely be sold south; even if his master was willing to forgive, the authorities would demand no less. Or, the sealed box might become Brown's coffin.[7]

Samuel Smith was skeptical at first. He told Brown that "he did not think I could live in a box for so long a time as would be necessary to convey me to Philadelphia." Brown insisted. "I had already made up my mind," he said, and Smith "consented to accompany me and keep the box right all the way."[8]

The 1849 *Narrative* states that Brown went to the railroad depot and noted the dimensions of "the largest boxes, which commonly were sent by the cars." He "repaired to a carpenter," who constructed a box to his specifications. "When the box was finished, I carried it, and placed it before my friend, who had promised to assist me, who asked me if that was 'to put my clothes in?' I replied that it was not, but to *'put Henry Brown in!'*"[9]

Less dramatic, but more likely, is the scenario suggested by the testimony of John Mettauer, "a mulatto man, a carpenter by trade," who recalled that Samuel A. Smith

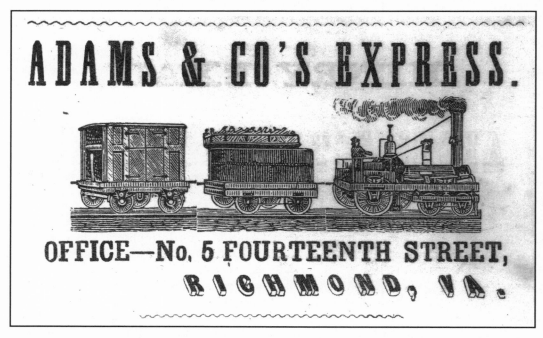

Adams Express, from advertisement in 1852 Richmond City Directory. In 1849, railroad equipment was evolving and not yet uniform; as yet, not all locomotives had cabs and variety typified passenger and freight cars.

had "employed him to make a pine box for him." Smith was "in a great hurry for the box," and Mettauer "worked after dark to finish it." The carpenter "did not know for what purpose Smith wanted the box." One man who examined the box described it as "a regular old store box . . . grooved at the Joints & braced at the ends leaving but the very slightest crevices to admit the air." The inside was lined with canvas. Eyewitness reports of its dimensions vary slightly; one detailed measurement was that the box was "3 feet long, 2 ft 8 inches deep, and 23 ½ inches wide—in the clear."[10]

For Brown's plan to work the box needed a destination. To find one Samuel Smith traveled to Philadelphia at the beginning of March 1849, probably funding the trip from Brown's payment. Smith called at 31 North Fifth Street, the office of the Pennsylvania Anti-Slavery Society. At the office that day were two of the society's activists, James Miller McKim and Cyrus M. Burleigh.[11]

J. Miller McKim was the "Resident Agent" of the Pennsylvania Anti-Slavery Society and ran the office. Miller McKim was from Carlisle, Pennsylvania, and thirty-eight years old. After graduating from Dickinson College, he became "an ardent and pronounced disciple of the 'New School' of Presbyterians." He had entered antislavery work in his early twenties, sparked by seeing copies of the *Liberator* at a black barber's shop, and he was also influenced by Lucretia Mott, the Philadelphia Quaker activist. McKim was the youngest delegate at the convention that formed the American Anti-Slavery Society in 1833, and in 1836 began working for the society as a lecturer. He was paid only eight dollars a week and expenses, and his meetings were disrupted by anti-abolitionist mobs wielding "stale eggs and other more dangerous missiles." In 1840 McKim went to work in the Philadelphia Anti-Slavery Office.[12]

Cyrus M. Burleigh, the other man present when Samuel Smith called, was an editor of the *Pennsylvania Freeman,* the society's weekly newspaper. A third employee at the office was William Still, a black man who worked as a clerk. All three were involved with the society's secretive Vigilance Committee, which aided fugitive slaves. The southernmost free city on the East Coast, Philadelphia was an active station on the Underground Railroad. Through the Vigilance Committee, fugitives found welcome there and assistance to travel on to New York, New England, and Canada.[13]

Once Samuel Smith determined that he had come to the right place, reported McKim, he told them "that he was a resident of the city of Richmond, and that he was very desirous to secure the escape of a man in that city who was held as a slave. He proposed to ship him by over-land express in a box to this city." McKim questioned "the risk & danger of such a scheme." Smith "overruled" McKim's objections, and satisfied him "that the plan was feasible. Said as a merchant he regularly shipped large boxes in that way &c &c. All he wanted he said was a man in Phila who would engage to receive the box." The slave, added Smith, "had saved a good deal of money by doing over-work & wd give any one $100. that wd receive the box." McKim told Smith that he could send the box to him "and let the man keep his $100." They agreed that "the box should be shipped" on the following Tuesday, 13 March 1849, and Smith departed for Virginia.[14]

After arriving back in Richmond, however, Samuel Smith wrote to McKim on Saturday, 10 March, that the attempt would have to be postponed. There was a problem with ice on the Susquehanna River. "Therefore I shall not send your Goods until the Cars can cross at Havre de grace," Smith explained. "The only Difficulty in the present rout[e] to philadelphia now is Good[s] have to be handled too often But when the Ice is out of the susquehanna they Go strait Through."[15]

McKim was not disappointed. He "had been in mortal fear for the previous day or two, lest the man should die of suffocation in the box, & we should be compelled on his

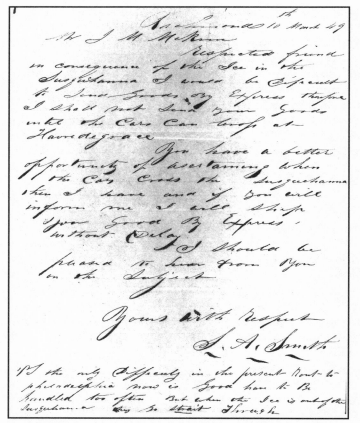

Samuel Smith wrote to McKim on Saturday, 10 March.

arrival to submit to the exposure of a coroners inquest." On Tuesday, 13 March, McKim wrote to Smith that the risk was too great and that he would no longer "consent to be a party to the scheme." The executive committee of the Pennsylvania Anti-Slavery Society met that day, and some of its members were also on the Vigilance Committee. McKim may have reflected on what he would tell them about the planned box escape. An associate later described McKim as a "prudent rash man," and perhaps it was a combination of his own fears—"How horrible I thought it wd be, & how deeply should we be censured, if the man were to come to us dead!"—and concern about the reactions of Vigilance Committee members that caused McKim to withdraw his endorsement.[16]

What Samuel Smith told Henry Brown about his visit to Philadelphia or about McKim's retreat from the scheme is not known. Brown's determination to make the attempt regardless of risk no doubt bolstered Smith's response on Thursday, 15 March 1849: "I feel perfectly safe in sending the Box and shall ship it on Tuesday next if there is any name or number to which you would prefer its Being consigned please answer by return mail if not I shall certainly send it on Tuesday morning and it will arive in your city Either at 3 o clock on Wednesday morning or 3 o clock Wednesday afternoon and I hope you will be on the spot to Receive the Box please answer by Return mail and let me know if you will attend to the Box as I wish to satisfy him on that subject Befor Shipment." Smith also noted that, "Unless you send some other direction," he would "mark the box James Johnson, 31 N. 5 Street, Phil"—the street address of the Anti-Slavery Society.[17]

The Tuesday specified for shipment would be 20 March. McKim realized that the men in Richmond intended to do this thing no matter what the danger, and made preparations in Philadelphia to receive the box. "My mind continues unchanged as to the risk of injury to the contents of that box if kept so long confined," McKim wrote Smith on Saturday, the seventeenth. "However, you can do as you choose about sending it, as long as it is not your intention to send it to me." A merchant friend had agreed to "send his porter to the depot . . . who will see to the safe delivery of the box." Address the box to "James Johnson, 131 Arch St," he told Smith. "If you are determined to send it," he concluded, "had you not better see that there is a crack or two at the joints of the box?"[18]

McKim was not at all sure about the venture. He was worried about tragic consequences both for the escapee and the Anti-Slavery Society and sought to exonerate "myself & the office from all legal responsibility." If Smith "was determined to send this box on his own responsibility—I of course wd make no objection." Simultaneously he was thinking about liability and the practical aspects of escaping in a box and how to make the attempt successful. "I had things put in train to receive the box & take it out of the cars immediately on its arrival."[19]

James Miller McKim

The friend and merchant who agreed to help out McKim was Edward M. Davis, the son-in-law of Quaker activists Lucretia and James Mott. Davis had attended the meeting of the society's executive committee, where he probably learned about the scheme. According to William Still, Davis was "extensively engaged in mercantile business" and could "talk about 'boxes, freight, etc.' from any part of the country" without arousing suspicions. He did business daily with Adams Express and was "well acquainted with the firm and some of the drivers." Davis arranged for "Dan, an Irishman, one of Adams' Express drivers," a man whom he trusted, "to go to the depot after the box."[20]

In Richmond, the box was ready. Samuel Smith made arrangements to have the box conveyed to the Express office. Now Henry Brown had to ensure that his disappearance would go unnoticed for a few days. The 1849 *Narrative* states that Brown went to overseer John F. Allen and "requested of him permission to refrain from labor for a short time, in consequence of a disabled finger." Allen refused, "on the ground that my hand was not lame enough." Allen's refusal may explain why the box was not shipped on Tuesday, 20 March, the date Smith had set in his letter to McKim.[21]

Meanwhile the box was expected in Philadelphia. That Tuesday there was another meeting of the executive committee, probably in the early evening. One imagines that McKim was somewhat distracted from the regular business of the committee, "for there was no room to suppose that Adams' Express office had any sympathy with the Abolitionist or the fugitive." Later that night McKim and Dan the porter went to the depot of the Philadelphia, Wilmington, and Baltimore Railroad at Eleventh and Market Streets.[22]

"Wednesday morning at 3 o'clock was the time at which—in due course—it should have arrived," wrote McKim, whose aim was "to deliver the box immediately on its arrival, without waiting as usual till after daylight." William Still recalled of McKim that "one of the most serious walks he ever took—and they had not been a few—to meet and accompany passengers, he took at half past two o'clock that morning to the depot. Not once, but for more than a score of times, he fancied the slave would be dead." As the freight was unloaded from the cars, McKim scanned anxiously for a box large enough to contain a man. "One alone had that appearance, and he confessed it really seemed as if there was the scent of death about it," wrote Still. But it was not the one, and "he was free to say he experienced a marked sense of relief."[23]

Later on Wednesday, McKim received a letter from Smith, sent the previous day, stating that the box would arrive in the wee hours of Thursday morning. "So we were on hand," McKim wrote, "but with the like result." By now he was "so nervous from loss of sleep & apprehending that the man would come to us dead" that he wrote Smith on Thursday evening "declining to 'accept the consignment.'"[24]

In the meantime in Richmond, after John F. Allen had judged Henry Brown's finger not lame enough to miss work, James Smith acquired some oil of vitriol and passed it on to Brown. Intending to pour but "a few drops upon my finger," Brown applied so much of the caustic sulfuric acid that his finger "was soon eaten through to the bone." Overseer Allen had no choice but to send him home, with advice to "get a poultice of flax-meal to it, and keep it well poulticed until it got better." Bought with a painful wound, Brown now had his opportunity.[25]

"This side up with care"

One can only imagine Henry Brown's thoughts and feelings as he prepared to be sealed into his box. Between the hurried departure and the completion of the arrangements, he probably did not have much time to reflect, but surely he thought of the fate of his family and of friends and relatives he would leave behind as he was transported to an unknown future. Brown recalled later that he imagined the scene as he emerged to freedom and he selected a hymn of thanks to sing. A strong vision of a happy outcome would help him to endure the suffering of the journey.

In the early morning of Friday, 23 March 1849, Henry Brown likely slipped by dark back ways to the clandestine rendezvous. Brown, Samuel Smith, and James Smith met at 4 A.M., probably at Samuel Smith's residence or at his shop. Attending to the final details perhaps helped to allay their apprehensions. The box was to be addressed to "James Johnson, 131 Arch St," Philadelphia, and marked "This side up with care." The specifics of the parting are not recorded, but Brown's recollection suggests a somber scene: "I laid me down in my darkened home of three feet by two, and like one about to be guillotined, resigned myself to my fate." As McKim described it later, Brown "placed himself in it in a sitting posture, his back shoulder & head resting against one end & his feet braced against the other." James C. A. Smith and Samuel Smith nailed the lid on the box and wrapped it with five hoops of hickory wood.[26]

Shortly after, the collaborators loaded the box onto a wagon. It is likely that a hired driver and team carried the box to the Express office, and that the driver was given a note containing shipping instructions to present to the clerk. Although Samuel Smith said that he often shipped parcels by express, the note probably did not identify him as the shipper of this one. Nor did Smith give the driver money to pay the shipping charge; the box was shipped freight due.

The Adams Express office was in the Exchange Hotel at Fourteenth and Franklin Streets, which Brown said "was about a mile distant from the place where I was packed." Freight for northern destinations was received at the office and then transferred to the terminus of the Richmond, Fredericksburg, and Potomac Railroad, seven blocks away at Eighth and Broad Streets. The railroad did not yet have a depot; the tracks ran down the middle of Broad Street to Eighth, and the cars were loaded in the street.[27]

"I had no sooner arrived at the office than I was turned heels up, while some person nailed something on the end of the box," Brown recalled. The trip from the office to the train tested Brown immediately. Despite the box lid's injunction of "This side up with care," the box was set on the wagon on end, putting Brown on his head. As the wagon bumped to train-side "he felt strange pains" but "gave no sign." The box was roughly loaded from the wagon to the train freight car, but this time placed right side up.[28]

Although Brown later stated that Samuel Smith had "consented" to accompany the box on the train, Smith did not go. He could not have ridden with the box without calling attention to it, but whether Brown knew when he embarked that Smith would not be along is unclear. Samuel Smith probably watched as the cars slowly pulled out about 8 A.M. He then walked to the office of the Washington and Petersburg Telegraph Line and wired Miller McKim in Philadelphia: "Those goods were shipped this morning & will be in Phila tomorrow morning."[29]

The first leg of the journey north was from Richmond to the Potomac River. The seventy-eight miles usually took about four hours. At best, if the train schedule held, Henry Brown would be entombed for nearly twenty-four hours, with his survival at the mercy of events he could not control. He took with him some crackers, about a half-gallon of water in a beef bladder (which being soft would not bang about), a small gimlet, and his hat. Once en route, Brown decided not to eat the crackers for fear he would become thirsty. He used the gimlet to bore four small holes in the box "to let in a little air," stated a later account. He used his hat to fan himself. "Nothing saved him from suffocation but the free use of water . . . with which he bathed his face, and the constant fanning of himself," wrote McKim. "He fanned himself unremittingly all the time."[30]

During the trip from Richmond to the Potomac, as the train took on more freight at stops along the way, twice the box was shifted so that Brown was "set down with his back, shoulders & head downwards." There was little regard paid to the "this side up," which McKim observed "was written very indistinctly." Amid the noisiness of the freight car Brown "turned in the box & fixed himself right," but not, said McKim, without "a very considerable struggle."[31]

At Aquia Creek on the Potomac, passengers and goods were transferred from the railroad to the Washington and Fredericksburg Steamboat Company. The steamboats were wooden side-paddlers that made the approximately forty miles upriver to Washington city wharf in about four hours. The box was set end down on the steamboat, again putting Brown on his head, but here, wrote McKim, "he was surrounded by a number of passengers; some of whom stood by & often sat on the box. All was quiet & if he had attempted to turn he would have been heard."

"In this dreadful position," recalled Brown in the 1849 *Narrative*, "I remained the space of an hour and a half, it seemed to me, when I began to feel of my eyes and head, and found to my dismay, that my eyes were almost swollen out of their sockets." He could not take a full breath and, he later told McKim, "the veins in his temples . . . were swollen as 'thick [as] his finger and beat like hammers.'" After another half hour Brown "attempted again to lift my hands to my face, but I found I was not able to move them. A cold sweat now covered me from head to foot. . . . Every moment I expected to feel the blood flowing over me, which had burst from my veins."[32]

Then he heard two men in conversation. One said that they had been on the boat for two hours and traveled twenty miles. He proposed that they sit. "They suited the action to the word, and turned the box over, containing my soul and body, thus delivering me from the power of the grim messenger of death." One of them asked what the box might contain. Probably the mail, guessed the other. "Yes," thought Brown to himself, "it is a male, indeed, although not the mail of the United States."[33]

The steamboat finally reached the wharf at Washington, and the box was put on a wagon for transfer to the railroad depot. It was about 4 P.M. The terminus of the Baltimore and Ohio Railroad at Second Street and Pennsylvania Avenue was upward of a mile from the landing. On arriving at the depot, the driver called for help to unload the box. "Some one answered him to the effect that he might throw it off," Brown recalled in the

Washington Steamboat Wharf. On 23 March 1849, the Potomac River steamboat conveying Henry Brown arrived at Washington in the afternoon.

1851 *Narrative*, "but, says the driver, it is marked 'this side up with care.'" The driver's concern was eased when "the other answered him that it did not matter if he broke all that was in it, the railway company were able enough to pay for it." With that, Brown felt himself begin "to tumble from the waggon." The porter "threw or dropped" the box "with violence to the ground, and it rolled down a small hill, turning over two or three times." The box landed "on the end where my head was. I could hear my neck give a crack, as if it had been snapped asunder, and I was knocked completely insensible."[34]

Perhaps it was Brown's great sense of mission that kept him from crying out even as he lost consciousness. Yet no matter with what strength he might exercise self-control, he was not the master of events. As he came to, he heard words that made him despair. The box was so heavy, said the porter at the depot, that there was no room for it on the train. It must lay over until the next day.

"My heart swelled in my throat; I could scarcely breathe; great sweats came over me; I gave up all hope," related Brown later. Then he remembered "the preacher had said 'it is good to pray at all times.' So I tried to pray, 'Lord Jesus, put it into the hearts of these men to find a way to send this box forward.'" As he was praying a man's voice declared "that box must go on; it's the express mail." Brown recalled, "Oh, what relief I felt."[35]

But each victory over circumstance seemed to lead to a new challenge. The box was loaded onto the freight car with Brown again "placed head downwards," and the train pulled out. After a while Brown found his "eyes were swollen almost out of my head, and I was fast becoming insensible." McKim wrote that at such times "the water was of special use to him & without it & the fanning he must have died." But the train did not proceed far, only "the space of half an hour," before more baggage was loaded on and Brown's "box got shifted about and so happened to turn upon its right side."[36]

Brown remained in his "proper position" for the rest of his journey. The train proceeded the thirty-seven miles from Washington to Baltimore, where the Baltimore and Ohio terminated and the Philadelphia, Wilmington, and Baltimore Railroad picked up the line to the north. In 1849 the two railroads shared a depot, but it is not clear whether the same train cars continued on, pulled by a new locomotive, or if passengers and parcels were transferred to new cars. Brown's accounts of his journey do not mention trouble at Baltimore.[37]

The barge crossing at the Susquehanna River about two hours out of Baltimore was also uneventful. Brown may have fallen asleep after Baltimore, for it had been a long and arduous day, and his account of the ninety-five-mile leg to Philadelphia in his *Narrative* is very brief. At long last Brown heard a voice call out, "We are in port and at Philadelphia." McKim expected the train at 3 A.M. but reported that "the cars were a good while behind time hour." By 5 A.M. Brown had been in his box for twenty-four hours. "I wondered," he said, "if any person knew that such a box was there."[38]

Philadelphia

In Philadelphia, Miller McKim's Thursday letter to Samuel Smith calling off the plan had become immaterial because "on Friday fore-noon came a telegraphic despatch." The box was on its way north. "There was now no backing out." For greater safety, McKim decided not to go again to the depot, "which might excite suspicion," but rather to have the box delivered to the Anti-Slavery Society's office.[39]

Dan, the porter who had gone with McKim to the depot on Wednesday and Thursday mornings, met the cars again Saturday morning. Henry Brown recalled that "a person inquired for a box directed to such a place, 'right side up.'" It was soon on the wagon. "This express man suspected I suppose what was going on," wrote McKim, "but had sense enought to know nothing." The box was "soon whisked round to the Anti-Slavery office. A man was there to unlock the door & help to lift it in," reported McKim. "A little before 6 the box was set down 'this side up' inside of the office door. It was just clearly day light and no one was out moving on the streets." For his trouble—and lack of curiosity—the porter accepted a five-dollar gold piece and departed.[40]

Inside the box, Brown "heard voices whispering" during the delivery, but he "lay still, not knowing who the people were." McKim entered the office where the box had been placed, "dreading lest I should find the man inside dead." He rapped on the box and called, "all right?" The reply promptly "came from within—'all right, Sir.'" "I never felt happier in life hardly," McKim declared. "It was an immense burden off my mind."[41]

At this point McKim, by his account, was joined by William Still, clerk at the Anti-Slavery Office and a mainstay of the Vigilance Committee, and Lewis Thompson, who lived upstairs and whose firm, Merrihew and Thompson, printed the society's newspaper and tracts. Arriving at the office a short time later was Professor Charles Dexter Cleveland, who operated a school for young ladies.[42]

Using a saw and hatchet, the men cut away the five hickory hoops and pried off the lid. Then "the marvelous resurrection of Brown ensued," as Still put it. "We opened the box," wrote McKim, "& up rose—with a face radiant with joy & gratitude—one of the finest looking men you ever saw in your life." Still recalled that "he was about as wet as if he had come up out of the Delaware." Brown extended his hand and said, "Good morning, gentlemen!"[43]

"It was a most thrilling scene," wrote McKim. An abolitionist who learned about the escape shortly afterward said that McKim's reaction was "so great as to stop his breath; but when he could speak, he wildly exclaimed, 'You are the greatest man in America.'" Brown recalled in the 1851 *Narrative* that "I rose a freeman, but I was too weak, by reason of long confinement in that box, to be able to stand, so I immediately swooned away." His welcomers helped him out of the box, and he paced the room several times to clear his head.[44]

"Then hadnt we a time of congratulations & mutual rejoicing," wrote McKim. "I wish all the world could have witnessed the scene of opening that box." Brown's first impression, after recovering from fainting, was of "a number of friends, each one seeming more anxious than another" to render him assistance and bid him "a hearty welcome to the possession of my natural rights." McKim wrote, "The man was so full of gratitude to us & to his God." In Brown's words, "I felt much more than I could readily express," and he gave thanks to "the kindness of Almighty God."[45]

Brown told the group he had chosen a hymn to sing "if he should get through in safety," and proceeded to sing part of it. "It was beautiful & appropriate," stated McKim. Still reported that he sang "most touchingly" and "to the delight of his small audience." The hymn's words, from Psalm 40, began, "I waited patiently, I waited patiently for the Lord, for the Lord; And he inclined unto me and heard my calling."[46]

McKim then took Brown to his home and "gave him refreshment & a bath." Brown's "happiness seemed greater than he could express." There Brown sang the complete hymn. "It was exceedingly affecting. He has a fine voice," wrote McKim. "It was impossible to listen to him without tears.[47]

McKim next took Brown to the home of James and Lucretia Mott, which was adjacent to the house of their son-in-law Edward M. Davis, the merchant who had facilitated the reception of the box. These homes were a stopping place for many abolitionists while in Philadelphia. Visiting at this time was the Reverend Samuel Joseph May, a Unitarian minister from Syracuse, and a leading abolitionist, who was in town to deliver a lecture. At the Motts' residence, reported Still, Brown "met a most cordial reception . . . and delight and joy filled all hearts in that stronghold of philanthropy." Brown, "so

Executive Committee, Pennsylvania Anti-Slavery Society. 1851. Standing fifth from left is J. Miller McKim, Samuel Smith's Philadelphia contact. Standing second from left is E. M. Davis, the merchant who did business with Adams Express. Seated from left are Oliver Johnson, Mrs. Margaret James Burleigh, Benjamin C. Bacon, and Robert Purvis. Seated farthest right are Lucretia Mott and James Mott. Standing, left to right, are Mary Grew, Davis, Haworth Wetherald, Abby Kimber, McKim, and Sarah Pugh.

long doubled up in the box," desired fresh air, so James Mott gave him "one of his broad-brim hats" and "Brown promenaded the yard flushed with victory." After some time there, Brown went to the home of William Still, where he spent his first two nights out of slavery.[48]

William Still

There was a great deal of excitement among Philadelphia abolitionists at the escape, but they tried to keep the story to themselves. Legally Henry Brown was still the property of William Barret. Under the federal law Brown remained a slave bound by the laws of Virginia. Publicity might risk recapture and could inhibit future efforts of the Vigilance Committee.

As was probably inevitable, the number of those in the know gradually increased. They included the four men who opened the box, the Mott and the Davis families, Samuel May, and Still's wife. No doubt selected members of the Pennsylvania Anti-Slavery Society were informed, as were other antislavery friends. One, a physician, Dr. Charles Noble, stated that "if he had been consulted, he should have said it would be impossible for the man to be shut up and live twenty-four hours." Over the next few days McKim and Lucretia Mott, and likely others, sent letters to people outside Philadelphia that told about the escape.[49]

One other person who learned of Brown's successful outcome was Samuel Smith. The day of the arrival McKim sent both a telegram and a letter to Smith in Richmond. Although he continued to correspond, McKim changed his view of Smith's role in the escape after talking with Brown. "I had supposed that the white man who made the arrangements with me was the principal one in devising & executing the project," McKim wrote to a friend. "But this was not the fact. The whole plan was conceived & nearly the whole of it executed by the slave." Smith's contribution was simply "to engage some one in Phila to receive the box, & then to mark & ship it." As Brown explained it to McKim, "all the rest was done by the slave—excepting some trifling services which he received from a brother colored man." McKim concluded that "the white man was a mere mercenary in the affair."[50]

Brown's reasons for minimizing the roles of the two Smiths in his escape are not clear. It may be that in correcting McKim's perception that Samuel Smith was the "principal one" Brown was especially emphatic. As a fugitive among strangers, sympathetic though they were, Brown may have felt the need to assert his own responsibility in initiating and carrying out the plan as a way of asserting also his own capability and independence.

Brown rested Sunday and Monday at Still's residence. While there he may have been welcomed by other black Philadelphians. For safety, however, Brown needed to go farther north, and it was arranged that he would be sent to Sydney Howard Gay in New York. Gay was a member of the New York Anti-Slavery Society and editor of the weekly *National Anti-Slavery Standard*. On Monday, 26 March, McKim composed a letter of introduction for Brown to carry north with him.

"Here is a man who has been the hero of one of the most extraordinary achievements I ever heard of," he wrote. "He came to me on Saturday morning last in a box tightly hooped marked 'this side up' by *overland express from the City of Richmond*! Did you ever hear of any thing in your life to beat that? Nothing that was done on the Barricades of Paris exceeded this cool & deliberate intrepidity. To appreciate fully the boldness & risk of this achievement you ought to see the box & hear all the circumstances. . . . He will tell you the whole story." From New York, Brown was to go on to Boston, where McKim expected he could find work. "And now I have one request to make," he told Gay, "for Heaven's sake don't publish this affair or allow it to be published—It would compromise the express & prevent all others from escaping the same way."[51]

Brown departed from Philadelphia Tuesday morning, three days after he had arrived. He probably traveled to New York by railroad. William Still or another friend may have helped him safely aboard, and then alerted the New York friends by telegraph, or a friend might have accompanied him. As a fugitive traveler, Brown could not relax his guard, but compared to the life-or-death stakes of the journey to Philadelphia, the trip to New York was far easier. He must have felt exhilaration to think of his successful exit from Richmond and the move from baggage car to passenger car, and from box to seat. His future was still unknown even if the possibilities were far more favorable than before, but it is likely Brown did not dwell on what might become of him. The rush of the scenery outside the windows and the speed at which events were unfolding probably kept his mind firmly in the present.

Connections in New York occurred without incident. In the 1851 *Narrative*, Brown said that there he "became acquainted with Mr. H. Long, and Mr. Eli Smith, who were very kind to me the whole time I remained there." He traveled on to Boston and spent a few days under the auspices of Francis Jackson, an abolitionist leader. From there Brown went down to New Bedford, Massachusetts. He arrived on the evening of 29 March at the home of Joseph Ricketson, another abolitionist and a merchant of whale oil. Ricketson wrote to Sydney Howard Gay the next day that Brown had "staid at my house last night and took breakfast this morning." Brown's finger was "still bad from the effects of the oil of vitriol," and Ricketson said that Brown had gone to see a doctor that morning. One wonders if the fugitive followed John F. Allen's advice to treat the wound with a flax-meal poultice, or if Brown's New England doctor offered an alternative remedy.[52]

"Wonderful Escape"

Miller McKim was emphatic in his letter to Sydney Howard Gay that the story of Henry Brown's escape not be published. Gay, though he was the editor of the *National Anti-Slavery Standard,* complied. Abolitionists understood the reasons for keeping Brown's escape out of print, but it was a tale too good not to pass along. The circle expanded of those who had heard it, and very soon reached the ears of a newspaper writer. The story of Henry Brown's courageous journey was more than remarkable. In less than three weeks McKim's plea for secrecy was undone.

On 12 April 1849, the *Burlington Courier*, in Vermont, published an article entitled "Wonderful Escape of a Slave." The article contained no names, was vague about places, and emphasized the method and valor of the escape. "When did Spartan intrepidity show greater firmness and fortitude under bodily suffering, than did this poor slave, when animated by the inspiring hope of freedom? We are glad to have assurance that this story is no flight of fancy," the article stated, "but is absolutely true."[53]

A reader of the article apparently contacted Adams Express. By 16 April officials of Adams Express in Philadelphia communicated their displeasure over box shipments to Miller McKim, who "promised them that I should never have another sent to me." Journalists in 1849 gathered news from distant places by exchanging newspaper subscriptions and reprinting articles of interest, and an editor at the *New York Daily Tribune* spotted the article in the Vermont newspaper. On 17 April the widely distributed *Tribune* reprinted "Wonderful Escape of a Slave." With that, the story was out.[54]

Once the story was public, the antislavery press quickly printed it. The *Pennsylvania Freeman* reprinted "Wonderful Escape of a Slave" on 19 April, the *Liberator* published it on 20 April, and a week later the *National Anti-Slavery Standard* reprinted the article from the *Freeman.* The editors of each of these papers knew more about the escape than the article disclosed but refrained from adding to the original story. Editor Cyrus M. Burleigh, of the *Pennsylvania Freeman,* did add an introductory note vouching personally for the story's truth.[55]

A letter criticizing the *New York Daily Tribune* brought further attention to the story. A correspondent, who used the pseudonym "Conscience," complained that by reprinting the *Courier* article, the *Tribune* seemed "to sanction and approve" the illegal acts of those who helped the slave escape. The *Tribune* replied that "we publish all sorts of doings" and that to record the news was not necessarily to approve of it. "But as to the general question involved," the *Tribune* continued, "we say, once for all, that we hold every innocent man's right to himself paramount to any right to his body which can be vested in another; and if a box should come directed to us with a live man in it, we should at the very least presume him the owner of himself until somebody else proved title to him." Even then, "we should let that somebody take his property running, recognizing no obligation resting on us to help him catch it."[56]

The *National Anti-Slavery Standard* noted the exchange. Referring to the correspondent's pseudonym, editor Sydney Howard Gay commented, " ' 'Tis conscience makes cowards of us all,' says Shakespeare, but he would have said no such thing had he been an American of the nineteenth century. The only brave thing about us is our conscience."[57]

In the meantime, Henry Brown discovered that he was not entirely among strangers in New Bedford. Before leaving Richmond, he had heard that one of his sisters lived in New Bedford, and Joseph Ricketson wrote that "Henry's sister is at service here and is a very nice woman." Brown knew others as well. "He has many friends here who former [*sic*] lived in Richmond," wrote Ricketson. "He will remain with them for a while— & I think with their assistance & my own he can get along." On 29 April, Ricketson asked a friend in Boston if she had seen the story in the *National Anti-Slavery Standard.* "The said slave came consigned to me about three weeks since," he reported. Brown "appears to be a fine fellow, has found considerable employment—he has worked several days for me." The manner of the escape excited great interest in New Bedford. "Every one that hears of it or seen him are astonished. They all glorify in it & I think it will have a strong tendency to cement the Anti Slavery feeling here." Ricketson was torn between prudence and the wish to proclaim Brown's feat. "Were it not for exposing the express I would call a town meeting," he declared.[58]

Despite Ricketson's and other abolitionists' caution, the consequences of "exposing the express" were apt to be felt, for the tale was on the streets. It was the sort of story people noted and remarked on to others. Moreover, it was an item that fed the controversy that was coming to dominate American politics, the sectional conflict over slavery.

The treaty that ended the war with Mexico early in 1848 conveyed to the United States vast western territories. The question of whether the system of slavery would expand into these new territories was an underlying issue of the 1848 presidential election. In the North, the new Free Soil Party stood for the exclusion of slavery from the western territories. The candidates of the major parties did not directly address the matter, for the Democrats and the Whigs were both divided into northern and southern wings and avoided issues that might split them apart. The abolitionist pamphleteer Charles Stearns mocked the Whig candidate for president, General Zachary Taylor, a native of Virginia and a commander in the Mexican War, for saying that he had "been so occupied in military exploits, that 'he never had been able to attend the merits of the controversy between the Whigs and Democrats!' " The busy Taylor's strategy of remaining aloof from partisan issues proved effective and he was elected president.[59]

Taylor's inauguration as president occurred a little more than two weeks before Henry Brown's journey in the box. The new Congress would convene in December 1849 to face a legislative agenda driven by the sectional conflict. The House of Representatives was so closely divided that the Free Soil Party's thirteen congressmen held the potential balance of power. In a political atmosphere that was increasingly fractionalized and even combustible, the story of the escape of a slave in a box spoke to all sides: a tale of bravery and ingenuity, and of lawbreaking and conspiracy.[60]

"Miracles in the Line"

On 24 March Miller McKim sent word to Samuel A. Smith by both telegraph and mail that Henry Brown had arrived safely that day in Philadelphia. Not hearing back from Smith, he wrote again on 3 April. He asked if Smith had heard of a rumor about the escape and inquired after the remaining half of Brown's money.[61]

Samuel Smith replied on 6 April. He had received both of McKim's letters, but the telegram "did not leave the office in your city as the wires was out of order between Richmond and Phila." Smith had also tried unsuccessfully to send a telegram that day and he advised McKim that "the money you paid for the Dispa[t]ch would be returned to you as <u>mine</u> was to me."

"As regards the <u>rumor</u> about the shipment from here or Charleston I have heard <u>nothing</u> of the kind," wrote Smith. Indeed William Barret seems to have placed no runaway advertisements in the Richmond newspapers after Brown disappeared, and Smith noted "there has scarcely been an Enquiry about" him. Smith had "called to see about the money being sent on and am assured it will sent on a weeks time," a statement implying that the process was out of his hands. "Remember me to the person," Smith told McKim. "I have no fear as regard addrssg you at your place and any business I can attend to for you or your <u>friends</u> in any <u>part</u> of Virginia or N. Carolina can be attended to."

The next line in Smith's letter McKim probably had to read more than once. "Next week you will receive from me some Goods and the <u>money</u> <u>in</u> <u>advance</u> to pay the charges." That Smith intended to send another fugitive in a box surely shocked and alarmed McKim. Not only that, but Smith seemed to look forward to making a regular practice of such shipments. "It is in my <u>power</u> to work <u>miaricles</u> [*sic*] in the Line for a <u>small</u> compensation Being acquainted all south from Washington to New orleans." In closing Smith enjoined McKim "to <u>Burn</u> up <u>all</u> my letters as I <u>do</u> yours."[62]

McKim responded immediately: "I must positively decline however receiving any consignments; and I advise you for your own sake not to send any." Brown's escape was "known to a multitude in this city & there is every reason to believe it will reach Richmond." Smith should not make another attempt "till you know all the circumstances of the last shipment." McKim invited him to visit next time he came to Philadelphia. "I am glad that money is coming on for that man," McKim said. "He feels badly about it."[63]

Smith had not yet received that letter when he wrote again to McKim on 11 April: "tomorrow morning I shall send you a Box of Goods directed to Jas Miller 231 Arch St." Smith was confident that it would arrive safely. "The line is so straight and I being engaged in the merchantile Business and so frequently shipping good that there can be no suspicion." This time there would be "money amongst the Goods to repay <u>all</u> expenses."[64]

McKim responded the next day, probably as soon as he finished reading Smith's letter. "Your letter of the 11<u>th</u> surprises me," wrote McKim. "You say you know there is no danger. I tell you you know nothing about it. It was a miracle that your friend did not lose his life. You dont know half the dangers that he escaped; and it is absurd to attempt a similar project till you know the particulars of this. I can not allow you to compel me against my will to be a party to what I so strongly disapprove. When I see you I can explain more particularly; but I again tell you for your <u>own</u> sake, <u>forbear</u>."[65]

Smith did not make the shipment as quickly as he had promised, and he had McKim's two letters of refusal in hand when he wrote to McKim on 14 April. "I am sorry you cannot receive <u>one</u> more as it is a very hard case and one which in <u>Justice</u> to Humanity should be attended." If McKim could only "find a <u>consignee</u>," he would trouble him "no more." McKim had labeled Smith a mercenary, based on Henry Brown's account, but Smith's appeal countered that impression. "God <u>will</u> reward us both for it I obtain nothing in this case only the expences of shipment," Smith implored. "Friend McKim use your best endeavors."[66]

McKim was certainly relieved to learn that another shipment was not imminent. Yet he also knew that Henry Brown had instigated his own escape and he did not wish to block a slave's way to freedom. Should the scheme be tried again, it would have to be done better. He wrote back to Smith at length on 16 April with a promise to try "to find a consignee for your goods." He also delivered "a few directions," based on what Brown had told him about his experience. Although the box itself was "of the very best size & shape that could have been hit upon," McKim advised, "don't send unless you allow much more breathing space." Brown nearly suffocated, and "any common man would have died." Inside the box the gimlet was useful and the bladder of water and the hat were essential. Heat could be deadly, so the box "should be sent in cool weather." The slave should be informed about the transfers of the box en route. "Don't send unless your man knows every thing to which he will be liable. He must have immense patience, courage, and endurance. He must understand that on the way no regard is paid to the words 'this side up.' "[67]

McKim explained that since "Adams & Co. know" of Brown's escape, receiving the box in Philadelphia had become more complicated. "We called for him," he wrote, but "the next man wd have to take the regular course of delivery & would not probably be released before 10 o'clock in the forenoon." For that reason, too, "the box should not be sent as before to a fictitious name & address; but to a real name and address." Above all, he continued, "don't send unless you are sure that there will be somebody here willing to receive it; and that he will be <u>in town</u> & <u>on hand when it comes</u>," a warning to Smith not to act without clearance from Philadelphia.

McKim closed with several requests for more information. "You say this is a case of peculiar injustice that you now have on hand. Please let me know as much about the case as you can." He also asked Smith for "particulars" about the present owner of Henry Brown's "wife & children & where they are; & whether they could be got & how."

Smith responded with two letters on 19 April. A short letter, signed "S. A Smith," was probably written as cover for Smith's by-now-regular correspondence to Philadelphia, perhaps while under the observation of a nosy Richmonder. "I find," the note said, "that a good article of wrought iron could be purchased at as low as $22.40 per ton which if you can pay that price and Expence of shipment I have no doubt but there could be a considerable quantity bot up here."[68]

In the other letter, which he signed "Jas Johnson," Smith responded to McKim's interest in the slave waiting to be sent to Philadelphia. "<u>He</u> was the person whom <u>Blevins</u> was to release he was confined in Jail 4 months and received 200 Lashes and nearly starved to death all to make him reveal the <u>Secrets</u> of Blevins. (all to no effect)," Smith explained. The slave had since then been "kept in the most <u>sevear</u> servitude and scarcely allowed to speak." If he could not escape in the next four or five days, "he will be sold to some of these Fiends of Hell who trade in <u>Human</u> <u>Flesh</u> his master says he <u>shall</u> be sold." McKim's reply would be "anxiously Looked for," and Smith promised he would write about Brown's family "in a few days."[69]

There is no extant reply from McKim to this letter. In the meantime, the reprinted article about the escape by box appeared in the *New York Daily Tribune*. The publicity changed the circumstances for attempting another such escape, and McKim may have wished to consult with his committee before proceeding. It is possible, too, that the name Blevins did not register with him, as Smith assumed it would. The slave described in Smith's letter was likely someone caught up in the investigations following the escape of the four slaves in June 1848. John A. Blevins's case had not been reported in the newspapers, and whether McKim knew of his service to the Underground Railroad is unknown.

In mid-April, Samuel Smith moved to new quarters, on Broad Street between Third and Fourth Streets, the same block in which James C. A. Smith's cake shop was reported to have been located. Samuel Smith lived upstairs over a shoe shop operated by Stephen H. Fisher. Smith worked on shoes and kept the books for Fisher, who lived a few miles away on Church Hill. Smith shared his home with Catharine Dolbow, who had been living with him for six months, although they were not married.[70]

Smith wrote to McKim again on 26 April, requesting "word to whom I shall consign my goods." He reminded McKim that "this is an urgent case and if not attended in a <u>few</u> days will be forever too late." To this letter came a reply from Philadelphia, though who wrote it is not known. The contact in Philadelphia was now to be Cyrus M. Burleigh, whom Smith had met when he visited the antislavery society's office in March. McKim would be out of town for a meeting. The letter also provided an address: "P. Williamson, No. 32, Buttonwood Street, Philadelphia." A second escape by box could proceed.[71]

In Richmond, Samuel Smith and James C. A. Smith carried the plan forward. Boldly—and probably without informing Burleigh—they decided to ship two slaves in two boxes. One was Alfred, who was hired out to John Talman at the Washington Hotel. The other was Sawney, a friend of Alfred and "a fine hotel-waiter," hired out to J. M. Sublett at the Columbian Hotel. James C. A. Smith introduced them to Samuel Smith. One paid Samuel Smith $65, and the other about $30 or $40. Which of them, if either, was the "urgent case" Smith wrote about to McKim is unknown.[72]

The boxes for the scheme were apparently constructed in Samuel Smith's kitchen, a separate building on the alley behind Fisher's shoe store. They were made of yellow pine, and each was somewhat longer than Brown's box, perhaps in response to McKim's advice about providing air to breathe. The completed boxes were hidden in the kitchen.[73]

The shipment was set for Tuesday, 8 May 1849. Some days before, Sawney brought his trunk of personal possessions to James C. A. Smith's cake shop. James Smith wrapped it in canvas and "had the initial letters J. M. F. marked in two places on the canvass." On Saturday, 5 May, Alfred and Sawney visited Samuel Smith's shoe shop, ostensibly to have a pair of boots stretched for a better fit. A witness said that "they were talking of dogs" and went with Smith to the backyard, returning about twenty minutes later. Probably they ducked into the kitchen to look at the boxes. The next day, Sunday, Alfred and Sawney were seen in conversation outside the Columbian Hotel.[74]

James C. A. Smith had told Alfred and Sawney that they must "tell their masters they were sick," to "get leave of absence for a day or two." Unless they bought time that way, "they would be discovered, pursued and brought back." Acting on these instructions, Alfred departed the Washington Hotel on Thursday evening saying he was ill, and early Monday morning Sawney left the Columbian Hotel "complaining of being sick" and said he was going home to take some medicine.[75]

Samuel Smith spoke with a drayman, an older black man named David Henderson. About 5 A.M. on Monday, 7 May, Smith met with Henderson at the stable where he worked. Witnesses reported that Smith told the drayman "he must be sure to do it, that he must not deceive him, that he (Smith) depended on him." On Tuesday morning, Henderson was to pick up two boxes at Smith's kitchen and convey them to the express office. If asked, he was to say they came from the armory. "He must certainly do so and so, and not disappoint him." Later on Monday, Samuel Smith purchased some stationery from P. W. Grubbs, whose store was a few doors away from the shoe shop. They talked a bit, and Grubbs recalled Smith's telling him that he was connected with a large policy office in Philadelphia, and that he planned to go up there on Tuesday morning.[76]

On Monday, Samuel Smith sent a telegram to "C. M. Burleigh" in Philadelphia "with regard to the payment of a draft." Finally, on Tuesday, James C. A. Smith carried Sawney's trunk to the depot, put it aboard the cars bound north, and "procured a check for it." He probably did the same with Alfred's trunk.[77]

In the early hours of Tuesday morning, the four men gathered at the kitchen behind the shoe shop. Alfred and Sawney fit themselves into the boxes and the Smiths fastened the lids. Each slave took with him "a small bundle of clothes, a pair of boots, a fancy fan, and a bladder filled with water." They also had the claim checks for their trunks. There were holes at the ends of the boxes, partially concealed by a rope knot, which they could pull away to allow more air into the box. The boxes were addressed, per arrangement, to "P. Williamson, No. 32, Buttonwood Street, Philadelphia." One imagines also that the boxes would have been marked to the effect of "This side up with care."[78]

David Henderson, the drayman, drove his wagon to the gate on the alley behind the kitchen before 7 A.M. James C. A. Smith and Henderson loaded the boxes onto the cart. Covering "one box there was matting, on the other a blanket." Samuel Smith gave the drayman a note written on the stationery purchased the day before that read "two cases from H. Tyler to Express office. May 8th, '49." Henderson set out down the alley to Fourth Street. Samuel Smith probably instructed him to drive south on Fourth Street until he reached a street that a wagon coming from the armory might logically take eastward to the express office.[79]

Samuel Smith was standing in the doorway of the shoe shop when Stephen Fisher arrived about 7 A.M., not long after the wagon had left. Smith read the newspaper for a while and then went out. The drayman arrived at the Adams Express office, under the Exchange Hotel, about 7:30. He gave Samuel Smith's note to the clerk, a man named James A. Morrison. As Morrison began to transfer the boxes to the express company's wagon for transport to the railroad depot, he "found one end heavier than the other." He later testified that he "asked the drayman what was in the boxes—he answered glass." Morrison turned one of the boxes over roughly and thought he heard a grunt from within. At this point Morrison called over William B. Barroll, his supervisor and the agent in charge of the Richmond office.[80]

Barroll had recently received a letter from the Philadelphia office of Adams Express warning of slaves shipped in boxes and "directing him to be upon his guard." It is likely that similar letters went to other express agents in slave states, probably about the time McKim was warned in mid-April.[81]

Under questioning, the drayman, "after hesitating sometime," held to his story that the boxes came from the armory. Barroll testified later "my suspicions were excited" when he "read the name of the person to whom they were directed," although it was probably not the person but the city that caught his eye. The uneven distribution of weight, the grunt heard by Morrison, the drayman's hesitation, and the Philadelphia destination all added up. Barroll told Morrison to get a hatchet and to take the drayman's wagon with the boxes to the depot.[82]

About this time, Samuel Smith called at the express office and inquired if a bag of meal for a lady in Baltimore had been sent the day before, which it had. It is uncertain whether Smith realized at this point that the scheme was about to be undone or if it came to him as he passed the railroad depot on his walk back to the shoe shop. At the depot, Morrison used the hatchet to open one of the boxes, and the slave within was discovered. The lid was resealed, and the wagon with the boxes and their human cargo was driven to the mayor's office.[83]

By one account Smith was "present at the opening of the boxes and immediately went up the street." About 8 A.M. the northbound train pulled out of the depot without the fugitives. It moved at a slow speed as it traveled down Broad Street. The shoe shop was about two hundred yards from the depot, and, as the train passed the shop, Samuel Smith climbed aboard.[84]

At the mayor's office, the boxes came open. Under questioning Alfred and Sawney gave up Samuel Smith. An officer hurried to the shoe shop, but "the bird had flown." Witnesses came forward to describe Smith's opportune boarding of the train.[85]

Telegrams went out to Fredericksburg and other cities north along the line about 10 A.M. The train reached Fredericksburg about noon. City Sergeant John S. Caldwell, accompanied by Lieutenant Robert F. Coleman, boarded the cars. A young man pointed

Broad Street Depot, ca. 1865. The Richmond, Fredericksburg, and Potomac Railroad loaded its trains in the middle of Broad Street, between Seventh and Eighth Streets. The large building with the flag is the Richmond Theater at Seventh Street. Note the telegraph pole and wires.

out Samuel Smith, and Caldwell told Smith he was "my prisoner, and to get his baggage." According to Caldwell, Smith "expressed great surprise" and "could not conceive for his life, why he was thus seized, on the public highway." In the depot, Coleman read Smith the dispatch from Richmond and sent a telegram back to Richmond.[86]

Smith was brought back on the evening train. During the return, an observer said, he "conversed fluently with the spectators," particularly about lottery tickets. His "high flow of spirits" lasted to the outskirts of Richmond, "when all his self-possession vanished." The imminence of his fate caused his eyes to roll "as if in great tribulation, and remorse and despair seemed to have fastened themselves so strongly upon him that he appeared almost dumb."[87]

News of the slaves hidden in express boxes and Smith's arrest spread throughout Richmond during the day. A large crowd—described in one report as "thousands of enraged citizens"—gathered at the depot to await Smith's arrival. "Many persons began to mutter about 'a rope,' &c." Cooler heads thought it "expedient that he should be taken out of the cars on the opposite side from the assemblage, placed in the Express wagon, and driven to the jail at all speed."[88]

Smith's preliminary hearing took place the next morning in the mayor's court. Many people were there early, reported the *Richmond Republican,* "impatiently awaiting the arrival of the great man of the 'Red Boot.'" Smith entered "escorted by a strong police force" and was seated "on the criminal's bench" beside Alfred and Sawney. According to the *Richmond Whig,* "his appearance was rather dejected." Some of the witnesses were not present, and the mayor put off a full hearing for three days until Saturday, 12 May.[89]

There were so many spectators on Saturday that even the rotunda room of city hall proved scarcely sufficient to hold them. "Half an hour's squeezing," wrote the reporter for the *Richmond Examiner,* "enabled us to get within imperfect *hearing* distance," but in the press of people "it was impossible to use one's pencil in taking a solitary note." The crowd's determination was of guilt, and the mayor agreed and sent the case on for trial. Samuel Smith was transferred to the Henrico County Jail, where, by one account, he was held in irons in solitary confinement. Smith remained in jail until his trial at Superior Court in the autumn.[90]

James C. A. Smith escaped immediate implication in the affair. Nevertheless, he ceased operating the cake shop and laid low. The punishment inflicted upon Alfred and Sawney, the would-be freemen, is unknown. They were saved from being sold south immediately by the need for their testimony.

The *Richmond Republican* reported that a Richmonder in Philadelphia on business had looked up the address "P. Williamson, 32 Buttonwood Street, Philadelphia" that Smith had written on the boxes. To his surprise at that address there was a "handsome three story brick house," with a sign identifying Passmore Williamson as a "General Conveyancer." The *Republican* observed that "such a sign, in the Northern Cities, usually indicates the transfer and conveyance of Real Estate, but in this case, it would seem, it has reference to personal as well as real effects." On 25 May, the *Richmond Enquirer* reprinted the article "Wonderful Escape of a Slave" from the *Burlington Courier* but changed the headline to "Not Original." The *Enquirer* introduced the story with the observation that "the scheme of S. A. Smith . . . does not seem to have originated in this city." It seems clear that Samuel Smith had not revealed his involvement in Henry Brown's escape.[91]

A journalist with special interest in the affair was Cyrus Burleigh, editor of the *Pennsylvania Freeman* and Samuel Smith's Philadelphia contact. The *Freeman* reprinted an article from the *Richmond Republican* about the interception of the boxes and the arrest of Samuel Smith that, wrote the *Freeman,* "talks of these happy slaves having been 'coaxed' to escape from slavery to freedom. We hardly know whether this is stupidity, or downright dishonesty, or a mixture of both." The *Freeman* also condemned the Philadelphia official of Adams Express who had "set the watch-dogs of the slave pen on the watch for fugitives and their helpers," calling the official's actions "a gratuitous offering to slavery." The deed "will insure you Richmond custom and the blood-stained money of the slaveholders, but every dollar of it will bring poverty to your soul," pronounced the *Freeman,* "and seas will not wash that stain from your name."[92]

Chapter Three

Among The Abolitionists

"A Noble Man"

The Richmond newspapers did not report the June 1848 slave escape facilitated by John Blevins. In contrast, stories about the interception of Alfred and Sawney and the arrest of Samuel Smith played for days. A failed attempt was evidently more worthy of public exposure. The tale of slaves seeking to flee in boxes had a wider interest, too. Newspapers elsewhere, including the *New York Herald*, the *Boston Daily Evening Transcript*, and the *New Hampshire Patriot*, picked up the story from the Richmond articles.[1]

On 10 May 1849, two days after Smith was taken off the train, the *New York Tribune* headlined a front page account "Great Excitement—An Attempt to Run Negroes to the North Detected." In session that day in New York was the annual meeting of the American Anti-Slavery Society. Among the Philadelphians present were Miller McKim and Lucretia Mott. Samuel May Jr. read the *Tribune*'s article to the meeting. "A fine story for Europe that," declared William Lloyd Garrison to the abolitionist audience. "What a love for liberty must not those men have had to be boxed up there."[2]

The abolitionists who met in New York, and among whom Henry Brown had arrived, represented the radical wing of the antislavery movement. With other abolitionists they believed that the absolute immorality of slavery required immediate and universal abolition. The radicals pushed further when they set aside practicality and applied antislavery logic regardless of social propriety. If slavery was immoral, institutions that supported the system were immoral, and the government and the churches in particular earned condemnation for their compromises with slavery. The minister's collar was no shield against radical denunciation.

Despite their militancy, a large portion of the radical abolitionists believed in nonviolent means to overthrow slavery. They fought their crusade through rhetoric and agitation; they wrote, spoke, and rallied. They circulated petitions and sent out lecturers. Their newspapers reported mistreatment of slaves, reprinted advertisements for fugitives from southern newspapers, and noted signs of slave resistance. The *Richmond Republican*'s article about Samuel Smith's arrest was reprinted not only in the *Pennsylvania Freeman*, but also in the *Liberator*, the *Anti-Slavery Bugle* of Ohio, and, true to Garrison's comment that it was "a fine story for Europe," in the *London Anti-Slavery Reporter*.[3]

When fugitive slaves went to Boston, an abolitionist remarked, "who did they enquire for? Not the clergy or any of the several denominations, but the Abolitionists. They knew who were their friends." The public support that the radical abolitionists rallied for fugitive slaves and the Underground Railroad was especially provocative to the southern slaveholders. Compared to the total population of slaves in the United States, successful escapes were few, but the numbers did not measure the affront to southern interests. The *Edgefield Advertiser* of South Carolina reprinted the *New York Tribune* article about the arrest of Samuel Smith with the single word "Madness" as a headline, and expressed its opinion in angry italic. "The following rascally attempt of an

Abolitionist to *steal* the property of a Virginia slaveholder," wrote the editor in preface, "was commented upon in the late *Anti Slavery Convention* as a laudable effort made for *liberty*, and the *'inalienable rights of man!'* "[4]

At the end of May, two months after Henry Brown's escape, another gathering of abolitionists took place in Boston. The American Anti-Slavery Society, which had met three weeks earlier in New York, was composed of numerous regional and local affiliates. Among them was the Pennsylvania Anti-Slavery Society, in whose office Brown had been released. The Massachusetts Anti-Slavery Society was the largest and strongest of the regional affiliates and the host for the Boston meeting.

The New England Anti-Slavery Convention of 1849 opened on 29 May at the Melodeon, a theater rented for the occasion. The convention lasted for three days, with a morning, afternoon, and evening session each day. A continuous cold rain fell the whole time. "There was no cessation—not a gleam of sunshine—not a comfortable hour," reported the *Liberator*. Wendell Phillips, the famed orator, presided. Francis Jackson, president of the Massachusetts Anti-Slavery Society and the man to whom McKim had sent Henry Brown from Philadelphia, opened the meeting. Present were Frederick Douglass and William Wells Brown, both fugitives from slavery and well known as lecturers and authors, and Abby Kelley Foster, a female lecturer when women were usually expected to be silent at public meetings. In attendance, too, was William Lloyd Garrison, editor of the *Liberator* since 1831 and the most prominent and influential of the radicals.[5]

In New Bedford, Henry Brown heard about the "great Anti-slavery meeting . . . and being anxious to identify myself with that public movement," he traveled to Boston. There he joined attendees from a wide region, enthusiastically enumerated by the *Liberator* as "lawyers, physicians, divines, merchants, mechanics, and farmers!"[6]

At the opening session on Tuesday morning, Samuel May Jr., General Agent of the Massachusetts Anti-Slavery Society, reported on the previous year's activities and commented on several fugitive slave cases. He mentioned one in particular in which "a brother man" was "coffined and almost stifled in a scanty box" and shipped from Richmond to Philadelphia. "Thus bore he," stated May, "*his* witness to the *contentment* of the slave in his bondage, and his *reluctance* to leave it, even should a *good* chance of doing so offer!" May noted that "others have attempted a similar experiment, but failed."[7]

In his presentation, May was the first to identify Richmond publicly as the place of origin of the fugitive in the box. His statements confirmed the vaguer reports that had appeared in the newspapers. Whether there was any discussion prior to May's talk about the wisdom of revealing details of Brown's escape is not known. Concerns about "exposing the express" and thereby precluding future escapes may have been thought dissolved by the failed second attempt, which caused Brown's method to become widely known to southern authorities. There was a strong impulse to publicize courageous escapes, for such stories conveyed every message abolitionists wished to send to northern audiences. Three months before Brown's journey, Ellen and William Craft had boldly escaped from Georgia by posing as a sickly young man—Ellen Craft looked white—traveling with a servant. Within weeks of their arrival, William Wells Brown was presenting them on the abolitionist lecture circuit.[8]

The convention's Tuesday evening session opened with three fugitive slaves singing antislavery songs. Edmund Quincy offered a resolution that pledged the abolitionists "to trample under foot any law which allows the slaveholder to hunt the fugitive slave through our borders" and "to make New England . . . an asylum for the oppressed." William Wells Brown took the stage to speak in support of the resolution. In the course of his remarks, Brown presented to the audience the fugitives William and Ellen Craft.[9]

William Wells Brown, 1849

Brown then "introduced Henry Brown, who procured his freedom by causing himself to be enclosed in a box." The *Liberator* noted that "at this time, *six* fugitive slaves were standing together on the platform." The *National Anti-Slavery Standard* reported that "their appearance on the platform created a marked sensation."[10]

When Henry Brown walked onto the Melodeon stage, he took his first step toward becoming a public figure. People knew of his story and now they could also identify the man. It was not Brown's first time in front of an audience, for he had performed before larger gatherings at the African Church in Richmond, but this platform was wholly of his own choosing.

That evening, too, as they stood on stage, William Wells Brown "jocularly termed" Henry Brown "Boxer." The idea of such a moniker struck a chord, although, strictly speaking, Henry Brown was not the boxer, he was the boxed. By the convention's end, William Wells Brown's concept had been resolved into Henry "Box" Brown. As the official report of the convention put it, "the middle name of Box, in honor of his method of escape, has been accorded by general assent." It was a name that Brown accepted and kept.[11]

At the evening session the next day, on Wednesday, 30 May, William Wells Brown brought him on stage again. "Henry Brown then came forward, and gave a brief, simple but very interesting account of his escape, and of the circumstances which led to it." Brown "told his story in an artless manner and with some diffidence," the *National Anti-Slavery Standard* reported. "He is, of course, unlettered, but his adventures and the fortitude with which he passed through an unparalleled journey of suffering and extraordinary danger, exalted a thrill of sympathy and admiration in every one who listened. . . . The finale of this simple tale was received with deafening shouts."[12]

The Reverend Samuel J. May stood to corroborate Brown's tale, stating that "he was in Philadelphia in the midst of the excitement caused by this wonderful adventure." Concluding to "loud huzzas," May asked "shall we not receive him as a brother beloved?" Wendell Phillips then told the hall that Brown "had been wronged out of the whole of his money" and "proposed a collection in the audience" to provide him "a little capital to commence freedom with." The response was "a generous contribution."[13]

Next Frederick Douglass introduced William and Ellen Craft, and William Craft gave an account of their escape. "What an exhibition!" exclaimed Douglass. "Are the slaves contented and happy? Here are three facts that sweep away all the sophistry." The *Dover Morning Star* of New Hampshire commented, "Never did we see an audience so stirred as was that audience by those simple, artless narratives."[14]

After the speeches, "Henry Brown, by request of many in the audience, again came forward," reported the *Liberator*, "and sang, with much feeling and unexpected propriety," the hymn of thanksgiving he had sung on his arrival in Philadelphia. The *National Anti-Slavery Standard* stated that "he sang amid profound stillness, but when he concluded, the air was rent with loud applause."[15]

On the previous night Brown had stepped into the public sphere, and this night he first performed as a freeman. Brown's hymn probably had both familiarity and unfamiliarity for his listeners. No doubt many whites in the audience had heard African American church music before. It could not have been a frequent opportunity, nonetheless, to hear a strong singer perform music so directly from the black South.

On Thursday evening the convention moved to Fanueil Hall for a well-attended final meeting. The Reverend Samuel J. May, Frederick Douglass, and Wendell Phillips delivered major speeches. "To those who were eye-witnesses and hearers," the *Liberator* wrote, the report of the Fanueil Hall meeting "will seem to be but a faint representation of what transpired. . . . No pen can trace, no pencil portray, the electric glow and stirring enthusiasm of the occasion."[16]

The Reverend Samuel J. May spoke extensively on the man he called "Henry Box Brown." He told of Brown's trials during his journey in the box: "Such was the intensity of the love of life and liberty in his bosom, that it seemed to set at defiance all the principles of physiology itself, and to live without air, that he might for one moment, at least, breathe the air of liberty." Who "can doubt," he declared, "that there must be in him not merely the heart and soul of a deteriorated man—a degraded, inferior man—but the heart and soul of a noble man? Not a *nobleman*, sir, but a NOBLE MAN! Who can doubt it?"

Wendell Phillips brought Brown on stage and spoke of his escape with the fugitive standing next to him. "He dared to die, alone and unpitied, for liberty. (Applause.) He took his life in his hand—looked in the faces of the white race around him, saw in none the lines of sympathy or tear of pity—and yet he shrank not. We say, in behalf of this man, whom God created, and whom law-abiding Webster and Winthrop swore should find no shelter on the soil of Massachusetts—we say that they may make their little motions, and pass their little laws, in Washington, but that FANEUIL HALL REPEALS THEM, in the name of the humanity of Massachusetts. (Great Applause.)"[17]

For Henry Brown, the New England Anti-Slavery Convention of 1849 was a signal event. He attended by his own choice, and for the first time as a free man he appeared and performed in public. He saw Frederick Douglass, William Wells Brown, and other fellow fugitives speak compellingly and act as leaders. At this meeting, it seems, he began to envision the possibilities for his life in liberty. And there was the crowning touch: he was now Henry Box Brown.

"Brown of the Box"

Henry Brown's appearance at the convention spread the story of his escape more widely and brought him a measure of fame. William Lloyd Garrison wrote to a friend in England that "we have never had so many runaway slaves on our platforms" as at the New York and Boston meetings. "The remarkable case of the one who escaped in a box from Virginia," said Garrison, "created a powerful sensation," and he expected that the story would be "extensively noticed" in England. "What a country is this, what a people we are, that such expedients should be necessary to obtain liberty, even at the almost certain loss of life!"[18]

Several newspaper stories about the New England Anti-Slavery Convention featured Henry Box Brown. "One of the most thrilling events of the week was the appearance of the heroic man," reported the *Boston Emancipator and Republican*. "Shame on Virginia," the article continued. "She proudly claims to be the mother of statesmen and heroes, but no son of hers ever gave greater evidence of heroism than this poor despised son of hers." The *Boston Chronotype* related Brown's story and concluded, "What heroism, what self-denial, what energy of purpose are here manifested." The *Boston Post*, the *Boston Daily Evening Transcript*, the *Worcester Massachusetts Spy*, the *New York Express*, and the *New York Herald* also reported on Brown's escape. The *New York Daily Tribune* provided the measurements of the box and reported that Brown "told his story in a simple, artless manner, that thrilled through the heart of the audience."[19]

News stories about the Boston meeting were not long in reaching Richmond. On 7 June 1849, the *Richmond Republican* noted that one of the fugitives "paraded on the stage" in Boston apparently "escaped in a box after the fashion of the Red Boot man." The *Republican* observed that this method of escape "seems to be the prevailing fashion," and called for "a vigilant eye" against abolitionist agents "at the South." Such "rascally white men" make "contented slaves dissatisfied" and then "induce them to escape to a country where they . . . starve and die in filth and misery." On 12 June the *Richmond Enquirer* reprinted the *New York Evening Post*'s account of Henry Box Brown's appearance at the convention. The newspaper apparently realized that the fugitive in Boston had been assisted by Samuel Smith, for its headline was "Another 'Red Boot' Box." One imagines that William Barret and John F. Allen learned then how Brown had escaped.[20]

View of Boston, ca. mid-1850s. Taken from the roof of the Massachusetts Statehouse, at the crest of Beacon Hill, the view looks northwest toward the Charles River. The prominent building at the center, outlined against the river, is the jail. The incline indicated by the descending row of houses, midground at right-center, is the western slope of Beacon Hill, the main locus for the black community. The larger building left-center—in the picture, just below and to the left of the jail—is Smith School, designated for African American students.

Henry Box Brown took up residence in Boston, likely staying in the city after the convention. Though Brown lived in Boston only a year or so, it was while there that he found direction for his career. The name Henry Box Brown was initially bestowed in a celebratory spirit to honor his means to freedom. In Boston the new name came to represent more profoundly the former slave's transformation into a new man.[21]

Where to live was a weighed decision for a fugitive slave. Safety was a concern because there had been incidents of fugitives recaptured in the North and taken back to slavery. To live in a community with antislavery friends provided security. In addition Brown needed to make a living. He had escaped with only the clothes on his back and could not depend long on the collection taken up for him at the convention. As an English newspaper story about Brown later expressed it, he wished to "obtain a respectable livelihood, and, if possible, benefit the suffering creatures he had left in bondage." While New Bedford was relatively safe, Boston offered Brown better opportunities.[22]

Newly arrived fugitives were often put up by black Bostonians. In 1849 African Americans comprised about 2,000 of the city's population of 137,000. Brown may have stayed first with Lewis Hayden, whose house was called the Underground Railroad's "main Boston depot." As many as half a dozen or more fugitives at a time found refuge there. Hayden had himself escaped from slavery in Kentucky and settled in Boston in 1846. His home at 8 Southac Street was in the neighborhood where most of the African Americans in Boston lived, on the western slope of Beacon Hill not far from Boston Common. Hayden operated a clothing store on Cambridge Street, which "provided garments for fugitive slaves, while the profits were used to feed runaway slaves while they were in Boston."[23]

In time Brown moved to a rooming house nearby at 41 Southac Street. His fellow residents included Louisa Freeman, a tailoress, and Henry Hall, who sold clothing. A short distance up Southac was the Twelfth Baptist Church, which came to be known as the "fugitive's church" in large part through the activism of its minister Leonard Grimes. Born free in northern Virginia about 1815, Grimes worked as a hackman in Washington, D.C., where he became involved in the Underground Railroad. He was arrested by Virginia authorities in 1839 and served two years in the penitentiary in Richmond. By 1846 he had had moved north to New Bedford and in 1848 became pastor at Twelfth Baptist. Perhaps Brown lent his voice to services at Grimes's church.[24]

When Henry Box Brown entered the Boston black community, he arrived known as a heroic resistant to slavery with a link to the abolitionist movement. Such credentials likely brought him into contact with the city's African American activists. More than anything else, what distinguished the black abolitionist perspective from the white was recognition that fighting prejudice at home was as important as ending slavery afar. Though Boston was a center of antislavery work, within the city itself racial equality was far from a reality. White laborers viewed blacks as unwelcome rivals for jobs, and the influx of Irish emigrants fleeing famine intensified competition for openings. In addition to "daily insults met in the streets of Boston," laws and customs of the city discriminated against African Americans. Theaters and other public places had segregated seating, for example, and blacks were excluded from juries.[25]

Black Bostonians did not simply accept the situation. In 1843 a "Garrisonian-led ride-in, boycott, and legislative campaign" ended segregated seating on railroads in Massachusetts. Similar tactics of nonviolent protest challenged Boston's segregated public schools. A petition campaign to the school board began in 1844, followed by a boycott of the all-black Smith School on Beacon Hill in 1845. In 1848, Benjamin F. Roberts, a black printer, filed a lawsuit against the school board on behalf of his daughter, Sarah C. Roberts. "On the direct route from her home to the primary school" to which black students were assigned, Sarah Roberts "passed no less than five other primaries." Roberts attempted four times without success to enroll her in the schools closer to her home and then sued under a law that provided damages from the city if a child was illegally excluded from public school. By June 1849 lower courts had rejected Roberts's argument, and an appeal was filed to the Massachusetts Supreme Court.[26]

Though there is no evidence that Henry Box Brown became involved in any local Boston issues, he was bound to have been exposed to them. If he visited Lewis Hayden's house, or attended services at Leonard Grimes's church, or went to the mass meetings called that summer to protest school segregation, Brown would have associated with politically aware African Americans who were working for change. Such influences would have augmented the examples of black leadership he had witnessed at the Boston convention.

Not every fugitive slave became an antislavery activist. Most fugitives sought simply the chance to live peaceably in freedom and were disinclined to seek a public role close to controversy. Henry Brown was motivated toward the cause from the first. When he learned in New Bedford of the Boston meeting, he decided to attend. When presented the opportunity to take the stage in Boston, he stepped forward. Not only did he have a remarkable story to tell, but Brown had too the vital drive to bring it before the populace.

Public meetings were one of the primary tools of the abolitionists. They used lectures

Handbill for 4 July Rally. The bill was for the 1848 gathering; the meeting format was the same in 1849.

and rallies to sustain the fervor of their supporters and to convince the unconverted. Public meetings were especially effective in small towns where people might attend any event that promised diversion. For such purposes Brown's tale was a strong draw. During the summer of 1849 Brown made a number of public appearances in Massachusetts and at least one in Maine. He had help in facilitating these activities from "several ministers of religion," who "took a great interest in Mr. Brown, and did what they could to bring the subject of his escape properly before the public."[27]

On Independence Day, 4 July 1849, the Massachusetts Anti-Slavery Society held a "Grand Celebration" at the Abington Grove, a waterside park outside Boston. The Old Colony Railroad offered half-fare tickets from the city, and "the weather was extremely fine, being precisely the right temperature for an open air meeting." Also at Abington Grove that day were the Sons of Temperance, a group with ideals that many abolitionists shared, and the grounds were "thronged with holiday groups." Samuel May Jr. estimated the crowd in the morning at 4,000 persons, with as many as 6,000 over the day. "The masses around the platform were densely packed and profoundly attentive," stated one report. The program consisted of speeches, "interspersed by Anti-Slavery Songs by the Assembly," with a midday break for picnic dinner.[28]

Toward the end of the program Henry Brown, "now generally known here as Henry Box Brown, in allusion to the manner of his escape from slavery," took the platform. "Brown of the Box occupied all the time the meeting could spare with his Narrative," but his speech was "unluckily cut short" by the schedule of the "inexorable cars" of the railroad for return to Boston. Brown's account of his final parting from his wife and children "was deeply affecting," reported a newspaper, "and brought tears into many eyes."[29]

Although Brown was well received at this appearance, not all abolitionists thought his public activities were a good idea. The *Pennsylvania Freeman* voiced its concern on 5 July, the day after the Abington Grove meeting. The *Freeman* noted that "several thrilling and interesting narratives" of slave escapes "have been recently published in anti-slavery papers or meetings, and widely copied by the public press, both at the North and South." Now some of the fugitives were "attending meetings in Massachusetts" and "proclaiming in public halls and churches, to friend and foe, the devices which they planned in secret, and once hardly dared to whisper in the ear of their nearest friend."[30]

The *Freeman* thought such publicity to be "inconsiderate, or ill judged, and calculated to do serious harm." For slaves who sought a means of escape, the "field for stratagem" was already narrow. If "whenever a new one is discovered by some genius among them, their masters are immediately advertised of it," such a revelation "must necessarily make their means still fewer and that field narrower." The *Freeman* counseled that "our incautiousness or imprudence may cut off the best hope of another Ellen Craft or Henry Brown," and, as evidence, cited the recent "recapture of two slaves in Richmond and the arrest of a white man suspected of aiding them." The *Freeman* commended the example of Frederick Douglass, who in his writing and his lectures continued to conceal "that (probably most interesting) passage of his history."

On the other side of the debate were the abolitionists who believed that publicizing these cases benefited the overall cause. The *Freeman* was incorrect to imply that Henry Brown's presence at meetings had led to the arrest of Samuel Smith and the recapture of Alfred and Sawney, for Brown did not appear in public until after the second boxing scheme had already been foiled.

In its argument for protecting escape methods the *Freeman* was aligned with Frederick Douglass, who restated the case in 1855 in his revised narrative, *My Bondage and My Freedom*. In a chapter entitled "Manner of My Escape Not Given," Douglass wrote that there was "neither wisdom nor necessity" in "publishing every new invention" by which slaves made their escape. "Had not Henry Box Brown and his friends attracted slaveholding attention to the manner of his escape," said Douglass, "we might have had a thousand *Box Browns* per annum." Douglass was more rhetorical than practical in this passage, taking no account of the suffering and danger that Brown overcame. At any rate, as the *Freeman* concluded, in the case of "the Man of the Box, it is doubtless too late to begin to be cautious." Brown was committed to public presentation and there was nothing to do but press on.[31]

Abolitionists gathered again later that summer at Hospital Grove, in Worcester, Massachusetts, on 3 August 1849. The purpose was to commemorate the anniversary of emancipation in the British West Indies, which commenced on 1 August 1834. The anniversary assembly was held on the third of the month, instead of the first, because President Zachary Taylor had proclaimed a national day of fasting on 3 August for the victims of the cholera epidemic. The abolitionists expressed their low regard for Taylor by scheduling their picnic for his day of fasting.

"The day was fine and the gathering very large, amounting, in all, ... to some three or four thousand persons," stated the *Worcester Massachusetts Spy*. "An extra train was run from Boston, . . . consisting of *fourteen* cars." The morning speakers included the abolitionist lecturer Charles C. Burleigh and the Unitarian minister Theodore Parker. The afternoon speakers were William Lloyd Garrison and Wendell Phillips. The writer and former preacher Ralph Waldo Emerson followed with "a brief speech marked by his peculiar tone of thought and expression."[32]

Also in attendance was Henry Box Brown, who "in the intervals of the meeting, related the story of his escape to various listeners, and distributed his narrative song." This song was the second one associated with Brown. The *Massachusetts Spy* reported that after the morning session there was an hour recess, "during which those who remained on the ground were entertained with songs, &c., one of them by Wm. *Box* Brown, the fugitive slave who escaped in a box. The song detailed his escape, and was sung to the tune of 'Poor Old Ned.'"[33]

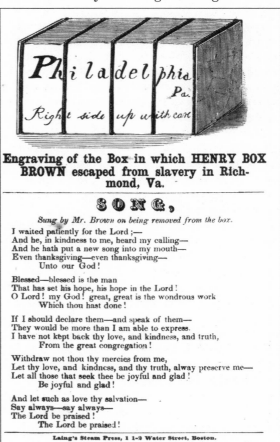

Engraving of the Box in which HENRY BOX BROWN escaped from slavery in Richmond, Va.

SONG,

Sung by Mr. Brown on being removed from the box.

I waited patiently for the Lord ;—
And he, in kindness to me, heard my calling—
And he hath put a new song into my mouth—
Even thanksgiving—even thanksgiving—
    Unto our God !

Blessed—blessed is the man
That has set his hope, his hope in the Lord !
O Lord ! my God ! great, great is the wondrous work
    Which thou hast done !

If I should declare them—and speak of them—
They would be more than I am able to express.
I have not kept back thy love, and kindness, and truth,
    From the great congregation !

Withdraw not thou thy mercies from me,
Let thy love, and kindness, and thy truth, alway preserve me—
Let all those that seek thee be joyful and glad !
    Be joyful and glad !

And let such as love thy salvation—
Say always—say always—
The Lord be praised !
    The Lord be praised !

Laing's Steam Press, 1 1-2 Water Street, Boston.

Song, Sung by Mr. Brown on Being Removed From the Box. Probably June 1849. The woodcut of the box is the first visual representation of Brown's escape. The picture implies what it does not show: Brown inside the box. Thus the image symbolizes his journey, and his courage in facing its difficulty.

Singing was an integral part of antislavery meetings. Songs served as a break from speeches and as a way for an audience to express solidarity. Antislavery songs were mostly "old-fashioned hymns and compositions . . . resembling hymns," and several collections were in print in 1849. George Whitfield Clark's *Liberty Minstrel* was first published in 1844 and by 1850 had gone through seven editions. William Wells Brown's forty-six-page compilation, *The Anti-Slavery Harp: A Collection of Songs for Anti-Slavery Meetings*, went into a second edition by 1849. Songs were also published individually as song sheets, typically a single page of lyrics without musical notation, and often illustrated.[34]

Henry Brown's performance of his arrival hymn had met with favor at the New England Anti-Slavery Convention, and one imagines he continued to feature it. A song sheet of the hymn was a logical step. "SONG, Sung by Mr. Brown on being removed from the box" was printed in Boston, probably in June 1849. It was illustrated with an "Engraving of the Box." How the publication came about is not known. It is possible that one or more of the clergymen who had taken an interest in Brown played a role, and that an intention was to provide Brown a means to earn income by selling copies at his appearances.[35]

In truth, the song sheet, "SONG, Sung by Mr. Brown on being removed from the box," was more of a memento than a guide to performance. The printed lyrics are a selection of verses from Psalm 40 as found in the King James Bible. They represent the source for Brown's song but not the song as he performed it. A different version of the lyrics to this song appeared in Brown's 1849 *Narrative*, entitled "Hymn of Thanksgiving, Sung by Henry Box Brown." Those lyrics adapted the biblical verses, repeating and recombining words and phrases. The book lyrics, described as "the identical words uttered by him," have much more the feeling of Brown's southern Baptist psalmody, and were undoubtedly truer to his performance. The song sheet lyrics, in that they favor the biblical source over the hymn as sung, suggest that the handbill may have been produced by someone more evangelistic than musical, such as one of Brown's engaged clergymen.[36]

Not long after the first song sheet, a second one was printed for Brown. While most antislavery songs, like Brown's hymn, were religious in origin, Brown's second song had a secular source. By the late 1840s a number of new tunes had begun to appear in the abolitionist repertoire. They were borrowed from the blackface minstrels, themselves borrowers from the African Americans they demeaned.

Blackface minstrelsy evolved from a long tradition of white entertainers performing with darkened faces. In 1843 a four-man group called the Virginia Minstrels presented a blackface variety of song, dance, and dialogue that proved a resounding success. Their format was widely adopted. In short order followed the Christy Minstrels, the Ethiopian Serenaders, and many more. By 1849 minstrel shows were the most popular form of entertainment in the North. The minstrels delivered their parodies and lampoons with humor, but their portrayals of blackface characters who pined for their old plantation homes and who were "foolish, stupid, and compulsively musical" had a deep effect on the whites who enjoyed the performances. As the historian Robert C. Toll puts it, "Minstrels shaped white Americans' vague notions and amorphous beliefs about Negroes into vivid, eye-catching caricatures."[37]

Abolitionists condemned the minstrel shows but could hardly ignore their popularity. In Boston, "where Negro minstrels were always welcome," a few days after the 1849 New England Anti-Slavery Convention concluded at the Melodeon Theater the stage was occupied in turn by Dumbolton's Celebrated Ethiopian Serenaders. Even abolitionists who agreed with Frederick Douglass that the minstrels were "filthy scum"

"Hymn of Thanksgiving, Sung by Henry Box Brown, After being released from his confinement in the Box, at Philadelphia."

The lyrics as recorded in Charles Stearns,
Narrative of Henry Box Brown (Boston, [1849]), ix–x.

I waited patiently, I waited patiently for the Lord, for the Lord,
And he inclined unto me, and heard my calling;
I waited patently, I waited patiently for the Lord,
And he inclined unto me, and heard my calling;
And he hath put a new song in my mouth,
Ev'n a thanksgiving, Ev'n a thanksgiving, Ev'n a thanksgiving unto our God.

Blessed, Blessed, Blessed, Blessed is the man, Blessed is the man,
Blessed is the man that hath set his hope, his hope in the Lord;
O Lord my God, Great, Great, Great,
Great are the wondrous works which thou hast done,
Great are the wondrous works which thou hast done, which thou hast done;
Great are the wondrous works,
Great are the wondrous works,
Great are the wondrous works, which thou hast done,

If I should declare them and speak of them, they would be more, more, more
than I am able to express.
I have not kept back thy loving kindness and truth from the great congregation,
I have not kept back thy loving kindness and truth from the great congregation.

Withdraw not thou thy mercy from me,
Withdraw not thou thy mercy from me, O Lord;
Let thy loving kindness and thy truth always preserve me,
Let all those that seek thee be joyful and glad,
Let all those that seek thee, be joyful and glad, be joyful, be glad, be joyful and
glad, be joyful, be joyful, be joyful, be joyful, be joyful and glad, be glad in thee.

And let such as love thy salvation,
And let such as love thy salvation, say always,
The Lord be praised,
The Lord be praised:
Let all those that seek thee be joyful and glad,
And let such as love thy salvation, say always,
The Lord be praised,
The Lord be praised,
The Lord be praised.

who "pander to the corrupt taste of their white fellow citizens" had to admit that the tunes were lively and appealing. "These tunes," writes William Austin, "functioned and survived . . . far beyond the shows." Antislavery musicians recognized the innovation. The Hutchinson Family, who sang at many abolitionist gatherings, revised the minstrel song "Jordan Is a Hard Road to Travel" into "Slavery Is a Hard Foe to Battle." Minstrel tunes fitted with new lyrics appear in the later editions of both George Whitfield Clark's *Liberty Minstrel* and Brown's *Anti-Slavery Harp*. William Wells Brown's best-known adaptation, entitled "The Northern Star," was based on "Susanna" by Stephen Foster, the young minstrel genre composer: "Oh! Star of Freedom, 'Tis the star for me; / 'Twill lead me off to Canada, There I will be free."[38]

Another Foster song widely performed in 1849 was "Old Uncle Ned." A new antislavery song borrowed its tune and adapted its lyrics; it was entitled "Escape from Slavery of Henry Box Brown." The lyrics were printed as a song sheet, probably in July 1849 as Brown had copies to distribute at the Worcester meeting on 3 August. The new song sheet was illustrated with the same box engraving as the hymn song sheet, indicating a link between the two, but there is no information about the process of publication. One writer called "Escape from Slavery of Henry Box Brown" "an old tune to new words," and another thought the song "both touching and witty." Foster's chorus to "Old Uncle Ned," as published in 1848, went: "Den lay down de shubble and de hoe-o-o / And hang up de fiddle and de

"Escape From Slavery of Henry Box Brown." June or July 1849. The song sheet uses the same illustration of the box as the arrival-hymn song sheet.

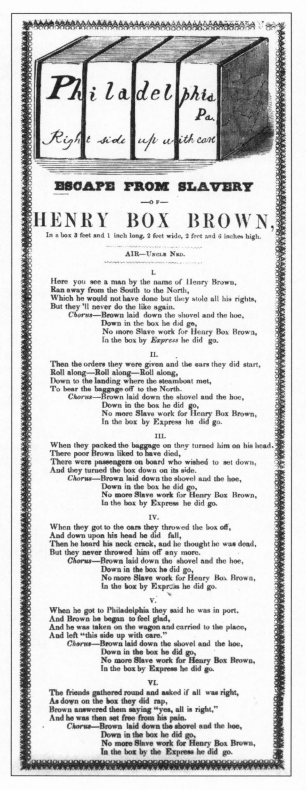

ESCAPE FROM SLAVERY

—OF—

HENRY BOX BROWN,

In a box 3 feet and 1 inch long, 2 feet wide, 2 feet and 6 inches high.

AIR—UNCLE NED.

I.

Here you see a man by the name of Henry Brown,
Ran away from the South to the North,
Which he would not have done but they stole all his rights,
But they 'll never do the like again.
Chorus—Brown laid down the shovel and the hoe,
Down in the box he did go,
No more Slave work for Henry Box Brown,
In the box by *Express* he did go.

II.

Then the orders they were given and the cars they did start,
Roll along—Roll along—Roll along,
Down to the landing where the steamboat met,
To bear the baggage off to the North.
Chorus—Brown laid down the shovel and the hoe,
Down in the box he did go,
No more Slave work for Henry Box Brown,
In the box by Express he did go.

III.

When they packed the baggage on they turned him on his head,
There poor Brown liked to have died,
There were passengers on board who wished to set down,
And they turned the box down on its side.
Chorus—Brown laid down the shovel and the hoe,
Down in the box he did go,
No more Slave work for Henry Box Brown,
In the box by Express he did go.

IV.

When they got to the cars they throwed the box off,
And down upon his head he did fall,
Then he heard his neck crack, and he thought he was dead,
But they never throwed him off any more.
Chorus—Brown laid down the shovel and the hoe,
Down in the box he did go,
No more Slave work for Henry Box Brown,
In the box by Express he did go.

V.

When he got to Philadelphia they said he was in port,
And Brown he began to feel glad,
And he was taken on the wagon and carried to the place,
And left "this side up with care."
Chorus—Brown laid down the shovel and the hoe,
Down in the box he did go,
No more Slave work for Henry Box Brown,
In the box by Express he did go.

VI.

The friends gathered round and asked if all was right,
As down on the box they did rap,
Brown answered them saying "yes, all is right,"
And he was then set free from his pain.
Chorus—Brown laid down the shovel and the hoe,
Down in the box he did go,
No more Slave work for Henry Box Brown,
In the box by the Express he did go.

bow, / No more hard work for poor old Ned / Hes gone wha de good niggas go." The revised chorus went: "Brown laid down the shovel and the hoe, / Down in the box he did go, / No more Slave work for Henry Box Brown, / In the box by *Express* he did go."[39]

The authorship of the lyrics for "Escape from Slavery of Henry Box Brown" is uncredited. The song may have been a collaborative effort that included Brown, because the song was clearly intended as one for him to perform. Whether or not Brown was the one who suggested the popular minstrel-genre tune that was used, the choice certainly had his approval. Prior to his arrival in the North there is no evidence that he had sung anything but church music. That he borrowed from minstrelsy for his signature song showed that Brown was neither inhibited by religious proscriptions nor reluctant to appeal to popular taste.

Only a few months after he had last twisted tobacco as a slave in William Barret's factory, Henry Box Brown was an active abolitionist, appearing at large antislavery rallies and small meetings. He was making his mark as a singer and all the while his education in liberty proceeded. He had learned that even if African Americans in the North did not "starve and die in filth and misery," all was not as it ought to be.

The Narrative

Henry Brown had scarcely arrived in Philadelphia before he was asked to tell the story of his life. Miller McKim's request then was the first of many. Brown told his story often through the summer of 1849. If his escape was the most thrilling part, audiences listened closely as well to Brown's narration of the events that persuaded him to make his dangerous attempt and to his eyewitness descriptions of slave life.

Though repetition Brown's narrative of his life took a regularized form. He based it naturally on his memories, but one imagines he also fashioned it to reflect the responses of his predominantly white and antislavery audiences. Brown's listeners expected him to testify to the evils of slavery, and some of his experiences were more suited to the antislavery argument than others. He would have grasped which incidents most moved his listeners and refined the stories of those incidents to tell again to subsequent audiences. He probably discovered that his many religious listeners were especially attentive to examples of the self-serving piety of the slaveholders and to specimens of the twisted Christian doctrines they taught to the slaves. He may have learned that audiences readily identified the evil of a cruel overseer and therefore emphasized the character of John F. Allen. As Brown developed his oral presentation, his personal narrative was both informed by the facts of his life and influenced by the preconceptions of his audiences.[40]

Already his escape was celebrated in two song sheets. A further step, likely suggested to him by antislavery friends and by those who heard his talks, was to recount his story in a book. Brown's oral narrative might form the basis for a book, but as he could not read or write he needed an amanuensis, someone to lay the words on paper. An unusual man named Charles Stearns served as the writer for Brown's book and indeed played a more significant role.

Charles Stearns worked in Boston as a printer and was an antislavery activist aligned with the radical abolitionists. Exactly when Brown met Stearns is not known. It may have been at the New England Anti-Slavery Convention in May or shortly thereafter. The book came out early in September so Brown and Stearns had worked together for some time before then. Their relationship was more extensive than simply the preparation of text, for the two were also business partners on the project. The publishing credit is "Brown and Stearns," and after publication the men traveled together on a month-long tour to sell the book.[41]

At the least, Charles Stearns was the writer, co-publisher, and co-promoter for Henry Box Brown's book, and he may have set the type for it as well. Raised in Greenfield, Massachusetts, Stearns was about thirty-one years old in 1849, a few years younger than Brown. Stearns's father died in September 1818 shortly before Charles was born, leaving his mother to raise four children. Sarah Ripley Stearns was a devout Christian and active in reform causes such as the temperance movement and abolitionism. Her brother was George Ripley, a founder of the utopian community of Brook Farm. Stearns recalled that his mother, who had moved to Springfield, was one of the first in that town "to extend a welcome hand" to the antislavery activist Sojourner Truth, and that "her house was the home of the wayfaring one, and never was a meal so scanty, that it could not be shared with those more needy."[42]

Where his mother was humanitarian, Stearns was radical. His religious faith was deep but very individual, and he did not hesitate to question received values. In January 1840, then living in Connecticut, Stearns refused on pacifist principles to perform his required militia duty and then refused to pay his fine. From Hartford County Jail he wrote William Lloyd Garrison for advice and asked if "by paying the fine, I do *not* countenance the military system." There was no provision in the state's law that time served could substitute for paying a fine, Stearns explained, thus "I must either pay this fine, or remain here *as long as I live*." Garrison published Stearns's letter in the *Liberator* and responded that he saw "no reason why a military fine may not be paid, as well as any other exacted by a government based on physical force." Just as the young Miller McKim was influenced by the *Liberator*, so Stearns wrote in 1841 that he was "a constant and attentive reader" of it and found "most beneficial" its effect "in instructing me as to what our duty to God and man requires of us in this age."[43]

For several years Stearns traveled in Kentucky and perhaps other slave states, where he "preached constantly," attended "many revivals of religion," and married. By 1844 Stearns was again living in Massachusetts, probably at his mother's house in Springfield, and had become interested in the millennialist fervor of the "Millerites." William Miller's prophesy that the second coming of Christ would occur in 1843 led to many mass gatherings of hopeful believers. The predicted date became the "Great Disappointment," but Miller issued a revised prophecy for 22 October 1844, and many of his followers renewed their faith. On 4 October, amid popular frenzy as the day approached, Stearns wrote to the *Liberator* expressing sympathy with the idea of the Second Advent, though he stopped short of endorsing Miller's designated date.[44]

Stearns's Christianity drew on the ecstatic meetings of the tents and was molded by his pacifism and abolitionism. He was probably influenced as well by the writings of his uncle George Ripley and the other Transcendentalists who emerged in the 1830s. Stearns was outside that movement but remained close if only by kinship. The original members of the Brook Farm community, founded under the banner of Transcendentalism in 1841, and located in West Roxbury near Boston, included Stearns's uncle, two aunts, and his sister.

Stearns expressed his own unconventional beliefs in a series of controversial letters to the *Liberator*. In March 1845 Stearns wrote that true Christianity was opposed to all slavery and war and required temperance. That October he wrote "we are not *radical enough*," that the "war part" of the Old Testament was "the stumbling block in the way of peace," and that therefore "the Old Testament should be laid aside" and "hurled to the pit of woe from whence *its war part* sprang." In statements that inspired numerous rebuttals, he declared that "God never punishes men for sin," and that it was the duty of Christians *"to abolish every prison at once."* In December 1848 Stearns wrote that he regarded "the Bible as a good book, in part; but there is so much bad in it, that, in its present form, I doubt its utility to the world."[45]

By 1847 Stearns had become a printer in Boston. His access to the press enabled him to become an active pamphleteer, publishing tracts about slavery and about the 1848 presidential election. At a meeting of the Massachusetts Anti-Slavery Society in January 1849 Stearns called for "the working-men of the North" to oppose slavery and for "Abolitionists to advocate the claims of the free laborer." In 1849, probably before beginning work with Henry Box Brown, Stearns published *The Way to Abolish Slavery*. In it Stearns blamed "both church and state" as "the props of Slavery," advocated "Dis-Union," a radical abolitionist argument that the North should secede from the South, and attacked the "noisy politicians" who valued "preserving our glorious Union, at whatever expense to the crushed and manacled Slave."[46]

Henry Box Brown likely found that, different from white men such as William Barret or Samuel Smith, Charles Stearns met him with sincere respect. When Brown agreed that Stearns should bring his narrative before the public in print, he probably saw Stearns as an earnest and strongly antislavery partner. Unknown is how fully Brown was aware of Stearns's singularity, that his path deviated not only from mainstream northern opinion but also from organized antislavery. Stearns wrote of himself that he "does not write for party purposes; neither is he the agent, or the organ of any Anti-Slavery society, but writes on his own authority, and that of truth." Stearns's often-extreme opinions on a variety of subjects probably did not matter much to Brown, who never displayed any interest in fine points of doctrine. More relevant to Brown would have been the Stearns who advocated the workers' plight and who had been swayed by religious frenzy. In summer 1849 these two individuals produced a book.[47]

By 1849 the books known as slave narratives were becoming numerous and had gained significant readership. The typical slave narrative is a first-person account of a life in bondage that ends with the narrator in freedom. The narratives were effective weapons in the abolitionist campaign by refuting the proslavery argument that slaves were satisfied in their condition; and when they showed their narrators to be conscious and perceptive, the narratives countered racist assumptions about African Americans. They had appeal as inspiring stories of people who achieved despite great obstacles, and as nonfiction were acceptable to readers who for religious reasons eschewed the novel.[48]

Two men who spoke at the 1849 New England Anti-Slavery Convention were authors of well-known narratives. The *Narrative of the Life of Frederick Douglass* appeared in 1845. An Irish edition and an English edition followed the same year, and the book was translated into French in 1848. The Anti-Slavery Office in Boston published *Narrative of William W. Brown* in 1847. By the fourth edition in 1849, some ten thousand copies had been sold. The year 1849 saw more slave narratives published than in any year before. Two were the stories of leaders of the fugitive communities in

"Just Published." The advertisement for the *Narrative of Henry Box Brown* ran four times in the weekly *National Anti-Slavery Standard* from 20 September to 11 October 1849.

> **HENRY BOX BROWN.**
>
> JUST PUBLISHED, The *Life and Travels* of the man who fled from bondage in a Box, a portion of the time on his head; with remarks upon the cure for Slavery, by Charles Stearns.
>
> For sale, wholesale and retail, by Bela Marsh, 25 Cornhill, Boston: Single copy 25 cents. Sep. 20.

Canada: the *Narrative of the Life and Adventures of Henry Bibb*, published in New York, and *The Life of Josiah Henson*, published in July in Boston. In England, the first edition of *The Fugitive Blacksmith, or, Events in the History of James W. C. Pennington* quickly sold out and a second edition was issued.[49]

The renown of his escape and the healthy sales of other slave narratives boded well for a book telling Henry Box Brown's story. The partners may have paid for its publication by combining Brown's fund-raising on the abolitionist circuit with cost-saving measures made possible by Stearns's double duty as the book's printer. The full title is *Narrative of Henry Box Brown, Who Escaped from Slavery Enclosed in a Box 3 Feet Long and 2 Wide. Written from a Statement of Facts Made by Himself. With Remarks upon the Remedy for Slavery.* The preface is dated 1 September 1849, and the published book appeared soon after. On 13 September the *Boston Emancipator and Republican* noted: "NARRATIVE OF HENRY BOX BROWN. . . . We have not had time to read it, but so far as we can judge by a hasty glance at its contents, we think it will be read with interest."[50]

Ninety-two pages long, *Narrative of Henry Box Brown* sold for twenty-five cents. The narrative is told in Brown's voice and occupies fifty-six pages. Stearns's preface takes up six pages and concludes with Brown's "Hymn of Thanksgiving." Following the narrative is a twenty-five-page essay by Stearns entitled "Cure for the Evil of Slavery," which restates arguments he had made in his 1849 pamphlet *The Way To Abolish Slavery.* On the next-to-last page is an excerpt from the speech of the Reverend Samuel J. May at Faneuil Hall during the 1849 New England Anti-Slavery Convention. There are two illustrations. The frontispiece portrait of Henry Box Brown appears to have been engraved from a daguerreotype, and the *Liberator* described it as "a pretty good likeness of the hero of the box." The final page has a "Representation of the Box," which recycles the illustration from the two song sheets.[51]

The *Narrative of Henry Box Brown* proves that good intentions do not guarantee literary achievement. The story begins with Brown's childhood in Louisa County and closes with his safe arrival in Philadelphia; and it is purposefully vague on

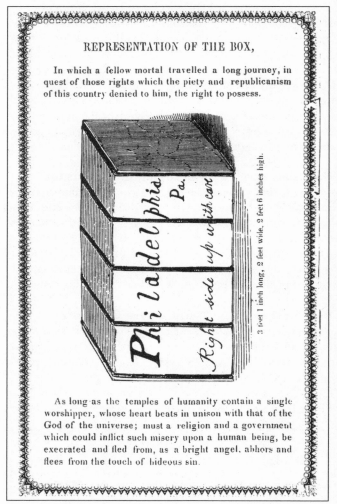

REPRESENTATION OF THE BOX,

In which a fellow mortal travelled a long journey, in quest of those rights which the piety and republicanism of this country denied to him, the right to possess.

Philadelphia Pa.

Right side up with care.

3 feet 1 inch long, 2 feet wide, 2 feet 6 inches high.

As long as the temples of humanity contain a single worshipper, whose heart beats in unison with that of the God of the universe; must a religion and a government which could inflict such misery upon a human being, be execrated and fled from, as a bright angel, abhors and flees from the touch of hideous sin.

Last Page of the 1849 *Narrative*. The illustration of the box is the same one that appeared on the song sheets.

a number of details. A final paragraph describes his activities in Massachusetts. Stearns positioned the 1849 *Narrative* in the context of prior slave narratives. Rather than a tale of terrible abuse, the book professes to show the evil of the system under even the best of slaveholders. Brown was only whipped once, and William Barret, who goes unnamed, was a "kind master." Stearns's intent is obscured, however, by his overheated style. Stearns was a tract writer and a preacher not blessed with the skills of a storyteller. The 1849 *Narrative* is awash with purple prose:

> My master, one of the most distinguished of this uncommon class of slaveholders, hesitated not to allow the wife of my love to be torn from my fond embrace, and the darling idols of my heart, my little children, to be snatched from my arms.

It is hard to imagine Henry Brown expressing himself in this way; the descriptions of Brown's early public speaking as artless suggest a less embellished manner. Stearns's rhetorical excesses weaken the book. As the historian James Olney puts it, Stearns "laid on the True Abolitionist Style very heavily." In fact, Olney hardly exaggerates when he says that "for every fact there are pages of self-conscious, self-gratifying, self-congratulatory philosophizing," to the extent that "there is precious little of Box Brown (other than the representation of the box itself) that remains in the narrative."[52]

If, measured for literary quality, the 1849 *Narrative* falls short, it seems generally reliable for its factualness. Every indication is that the book was indeed "Written from a Statement of Facts Made by Himself." Records corroborate names, places, and events that only Brown could have provided. The present volume uses the 1849 *Narrative* as a source. Nonetheless there are questionable aspects to its accuracy. One deficiency is the reconstructed dialogue. In the manner of many nineteenth-century (and modern) books, conversations are presented that it is doubtful could have been remembered verbatim. An example is the warning Brown's mother gave him when he was very young that slave families were doomed to be broken up. That Brown recalled the effect of what she said seems certain, yet surely Brown's memory was not of her precise words, and in the book her quoted language has the ring of Stearns.

At other points besides dialogue the 1849 *Narrative* engages in what William L. Andrews has discussed as fictionalization in the slave narrative. Shortly after he escaped Brown told J. Miller McKim that a slave trader had purchased his family and taken them to North Carolina where a preacher had bought them. The 1849 *Narrative* merges the two and has the preacher taking the slave coffle south himself. In addition, the book's purpose produced a less-than-comprehensive account of Brown's life. Many Richmond slaves gambled, for instance, and it would be more surprising if Brown abstained rather than played; but telling of this would not have served the antislavery argument, and there is no mention of gambling in the book. In

> ### ANTI-SLAVERY MEETINGS.
> HENRY BOX BROWN and CHARLES STEARNS will hold anti-slavery meetings as follows:—
>
> | | | | |
> |---|---|---|---|
> | Feltonville, | Friday | evening, November | 2. |
> | Berlin, | Saturday | " " | 3. |
> | Bolton, | Sunday | " " | 4. |
> | Lancaster, | Monday | " " | 5. |
> | Leominster, | Tuesday | " " | 6. |
> | Fitchburg, | Wednesday | " " | 7. |
> | Westminster, | Thursday | " " | 8. |
> | Ashburton, | Friday | " " | 9. |
> | Gardner, | Saturday | " " | 10. |
> | So. Gardner, | Sunday | " " | 11. |

"Anti-Slavery Meetings." Brown and Stearns placed notices for their tour—without mention of the book—in the *Liberator* 7–21 September and then weekly from 12 October to 9 November 1849.

seeking its historical value, the 1849 *Narrative* must be read with an ear both to Stearns's rhetorical overlay and to his method, which common to the period did not place foremost strict veracity.[53]

In its brief notice of the book, the *Liberator* commented succinctly that "it is to be regretted that it was not prepared with more care, as its loose and declamatory style greatly mars its interest." Nonetheless the story would "affect the heart" and "excite an intense moral abhorrence of the cruel system of slavery." The reviewer for Frederick Douglass's *North Star* of Rochester, New York, was sympathetic to the message of the *Narrative*. "Slaveholders tell us that slaves are contented and happy," he wrote, "Behold the proof!" The review summarized the story of Brown, "who has dared and suffered for freedom in such a way as was never before dreamed of," and concluded, "We say to all our readers, Get the book."[54]

After publication, Brown and Stearns worked to sell the book. They placed an advertisement in the *National Anti-Slavery Standard* and then, books in hand, set out on an ambitious series of antislavery meetings. Their first venture, from 9 through 24 September, took them north of Boston in a loop from Newburyport to Lawrence and along the coast to Manchester, Massachusetts. Starting on 12 October 1849, Brown and Stearns appeared in a different place every day for thirty-one consecutive days. They opened in Norton, Massachusetts, and for ten days circulated in the southeastern part of the state between Boston and Attleboro. After dipping into Rhode Island for three days, they headed north through central Massachusetts, closing on 11 November in South Gardner, near the New Hampshire border. The tour seems to have been suc-

Henry Brown Arrives, from *Cousin Ann's Stories for Children* (1849). The first published representation of Brown rising in the box. In contrast to the illustration of Brown's box by itself, symbolizing the journey, the focus of this image is the culmination, his arrival to liberty. Befitting a book of moral instruction, Brown's welcomers exhibit proper decorum. The setting is indeterminate, and the box is inaccurately addressed to "Thomas Wilson"; Miller McKim, the publisher, probably remained cautious about the case.

cessful, for the 1851 *Narrative* states that "an edition of 8,000 copies sold in about two months." The size of the print run cannot be confirmed, but it seems likely that the partners sold out the first printing on their tour.[55]

The book campaign was the first time Brown spent a sustained period—a solid month on the second leg—on the performing circuit. He probably learned much about the basic mechanics of touring. The pair may have traveled by rail on occasion, but to get to all the towns they visited, they likely hired a buggy or wagon, loaded the books in the back, and drove from site to site. Brown's youthful training as a teamster probably proved useful. The partners would have arranged with local antislavery activists and ministers for halls and church rooms in which to speak, for a place to stay, and for publicity to bring out an audience. One imagines the egalitarian Stearns insisted on equal accommodations for Brown and himself. On this tour Henry Brown had the opportunity to gain invaluable experience in fulfilling the expectations placed on the headline performer and in the art of handling antislavery hosts. He probably realized, too, that traveling as a lecturer was an occupation at which he could succeed.

Though there is no record that Henry Box Brown ever returned to Pennsylvania, he was well remembered there. On 16 October 1849, during the annual meeting of the Pennsylvania Anti-Slavery Society in Norristown, the box in which Brown had escaped was exhibited to the audience, and a speaker related "its history." At a later date the box was shipped north to Brown's custody.[56]

That year also, an account of Brown's escape was published in Philadelphia. Issued anonymously (although several sources credit Ann Preston as the author), *Cousin Ann's Stories for Children* is a thirty-six-page volume of entertaining moral instruction. The printer was Merrihew and Thompson—the Lewis Thompson who was present at Brown's resurrection—and the publisher was J. Miller McKim. As the father of a seven-year-old daughter and a two-year-old son in 1849, McKim had a personal interest in books for children that reflected his values.[57]

Cousin Ann's Stories contains a variety of sketches, fiction, and poetry. A verse on one page promises "I'll never use tobacco," and another declares "Drink only cold water, / And joy it will bring." The story entitled "Henry Box Brown" tells in five pages of his journey in the box and conveys to the young readers that slavery is wrong: "His heart will always ache when he thinks of his wife and dear children. No one in Carolina is allowed to teach a slave to read or write; so he will never get a letter from any of his family, and it is not likely they will hear from him, or ever know that he is free." The story's conclusion echoes the sentiment of the abolitionists who had met Brown in the months since his escape: "We call people heroes who do something that is brave and great, and Henry is a hero."[58]

"Feloniously Advising"

While Henry Box Brown was touring New England and selling his book, the men in Richmond who had shipped him north faced the consequences of their failed second attempt. Samuel A. Smith had been held in solitary confinement at the Henrico jail since shortly after his arrest in May. Through the summer months of 1849 James C. A. Smith "kept very close quarters." Early in September two Richmond police officers obtained information "which led them to suspect" that James Smith was involved "in the plans of certain white persons who were engaged in running off slaves to free States." After an investigation they "determined to arrest him." Despite Smith's efforts to stay scarce, on 25 September 1849 one of the officers "accidentally met him, and at once took him into custody."[59]

16   [Doc. No. 11.]

[IV.]

Of the Persons received into the Penitentiary from the 1st of October 1849, to the 30th September 1850, there were :

Whites.	Blacks.	Total No. of both colors.	CRIMES.
3	1	4	- - - For murder in the second degree.
3	–	3	For voluntary manslaughter.
–	–	–	- - - For shooting.
1	–	1	For stabbing.
–	–	–	- - - For maiming.
2	–	2	- - - For rape.
2	1	3	- - - For burglary.
3	–	3	- - - For burglary and larceny.
–	–	–	- - - For slave stealing.
1	–	1	- - - For carrying off slaves.
–	–	–	- - - For aiding slaves to abscond.
5	1	6	- - - For horse stealing.
13	3	16	- - - For larceny.
3	–	3	- - - For forgery.
–	–	–	- - - For passing counterfeit money.
–	–	–	- - - For passing counterfeit bank notes.
–	–	–	- - - For burning stacks,
1	1	2	- - - For malicious cutting.
1	–	1	- - - For bigamy.
1	–	1	- - - For arson.
1	–	1	- - - For barn burning.
	1	1	- - - For highway robbery.
1	–	1	- - - For enticing slaves to be boxed up.
3	–	3	- - - For robbery.
1	–	1	- - - For malicious and unlawful shooting.
	2	2	- - - For store breaking.
1	–	1	- - - For horse stealing and larceny, second offence.
1	–	1	- - - For having a ½ dollar die to counterfeit with.
	1	1	- - - For setting fire to house.
1	1	1	- - - For carrying off slaves and barn burning.
	1	1	- - - For furnishing register to slave.
48	12	60	- - - Whole number received.

"For Enticing Slaves to be Boxed Up." From an official report, the table summarizes the criminal convictions of "persons received into the Penitentiary" from October 1849 to September 1850, including Samuel A. Smith's offense.

James C. A. Smith was arraigned the next day before the Mayor's Court of the city of Richmond. Alfred and Sawney, the slaves who had been discovered hidden in the boxes in May, were brought to court and compelled to testify. The two men likely knew that they had avoided the punishment of being sold away only because the authorities needed their testimony. Even though self-protection must have been on their minds as they came to the hearing, Alfred "denied all knowledge of the prisoner, and stated that he had taken no part in the arrangements, as far as he knew." While Alfred stood firm, Sawney told all. He testified that James Smith "was connected in this business with Samuel A. Smith—that he introduced Alfred and himself to Smith, &c." James Smith had handled the shipping of Sawney's trunk to the North, and with the claim check Smith had given him, Sawney said, he was able "to get his trunk after the plan miscarried."[60]

The mayor deemed the evidence "sufficiently strong" to hold Smith for trial. "If Jim Smith had any connection with it," the *Richmond Examiner* declared, "he is certainly a candidate for the Penitentiary." As a free black charged with a felony, Smith would go before a court of oyer and terminer. There would be no jury but rather a panel of justices, who were not necessarily judges, at least five of them, by law, and at Smith's trial, eight. Conviction required a unanimous decision by the justices.[61]

The trial took place on 15 October 1849. To prepare his defense, James Smith hired three prominent white lawyers at a reported cost of $900. The defense strategy was to impugn Sawney and make his incrimination of Smith the issue. "Sawney was the only witness to prove the guilt of the prisoner," reported the *Richmond Examiner*, and testimony from blacks was mistrusted. "It is surmised," continued the account, that Sawney "was prompted to appear as a witness in the case for the reason that he was chagrined on account of the failure of the scheme to obtain his own freedom, and a desire to regain the favor and lost confidence of his master in him." Only a single justice had to be convinced, and the strategy proved successful when the verdict came back that "seven Justices voted to convict, and one to acquit."[62]

The vote of a single magistrate had saved James C. A. Smith from prison but not from notoriety. Within two weeks Smith was back in court, this time charged with traveling to "Pillsbury," Pennsylvania. Under Virginia law, a free person of color who went to a nonslaveholding state for any purpose could no longer reside in Virginia. On 24 October 1849 the *Richmond Republican* reported Smith's arrest and expressed the hope that he would be required "to spend the balance of his days in Boston, or some other place, where negroes are so much admired and beloved." The case was dismissed for insufficient evidence, but with this second charge the authorities made clear to James Smith that it would be difficult for him to continue to live in Richmond.[63]

Meanwhile Samuel A. Smith's situation was unpromising, for the authorities had seized his property, and he faced two trials, one for each of the captured fugitives. Given the publicity of his case and its political ramifications he had little chance of escaping conviction. The first trial, on the charges related to Alfred, began on 30 October 1849. An account published some years later in the *New York Tribune* claimed that Smith's two lawyers called no defense witnesses because "no officer could be found who would serve a summons on a witness." The jury found Smith guilty, and on 1 November he was sentenced to four and a half years in the penitentiary. The second trial, 8–10 November, for aiding Sawney, added two years to his term. Smith's lawyers appealed without success, and Samuel A. Smith entered the Virginia State Penitentiary in Richmond to serve consecutive sentences totaling six and a half years.[64]

The historian Herbert Aptheker, a pioneer in the study of slave resistance, lists Samuel Smith in his accounting of "political prisoners and martyrs" who fought against slavery. "It is not customary in the literature to consider these people political prisoners or refugees or martyrs," he writes, "but that is what they were." On 23 November 1849, the *Liberator* reported Smith's conviction. "So much for endeavoring to deliver the spoiled out of the hands of the oppressor in this Christian country! Talk of Austrian and Russian atrocities! Where is Daniel Webster?"[65]

Chapter Four

The Moving Panorama

Picture Shows

Black and white abolitionists had assisted and guided Henry Brown during his first months in freedom, providing accommodations, arranging appearances, and helping him to earn money. By the end of 1849, with the profits from his *Narrative,* Brown was able to become more self-reliant and to begin to plot his own course. In Richmond, his savings had been the means to effect his escape. Now in Boston he again had funds and conceived a new plan. In it he envisioned himself in a public role quite different from the ones that abolitionists usually assigned to fugitive slaves.

Henry Box Brown determined to produce and exhibit an antislavery moving panorama. The moving panorama was a theatrical presentation widely current in 1849. Brown later told an English newspaper that he "wrote and published a narrative of his life, and with the proceeds of the sale procured the execution of a panorama illustrative of African and American slavery." In this explanation Brown underplayed his accomplishment, for no one before had used a moving panorama for abolitionism, and his panorama was a remarkable and original work.[1]

Brown's project brought the antislavery appeal to a medium of entertainment best known for travelogue and associated with the likes of promoter P. T. Barnum. Although the abolitionists were similar to any political activists in seeking to catch the public's attention, their methods reflected a concern for propriety. The antislavery mass meetings with stirring speeches and uplifting songs were popular, attracting thousands, yet even so were guided by religiously influenced decorum. Prior to 1852, when the spectacular success of Harriet Beecher Stowe's novel *Uncle Tom's Cabin* inspired numerous offshoots, there are few examples of popular entertainments with an antislavery message.[2]

Henry Box Brown envisioned an enterprise with a lectern and a ticket box. He had learned from his experiences on the book tour, and before then from selling his song sheets, that commerce and advocacy could be combined. There were certainly precedents for an entrepreneurial approach to abolitionism, including not least William Lloyd Garrison's operation of the *Liberator* and Frederick Douglass's of the *North Star.* To tour with an exhibition would take advantage of his fame, serve the cause, and earn him a living.

The moving panorama as an exhibition was the latest in a series of formats featuring large paintings that entertained and educated. The big paintings started in Europe. In 1794 Robert Barker had opened a new circular building in London to exhibit his innovation the "Panorama." Patrons climbed a tower inside the exhibition hall to look at the Panorama, a huge 360-degree painting of a detailed view in all directions from a high vantage point. Barker's first painting was of London seen from the top of the Albion sugar mills, the highest point between Westminster Abbey and Saint Paul's Cathedral, and new paintings were installed annually. Some years later in Paris another format appeared. Louis Daguerre, a painter of theater sets and later an inventor of photography, opened the "Diorama" there in 1822. Seated in a darkened hall, an audience viewed a large and vivid landscape painting. Gradually the illumination of the image altered to suggest clouds passing before the sun, the approach of a storm, or a daytime scene transforming into evening.[3]

Both the Panorama and the Diorama, as originally conceived, required specially designed buildings for their full realization, and these were constructed only in major cities. Other promoters developed large new displays that were mobile. Though the effects were not as grand, the exhibitions could be toured to many places. These promoters borrowed the names *panorama* and *diorama* to advertise their exhibitions, and in time the terms came to refer not only to Barker's and Daguerre's specific formats but more broadly to a wide variety of painted exhibitions.[4]

One variation was to display a painting in motion. In London by 1820 some shows used as a backdrop a rolling painted canvas, with actors walking in place as the scenery passed behind them. A New York production in 1828 used a similar idea. The characters in William Dunlap's work *A Trip to Niagara; or, Travellers in America* sat in a stationary boat onstage and moved "from the wharf in New York and up the Hudson" by means of "moving diorama." Dunlap himself admitted that the piece was "merely a device for the employment of dioramic scenery." From such applications evolved the format known as the moving panorama. In 1841 P. T. Barnum purchased the American Museum in New York. Along with its galleries of curiosities, the renamed Barnum's Museum offered variety shows, which often included moving panoramas between live acts. At Barnum's the panoramas, though primarily entr'acte diversions, seem to have been presented as attractions in themselves.[5]

In 1846 the moving panorama took center stage as an entertainment phenomenon. That year John Banvard's mammoth *Panorama of the Mississippi River* debuted in Louisville and went on to Boston. Advertised with exaggeration as having a canvas "Three Miles Long," its length was nonetheless exceptional. In Boston, "thousands upon thousands visited it," claimed Banvard's literature, "many coming hundreds of miles,—from the remotest parts of New England." Banvard played New York with great

 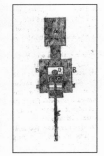

Banvard's Panorama Machinery, 1848. **Left:** Frame with Canvas and Gearing. **Right:** Pulley Sideview. To prevent sagging of the canvas, beneath the crossbeam of the frame "are set a double row of pulleys." At the upper edge of the canvas "is sewed a thick cord or small rope," which rests atop the pulleys while the canvas passes between them. Thus "the canvass is rolled up along the whole length of the line without any sensible dropping of it at one place more than another."

result in 1847 and then took the panorama to London, where it created a sensation. *Scientific American* reported that "the Panorama of the Mississippi has had an astonishing effect upon all classes in London." During Banvard's run, a competitor opened *Smith's Leviathan Panorama of the Mississippi River* with "over four miles of canvas," and the well-advertised rivalry "engaged the attention of all London."[6]

Banvard's conspicuous success inspired a number of American and English productions and set off the boom era of the moving panorama, which lasted for about a decade. Popular interest in foreign and unfamiliar lands had been spurred by the growth of international trade and by the march of imperialism. By the end of the 1840s stories of events from around the globe were in the newspapers. At the same time, compared to the modern era, pictures were a scarce commodity. Photography was new and its scope remained limited, and new advances in printed reproduction were only beginning to show up in the illustrated press. The moving panorama met the public's great curiosity for glimpses of places unseen.

Though the moving panorama was, in one sense, a "moving picture," the scenes were not moving when viewed. Thus, the closest modern analogy is to a photographic slide show, a sequence of still images with commentary. In its mechanics, a moving panorama was a kind of giant scroll. A large frame held two vertical rollers. The canvas, usually between eight and twelve feet high, was wound from one roller to the other, revealing a sequence of painted scenes. When available, side and top curtains on the stage hid the mechanism and framed the painted scenes. In some exhibitions the curtains fell to hide the working of the machinery altogether and then reopened to reveal the next view. Banvard's presentation became the standard. He sat on a platform and explained the scenes, enlivening his narrative with "jokes, poetry and patter." In London, piano music accompanied, and with the theater darkened the panorama was illuminated "with the aid of strong gas light."[7]

The moving panorama apparatus was designed to be easily disassembled and shipped. A touring panorama promoter had the flexibility of renting a theater, a music hall, or a meeting room for an exhibition. An engagement might last from several days to many months, with shorter stays typical for smaller towns and longer runs in large cities.

In 1849 a Philadelphia abolitionist explained the attraction of the moving panorama in a world of "steamships, railroads, and magnetic telegraph, and all the many improvements of modern times." It was not enough, he said, that distant places could "whisper in each other's ears, over magic wires." With the panorama "we would see the far off cities and nations as well as hear their voices." The moving panorama had special benefit for "the masses of people," he believed. "Rich and poor alike can partake of the feast of beauty and knowledge which the hand of Art has here spread for them." The panoramas, he concluded, brought "the beauties and glories of the old world" and "the wonders of our own Continent" to all.[8]

The English novelist Charles Dickens in 1850 wrote of a visit that his character "Mr. Booley" made to a panorama of the Mississippi River. It pleased Mr. Booley that "new and cheap means are continually being devised, for conveying the results of actual experience, to those who are unable to obtain such experiences for themselves; and to bring them within the reach of the people—emphatically of the people; for it is they at large who are addressed in these endeavours, and not exclusive audiences." Mr. Booley continued that "even if I see a run on an idea, like the panorama one, it awakens no ill-humour within me. . . . The more man knows of man, the better for the common brotherhood among us all."[9]

At one point in the Mississippi panorama, Mr. Booley observed "the doomed Negro race . . . working in the plantations, while the republican overseer looked on, whip in hand." Panoramas that depicted life in the southern United States inevitably presented images of slavery. "Hundreds of slaves are seen carrying earth, trees, &c., to fill up the gap," stated the *Descriptive Pamphlet* about a scene in *Smith's Leviathan Panorama of the Mississippi River*. Dickens was unsympathetic to slavery and recorded its depiction with reproach, but the panoramas themselves expressed no such disapproval. In a scene of "a splendid plantation," Smith's *Descriptive Pamphlet* noted "three sugar mills, a jail, saw mill, the overseer's house, and owner's villa," and spoke of the production capacity, but did not touch on the reasons why this sugar plantation had its own private jail.[10]

The black abolitionist William Wells Brown attended an exhibition of Banvard's Mississippi panorama during its Boston run in 1847. "I was somewhat amazed at the very mild manner in which the 'Peculiar Institution' of the Southern States was there represented," he wrote later. Brown recognized that Banvard's depiction was not neutral. To show slavery in a "very mild manner" was an implicit endorsement of the status quo. It occurred to him that a moving panorama "with as fair a representation of American Slavery as could be given upon canvass, would do much to disseminate truth upon this subject." In England William Wells Brown produced a moving panorama about slavery that he began showing in the autumn of 1850.[11]

Before the end of 1849 Henry Box Brown was already at work on his own antislavery moving panorama. How he conceived the notion can only be guessed. The idea might have been in circulation among Boston abolitionists. William Wells Brown may have conveyed to his colleagues his thoughts on Banvard's panorama, but because he departed for England in July 1849, when Henry Box Brown was still new to life in the North and to antislavery activism, it seems unlikely that Wells Brown was the direct inspiration for Box Brown's concept. The *Narrative of Henry Box Brown* did not mention any plans for a panorama, which suggests that the project probably originated after the book's publication early in September.

The moving panorama would have been particularly appealing to Henry Box Brown as one who was not a reader. Because the panorama performance was visual and aural, Brown would have been able to take its full measure. Undoubtedly he attended moving panoramas in Boston, for there was ample opportunity, and one imagines he learned for himself that a panorama could both entertain and educate. "Ever since the advent of Banvard, this city has been literally over-run with panoramas," wrote the Boston correspondent of a Saint Louis newspaper in October 1849:

> I cannot enumerate them all, but there is always two or more open at the same time. With the exception of "Bayne's Panorama of a Voyage to Europe," all have lost money. Two *Mexican Panoramas* were failures. "Champney's Rhine," the "Shores of the Mediterranean," a "Voyage to California," the "Creation and the Deluge," "Ireland and her Shores," Hudson's "Ohio and Mississippi," "A Voyage round the World," "A walk through the Garden of Eden," are anything but successful. . . . The panorama rage, however, is still high. The Panorama of the "River St. Lawrence and Falls of Niagara," and another called "American Scenery, embracing all that is grand and wonderful in America," also "Stockwell's colossal Panorama of the Mississippi river" are yet in full blast. "Skirving's overland journey to California" was opened October 1st.[12]

For his *Narrative* Brown had needed an amanuensis. As a panorama exhibitor, he could express himself directly. A newspaper interview with Brown ten years later suggests that he sought to sustain the positive results of the summer and of the book tour during October and November. Brown "determined to deliver lectures, which were the more interesting, inasmuch as they contained the experiences of his own life. His first efforts being successful, he had a panorama painted, illustrating scenes in his own life, and in slave life generally."[13]

Henry Box Brown may have simply had a moment of inspiration. It likely came at the end of the book tour, when his publishing profits presented new opportunity. Circumstances suggest one possibility. When Brown and Stearns returned from the tour to Boston, the *Panorama of the Bible* was playing there.

> ## Second Week at Boylston Hall.
> ### J. INSCO WILLIAMS'S
> ## PANORAMA OF THE BIBLE.
> THIS Painting, which is over a mile in length, will commence moving every evening, at 7 1-2 o'clock, precisely.
>
> Tickets 25 cents   Children under 12 years of age, half price.
>
> Exhibition every Wednesday and Saturday afternoon, at 3 o'clock.
>
> ☞ Parties and schools admitted on reasonable terms.
>
> See small bills.
> November 16

Panorama of the Bible. The advertisement appeared in the *Liberator,* 16 November 1849.

An advertisement for *Panorama of the Bible* appeared in the *Liberator,* exactly where their book tour schedule had been listed for the previous five weeks, and the *Liberator* noticed the panorama in a short article entitled "Well Worth Seeing," calling it "truly felicitous." With that endorsement and his own interest, Brown might have attended *Panorama of the Bible.* This exhibition could have prodded his thinking, for it demonstrated that travelogue was not the only content fit for a panorama, and further that a moving panorama might convey moral issues.[14]

However the revelation came about, Henry Box Brown had once before in Richmond made an imaginative leap. The idea may have popped into his head: "Go and get a panorama, and put yourself in it."

Into Production

Just as Henry Box Brown began work to create a panorama, he propitiously gained a comrade. James C. A. Smith heeded the signal from the authorities after his second arrest in Richmond and left Virginia for the North. Smith probably went first to Philadelphia to learn of his friend's current whereabouts. He arrived in Boston by December 1849. The city directory published in April 1850 recorded him living in the same building as Brown at 41 Southac Street.

James C. A. Smith joined the panorama project right away and essentially became a partner with Brown, although it seems unlikely that there was any formal agreement. Smith's varied experiences—as a shopkeeper and dentist, as a leader and singer in the First African Baptist Church choir, and as a conductor on the Underground Railroad—gave him abilities that complemented well those of Henry Box Brown. It was particularly valuable that Smith had some education since he could read and write for Brown.

Smith had known Nancy Brown and reported later that one of the first letters he wrote for Brown went to "the man which own H. Box Browns wife to know if he would sell the woman and her children." Smith said Brown had told him "that the man would not answer any letters upon the subject of buying his wife and children," but a reply came to Smith's letter "in a very short time." Smith recalled that "both of us look over the contents and the master of his wife—said in his letter to us that he would take $1500. for the woman and her children if Brown would promise to treat them kindly."[15]

It was an offer that Brown did not pursue. Although his reasons are unrecorded, Brown's intent was to be an exhibitor, not a supplicant. The master's asking price for

Nancy Brown and the children was certainly well more than the proceeds from sales of the book. Abolitionists had at times purchased freedom for slaves, but many potential contributors were unwilling to become complicit in the slave system by paying for a human being. For Brown, not only would an attempt to purchase his family have been difficult, it would have also scuttled the panorama, his means to become independent. Perhaps Brown thought to get on his feet and then return to the offer.[16]

Brown's funds were sufficient to start the panorama and to provide living expenses for himself and Smith for a time, but they were not enough to carry the project through to completion. Hence the effort moved on two fronts: the creation of the moving panorama and the raising of money to pay for it. Aided by James Smith, Brown shouldered the primary responsibility to solicit funds for the panorama. As Smith wrote later, "During the time we were traveling to geather from december 1849 to the time the Panorama was finished I used every thing to help get the means to finish paying for the Panorama." Smith's words suggest that the two men were on the road much of the time. Brown reported that he "attended large meetings in different towns in the states of Maine, New Hampshire, Vermont, Connecticut, Rhode Island, Pennsylvania, and New York, in all of which places I have found many friends."[17]

As Brown and Smith sought money to complete it, the panorama was underway in Boston. Brown said that he "procured the execution" of the panorama, and in executing the panorama the most important participants were the artists. A Liverpool newspaper in 1850 stated that the panorama was "painted by Willcott, Rouse, and Johnson, Artists, of Boston." Earlier that year the *Liberator* reported that the panorama "has been for several months past in process of completion by the artist, Mr. Josiah Wolcott,

Above: Josiah Wolcott, *Brook Farm,* 1844. The painting shows "the entrance to the community, along with the various buildings—the Hive, Shop, Eyrie, Cottage, and Pilgrim House—and the foundations for the new building, the phalanstery, which was begun in 1844.... On the back of the painting panel is a pencil sketch detailing the specific buildings."
Opposite: Samuel Worcester Rowse, *Henry David Thoreau,* 1854. Among Rowse's other portrait subjects were Nathaniel Hawthorne and Ralph Waldo Emerson.

who has been employed for that purpose by the celebrated Henry Box Brown." Wolcott seems to have been the primary artist, with the other two artists assisting.[18]

Josiah Wolcott was about thirty-five years old in 1850 and made his living as an ornamental sign-painter. By April 1850 he was working out of a studio on Court Street at the corner of Sudbury Street, where Brown's panorama was likely painted. Wolcott had previously put his talents to work for abolitionism. In December 1842, Caroline Weston, an organizer of the Anti-Slavery Bazaar, an annual fundraising event in Boston, wrote to her sister that "a young man called, who announced himself as Josiah Wolcott & offered his services to make all the motto's—we don't know who he is, but Maria thinks he has saved her life." Wolcott later provided illustrations in 1851–1852 for a Boston weekly, the *Carpet-Bag*, whose editors wrote that Wolcott had "a peculiar genius for designing."[19]

As a fine artist, Wolcott exhibited three landscapes at the Boston Athenaeum in 1837. His best-known works are two landscapes of Brook Farm, one painted in 1843 and the other circa 1844–1846, the only extant contemporary views of the utopian community. He was associated with Brook Farm from 1843 until its dissolution in 1847, purchasing shares and serving on a committee there in 1845. It was probably through Wolcott's connection to Brook Farm that he came to work for Henry Box Brown. Charles Stearns, Brown's book partner, had been close enough to the community by his kinship ties that he likely knew of Wolcott and could have steered Brown to the painter.[20]

Identification of the other two artists, "Rouse" and "Johnson," is less definite, but two candidates stand out. Samuel Worcester Rowse was about twenty-seven years old in 1850 and had moved to Boston from Maine to learn lithography. Of his crayon portraits of literary people, including Nathaniel Hawthorne and Henry David Thoreau, it was said that he "seized upon character and rendered the soul in the faces he portrayed." The most prominent among the several artists named "Johnson" in Boston at the time was David Claypoole Johnston, who was then about fifty-one years old and who had exhibited regularly at the Boston Athenaeum since 1828. Known as a graphic humorist, D. C. Johnston worked in a variety of mediums and was called "the American Cruikshank" by his biographer. Johnston designed the *Liberator*'s second masthead. He began teaching in the mid-1840s, and it is possible that he stood in that relationship to Rowse or Wolcott, which might explain how the older and more established artist became involved with the panorama and why he had a secondary role.[21]

Six names—Brown, Smith, Stearns, Wolcott, Rowse, and Johnston—can be linked to some degree to the creation of the panorama. Other people undoubtedly also contributed, for there were many tasks. An inventory in an 1848 contract describes the components of a panorama, and thus indicates the variety of skills necessary to produce one. The sale contract for *Hutching's Pictorial Map and Chart, or Grand Classical Panorama of the Sea and Shores of the Mediterranean* recorded "the original sketches, drawings, plans, descriptions printed and written, with the leases, copyright, curtains, canvass, machinery, paint, brushes, signs, and all other articles, goods, & chattels thereunto belonging."[22]

From this list the stages of production can be identified. The work began with "the original sketches, drawings, plans." Painting the panorama required "canvass" and "paint" and "brushes." The means of presentation included "machinery" and "curtains." Needed for exhibition were "descriptions printed and written," "leases," and "signs."

Before Wolcott and his associates began to paint Brown's panorama, they would have developed a plan for the sequence of illustrations. Such a plan would roughly correspond to the shooting script in modern cinema because it would have included draft sketches of the scenes and an overall concept for the story line. William Wells Brown wrote that when he decided to create a panorama he "commenced collecting a number of sketches of plantations in the Slave States, illustrating the life of the Slave." He obtained "sketches of beautiful and interesting American scenery, as well as of many touching incidents in the lives of Slaves." He then had the images "copied by skillful artists in London" to "form the subjects of the Panorama."[23]

One imagines a similar process for Henry Box Brown's panorama. At the beginning the group collected drawings, prints, and published illustrations. Charles Stearns was versed in antislavery and if he contributed to the project it was probably at this stage. Images in circulation among abolitionists could be borrowed and then copied or adapted by the artists. Whereas William Wells Brown intimated that he alone selected the images and developed the plan for his panorama, Henry Box Brown lacked Wells Brown's wider knowledge of the subject. The creative process behind the plan for Box Brown's panorama was probably more collaborative, though in all likelihood Wolcott and the other artists made most of the significant choices. The artists would have made a drawing for each scene, worked them into a sequence, and then proceeded to the painting.[24]

Later advertisements for Henry Box Brown's panorama claimed it was 50,000 square

D.C. Johnston, from *Scraps*. 1849: "Raffaelle Viledaub, painting the first section, six miles in length—of his monster panorama of ALL CREATION. ("This section)" says the *Daily Snob,*— "which for strength, & force of color, is unequalled by the most powerful of the old masters, embraces that portion of time when DARKNESS WAS UPON THE FACE OF THE DEEP, & truly may it be said that the artist has left nothing to be desired, save a mile or two more of canvas."

feet in size, but a tenth of that seems more likely. Amid the hyperbole of panoramic advertising, with announcements of lengths in miles, the 1849 pamphlet for *The Nile* stated that the panorama was "above 800 feet in length, by 8 feet in breadth." The pamphlet quoted an observer who judged that "the cloth appears to be as long, or even longer, than those said to be of miles' extent."[25]

Even if Brown's panorama was smaller than *The Nile*, a canvas on the order of 8 feet high and 600 feet in length was a lot of surface to paint. How Brown's artists divided the work is unknown, though their prior work offers hints. D. C. Johnston may have assisted primarily with laying out scenes for the plan, or possibly in his teacher's role offered critiques of the work in progress. Rowse was skilled at portraiture and may have concentrated on the human figures in the scenes. As a sign painter Wolcott probably had the most experience working on a very large scale, and since the *Liberator* credited Wolcott alone with spending "several months" on the project, he probably took the biggest part in painting the canvas.

There was not only painting to be done. A panorama also required much sewing. Each section of painted canvas had to be attached securely to the next one. To the top of the canvas a rope was sewn to ride along the pulleys of the panorama apparatus. There might also have been curtains to hide the apparatus. Perhaps Brown recruited Louisa Freeman, the tailoress who lived in his building, or one of Boston's many sailmakers. Given the business difficulties that many panorama operators apparently faced, Brown might have obtained the display machinery from a retiring exhibitor. If not, construction of the apparatus and of shipping crates would have required the services of both a skilled mechanic and a carpenter. As exhibition neared, there would be need for preparation and printing of handbills, programs, and such.[26]

Beyond his financial responsibility, Henry Box Brown's part in the realization of the panorama is undocumented. He did make some contribution to the plan of the panorama, for there were two scenes of his own escape, and he had witnessed the subjects depicted in several other scenes. He probably did not paint or sew. As the primary fund-raiser, the one who presumably paid the bills, and, most likely, the final authority for the conduct of the project, Brown acted much as a film producer does in bringing a motion picture to the screen. Once the plan was set Brown may have left the execution of it to the artists and inspected progress when he was in Boston between trips. Yet if he did not paint each scene, if he was not the physical creator of the work, Henry Box Brown was the force behind this moving panorama, and his name appeared in its title.

The Nubian Slave

Most moving panoramas were travelogues, their painted views assembled as if they were the scenes of a journey. Henry Box Brown's panorama, with a different aim, had another kind of story line. His artists found their model in antislavery literature, in an illustrated poem published in Boston in 1845 and little remembered today entitled *The Nubian Slave*.

Charles C. Green was both author and artist of *The Nubian Slave*. Best described as an antislavery romantic tragedy, the poem in its title and conception reflected contemporary interest in ancient Egypt. Nubia is a region on the upper Nile, in present-day southern Egypt and northern Sudan. The Nubians are a dark-skinned people, and the westerners whose writings helped inspire interest in ancient Egypt linked the Nubians with Egyptian slavery. "The name of Nouba is given to all the Blacks coming from the slave countries to the south of Sennaar," explained John Lewis Burckhardt in his 1822 *Travels in Nubia*, a work that Green quoted in *The Nubian Slave*.[27]

In the United States popular awareness of ancient Egypt flowered during the 1840s. The Egyptian revival was manifested in lectures, books, and displays of artifacts at Barnum's Museum and similar institutions. Motifs drawn from Egyptian monuments found their way into home furnishings and architecture, exemplified by the obelisk design for the Washington Monument, begun in 1848. In Richmond the Egyptian Building was completed in 1846 to house the Medical College of Virginia. It was built diagonally across the street from First African Baptist Church, where Henry Brown and his fellow churchgoers observed each week the progress of its construction.[28]

Edgar Allan Poe satirized the Egyptian revival in his 1845 story "Some Words with a Mummy" and named one of the characters Gliddon, after one of the key agents in launching American interest in ancient Egypt. George Robbins Gliddon delivered a series of lectures on Egyptian archaeology in Boston beginning in December 1842 and returned to present the prestigious Lowell Institute lectures in October 1843. These lectures, augmented by exhibits of artifacts, were heavily attended—one account recorded nearly ten thousand subscribers to the 1843–1844 series—and reported extensively in the newspapers. Gliddon took his lectures across the country and published several books on ancient Egypt, including a version of his lectures that sold 24,000 copies.[29]

Gliddon's version of Egypt's history, however, had a pernicious subtext. He espoused a theory of permanent racial hierarchies. In the third of the Lowell Institute lectures, he declared that "no nation has ever become *permanently* subdued by any other that was *its inferior in Race*," and proclaimed that "no power can stem the progress of the *Anglo-Saxon* on the Asiatic and American continents." Gliddon contended that Egyptian culture was Caucasian in origin rather than African, and interpreted his exhibits of hieroglyphic translations and ancient art to reach conclusions seemingly buttressed with the imprimatur of scholarship. To justify ranking the peoples of the world by their color, Gliddon presented drawings of human figures copied from ancient Egyptian art. He identified these figures according to their ethnic origins and social status. The visual evidence, he asserted, demonstrated the permanence of natural hierarchies of race.[30]

At the fourth Lowell lecture, according to a newspaper account, Gliddon presented "various scenes of *Negroes* from the Scriptures, showing that, 2000 B.C, their social position 'was then what it yet is, that of plebeians, servants, and slaves.'" In this lecture Gliddon revealed that his supposed scholarship was on a par with that of the blackface minstrels. He closed, stated the report, "with a curious scene of Negros dancing in the streets of Thebes, proving that 'de Nigger' rejoined anciently, as he does now, and that to the music 'ob de Banjo' he 'Wheel about and turn about / And jump Jim Crow.'" The popular minstrel refrain, claimed Gliddon, had roots in ancient civilization.[31]

Gliddon's Evidence. In his 1840s lectures George R. Gliddon displayed an image of "Negroes Dancing in Thebes" that he linked to the minstrel refrain "jump Jim Crow." In a book Gliddon co-authored in 1854 this image illustrated similar comments.

Through the efforts of Gliddon, the Egyptian revival was implicated in contemporary issues of race and slavery. When the abolitionist Charles C. Green placed a prospectus in the *Liberator* in March 1845 for "a series of Anti-Slavery Designs, to be called, The Nubian Slave," he could expect that readers would understand the allusion to an Egyptian context. Green may have been mindful too of Gliddon's talk-of-the-town lectures of a year earlier, for his antislavery poem challenged Gliddon's appropriation of things Egyptian to justify prejudice and slavery. "These Designs are worthy of high praise," declared the *Liberator* on the book's publication in May 1845. "Encourage the modest but meritorious artist, and thus enable Genius to give a staggering blow to the foul system of slavery."[32]

The Nubian Slave is a thin volume with large pages displaying "seven Designs, drawn on stone." The lithographs and the text of the poem appear on alternate pages, and each print is linked by its title to a particular passage in the poem. The opening stanzas describe the author's awakening to the evil of slavery: "Indignant Truth inspires the song." In three parts, the poem tells the story of a Nubian family of father, mother, and son, and their passage from liberty in Africa to slavery in the United States. In Nubia the family lived freely near "lofty piles by Pharaohs reared, / . . . Huge relics of the mighty past." In part two the family is captured by "*Christian* robbers," shipped to the United States, and put up at auction. "Come, freemen! bid! they're bright and hale," enjoins the poem. A clergyman purchases the mother, and the family is separated.[33]

Title Page, Charles C. Green, *The Nubian Slave,* Boston, 1845.

In the third part, the husband and wife contrive to meet and plan an escape but are caught together and punished. Their "fellow bondmen" tell them about freedom in the North, and they reunite to attempt to escape. The accompanying print, *The Escape*, shows the father pointing out the North Star to his wife and son "as their guide to the land of Freedom." But tracking dogs and slave hunters overtake them, and mother and father die resisting their captors. "'Twas gold, not mercy, spared the child," the poem explains, and it concludes "O, christian sons of christian sires, / Thus, thus ye feed your altar-fires!!"[34]

To the creators of Henry Box Brown's panorama, *The Nubian Slave* offered a structure: a narrative with fictional protagonists. With its African beginning, the poem's plot encapsulated in a single story the whole cycle of slavery. Green portrayed the Nubians as noble and sympathetic and their fate as tragic; they symbolized the many. Contrary to Gliddon, the Nubian family's original freedom was natural, and their enslavement unnatural; they were not destined for servitude, rather they were robbed of liberty.

Green's description of his purpose could as well apply to the panorama: "The application of PICTORIAL ART to MORAL TRUTH is capable of producing a great, and, as yet, almost untried force, which the FRIENDS OF HUMAN FREEDOM have now an opportunity to test." Four years after the publication of *The Nubian Slave*, the creators of Brown's panorama similarly sought to apply "pictorial art to moral truth," and used the story of the Nubian family as the framework for the panorama's narrative. Copies of *The Nubian Slave* are rare today, an indication that the edition was probably not large. Charles C. Green's allegory of slavery surely found its broadest audience when adapted to Henry Box Brown's panorama.[35]

Preparation Amid Contention

As Henry Box Brown and his comrades made a panorama, events in Washington picked up pace. The Congress elected in 1848 convened in December 1849, and reports of its conflicts over slavery filled the newspapers. On Christmas Eve James Buchanan, the future president, declared to a correspondent that "the blessed Union of these States is now in greater danger than it has ever been since the adoption of the federal Constitution."[36]

On 4 January 1850 Senator James Murray Mason, of Virginia, introduced a Fugitive Slave Bill that would greatly enlarge the ability of slaveholders to recover runaways in the North. The bill added the issue of fugitive slaves to the controversial matters already before Congress that turned on slavery. Slave-state senators were blocking the admission of the territory of California to the Union as a free state, for its entry would tip against them the even balance of senators established in the Missouri Compromise of 1820. Antislavery congressmen from the North sought to ban slavery and the slave trade from the District of Columbia. And questions about the territories conquered from Mexico loomed above all, especially whether they would be open to slavery.[37]

On 29 January 1850 Senator Henry Clay of Kentucky introduced a series of linked resolutions on the major issues. Devoted to preserving the Union, Clay maintained that his package of resolutions balanced the interests of the sections. To win southern support, Clay's compromise endorsed Mason's Fugitive Slave Bill. Early in March Senator John C. Calhoun of South Carolina rejected Clay's compromise on the grounds that it would not protect the South's rights in the future against a more-rapidly growing North. In answer, Senator Daniel Webster of Massachusetts championed Clay's approach as the best means to preserve the Union. Webster's famous "Seventh of March Speech" would long be remembered by abolitionists in Massachusetts.[38]

The prominence of the slavery issue in national affairs probably helped Henry Box

Brown and James C. A. Smith to raise funds for the panorama. As part of that effort, early in January 1850 a lithographic print of Brown's arrival in the box was issued in Boston. *The Resurrection of Henry Box Brown at Philadelphia* is large and striking. The uncredited print was probably made by Samuel W. Rowse, one of the artists working on the panorama. Brown and Smith went to Syracuse, New York, for an abolitionist meeting shortly after and took with them copies to sell.[39]

The meeting in Syracuse, the "Anti-Slavery Mass Convention, of the Abolitionists of the State of New York," was called to resolve divisions within the radical wing of the abolitionist movement. The American Anti-Slavery Society had fractured in 1839. The part that kept the name rejected participation in electoral politics; this wing held the Boston convention that Brown attended. Another part organized as a single-issue abolitionist political party, the Liberty Party, and nominated candidates for president in 1840 and 1844. The Liberty Party itself splintered in 1848 when one faction joined the new Free Soil Party, which opposed the expansion of slavery into new territories but was not abolitionist. Those who remained with the Liberty Party saw the Free Soil Party as compromised and opportunistic. The Syracuse meeting at city hall on 15 January 1850 brought together members of the American Anti-Slavery Society, the antipolitical radicals, and of the Liberty Party, the political abolitionists. The conveners hoped, with so many slavery issues before Congress, that the groups might find common ground for action.[40]

Agreement proved elusive. The convention went on for three days during which a narrow, albeit fundamental, question occupied an inordinate amount of the delegates' time: whether the U.S. Constitution was a prop for the slave system or, as the adherents of the Liberty Party contended, an antislavery document. The Philadelphia monthly *Non-Slaveholder* saw little "practical importance" to the debate. The black abolitionist Samuel Ringgold Ward, in his *Impartial Citizen*, lamented the conflicts at the meeting but decided that "upon the whole the Convention did good." The tenor of the meeting is best expressed in the fate of a resolution "advising the Liberty party and American Anti-Slavery Society to cease their warfare upon each other, and devote all their energies to the overthrow of Slavery." A minority "vehemently opposed" the resolution, and it was withdrawn.[41]

In the midst of the factional disputes Henry Box Brown and James C. A. Smith were honored above the fray. At the opening of the second day's session, the president of the convention, the Reverend Samuel J. May, "introduced to the audience Henry Box Brown, who escaped from Slavery in Richmond, last spring, by being fastened up as Dry Goods in a Box about three feet long," and "James Boxer Smith, another colored young man, who boxed Brown up." The reporter who prepared the convention's proceedings described them as "good and intelligent looking young men." Smith later recalled that May had introduced him as "one of the conductors of the under ground rail road." For him the Syracuse event was a debut in the way that the Boston convention had been for Brown. Not only did he receive public credit for his antislavery efforts but also he gained a nickname. Samuel R. Ward stated later that at the meeting he "gave him the *sobriquet* of 'Boxer' Smith, because he is the man who nailed the box in which Henry Box Brown escaped from Virginia."[42]

Brown opened the third day of the convention by performing the "Escape from Slavery of Henry Box Brown," his song to the tune of "Old Uncle Ned." The afternoon session also began with a "Song, by Henry Box Brown." The *Syracuse Impartial Citizen* reported that "James Boxer Smith" sang with Brown and that their song was "encored with rapturous applause."[43]

At a meeting marked by disagreement, Brown and Smith provided the assemblage with a few moments of unanimity. The *Non-Slaveholder* found their performances

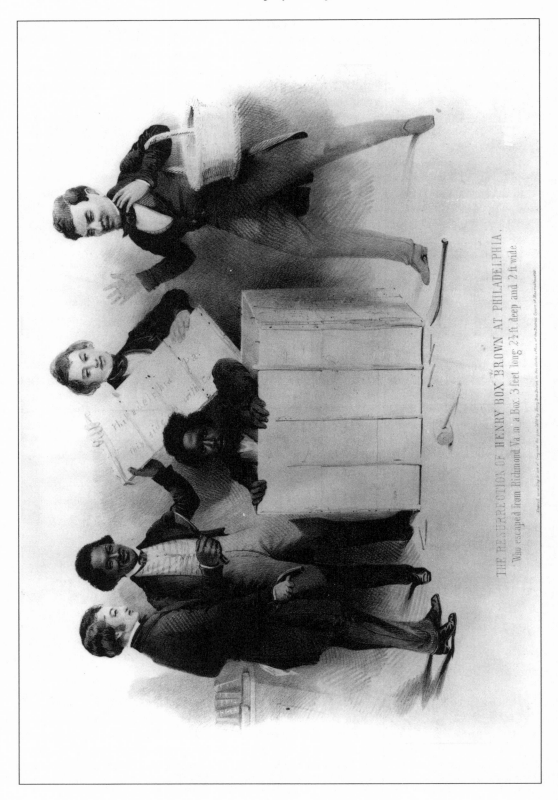

THE RESURRECTION OF HENRY BOX BROWN AT PHILADELPHIA.

Who escaped from Richmond Va in a Box 3 feet long 2½ ft deep and 2 ft wide "gratifying" for demonstrating that public sentiment in the North must be changing when "fugitives slaves appear openly" at meetings. Citizens in the North, it declared, now refrained "from executing the law of Congress relating to the recovery of such persons" and as a consequence, "efforts are no longer made by their claimants to seize them."[44]

Henry Box Brown's first public appearances had been under the auspices of the American Anti-Slavery Society, but he was not beholden to that group. His independence was such that he and James C. A. Smith also reached out to Gerrit Smith, a wealthy resident of Syracuse and the leading figure in the Liberty Party. After Brown and Smith returned to Boston they addressed to him a plea that James C. A. Smith penned in Brown's name. "Will you please to lend me the some of one hundred & fifty dollars until I can get out my panorama and I will faithfully return the same amount to you again soon," the letter requested. "I did not have as good success as I expect to meet with in my journey; and that is the reason I now ask this favor of you." Although Gerrit Smith was a generous contributor to causes in which he believed, his response to their letter is not known. This letter, the only one extant from Brown and Smith seeking funds for the panorama, was likely representative of similar letters sent out in the first months of 1850.[45]

At some point in this period of preparation and raising money Henry Box Brown decided to publish his narrative again. The exhibition had great potential as a means to sell a book. The literary project began early enough that on 3 April 1850 Brown could state, "I have the book all ready." He solicited letters of endorsement from the Reverend Samuel J. May and J. Miller McKim to include in the book. May's letter, dated 26

The Resurrection of Henry Box Brown at Philadelphia. Boston, January 1850. The print is not signed or otherwise credited. Given that Henry Box Brown was offering copies for sale less than a week after it was deposited for copyright, the edition was doubtless linked to the panorama project and created by one of the associated artists. Based on the visual style the artist was Samuel W. Rowse. Comparing the print to Rowse's 1854 portrait of Thoreau (page 75), the images have the same soft-edged look, and many features in common, such as the overhead yet diffuse illumination, the treatment of hair, the reflective expressions of the subjects, and the ubiquitous cravats.

Miller McKim's first version of the unboxing (page 64) symbolically represented Brown greeted to liberty. Rowse's illustration of the scene, drawn from Brown's recollection, is more concrete, describing the moment of the removal of the box lid. Brown emerges from the box, which not only appears to scale, but is probably the actual one (it was shipped to him from Philadelphia, though exactly when is not known). The reception party members are all impeccably (and improbably) dressed. On the right, Miller McKim steps forward in reaction. A portrait of McKim seems to have been available to copy. Second from the left, the man holding a small tool for prying is Frederick Douglass, substituting—probably too by means of a portrait—for the unavailable William Still. Stand-ins also represent Lewis Thompson and Charles D. Cleveland, the other figures. The reason McKim holds a basket can be guessed: Cleveland may have been on his way to market when he happened to drop by the Anti-Slavery Office that morning, and Brown remembered a man with a basket, though not who it was.

It is likely that Rowse, in order to work out the pictorial arrangement, had the scene enacted in a studio, which could help explain the print's theatrical presentation. Logic suggests that the studio was Josiah Wolcott's, where the panorama was being prepared. Did Rowse, in recruiting his models, use the people who were most available, the members of the panorama team, possibly D. C. Johnston or Charles Stearns on the left, or Josiah Wolcott behind the box?

Of the ten or so portrayals of Henry Box Brown that exist, Rowse's in this print is probably the only one taken from life. The other authentic portrait, the frontispiece to the 1849 *Narrative* (frontispiece), looks as if the engraver worked from a daguerreotype and thus would have been indirect. The rest of the Browns, by all indications, are copied or imagined.

April 1850, declared that "the narrative of such a man cannot fail to be interesting." McKim's initial response was apparently not what Brown needed. "I did not write to you for my character," Brown wrote back to McKim. "I did wished a few lines from some one in Philadelphia—But I dont wish you to give that—character which you know nothing of." Rather, Brown wanted "a few lines as I knew you know me to be the very man that came in the box." McKim took the criticism in stride and produced a more satisfactory endorsement on 8 April 1850. "I was pleased to learn, by your letter, that it was your purpose to publish a narrative of the circumstances of your escape from slavery," wrote McKim. "Such a publication, I should think, would not only be highly interesting, but well adapted to help on the cause of anti-slavery."[46]

As the endorsements indicate, the planned publication was a narrative of Brown's life and escape from slavery, but it almost certainly was not a reprint of Charles Stearns's 1849 *Narrative*. It is probable that the book that was "all ready" in April 1850 became the quite different *Narrative* published in England in 1851. At any rate the book project was set aside, likely overtaken by events. When Brown and Smith wrote the second time to McKim on 3 April, the first performance of the panorama was only a week away.

"Self-Effort"

It may have been through his efforts to publish a new narrative or to obtain handbills to advertise the panorama that Henry Box Brown crossed paths with the printer Benjamin F. Roberts. A leader in Boston's African American community, Roberts had sued the city on behalf of his daughter to overturn its policy of segregated schools. However the two met, their encounter led to Roberts's joining the collaborators on the panorama.

If Brown first called on Roberts for printing, their conversations probably expanded to other topics. Roberts was a man of forthright expression, and it is unlikely that Brown would have brought him into the exhibition unless Brown found his point of view compatible. Through Roberts, Brown encountered an abolitionist perspective that emphasized the need for African Americans to think and do for themselves. His exposure to the set of ideas that Roberts represented no doubt strengthened Henry Box Brown's inclination toward an independent course.

Benjamin F. Roberts saw the antislavery cause as inextricably bound up with battles to improve the status of free blacks. In 1838 he wrote that it was of no use to "say with the mouth we are friends of the slave and not try to encourage and assist the free colore[d] people in raising themselves." He was devoted to "improvement among this class of people, mental and physical." Essential to progress was fighting racism. It was, said Roberts, "altogether useless to pretend to affect the welfare of the blacks in this country, unless the chains of prejudice are broken."[47]

One of the themes Roberts assuredly expressed to Henry Box Brown was black "self-effort" as "an essential to our elevation." Roberts envisioned the printing office he had established in 1838 as a place where "colored lads shall be employed & taught the business of printing." He had also intended to issue "a small anti-slavery paper, edited & published entirely by colored men." Roberts's *Anti-Slavery Herald* was credited by one writer as "the first paper ever issued in Boston by a colored man," but it survived only five months. Roberts said publicly that the effort needed to start his printing shop caused the paper to be discontinued. Privately in a letter he also blamed "a combined effort on the part of certain professed abolitionists"—including, though not named by Roberts, William Lloyd Garrison, whose *Liberator* depended on black subscribers—"to muzzle, exterminate and put down the efforts of certain colored individuals effecting the welfare of their colored brethren."[48]

Roberts sustained his printing business largely through work for antislavery groups and for black churches and fraternal organizations. He also printed books. The year before he joined Brown's panorama, Roberts prepared a second printing of a book notable more for its aim than its execution. Written by Robert Benjamin Lewis and entitled *Light and Truth; Collected from the Bible and Ancient and Modern History, Containing the Universal History of the Colored and the Indian Race, from the Creation of the World to the Present Time*, it was first published in 1836 in Portland, Maine. A "Committee of Colored Gentlemen" from Boston obtained the copyright in 1843, and "Benjamin F. Roberts, Printer," issued it in 1844.[49]

Lewis's *Light and Truth* was a history of mankind that made Africans the central actors. Chapters such as "Modern Eminent Colored Men" had more substance than those on ancient times, for Lewis relied on biblical accounts and overcorrected for the omissions of previous histories by insisting on the prominence of blacks everywhere in the ancient world. The African American writer Martin Robison Delany, a former co-editor of Frederick Douglass's *North Star*, dismissed *Light and Truth* in 1852 as "a tissue of historical absurdities and literary blunders, shamefully palpable." Delany did find "one redeeming quality," stating that "it is a capital offset to the pitiable literary blunders of Professor George R. Gliddon . . . who makes all ancient black men, *white*; . . . this colored gentleman, makes all ancient great white men, *black*." In fact, the timing of the first Boston edition suggests that the "Committee of Colored Gentlemen" might have reissued *Light and Truth* as an answer to Gliddon's widely known Boston lectures of 1843.[50]

As the book's printer, Roberts knew the text of *Light and Truth* well and undoubtedly approved of Lewis's inclusion in his record of "Modern Historians" the names of David Walker, whose *Appeal* had so alarmed Virginians in 1830, and Hosea Easton. These men were representative of an activist movement in the Boston black community that emerged in the 1820s. Hosea Easton was also Benjamin Roberts's uncle, and a man he likely described to Henry Box Brown as an exemplar. Easton's father and Roberts's grandfather was James Easton, a Revolutionary War soldier and a manufacturer of iron afterward. James Easton conceived his foundry as a training school for young black men to gain the skills and academic learning they would need to claim their freedom in full. Roberts expressed a similar goal for his print shop. As late as 1870 Roberts recalled James Easton's "manual labor institution" as a pioneering effort to prepare young people, declaring that "if we mean success" it would come only with education, "which is power."[51]

Hosea Easton, James Easton's youngest son, worked with his father and then became an activist clergyman and an associate of David Walker. In 1833 Easton became pastor of a Congregational church in Hartford, Connecticut, and in 1837 he published *A Treatise on the Intellectual Character, and Civil and Political Condition of the Colored People of the U. States; and the Prejudice Exercised Towards Them*. Roberts's thinking in his 1838 letter had much in common with his uncle's book, and, at an appearance with Henry Box Brown, Roberts echoed the book's title when he lectured on the "Condition of the Colored Population in the United States."[52]

Written with much of the character of a sermon, Easton's essay overturned notions of racially determined civilization more profoundly than did *Light and Truth*. Viewing the history of the Europeans, Easton saw "a motley mixture of barbarism and civilization, of fraud and philanthropy, of patriotism and avarice, of religion and bloodshed." The superior civilization was the African, he argued, until Europeans destroyed it. The degraded condition of Africans in America was entirely due to the suppressing forces of slavery and prejudice. Easton refuted the contention that the intellectual capacity of blacks was inferior, in part by noting that the formation of the mind begins before birth and is affected by the health of the mother: "Contemplate the exposed condition

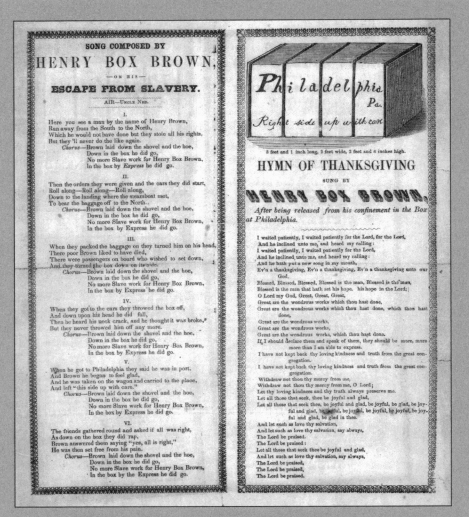

A Second Printing of the Song Sheets

On this undated broadside, the lyrics to Henry Box Brown's two featured songs were printed side by side, presumably to be cut apart into separate handbills. The unknown printer likely also produced the first "Escape from Slavery," for both versions of that song utilized the same typefaces, general design, and border pattern.

By the time of the second printing Brown had taken control of his songs, as indicated by the changes to each from the earlier versions. The later-arrival hymn replicates not the first song sheet of it but the fuller lyrics in the 1849 *Narrative*, including the title "Hymn of Thanksgiving." The second version of "Escape from Slavery" changes part of one line—from "he thought he was dead" to "he thought it was broke"—and significantly is headed "Song Composed by Henry Box Brown." Unlike the earlier, uncredited "Escape from Slavery," at the second printing Brown was in position to assert his authorship of the song.

The second printing probably came after the publication of the 1849 *Narrative* in September 1849, since it uses the book's Hymn lyrics. The song sheets were likely produced to sell, either for the book tour in fall 1849, to raise funds for the panorama, or at its exhibition, and thus appeared sometime between September 1849 and March 1850.

of slave mothers," he suggested. If "natural causes produce natural effects, then it must be equally true that unnatural causes produce unnatural effects. The slave system is an unnatural cause." Blacks were "Americans by birth, genius, habits, language," wrote Easton, and had equal claim to the privileges of American citizenship. "All Christendom" acknowledged, he said, that "God hath made of one blood all nations of men for to dwell on all the face of the earth."[53]

Easton presented a deep and thorough critique of American society from an African American perspective. In his view the abolition of slavery was necessary but was only a first step to freedom. For Benjamin F. Roberts, his uncle's passionate discourse was part of a family legacy that included his parents' abolitionism and his grandfather's commitment to self-effort. Two years after working with Henry Box Brown, he started a second short-lived newspaper called the *Self-Elevator*. It was consistent that Roberts should challenge, in his words, that "colorphobia deprived us of common school." In the autumn of 1849 a renewal of the boycott of the Boston school designated for black students focused attention on the school desegregation case in the name of Roberts's daughter. On 4 December 1849 the Massachusetts Supreme Court heard arguments on the appeal of *Sarah C. Roberts v. City of Boston*. Charles Sumner, chairman of the Massachusetts Free Soil Party Executive Committee and soon to become an important figure in the United States Senate, was lead counsel for Sarah Roberts. Many blacks attended the court hearings. No decision had yet come down by the end of March 1850, the time by which Roberts had probably already joined Brown's panorama.[54]

When the idea of collaboration arose, Brown and Roberts each likely recognized the mutual benefit. Brown's panorama made manifest Roberts's vision of African Americans speaking for themselves. At a time when Roberts had to depend on the attorney Sumner to argue his case and then wait for the justices to make a decision, he might have valued the panorama as a forum to speak for himself. In turn Brown probably appreciated Roberts both for his knowledgeable opinions and for his self-reliant independence. Brown remained unconcerned with intra-abolitionist rivalries. His first friends in liberty had been from the Pennsylvania and Massachusetts affiliates of the American Anti-Slavery Society. He next worked with the independent radical Charles Stearns and reached out to the Liberty Party's Gerrit Smith as a patron. That Benjamin F. Roberts stood apart from the Massachusetts Anti-Slavery Society and was represented in court by a prominent Free Soiler did not stop Brown from inviting his assistance in the presentation of the panorama.

Abolitionists read Daniel Webster's speech in Congress on 7 March 1850 in favor of Clay's compromise as an endorsement of the Fugitive Slave Bill. Among African Americans in Boston, where a significant minority were fugitives from slavery, the speech was nothing less than a betrayal. On 27 March 1850 the "Anti-Webster Meeting of the Colored Citizens of Boston and Vicinity" met at the Belknap Street Church on Beacon Hill. At the "crowded meeting" one of the speakers was Samuel R. Ward, who had coined the name "Boxer" for James C. A. Smith at Syracuse two months before. "That infamous bill of Mr. Mason, of Virginia, proves itself to be like all other propositions presented by Southern men," Ward declared. "It finds just enough of Northern doughfaces who are willing to pledge themselves, if you will pardon the uncouth language of a backwoodsman, to lick up the spittle of the slaveocrats, and swear it is delicious." Benjamin F. Roberts was present that day as a member of the meeting's Business Committee and he might have convinced Henry Box Brown and James Boxer Smith to attend as well.[55]

"Splendid Panorama"

The premier exhibition of *Henry Box Brown's Mirror of Slavery* was held in Boston on 11 April 1850. At the same time two other moving panoramas were advertised in the city's newspapers. One was a spectacle. Burr's extraordinarily long *Seven-Mile Mirror, or a Pictorial Tour of the 2000 Miles on the Great Lakes, the Niagara, St. Lawrence and Saguenay Rivers* was in its tenth week at Amory Hall. Advance publicity claimed of it that "seven or eight" painters worked for six months from some 400 "rough but faithful" sketches, and that it cost $30,000 to produce.

The other panorama was offered as scholarship. Direct from London, and just finishing its first week, was the *Egyptian Collection and Grand Moving Transparent Panorama of the Nile*. The exhibitor was none other than George R. Gliddon, the Egyptologist and racist ethnologist, on the circuit again with a new visual aid. For the period that the exhibitions of *Mirror of Slavery* and *Panorama of the Nile* overlapped, Bostonians had the opportunity to take in competing panoramic visions of Nubian slavery and of the rightfulness of that slavery.[56]

Henry Box Brown's Mirror of Slavery was exhibited at Washingtonian Hall on Bromfield Street, where two local chapters of the Sons of Temperance held their weekly meetings. The *Liberator* reported that attendance at the first two performances was "by special invitation" and that "a considerable number of ladies and gentlemen assembled" for the shows. "Considering the difficulties to be overcome, the time spent upon and the sum paid for it, it is very creditable to the industry, zeal and talent of the artist," the article stated, "and we trust, as it is the design of Mr. Brown to exhibit it in various parts of the country, this novel mode of advancing the anti-slavery cause, by a faithful delineation to the eye of the principal features of the traffic in human flesh, will be very successful." The *Liberator* judged that "some portions of the Panorama are very well executed," and commended "the last scene particularly."[57]

Following the two nights for invited audiences, *Mirror of Slavery* opened for the public on 23 April. An advertisement in the *Boston Herald* for the "New and Original Panorama" described the painting as "elegant," and stated that "as an exhibition, it has no superior." The *Herald* noticed it on 30 April: "This new exhibition having received mete notice from literary gentlemen, is becoming the topic of conversation in all parts of the city and vicinity." Brown evidently had advice from a friend who knew how to promote a show, for the newspaper also reported that "among those who have received complimentary tickets is Hon Daniel Webster, who is now at the Revere House. At this particular time, some portions of the exercise may not be uninteresting to the honorable Senator."[58]

On 29 April the *Boston Daily Evening Traveller* called *Mirror of Slavery* "one of the finest panoramas now on exhibition." Of Henry Box Brown, the *Traveller* stated that "many persons would walk a long way to see this curious specimen of American freedom," and commented "we wish all the slaveholders would go and view their system on canvass." On 1 May "the proprietor" announced in the *Boston Herald*,

FOR ONE WEEK!
Commencing on **FRIDAY** *Evening, June* 21.

LANDS SACRED & CLASSICAL !
THE NILE ! EGYPT & NUBIA !
1720 Miles !
TRANSPARENT PANORAMA !
PAINTED IN LONDON by Warren, Bonomi, Martin, Fahey, Corbould and Weigall ; with
EGYPTIAN MUMMIES,
Antiquities, Library, Models, Tableaux,
GLIDDON'S LECTURES,
ORIENTAL MUSIC, &C.
AT THE TEMPLE, PORTSMOUTH,
EVERY EVENING at 8 o'clock, *and* **WEDNESDAY & SATURDAY AFTERNOONS** *at* 3 o'clk.
Price of Admission—For Adults 25 cents ; for Children half price ; Schools, numbering over twenty pupils, 10 cents each.— Teachers with pupils, free.
June 22.

Gliddon's Nile, advertised in June 1850

because "so urgent has been the invitation of people in some of the neighboring towns," that "this will be the last night for the present," but promised a return engagement to begin on 28 May.[59]

After the Boston showings the exhibitors took the panorama on the road. There was likely one other venue—possibly in Lynn—before the next known performances in Worcester, Massachusetts, where *Mirror of Slavery* was presented for ten days in May 1850. The *Worcester Massachusetts Spy* announced on 8 May that it would open the next day: "This panorama under the direction of Henry Box Brown, is to be exhibited in the City Hall, Thursday evening. It is spoken of as being a very fine painting, and as giving a good idea of the workings of the 'peculiar institution.'"

A week later the *Spy* published a review. "No one can see it," the reviewer declared, "without getting new views and more vivid conceptions of the practical working of the system than he had before." The presence of a "very good audience" made the verbose reviewer glad, "because the proprietor deserves it as a reward for the indomitable energy of character, which impelled him, first to break away from the ignominious bondage in which he was held, and next to plan and carry out so ingenious a mode of providing for the public amusement at the same time that it brings home to the people a representation so faithful, of the great evil, to which most of them are, directly or indirectly, accessory." The reviewer closed by noting that "the low price at which the exhibition is afforded should commend it to the public."[60]

A correspondent to the *Liberator* by the name of Clarkson also reported on the Worcester exhibition. The "diorama," as he called it in a letter dated 25 May, "was well patronised," and "the painting is well executed and gives general satisfaction." At this early stage of presenting the panorama Henry Box Brown did not take the lead commentator's role. Clarkson reported that "the description of the various scenes was very handsomely done by Benjamin F. Roberts, a colored man." On Sunday "the gentlemen belonging to the Panorama gave an entertainment at the City Hall," apparently without the panorama. "The house was thronged," stated Clarkson. "Henry Box Brown related

FOR A SHORT TIME ONLY.
NEW AND ORIGINAL PANORAMA!
Henry Box Brown's
MIRROR OF SLAVERY,

DESIGNED and Painted from the best and most authentic sources of information, will be open for public exhibition at

HAMPDEN HALL,

Wednesday, Thursday, Friday & Saturday Evenings, May 22d, 23d, 24th, and 25th.

Also at 3 o'clock Saturday afternoon.—Vocal and Instrumental Music to accompany Exhibition.

Part I.

The African Slave Trade—The Nubian Family in Freedom—The Seizure of Slaves—Religious Sacrifice—Beautiful Lake and Mountain Scenery in Africa—March to the Coast—View of the Cape of Good Hope—Slave Felucca—Interior of a Slave Ship—Chase of a Slaver by an English Steam Frigate—Spanish Slaver at Havana—Landing Slaves—Interior of a Slave Mart—Gorgeous Scenery of the West India Islands—View of Charleston, South Carolina—The Nubian Family at Auction—Grand 4th of July Celebration—Separation after Sale of Slaves—Grand Slave Auction—March of Chain Gang—Modes of Confinement and Punishment—Brand and Scourge—Interior of the Charleston Workhouse, with Treadmill in full operation.

Part II.

Sunday among the Slave Population—Monday Morning, with Sugar Plantation and Mill—Women at Work—Cotton Plantation—View of the Lake of the Dismal Swamp—Nubians Escaping by Night—Ellen Crafts Escaping—Whipping Post and Gallows at Richmond, Va.—View of Richmond, Va.—Henry Box Brown Escaping—View of the Natural Bridge and Jefferson's Rock—City of Washington, D. C.—Slave Prisons at Washington—Washington's Tomb at Mount Vernon—Fairmount Water Works—Henry Box Brown Released at Philadelphia—Distant View of the City of Philadelphia—Henry Bibb Escaping—Nubian Slaves Retaken—Tarring and Feathering in S. Carolina—The Slaveholder's Dream—Burning alive—Promise of Freedom—West India Emancipation—Grand Industrial Palace—Grand Tableau Finale, UNIVERSAL EMANCIPATION.

The Panorama will commence moving at 8 o'clock.

Tickets 12 1-2 Cents.

May 22.   4d

"**Henry Box Brown's Mirror of Slavery.**" From the *Springfield Republican*, 22 May 1850.

89

many incidents about the peculiar institution, and sung [*sic*] several pieces of sacred music." At the Sunday event Roberts also delivered his lecture on "the 'Condition of the Colored Population in the United States.'"[61]

Clarkson concluded that "what makes this enterprise more interesting is the fact that the whole is conducted by colored men," a fact that Benjamin F. Roberts may have pointed out to the audiences. Henry Box Brown and James C. A. Smith were the mainstays for all the performances. For Roberts, there is only evidence that he appeared in Worcester. It is probable that he also presented the scenes in Boston and in any other exhibitions before Worcester. There is no record of his participation after the Worcester appearances.[62]

Roberts's departure from the exhibition was likely precipitated by the outcome of *Roberts* v. *City of Boston*. In April 1850 the Massachusetts Supreme Court ruled unanimously that the school board had the right to operate separate schools for blacks. The decision is remembered as the first to articulate the infamous legal principle of "separate but equal." Chief Justice Lemuel Shaw's opinion for *Roberts* v. *City of Boston* conceded that "colored persons, the descendents of Africans, are entitled by law, in this Commonwealth, to equal rights, constitutional and political, and civil and social," but held that the establishment of "separate schools for colored children" was not "a violation of any of these rights."[63]

In the *Liberator* of 14 June 1850, Roberts announced that he was "about to commence a mission to the several towns in Massachusetts, for the purpose of obtaining signatures to a petition, asking the Legislature of this Commonwealth to pass a law compelling those who have charge of public school instruction for children to make no distinction on account of color, in relation to the admission of children to the schools nearest their residences." His collaboration with Henry Box Brown, if not long, was undoubtedly influential.[64]

A week before *Mirror of Slavery* opened in Worcester, the annual meeting of the American Anti-Slavery Society took place in New York. The event was notable for the appearance of "a riotous assemblage of men and boys, in the rear of the hall." Wendell Phillips defended freedom of speech "amid much interruption from the mob." The Hutchinson Family's attempt "to restore order by the influence of their songs" was "ineffectual." The mob's "tumult increased until the hour of adjournment."[65]

Prior to the disruption, William H. Furness, pastor of the First Congregational Church, of Philadelphia, spoke to the meeting on what it meant to be an abolitionist. "It is only at great cost that this distinction can be obtained," he said. William Lloyd Garrison was an abolitionist because the price put on his head was "a crown of more than imperial glory." Frederick Douglass was an abolitionist because he "*has* abolished slavery—in his own person. But he is not alone," continued Furness. "A slave, worth a few hundred dollars, was put into a box. The box was nailed down; and, after being well shaken, and turned over a number of times, it was opened, and out leaped a freeman, whose value no man can compute. That box has magic in it." If "any man who loves and defends slavery could be induced to get into that box, and let himself be nailed down and well shaken for some thirty hours, with an occasional turn, over and over, the result would be the same. We should gain another freeman."[66]

Henry Box Brown, freeman and antislavery symbol, was now a performer on the road. After Worcester, *Mirror of Slavery* opened in Springfield, Massachusetts, on 22 May 1850. James C. A. Smith traveled with Brown, but it is not known if there were others in the company. In Springfield, the exhibitors may have stayed at the home of Sarah Stearns and Rachel Stearns, Charles Stearns's mother and sister. The show had a four-day run, from Wednesday through Saturday. An advertisement appeared in the *Springfield Republican* on the day of the first performance, noting that "the Panorama will commence moving at 8 o'clock." Admission was 12.5 cents, half the usual price for panoramas in Boston. There was also a matinee on Saturday, with "Vocal and Instrumental Music to accompany Exhibition." Nothing in the record suggests that either Brown or Smith played musical instruments, and they probably found local musicians, perhaps with the help of the Stearns family, for the afternoon performance.[67]

After the final exhibition at Springfield on 25 May 1850, documentation of the tour is scanty. The *Boston Herald* had stated that *Mirror of Slavery* would return there on 28 May, but no evidence of that engagement has been found. The exhibition reached Dover, New Hampshire, before 12 July, and the company was still on tour at the end of August. If Brown and Smith followed the pattern of Brown's and Stearns's book tour, they would have visited many New England towns between June and August 1850.[68]

Venue by venue, Brown and Smith learned how to tour successfully with a moving panorama. Transporting the crates containing the panorama and its apparatus from place to place was a repeated hard effort. They would have shipped the gear by railroad where possible and otherwise probably by a hired or donated wagon and driver.

Exhibition Nuts and Bolts

Expenses, June–July 1848, for a moving panorama at the Masonic Temple in Boston, from J. W .E. Hutchings, "Account Book."

Transporting panorama from Reading	4.00
Button slides	2.00
Lumber	3.30
Curtains	15.00
Rope	1.50
Nails	.40
Thread & tacks	1.35
Red bunting	3.00
Advertising Transcript	1.50
A. Blevin for Sewing &c	30.25
Screw & pulies	.50
Poles for flags	.75
Cleaning hall	3.00
Carpenter	8.00
Bill poster	2.00
Rent	25.00
Reflectors	.95
Services of boys	4.00
Cotton	.35
Pasting bills	1.50
For music	22.00
Flags	10.00
Printing	44.00

Brown and Smith would also have arranged with local sponsors for use of a hall, for help with publicity, and for accommodations, and contracted with printers for handbills, placed advertisements in newspapers, and recruited local musicians.

Some venues may have been scheduled before the tour began, but most would have been arranged as Brown and Smith went along. A network of abolitionists helped them make connections ahead of their travels. Antislavery ministers were especially important among the "many friends" who assisted them by making church halls available for the exhibition and by providing endorsements. On 12 July 1850, in a letter that Brown later published, the Reverend Justin Spaulding, of Dover, New Hampshire, wrote on Brown's behalf to two preachers in another town. "A coloured gentleman, Mr. H. B. Brown, purposes to visit your village for the purpose of exhibiting his splendid Panorama, or Mirror of Slavery. I have had the pleasure of seeing it," he wrote, and "in my opinion, it is almost, if not quite, a perfect fac simile of the workings of that horrible and fiendish system." Spaulding also testified that Brown was to be trusted. "I know very well, there are a great many impostors and cheats going about through the country deceiving and picking up the people's money, but *this* is of another class altogether."[69]

In addition to helping to arrange a venue, such letters could be valuable afterward as credentials. Letters of endorsement from respectable persons were a common means for travelers to establish credibility. Exhibitors of commercial panoramas often published endorsements in their advertising literature. A black performer professing anti-slavery on the northeastern circuit in 1850 had particular need for authenticating credentials. Under the headline "Imposter," in March 1850 the *North Star* of Rochester, New York, reported that "a colored man calling his name William Johnson, is on a tour of speculation among the friends of the colored race in the Northern and Eastern States. . . . He pursues his journey from place to place, repeating the same statements." The *Massachusetts Spy* reported in October 1850 of deception by "the colored man known as Charles W. Swift, who has created a good deal of sympathy in this community, as a recently escaped fugitive slave." Not only did Swift admit "the attempt to deceive," but also "it turns out . . . that he was in the eastern part of this state, and in the northerly part of this county, last June, and July, under the name of John Allen, and spoke at several anti-slavery meetings."[70]

With imposters about—indeed, in the case of the man using the names Swift and Allen nearly crossing his path—Henry Box Brown would have found letters such as the Reverend Spaulding's not only useful but also necessary. The need to prove his identity was likely only one of the unexpected problems with which Brown and James C. A. Smith had to contend on the exhibition circuit. On an earlier adventure on the road, the one that made him famous, however, Brown had shown himself well capable of prevailing over unforeseen difficulties as they arose.

Chapter Five

Mirror of Slavery

The Painted Panorama

His presentations of *Mirror of Slavery* in April and May 1850 started Henry Box Brown on his career as a panorama exhibitor. A good part of his new occupation involved traveling, meeting people, and managing money. Its defining work, however, was on stage, when Brown stood before an audience and presented the panorama. *Mirror of Slavery* was Henry Box Brown's contribution to Anglo-American debates over slavery and race, and during a vital period, the 1850s, Brown delivered its message to many thousands. It is difficult to understand Brown in this public role without a sense of his exhibition.

To recapture *Mirror of Slavery* exactly is impossible today, and even a general sketch is not without impediment. No portion of the painted panorama is known to exist. Nor has any contemporary account been found that describes the whole of its exhibition. *Mirror of Slavery* can be reconstructed only by piecing together numerous incomplete reports, and the results must remain tentative. Still there is evidence enough to proceed. Advertisements and reviews reveal the titles and sequence of the painted images of the panorama, and occasionally describe aspects of the performances.

"The real *life-like* scenes presented in this PANORAMA," stated one observer, "are admirably calculated to make an unfading impression upon the heart and memory." *Mirror of Slavery* was designed to convey an antislavery message, and thus it functioned at one level as political argument or, to say it more baldly, as abolitionist propaganda. At the same time it was a popular show, packaged to take good advantage of Brown's fame and to draw and entertain an audience. The reviewer for the *Massachusetts Spy* admired it for being "so ingenious a mode of providing for the public amusement at the same time that it brings home to the people a representation so faithful, of the great evil." A close look at *Mirror of Slavery* illuminates some of the ways that the exhibition was "admirably calculated" to achieve these different objectives and make its "unfading impression."[1]

In proceeding it is useful to distinguish between the *painted panorama* and the *performed panorama*, and to examine each in turn. The painted panorama refers to the sequence of scenes painted on canvas as produced by Josiah Wolcott and company. The performed panorama was the theatrical presentation before an audience, which enriched the display of the painted panorama with the narrator's description of the scenes, with music, and with the other performed elements of the show. Where the painted panorama was a constant, the performed panorama varied as Brown adapted to the circumstances of each presentation and evolved over time as Brown and his associates revised and refined the exhibition.

The painted panorama was a very long canvas, probably eight to ten feet high, containing forty-nine scenes. The key to its reconstruction is a list of scene titles, in sequence, that appeared in the advertisement for the exhibition in the *Springfield Republican* on 22 May 1850. The subjects depicted in the scenes can be inferred, with varying degrees of certainty, from the titles. For a number of scenes, the visual content

---

The Poem and the Panorama

Six scenes in *Mirror of Slavery* (listed in the *Springfield Republican*, 22 May 1850) corresponded by title and order with the six plates that illustrated Charles Green's work *The Nubian Slave*.

The Nubian Slave	*Mirror of Slavery*
Plate II: "Freedom."	Second scene: **The Nubian Family in Freedom**
Plate III: "'For Sale,' represents the Auction scene."	Sixteenth scene: **The Nubian Family at Auction**
Plate IV: "'Sold,' shews the Separation of the family after the Sale."	Eighteenth scene: **Separation after Sale of Slaves**
Plate V: "The Brand and Scourge."	Twenty-second scene: **The Brand and Scourge**
Plate VI: "'The Escape.' The Father is pointing out the North Star to his Wife and Son ..."	Twenty-ninth scene: **Nubians Escaping by Night**
Plate VII: "'Man Hunting,' shews the Family pursued with Blood-hounds, and fired upon."	Forty-second scene: **Nubian Slaves Retaken**

---

may be surmised fairly confidently. The thirty-ninth scene, for example, was titled **Henry Box Brown Released at Philadelphia.** That scene no doubt closely resembled *The Resurrection of Henry Box Brown at Philadelphia,* the lithograph issued in Boston during the making of the panorama.

The list of scene titles makes clear that the creators of the panorama used Charles C. Green's book *The Nubian Slave* as a basis for *Mirror of Slavery.* Pictorial sources for several other scenes can be identified with equal confidence. The forty-first scene in the panorama was titled **Henry Bibb Escaping.** Published in 1849, the *Narrative of the Life and Adventures of Henry Bibb* included an illustration of Bibb escaping from slavery. Another plate in Bibb's *Narrative* was entitled "The Sabbath Among Slaves," and was likely the model for the twenty-fourth scene of the panorama, entitled **Sunday among the Slave Population.** Other information about the visual content of scenes comes from contemporary newspaper reviews. For scenes without evident visual sources or written descriptions, the titles themselves usually suggest precedents in antislavery or popular picturesque imagery. An estimate of the content of nearly all the scenes can thus be deduced.[2]

The individual scenes of a moving panorama were sewn together to make a sequence. In this regard, *Mirror of Slavery* can be usefully compared to the commercial panoramas. The original idea of the moving panorama was a depiction of a journey, and the majority of moving panoramas followed this basic story line. The historian Richard Altick calls them "travelogues." One approach was to represent views that a traveler might observe in going from one place to another. Often the format was a voyage, such as Beale and Craven's *Panoramic Voyage to California! . . . and Return* (1850), or the especially popular voyage down a river, such as Banvard's *Panorama of the*

Mississippi River (1846), or Benjamin Champney's *Grand Panoramic Picture of Rhineland* (1849). Another approach to panoramic travel was the tourist's meandering movement from one highlight to the next, providing audiences with a grand tour on the cheap. The brochure for Bayne's *Gigantic Panorama of a Voyage to Europe* (1848) promised that "those whom inclination or circumstances have prevented" from seeing the sights depicted in the panorama "may glean a correct and comprehensive knowledge of some of the most interesting features on this continent, and that of Europe."[3]

A few moving panoramas varied from the predominant travel story line and offered a narrative more literary than geographical. John Insco Williams's *Panorama of the Bible* (1849) presented thirty-one scenes "commencing at Chaos" and "following each other in historical order to the Babylonish captivity." Biblical narrative, not location, governed its sequence. If Henry Box Brown and his collaborators attended *Panorama of the Bible* when it played Boston in the autumn of 1849, they might have seen not only that the medium was capable of addressing a subject of moral consequence, but also that a moving panorama could derive its structure from literature.[4]

The primary literary source for *Mirror of Slavery*, Charles C. Green's work *The Nubian Slave*, provided the narrative outline for the panorama but not the conclusion. The second half of *Mirror of Slavery* featured Henry Box Brown's own story of daring adventure and eventual liberty. Moreover, it supplanted the tragic ending of Green's work with a more hopeful vision that looked forward to universal emancipation in a changed society. That the ending of the panorama was set in a transformed future likely reflected the utopianism of the lead artist, Josiah Wolcott.

The *Liberator* stated that one of the final scenes in the panorama was "according to a plan of Charles Fourier." The French social theorist Charles Fourier (1772–1837) described in six volumes a complex, meticulously arranged, and sometimes fanciful vision of ideal communities. As Ralph Waldo Emerson put it, "Fourier carried a whole French Revolution in his head and much more." Fourier's American disciple Albert Brisbane distilled the more practical of Fourier's ideas into his *Social Destiny of Man* (1840) and helped win Fourier many adherents in the United States.[5]

Josiah Wolcott became involved with Brook Farm just when the community was moving to adopt Fourierist principles. The historian Nancy Osgood has described Wolcott's active role from 1843 to 1847 at Brook Farm and in related organizations such as the New England Fourier Society and the Boston Religious Union of Associationists. Wolcott was a charter member of the latter in 1847, along with Albert Brisbane and the founders of Brook Farm, George Ripley and Sophia Ripley.[6]

Utopian socialism did not attract many black abolitionists, who rejected the assertion that wage slavery and chattel slavery were comparable evils. Brisbane in *Social Destiny of Man* called slavery "not the foundation of social evil" and thought that to "abolish it suddenly" would "infringe on a great many other rights." Utopianism and abolitionism, however, were not inherently contradictory. A Massachusetts man in 1844 recorded his attendance within a month at meetings of temperance advocates, abolitionists, and Fourierists, crusades he believed were aligned in their aims: "first make all *sober* then equal & the philosophy of Fourier carried out will do the rest." Despite the demise of Brook Farm in 1847, Josiah Wolcott maintained a Fourierist vision along with his abolitionism.[7]

In sum, the creators of the painted panorama for *Mirror of Slavery* drew on a number of sources. There was the enabling idea that the panoramic format could tell a story, as possibly learned from *The Panorama of the Bible*. From the fictional work *The Nubian Slave* they derived the outlines of the story and from the true account of Henry Box Brown an expansion of that narrative. The literature and imagery of abolitionism

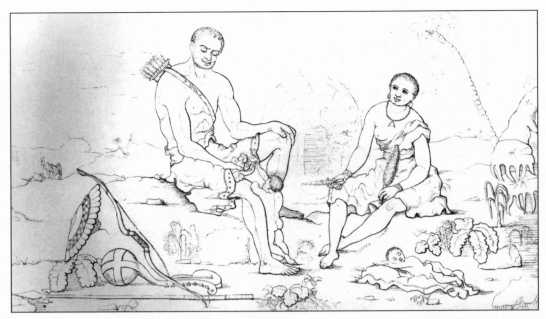

For the Second Scene, THE NUBIAN FAMILY IN FREEDOM. Plate II, *The Nubian Slave.* The book caption states: "'Freedom,' represents the African family sitting at the door of their hut, whose site is an oasis of the desert, in Nubia. The hour is sunset. By the Father's side are the implements of the chase, with musical instruments, which are still used in Africa. The Mother holds a spindle and distaff. In the back-ground, are seen the Slave-stealers, approaching the hut, unobserved."

provided incidents and topics, and Josiah Wolcott's utopian thinking offered a particular way to look forward. A writer for the *Boston Daily Evening Traveller* stated that *Mirror of Slavery* was "not a mere delineation of landscape, but a succession of scenes of human action, addressed to the whole mind, and especially to the highest faculties."[8]

The forty-nine scenes in *Mirror of Slavery* were organized in two parts divided by an intermission. The first part was mainly about the slave trade. The second began with the daily life of slaves in the South, showed slaves escaping, and closed with a series of more visionary images. The scenes of the panorama progressed geographically from Africa to America: from Nubia down the East African coast, across the Atlantic to Cuba, on to South Carolina, next to Virginia, where Brown's own experience became the primary narrative, and then northward to Philadelphia. The narratives of the Nubian family and Henry Box Brown were placed within this overall journey, and intermixed were picturesque segments akin to the grand tour style of commercial panoramas.

Few slaves' lives embodied all the aspects of slavery portrayed in *Mirror of Slavery*. The Nubian family illustrated freedom, capture, transportation, sale, separation, work, and punishment, and Henry Box Brown represented escape and ultimate freedom. The panorama's combination of actual and fictional scenes presented an archetypal narrative of the history of the slaves.

The painted panorama commenced with seven scenes set in Africa. The title of the first, **The African Slave Trade**, also described the general topic of the initial twenty scenes. The second, **The Nubian Family in Freedom**, introduced the fictional protagonists. In the corresponding plate in *The Nubian Slave*, Charles C. Green foreshadowed his narrative by depicting "Slave-stealers" skulking in the background. The panorama may have delayed such imagery to the third scene, **The Seizure of Slaves**. The gener-

For the Sixteenth Scene, **THE NUBIAN FAMILY AT AUCTION.** Plate III, *The Nubian Slave.* The book caption states: "'For Sale,' represents the Auction scene. The spectators are kept out of the picture that the interest may be concentrated in the group on the stand,— their shadow merely being cast upon the platform." Green represents the crowd at the auction by their shadows. Whether the panorama artists would have relied on such a delicate effect for a work to be viewed at a distance is questionable. Their borrowing from Green's images was probably more for content and composition than for visual style.

Probably the best clue to the visual style of *Mirror of Slavery* is the 1850 *Resurrection* lithograph attributed to Samuel Rowse (page 82), a print likely based on sketches made in the panorama studio. Compared to Green's restrained delineation, which takes a moment to grasp, Rowse's image pushes forward and is readily comprehended. Rowse's approach is much like that of the contemporary political cartoon. In this period the political cartoon tended to concentrate on faces and a few telling details, and to avoid busy backgrounds and complicated rendering. (Unnecessary for a panorama would have been another common feature, the expansive dialogue balloons.) Images with cartoon characteristics blown up to panorama dimensions would have been well suited to project to viewers in the back of a hall.

alized title suggests the scene did not show the Nubians but served the plot by implying their enslavement.[9]

The narrative then paused to offer a brief African picturesque in the mode of the grand tour. The fourth scene, **Religious Sacrifice,** probably appealed to interest in the exotic. It might also have been intended to show that, if not Christian, Africans had religion and were not without culture. A note in *The Nubian Slave* stated that "the pagans of Nubia worship the moon." The next title, **Beautiful Lake and Mountain Scenery in Africa**, would not have been out of place as a sublime landscape in a

For the Eighteenth Scene, **Separation after Sale of Slaves.** Plate IV, *The Nubian Slave*. The book caption states: "'Sold,' shews the Separation of the family after the Sale."

commercial panorama. The landscape's beauty reflected positively on the quality of life in Africa in freedom.[10]

The sixth scene, **March to the Coast**, resumed the narrative and began a ten-scene journey segment. Whether the Nubian family was specifically illustrated is unknown. Though most slaves bound for the Americas came from Africa's west coast, the next two titles indicate that the panorama followed the Nubian family along the east coast. The seventh scene, **View of the Cape of Good Hope**, was likely another picturesque landscape, and the eighth, **Slave Felucca**, depicted a coastal sailing vessel of Arabian origin. The scene showed the first of four of ships; the journey had become a voyage.[11]

The next two scenes moved to the Atlantic Ocean and the infamous Middle Passage. **Interior of a Slave Ship** represented a subject that had recurred in antislavery imagery since the late eighteenth century. The tenth title, **Chase of a Slaver by an English Steam Frigate**, was an action scene that referred to Great Britain's contemporary naval blockade of Africa against the slave trade, a commitment that was not matched by the United States.[12]

The journey continued to the Caribbean for the eleventh to the fourteenth scenes. Three of them, beginning with **Spanish Slaver at Havana**, depicted the slave trade in Cuba, a Spanish colony. Southern radicals advocated the acquisition of Cuba as a slave state to offset the admission of new free states to the Union. The context implies that the next two scenes were also set in Cuba: **Landing Slaves** and **Interior of a Slave Mart**. The final scene of the sequence, **Gorgeous Scenery of the West India Islands**, was a picturesque landscape that alluded to the emancipation of slaves in the British West Indies, which explained why the view was "gorgeous."[13]

The fifteenth scene, **View of Charleston, South Carolina**, culminated on American

For the Twenty-Second Scene, **BRAND AND SCOURGE**. Plate V, *The Nubian Slave*. The book caption states: "'The Brand and Scourge.' The husband and wife having met, and concerted an escape, are betrayed, and punished." Like Green's print, the makers of the panorama might have included a minister in their scene; perhaps, too, with a devilish expression as he holds his Bible and sermon text on "Servants, obey your masters."

soil the journey from Africa and set up the transition to the concluding scenes of the first part of *Mirror of Slavery*. The sixteenth scene, **The Nubian Family at Auction**, borrowed from the third plate in *The Nubian Slave*. By following the scene of Charleston with the scene of an auction, the sequence located the auction there and implied that South Carolinians, the most vocal of the South's defenders of slavery, were complicit in the illegal international slave trade.

 The Nubian Family at Auction began a series of eight scenes on the horrors of slavery in the American South. The story of the Nubian family was the thread that tied the sequence together. The next scene, **Grand 4th of July Celebration**, emphasized the irony, as described by a reviewer, of "the celebration of the independence of America under the figure of liberty, and a sale of slaves going on at the same time." The eighteenth scene, **Separation after Sale of Slaves**, corresponded to the fourth plate "Sold" in *The Nubian Slave*, and therefore likely showed the separation of the Nubian family. If the panorama followed Green's design for **The Nubian Family at Auction**, which excluded the spectators and concentrated on the family, the nineteenth scene, **Grand Slave Auction**, might have offered a more comprehensive view of a slave auction. A review of *Mirror of Slavery* described a scene that could have been either of the auctions: "'Heartless Knock-'em-off' officiating as auctioneer, at a sale of what he calls 'cattle (slaves) and other merchandise.'" The quoted phrases in this review probably derived, as seen in Green's print, from written signs within the panorama image.[14]

 The twentieth scene, **March of Chain Gang**, ended the long disquisition on the slave

For the Twenty-third Scene, Interior of the Charleston Workhouse, with Treadmill in Full Operation. *A Tread-Mill Scene in Jamaica*, 1834 engraving issued by Glasgow Ladies' Emancipation Society.

trade and introduced the theme that closed the first part of the panorama, the physical coercion of slaves. The next three scenes constituted a baleful sequence. By its plural title the twenty-first, **Modes of Confinement and Punishment**, seems to have been composed of two or more vignettes. The title for the twenty-second scene, **Brand and Scourge,** was the same as the fifth plate in *The Nubian Slave*. In Green's poem the Nubians were punished for conspiring to escape. The law specified branding for certain offenses in the South; to scourge was to wash a brine solution into the fresh wounds from a whipping. The twenty-third and final scene of the panorama's first half, **Interior of the Charleston Workhouse, with Treadmill in Full Operation**, depicted mass punishment meted to "runaway slaves . . . and disorderly persons."[15]

After the intermission, part two of the panorama opened with four scenes of slave life in the South. The first, **Sunday among the Slave Population**, was likely based on an illustration in the *Narrative of the Life and Adventures of Henry Bibb*. After Sunday came **Monday Morning, with Sugar Plantation and Mill**, undoubtedly a view of slaves at work, as were the following scenes, **Women at Work** and **Cotton Plantation**. Brown later retitled the latter scene as **Cotton Plantation Slaves at Work.**[16]

The twenty-eighth scene, **View of the Lake of the Dismal Swamp**, was a picturesque landscape, always appropriate in a panorama, that shifted the narrative geographically from cotton country to Virginia. In 1849 the *Liberator* described the Dismal Swamp as "full of wild birds, wild beasts, reptiles, and runaway slaves," and the scene introduced the primary theme of the second part of the panorama, slave resistance. The twenty-ninth scene, **Nubians Escaping by Night**, returned to the symbolic family's story and began an extended northbound narrative of escape. The next scene, **Ellen Crafts Escaping**, depicted the escape of Ellen Craft and her husband, William Craft, from Georgia in December 1848. Because the title mentioned only Ellen Craft, it

For the Twenty-fourth Scene, SUNDAY AMONG THE SLAVE POPULATION. *The Sabbath Among Slaves,* 1849 engraving from *Narrative of the Life and Adventures of Henry Bibb.*

may have shown her in disguise among the white passengers on the boat or on the train that conveyed them to freedom. The Crafts' was the other escape from slavery most celebrated among abolitionists in 1849–1850.[17]

The journey reached Henry Brown's Richmond in the thirty-first scene, **Whipping Post and Gallows at Richmond, Va.** An audience member later described two different scenes of whipping in *Mirror of Slavery*, and it is not clear which of them applied to this scene. In one, he said, "there were women represented with drops of blood falling, proceeding from flogging," and in the other there was "a representation of a man being whipped, with some blood." The panorama did not shirk from depicting violent punishment, a visual strategy that exposed slavery as a system of cruel exploitation and at the same time added emotional impact for the panorama's audiences.[18]

The next scene, **View of Richmond, Va.**, was probably when Henry Box Brown began to tell his own story. At the thirty-third scene, **Henry Box Brown Escaping**, Brown himself became a visible presence in the panorama. The scene was perhaps a tableau of two or three key events in the escape and might have been where James C. A. Smith appeared in the panorama. It was the first scene of eight that moved gradually northward, paralleling in a general way the route of Brown's escape.[19]

The thirty-fourth scene, **View of the Natural Bridge and Jefferson's Rock**, featured two landscapes of western Virginia associated with Thomas Jefferson. He had owned Natural Bridge, and one of the best views of Harpers Ferry was from Jefferson's Rock, so called because he once climbed it. The scene might have served to claim Jefferson for the antislavery cause. The next two scenes, **City of Washington, D. C.**, and **Slave Prisons at Washington**, juxtaposed symbols of liberty and the continuing presence of slavery in the nation's capital. "The noble House of Congress stands at the top of one picture, and in the fore ground is to be seen a slave auction," according to a newspaper review. The other showed "General Taylor (as President) driving in state into the city of Washington, whilst his four grey steeds are frightened by the cries and groans of a gang of slaves." The thirty-seventh scene, **Washington's Tomb at Mount Vernon**, was

For the Twenty-fifth Scene, Monday Morning, with Sugar Plantation and Mill. *Sugar Cultivation in the West Indies: Cane-holing,* 1849 engraving from *Illustrated London News.*

both a popular travelogue subject and a place that Brown, in his box, had actually passed on the steamboat up the Potomac River to Washington. As with Jefferson, abolitionists contended that this American icon was opposed to slavery.[20]

The thirty-eighth scene, **Fairmount Water Works**, was the first of three set in Philadelphia. The scene epitomized the progressive North of 1850. In the setting of a landscaped public park, hydropowered pumps filled elevated reservoirs to supply Philadelphians with pure drinking water. Josiah Wolcott probably offered the waterworks as an example of planned improvement to human living conditions.[21]

The thirty-ninth scene, **Henry Box Brown Released at Philadelphia**, was the climax to Brown's personal narrative. The fortieth scene, **Distant View of the City of Philadelphia**, was a landscape that ended the panorama's northward progression. The next two scenes concluded the subject of escapes. **Henry Bibb Escaping** was derived from an illustration in Bibb's *Narrative* and emphasized the danger of escape. The forty-second scene, **Nubian Slaves Retaken**, corresponded with the seventh and final plate in *The Nubian Slave.* The scene title says "retaken," a less violent outcome than the poem's in which only the son was recaptured and the father and mother were murdered. The scene would have been a reminder that many attempts at resistance were unsuccessful.[22]

Nubian Slaves Retaken also brought to an end the overall journey of the panorama. The final seven scenes contrasted futures of horror and hope. The first three of them returned to slavery's evils. The forty-third scene, **Tarring and Feathering in S. Carolina**, depicted a type of extralegal punishment suffered by persons who dared to espouse antislavery sentiments. The title of the forty-fourth scene, **The Slaveholder's Dream**, is intriguing but difficult to identify for content. The forty-fifth scene, **Burning Alive**, morbidly culminated the theme of violent repression. Such an incident was

For the Twenty-ninth Scene, **Nubians Escaping by Night.** Plate VI, *The Nubian Slave.* The book caption states: "'The Escape.' The Father is pointing out the North Star to his Wife and Son, as their guide to the land of Freedom."

illustrated and recounted in the 1840 *American Anti-Slavery Almanac*, which may have been an inspiration for the scene.[23]

Mirror of Slavery closed with four scenes that anticipated emancipation. The title of the forty-sixth scene, **Promise of Freedom**, was evocative of a number of abolitionist images in which a slave looked heavenward for deliverance. Religious iconography in the scene would allude to the true Christian attitude toward slavery and would have been an apposite sequel to the martyrdom just depicted in **Burning Alive**. The next scene, **West India Emancipation**, showed that an end to slavery was possible by offering Great Britain's action as a precedent.[24]

At a time when emancipation was not at all imminent in the United States, the panorama's multiple scenes of emancipation probably reflected Josiah Wolcott's forward outlook. According to the *Liberator*, the forty-eighth scene, titled **Grand Industrial Palace**, was "a view of a township, according to a plan of Charles Fourier, and given by the artist to indicate his idea of the fruition of emancipation." Wolcott's vision embodied Hosea Easton's conception of emancipation, as stated in his *Treatise*, which required more than "merely to cease beating the colored people, and leave them in their gore." Rather, wrote Easton, the process should provide equal opportunity: "emancipation embraces the idea that the emancipated must be placed back where slavery found them, and restore to them all that slavery has taken away from them." **Grand Industrial Palace** suggested that if emancipation was to include the restoration that Easton called for, its logic required fundamental change in economic and social relations.[25]

The panorama concluded with the forty-ninth scene, **Grand Tableau Finale**,

For the Forty-first Scene, **Henry Bibb Escaping.** *The Escape,* 1849 engraving from *Narrative of the Life and Adventures of Henry Bibb.*

Universal Emancipation. The title implies a visual design composed of a number of vignettes, perhaps reprising previous images of the Nubian family and Henry Box Brown.

Audiences brought their expectations of a moving panorama to *Mirror of Slavery* and in part they were met, with scenes of foreign lands, picturesque landscapes, heroic actions, and bloody violence. Yet *Mirror of Slavery* turned the conventions of the medium to its own purposes. Brown's panorama asked the viewer to imagine journeys forced and unwanted: marches in gangs chained together, voyages in dark holds, steps up to the auction block, and desperate bids for freedom.

Mirror of Slavery's heroes were the slaves. It was positive about their African origins, portrayed their natural state as freedom, and depicted the condition of enslavement as an unnatural imposition. Recognizing that females were equally repressed by slavery, *Mirror of Slavery* featured women at work, being punished, and escaping. It described a system based on coercion, threatened and overt, and without benevolence, even on Sunday. In opposition, the panorama presented the brave resistance of the slaves, some, like Brown, able to emancipate themselves by escape, and others not. To right the wrong, the panorama's answer was emancipation, transforming and universal.

The Performed Panorama

In performance the panorama became theater. Just as the painted panorama was central to *Mirror of Slavery* so too was the performance of Henry Box Brown, who held the stage and brought the paintings to life. Brown may have performed *Mirror of Slavery* as many as two thousand times.[26]

The standard presentation for a moving panorama featured a narrator who served as the audience's guide by explaining the contents of each scene. Within this format much variation was possible. For some performed panoramas the narrator delivered a prepared lecture, but other narrators were less formal, telling stories, making humorous remarks, reciting poetry, and singing.

For the Forty-second Scene, **N**UBIAN **S**LAVES **R**ETAKEN. Plate VII, *The Nubian Slave.* The book caption states: "'Man Hunting,' shews the Family pursued with Blood-hounds, and fired upon."

After the Worcester exhibition, where Benjamin F. Roberts presented "the description of the various scenes," Henry Box Brown assumed the role of the panorama's narrator. At first Brown probably drew from Roberts's model, though little evidence exists to know for certain how either man handled the job. A newspaper reported that "the Illustrations are described by Mr. Brown," accompanied "with a narrative of his own experience and sufferings." Another article referred to Brown's "verbal observations" on the views. One account indicated that at a scene near the middle of the panorama Brown paused in his narration to tell a story. During the show he took questions from the audience, the account went on, but he also preferred that questions be held to be answered at the end. Several reports said that local ministers took the stage to offer testimonials for Brown and to endorse his antislavery message. An advertisement stated that "the box may be seen, and Mr. Brown in it, after each exhibition."[27]

The only newspaper story that describes Brown's performance at any length was an attack that quoted him speaking in crude dialect. It is likely that Brown, denied an education, did speak with some grammatical improvisation, and, as a Virginian, his speech probably included southernisms. Such characteristics were enough for the predisposed in his audiences to hear him as if he were using the exaggerated language of blackface minstrels. The writer of the hostile article recorded Brown's speech as farcical. One reader of that article disagreed with its representation and declared that Brown spoke "not in the nigger style, but in English." After listening to him in court, a reporter judged Brown's "pronunciation altogether very correct." Another account stated that Brown spoke "with a simple, earnest, and unadorned eloquence."[28]

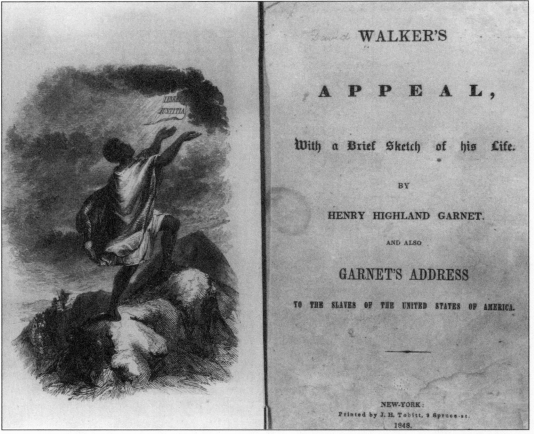

For the Forty-sixth Scene, PROMISE OF FREEDOM. Frontispiece engraving to 1848 edition of David Walker's *Appeal.*

Music was part of the exhibition from the beginning. Songs made the performance more complete as an entertainment. Henry Box Brown and James C. A. Smith had performed previously as singers, and in the early phase of the exhibition probably carried over their repertoire as a supplement to the panorama. A Worcester report noted that Brown had "sung several pieces of sacred music," among which was likely Brown's hymn of thanksgiving, and during the Worcester and Springfield runs weekend matinees featured expanded musical offerings.

Before long Brown added several songs that were keyed to scenes in the panorama and inherent to its presentation. An advertisement stated "Mr. Brown and Mr. Smith will Sing Pieces descriptive of several Scenes represented on the Mirror." A later advertisement listed the titles of these songs as " 'Freedom's Song!' 'Mr. Henry Box Brown's Escape!' and 'Song of the Nubian Family by the North Star!' " "Freedom's Song!" would have been appropriate for the panorama's second scene, **The Nubian Family in Freedom**, and "Song of the Nubian Family by the North Star!" fit the twenty-ninth scene, **Nubians Escaping by Night**. Undoubtedly "Mr. Henry Box Brown's Escape!" was a variant title for Brown's signature standard. Several reports said Brown closed the performance with this song.[29]

In the presentation of the show, one of Brown's programmatic songs would have come at the beginning, another near the start of part two, and another at the end.

Although the lyrics and music for the songs about the Nubian family are unknown, a report on the panorama likely referred to them when it stated that Brown periodically interspersed "some 'nigger' songs." Another account said that James C. A. Smith "joined Brown in singing one or two negro songs." For his songs about the Nubians, Brown might have used tunes that he knew from Virginia or alternately the report's use of the minstrel-propagated word "nigger" could suggest that, just as for his namesake standard, Brown borrowed minstrel-genre tunes. Even though Brown's exhibition was a corrective to the misrepresentation of African American culture put forth by the popular minstrels, he probably could not escape being seen in their light, especially since both his and theirs were shows with music on African American themes.[30]

Another similarity to the minstrels may have been by Henry Box Brown's choice. The few known contemporary descriptions of his perform-

For the Forty-seventh Scene, **West Indian Emancipation.** *Emancipation, Glorious First of August 1834,* mezzotint engraving by Stephen H. Gimber.

ance suggest that Brown's approach as narrator was neither didactic nor explicitly political, but rather anecdotal and, one might even say, folksy. He seems to have adapted to his own purpose the minstrels' style of mocking by exaggeration. The hostile newspaper article recorded Brown's commentary for the scene entitled **Sunday among the Slave Population**, a scene probably based on an image from the *Narrative of the Life and Adventures of Henry Bibb.* The book's illustration included a white man pouring a beverage, and the article reported Brown's explanation that some slaveholders "give their slaves money to buy rum to get drunk on the Sunday, in order to prevent them from attending a place of worship." Other slaveholders preached to the slaves, Brown said, "like his own master did every Sunday morning." The article then quoted Brown's comment about a preacher in the painted scene, who was apparently depicted with a ruddy complexion:

> Like an old-fashioned beef steak is de parson's face when he preaches to de slaves, and like it will they be roasted in the fire and be done infernally brown.[31]

For the Forty-eighth Scene, **Grand Industrial Palace**. *Vue générale d'un Phalanstère où village organisé d'après la théorie de Fourier.* The bird's-eye view of a Phalanstery was published in France and exhibited in the United States by Albert Brisbane. Given Wolcott's association with Brisbane, and the similarity of the *Liberator's* description of the panorama scene to this view, this print seems a likely source for **Grand Industrial Palace**. The Phalanstery is the large building at the center of the settlement.

Though the writer's transcription of Brown's spoken words cannot be completely trusted, as it stands Brown's imagery is both colorful and complex. The preacher is not white but "beef steak" red, and when the slaves have roasted in the fires of hell they will be not simply dark-skinned but "infernally brown." The simile of the "old-fashioned beef steak" attaches to the preacher and to the slaves and is perhaps also what the slaves actually thought about instead of the preacher's lesson. Brown here wielded well the weapon of satire. By his caricature of the preacher he illustrated the larger truth of the slaveholders' hypocritical religious teaching without preaching himself.

At the same performance Brown told a story midway through the panorama that set the stage for him to sing the "Escape from Slavery of Henry Box Brown" at the end of the show. His story was a parable that explained the meaning of the words "the shovel and the hoe" in the chorus of the song, words retained from the lyrics of Stephen Foster's "Old Uncle Ned." The story is rich in meanings and important enough that Brown published it as an appendix to his 1851 *Narrative*.[32]

The printed version of the story is a step removed from Brown's telling of it on stage, but such details as the recurring exclamation marks hint at his voice. Brown explained that his story was "the slave-holder's version of the creation of the human race."

> The slave-holders say that originally, there were four persons created (instead of only two) and, perhaps, it is owing to the christian account of the origin of man, in which account two persons only are

mentioned, that it is one of the doctrines of slave-holders that slaves have no souls: however these four persons were two whites and two blacks; and the blacks were made to wait upon the whites. But in man's original state, when he neither required to manufacture clothes to cover his nakedness, or to shelter him from storm; when he did not require to till the earth or to sow or to reap its fruits, for his support! but when everything sprung up spontaneously; when the shady bowers invited him to rest, and the loaded trees dropped their lucious burdens into his hands; in this state of things the white pair were plagued with the incessant attendance of the two colored persons, and they prayed that God would find them something else to do; and immediately while they stood, a black cloud seemed to gather over their heads and to descend to the earth before them! While they gazed on these clouds, they saw them open and two bags of different size drop from them. They immediately ran to lay hold of the bags, and unfortunately for the black man—he being the strongest and swiftest—he arrived first at them, and laid hold of the bags, and the white man, coming up afterwards, got the smaller one. They then proceeded to untie their bags, when lo! in the large one, there was a shovel and a hoe; and in the small one, a pen, ink, and paper; to write the declaration of the intention of the Almighty; they each proceeded to employ the Instruments which God had sent them, and ever since the colored race have had to labor with the shovel and the hoe, while the rich man works with the pen and ink![33]

With this mock-sermon, Brown did not so much condemn the slaveholders as make fun of them. His aim was at the whites who believed in a divinely ordained hierarchy of the races. When the white man is given pen, ink, and paper "to write the declaration of the intention of the Almighty"—a weighty charge, indeed—the story speaks to the shallow self-interest behind the religion that the slaveholders tried to teach the slaves. The story has resonance too with racist theories of the origin of humans. When George R. Gliddon, for instance, asserted that blacks were "always distinct from, and subject to, the *Caucasian*, in the remotest times," he did not refer only to ancient Egypt but also claimed the races were created separately. Theories of polygenesis, as this rationale for prejudice was called, were nicely satirized in Brown's fable.[34]

The story of "the shovel and the hoe" enabled Brown to address a difficult issue indirectly. Telling a tale was more his talent than essaying an argument. It is likely the visual imagery of the painted panorama was sufficiently forceful that the exhibition was effective anyway without an overly rhetorical commentary. Though Brown did not fool his way through a show like a minstrel, he leavened his presentation of slavery's horrors with music and enough acute comment to keep his audiences entertained.

Chapter Six

Expatriation

"The Slave-Catching Bill"

Throughout the spring and summer of 1850, as Henry Box Brown and James C. A. Smith toured with *Mirror of Slavery*, the news from Washington followed them to every town. Early in May the various bills of Henry Clay's compromise package, including the Fugitive Slave Bill, were grouped together in a single "Omnibus Bill." President Zachary Taylor opposed linking the issues but died unexpectedly on 9 July. The new president, Millard Fillmore, of New York, supported the Omnibus Bill.

Senator Thomas Hart Benton, of Missouri, described a subplot to the machinations in an anecdote reported in "substance" by the *National Era* of Washington, D.C. Benton used the meaning of "omnibus" as a passenger vehicle for his analogy:

> "Sir, there are four inside passengers in that Omnibus—there was California, sir; there was New Mexico; there was Texas; there was Utah, sir!—four inside passengers. There were two outside passengers, sir: There was the fugacious Slave Bill, and the District Slavetrade Abolition Bill. They could not be admitted inside, but they had outside seats, and the inside and outside passengers could be seen and known, sir. But there was another passenger under the driver's seat sir; carefully concealed in the boot, breathing through chinks and holes like Henry Box Brown, sir—the tariff, sir! But he had a worse fate than Box Brown— he was killed in the House, sir—and I hope we shall have no more Omnibuses and no more passengers in the boot, sir."[1]

Even without the tariff, the Omnibus Bill proved to be overloaded and lost in the Senate on 31 July 1850. Senator Stephen A. Douglas, of Illinois, and his allies promptly revived its components as separate bills and began to gather a different majority of senators for each. Legislative results came quickly. The Senate passed the Texas Boundary Bill on 9 August, approved the admission of California as a free state four days later, and organized New Mexico as a territory on 15 August. Debate opened on the Fugitive Slave Bill on 19 August, and seven days later the Senate approved it.[2]

The Fugitive Slave Bill, which now went on with the other bills for consideration by the House of Representatives, made it far easier for a slave owner to reclaim an escaped slave in the North. The existing law, the Fugitive Slave Act of 1793, was administered through state officers, rendering it ineffectual in states where officials declined to enforce it. The new bill called for enforcement by federal officers. Moreover, it mandated procedures that presumed that the accused person was a fugitive. Rather than requiring the slave catchers to prove their case, the bill obligated a person arrested as a fugitive to document his or her right to freedom.

On 28 August, in Rhode Island, the *Providence Republican Herald* reported the bill's passage in the upper house. "The Senate have done their duty in a prompt and efficient style," it declared, "since they have realized the danger they incurred by the defeat of the general Compromise Bill." In Providence at that time were Henry Box Brown and James C. A. Smith. Brown may have scheduled his panorama exhibition there to coincide with the Providence Anti-Slavery Fair on 4 and 5 September. Such fairs, with hand-made goods for sale, were a primary means for antislavery societies to raise funds. The *Providence Post* predicted that "several thousand folks" would attend the Anti-Slavery Fair "to get a view of the pretty things."[3]

On Friday afternoon, 30 August, as Henry Box Brown was "walking peaceably" on Broad Street in Providence, several men attacked him. Brown was beaten but managed to hold them off. A short while later the men assaulted Brown again, and "the attempt was made to force him into a carriage." Brown "proved too strong for them" and saved himself from being kidnapped.[4]

Two men were arrested. The *Providence Post* reported that the attackers' "purposes were not fully disclosed," but that Brown's "friends think the object was to get him on board a vessel bound to Charleston, or dispose of him Southward, in some other way." In court on Monday, one Thomas Kelton was fined fifteen dollars and costs for the assault. "Several persons swore positively to the identity" of the second man charged, Simon A. Bates, but they were "as positively contradicted by as many more." Even though Bates "advanced . . . in a threatening manner" toward Brown when the latter testified in court, the magistrate discharged Bates for insufficient evidence.

The assault signaled that the impending Fugitive Slave Law was no idle threat. Continuing to exhibit *Mirror of Slavery* had become a risky venture. Brown and Smith quit Providence. Two weeks after the incident they were in Springfield, Massachusetts. It is likely they went there to find refuge, perhaps at the Stearns home.

On the same day the *Providence Post* reported the attack on Brown, it carried a story from New York City about an attempt "to carry off a free colored woman" and "put her on board a schooner." Antislavery newspapers saw a pattern in such assaults. The *Boston Emancipator and Republican* suggested that "perhaps Webster's call upon the people of the North 'to conquer their prejudices,' and perform their constitutional duties, encouraged these kidnappers to engage in this outrage." The *Pennsylvania Freeman* saw "this species of land-piracy" as "the first fruits of the devoted efforts" of the advocates of compromise in Congress. "That these attempts will continue to grow more frequent, is very probable," the *Freeman* predicted, "especially if the House of Representatives are sufficiently wicked and demented to pass the Slave-Catching bill of the Senate."[5]

The *National Anti-Slavery Standard* also mocked Daniel Webster's language in defense of compromise, declaring that the men who had attacked Henry Box Brown had done so "with the purpose, doubtless, of fulfilling their constitutional duties by returning him to Slavery." In the case of Brown particularly, "we know what he has dared for the hope of freedom before he had tasted its reality," and the *Standard* warned, "Wo[e] be to them who attempt to deprive him of that reality!"[6]

On 12 September 1850 the House of Representatives took up the Fugitive Slave Bill. A vote was called immediately. With about thirty members from northern states conveniently absent, the bill passed, and on 18 September President Fillmore signed it into law. The Fugitive Slave Act changed life for all fugitive slaves but especially for one as well known as Henry Box Brown. Were he to be assaulted again, his attackers might well have the law on their side.[7]

Abolitionist friends advised Brown and Smith to leave the United States for England. To flee to Europe was a drastic decision, yet the possibility that Brown might be captured and reenslaved was an alarming prospect. The abstract debate in Congress had become hard reality for Brown. He and James C. A. Smith decided to leave. Friends took steps to help them, providing the address of a place to stay in New York, working to find them passage, and probably advising them on the preparations they should undertake. On 15 September Brown and Smith wrote from Springfield to Gerrit Smith, the Syracuse activist who may have been their benefactor previously. The letter expressed their fears and intentions in a single long sentence: "My dear friend & Brother I sirpose you have heard of my being kidnaped in R. I. or in city of Providence a few days sence, which has created a great excitement every where and sence that time the friends to Our Cause thinks that it is not safte for us to stay about here and speaking before the public as me & Mr. Smith is or has been ingage in doing) and as it is not very saft for us we have made an arraingement to go to England about the 24th inst."[8]

In England they could continue to exhibit the panorama. Brown and Smith's purpose in writing Gerrit Smith was to ask for "the favour" of a letter of introduction to antislavery friends in England, "as you know us and it may be of some good use to us." The pair apparently left Springfield shortly after the date of the letter, 15 September, for they requested that Gerrit Smith direct his response to Robert Meekins in New York City "and we will get it for we will be there about that time." Gerrit Smith did provide a letter of introduction, and it seems likely that Brown and Smith requested similar letters from other antislavery friends.[9]

Attempts to enforce the Fugitive Slave Act during the 1850s had a great bearing on the deteriorating relations between the North and the South. For Henry Box Brown, involvement in one of the early incidents was enough to convince him that the North was no longer a sanctuary. One account stated that "such was the vigilance with which the search for victims was pursued" (and perhaps on the advice of friends), "that Mr. Brown had to travel under an assumed name, and by the most secret means shift his panorama to prevent suspicion and capture." Brown's hope to bear witness to Americans was thwarted. He and James C. A. Smith prepared to take *Mirror of Slavery* across the Atlantic.[10]

More the Story than the Man. Engraving from *The Liberty Almanac for 1851.* The artist, likely working from written accounts, presents only a vague impression of Brown.

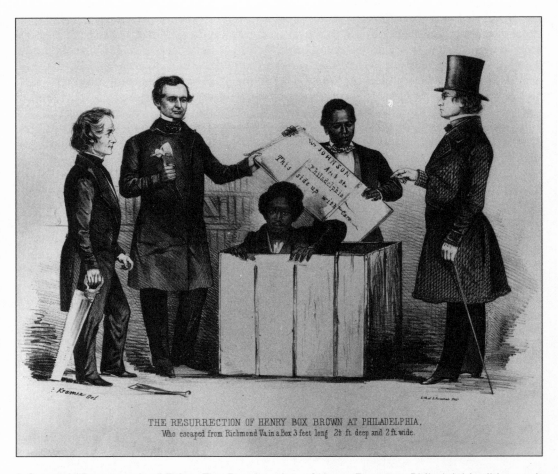

THE RESURRECTION OF HENRY BOX BROWN AT PHILADELPHIA.
Who escaped from Richmond Va. in a Box 3 feet long 2½ ft. deep and 2 ft. wide.

A Second "Resurrection" Print. *The Resurrection of Henry Brown at Philadelphia,* lithograph by Peter Kramer. The Philadelphia printer is identified by the historian Bernard F. Reilly as Thomas Sinclair, though the credit on the print is "Lith. of L. Rosenthal, Phila." The *Anti-Slavery Bugle* of Ohio had copies in hand prior to 8 March 1851. If distribution was expeditious once it was off the press, as seems likely, the date of publication was probably January or February 1851.

The artist Kramer was a German refugee from the political events of 1848 in Europe. His print replicates the design of the identically titled 1850 Boston print attributed to Samuel Rowse (page 82). A number of the components are different, however. If the new print is somewhat stiffer and less animated, in several respects it is more accurate. One change of substance is that Kramer in Philadelphia would not have required stand-ins. Except for Brown, whose likeness was copied from the Boston print, Kramer presumably had access to his subjects, all Philadelphians, and probably portrayed them with reasonable fidelity. Left middle is Miller McKim, and William Still stands right middle. One imagines that the gentleman on the right is Professor Charles D. Cleveland, operator of a school for girls, and that the man on the left is the printer Lewis Thompson. He holds a saw and McKim a hatchet, the latter a reprise from the first Philadelphia unboxing image (page 64). From the way McKim holds the hatchet, one can imagine that the print commemorates the actual tools used to open Brown's box.

In absentia Henry Box Brown would remain an American symbol. *The Liberty Almanac for 1851*, an annual put out by the American and Foreign Anti-Slavery Society, advertised "well executed wood engravings, prepared expressly for it," including one "illustrating the escape of Henry *Box* Brown." That the more moderate wing of the abolitionists featured his escape indicated Brown's appeal across the factional lines of the movement. The engraving appeared opposite the almanac's calendar for December, accompanied with text mostly drawn from the April 1849 *Burlington Courier* account. The *Almanac* was published in New York and advertised for sale in September 1850. Henry Box Brown and James C. A. Smith could have seen a copy when they were in that city preparing to go into exile.[11]

A few months later, a lithograph entitled *The Resurrection of Henry Brown at Philadelphia* was published in Philadelphia for the Pennsylvania Anti-Slavery Society. Miller McKim and his fellow abolitionists, some of them participants in Brown's escape, had not previously issued a broadside about it, although it was a natural subject, probably in deference to Brown's right to present his own tale. Brown seems never to have exhibited in Pennsylvania, however, and his various publications apparently did not reach there in any quantity. Likely the Philadelphians moved to produce their *Resurrection* print after Brown departed, intending it for distribution to areas Brown had not reached. In March 1851 the *Anti-Slavery Bugle*, of Salem, Ohio, announced that it had received the print, "a very life-like lithographic representation of one of the most extraordinary scenes which, we venture to say, ever occurred in the United States, if not in the world, and which affords a remarkable illustration of the old adage, 'Truth is stranger than Fiction.'" Offering copies at twenty-five cents per single copy, or fifteen dollars per hundred, the *Bugle* declared that "it ought to be framed and suspended on the wall of every dwelling and workshop in the land."[12]

To Liverpool

Henry Box Brown and James C. A. Smith did not sail on 24 September, the date they had given Gerrit Smith. The delay was likely caused by a lack of funds. The danger of appearing in public precluded exhibiting the panorama, their source of income, and they probably used up any previously accumulated money in the sudden departure from Providence and in getting themselves and the panorama to New York. The cost to their fugitive neighbors in Boston, William and Ellen Craft, for steerage passage in November 1850 from Halifax to Liverpool was seventy-five dollars each. Brown and Smith needed more than that because the voyage from New York was longer, and they also faced freight costs for the panorama.[13]

Eventually they managed to arrange to travel without paying in full. The shipper would hold the panorama on arrival in England until they paid for the passage. Their luggage also included the box in which Brown had escaped and a collection of Brown's publications: copies of the 1849 *Narrative*, of the Boston lithograph of Brown's arrival in Philadelphia, and perhaps of Brown's song sheets. Almost certainly Brown carried, too, the manuscript for a new edition of his *Narrative* that had been ready in April.

On 7 October 1850, Henry Box Brown and James C. A. Smith departed from New York for Liverpool on the packet ship *Constantine*. Their journey took more than three weeks, twice the time that steamships normally required crossing the Atlantic, indicating that the *Constantine* was a sail-powered ship. They undoubtedly traveled steerage class, the cheapest fare. If they were fortunate their experience on board might have been similar to that of the black abolitionist Samuel Ringgold Ward, who wrote of his voyage to England in 1853 that it was "most delightful," for he was "able *to do noth-*

ing, comfortably and perseveringly, without sea sickness." He ate, drank, and slept well, "great comforts, at sea." Brown and Smith arrived in Liverpool on 1 November 1850.[14]

Liverpool's miles of quays served the largest fleet of oceangoing ships in the world, and its 375,000 inhabitants made it England's second-largest city. Samuel R. Ward had expected a "strange aspect" to Liverpool but instead found "some resemblance to Boston and the Bostonians." One wonders if Henry Box Brown, finding himself in the bustle of an unfamiliar city, might not have thought back to his arrival in Richmond from Louisa County some twenty years before or to his first time in New York or Boston. Because Great Britain recognized no legal status of involuntary servitude, on disembarking Henry Box Brown was emancipated. "For the first time in my life I can say 'I am truly free,'" wrote William Wells Brown after he arrived from the United States in 1849. "England is, indeed, the 'land of the free and the home of the brave.'"[15]

It seems likely that a friend in New York had written ahead to Liverpool, for Brown and Smith made connections promptly after their landing. They arrived on a Friday, and on Tuesday, 5 November 1850, an article entitled "A Fugitive Slave in Liverpool" appeared in the *Liverpool Mercury*. It explained that Brown, "a fine intelligent-looking man," had "earned a subsistence" by exhibiting his panorama and lecturing against slavery. His activities made him "very obnoxious to the slaveowners of the states," who were now "armed with the powers of the Fugitive Slave Bill." After two attempts to arrest him, "Brown made his escape to this country" in the company of "James Boxer Smith, also a coloured man, but not a slave, who assisted to box him up at Richmond," whose "connexion with Brown" put him at risk, too. "These two men have landed on our shores almost penniless," the article stated, "unable to release" the panorama "unless they receive assistance from some benevolent friends of the coloured race."[16]

Word of their arrival quickly passed around British and Irish antislavery circles. An activist named Richard Webb wrote from Dublin to an American abolitionist on 12 November that Brown had come to England "without money to pay his passage so that by the last accounts his Panorama was a pledge in Liverpool." Webb observed that William Wells Brown had "also got up a Panorama of the same kind with great labor." He was of the opinion that William Wells Brown would "not be at all pleased by the competition."[17]

What William Wells Brown thought is unknown, but Webb's news was outdated even as he penned it. Before they had been a fortnight in England, Brown and Smith had redeemed the panorama and were about to begin exhibiting it. Some "benevolent friends" helped. On 14 November John Bishop Estlin wrote to an American correspondent that he had heard "H. Box Brown is in Liverpool penniless having started from Am. with his panorama from fear of the new Bill." Estlin had asked a friend in Liverpool "to give him some money for me," and said that his brother-in-law, a Mr. Bazehot, was on his way to Liverpool and would "find out B. Brown & his friend Boxer Smith, and give them advice & help." James C. A. Smith later reported that "we arrived in Liverpool safte with the <u>Panorama</u> and with the assistance of the friends we commence giving Exhibitions."[18]

Brown and Smith opened their first British exhibition on Tuesday, 12 November 1850. An advertisement appeared in that day's *Liverpool Mercury* for "the New and Original PANORAMA, or MIRROR OF AMERICAN SLAVERY" at the Concert Hall on Lord Nelson Street. Shows were scheduled through Friday evening, with matinees on Wednesday and Friday. "The box may be seen," the advertisement promised, "and Mr. Brown in it, after each exhibition." Brown and Smith would also "Sing Pieces descriptive of several Scenes represented on the Mirror."[19]

CONCERT-HALL, LORD NELSON-STREET.
HENRY BOX BROWN, THE FUGITIVE
SLAVE.
THIS EVENING (Tuesday), the 12th, TO-MORROW (Wednesday), the 13th, and FRIDAY next, the 15th instant, the New and Original PANORAMA or MIRROR of AMERICAN SLAVERY! Painted by Willcott, House, and Johnson, Artists, of Boston, United States. This elegant work of art will be described by Mr. Henry Box Brown, a fugitive slave, whose miraculous escape from slavery was effected by his friend Mr. James Boxer Smith (who accompanies him) packing him in a box three feet long, two and a half feet deep, and two feet wide, and forwarding him, by rail and steam-boat, to a gentleman in Philadelphia. The box may be seen, and Mr. Brown in it, after each exhibition.
Mr. Brown and Mr. Smith will Sing Pieces descriptive of several Scenes represented on the Mirror.
Admission:—Body, 6d.; Side Galleries, 1s.; Reserved Seats, 1s. 6d.
DAY EXHIBITIONS on Wednesday and Friday, at Two o'clock. Admission: Body, 1s.; Side Galleries, 1s. 6d.; Reserved Seats, 2s.

Liverpool Mercury, 12 November 1850

James C. A. Smith stated later that "we did not do so well at first." Perhaps that explains why, following the last advertised performance of the panorama on Friday, Brown and Smith appeared on Saturday evening with the "Minstrel Fairies giving their Fairy Entertainment." The Minstrel Fairies were "3 young and talented children" who had performed for Queen Victoria and Prince Albert. One sister played harp, the other played the violin, and their brother, Lorenzo, the youngest, played violoncello. A highlight was the six-year-old Lorenzo's performance of "Paganini's grand violin solo upon one string." Brown and Smith were musical guests and sang "some Anti-Slavery Songs and Duets, their own composition."[20]

A favorable notice in the *Liverpool Mercury* on the Friday of their first week of exhibition, however, helped Brown and Smith's own show find its feet. "The exciting scenes reflected on this mirror are such as description fails to convey to other minds," enthused the reviewer. "We would urge our readers to visit this panorama; and if any of them have thought lightly of the injustice done by America to three millions and a half of our fellow-creatures, we feel assured they will leave the exhibition in another frame of mind." The reviewer commented that "the entertainment is varied by the singing of Mr. Brown and Mr. Smith," and described their music in reference to the American blackface minstrels, who had become very popular in England. "The imitators of negro melodists have long delighted the public, and an opportunity is now afforded of hearing the originals."[21]

Brown and Smith apparently recognized that their music was a drawing card. They engaged the Concert Hall for a second week, and their advertisements now announced the music of "Mr. Henry Box Brown, The Fugitive Slave, and Mr. James Boxer Smith, Who sing Plantation Melodies, Serenades, Duets, and Anti-Slavery Songs." With the favorable review, new advertisements, and word of mouth, audiences improved, for the exhibition was extended a third week, billed as "Last Week," with Saturday, 30 November, announced as the "Last Night." Held over again, the advertisements for the first week of December stated: "Prices Reduced! Positively the Last Three Nights." Brown and Smith's month in Liverpool taught them that their exhibition could draw audiences in England, especially with music as an attraction. Even exiled, they could carry on.[22]

Chapter Seven

English Freedom

Britain, Slavery, and Panoramas

By 1850 southern Lancashire, including Liverpool, had become, in the words of a contemporary, "the principal manufacturing district, not only of England, but of the world." The major industry was cotton milling, and in that fact abolitionism confronted a key British economic interest. Cotton, the product of slave labor, was the United States' largest export, and the primary purchasers were English manufacturers of cotton cloth, which was Britain's largest export. By 1852, Liverpool was shipping "over 1,000 million yards of cotton piece-goods" annually.[1]

The economic importance of cotton was one factor that influenced Great Britain's policy toward American slavery. Another was an antislavery movement that had pushed Britain to abolish slavery in the British West Indies and other colonies in 1834 and to continue to employ its navy to suppress the international slave trade. Public opinion played an ever-larger role in British politics, and abolitionists sought to trump economic interests by convincing the populace, especially the middle classes, that slavery was foremost a moral question.

After West Indian emancipation the antislavery societies in Great Britain directed their efforts against slavery elsewhere and in the United States in particular. The numerous local groups, often based in dissenting churches, were spread throughout Britain and helped make possible an active antislavery lecture circuit. A number of American abolitionists, black and white, made speaking tours. Frederick Douglass traveled the British Isles from 1845 to 1847 and said that he had come to Great Britain "because you have an influence on America that no other nation can have."[2] Many of the other black abolitionists who went to Britain did so following the enactment of the Fugitive Slave Law. One London newspaper thanked the law "for having sent amongst us a band of zealous and intelligent witnesses against slavery, who will not allow public feeling here to subside on the question." Among these advocates were Henry Box Brown and James C. A. Smith; though they had fled the United States, they could yet play a part in the antislavery movement.[3]

Their intention to exhibit the *Mirror of Slavery* was well timed, for the British public was much interested in moving panoramas. The concept of a moving panorama as a feature presentation had arrived from the United States late in 1848, when John Banvard opened his *Panorama of the Mississippi River* in London. Banvard's "three-mile painting" and his publicity battle with the four-mile claims for John R. Smith's *Mississippi River* helped to spark a panorama boom. "Strange it is that we should have received such a hint from a nation by no means distinguished for its school of painting," commented the *Illustrated London News*. One of the first British moving panoramas was *The Nile*. In the spring of 1850, *The Overland Route to India* opened in London and was a great success; twelve panoramas competed for audiences there in January 1851. Many of the panoramas toured the country after their London runs.[4]

Henry Box Brown's *Mirror of Slavery* was the first antislavery panorama in the United States, but at least two others preceded it in Britain. Attending Banvard's

Mississippi River in Boston had first set William Wells Brown to thinking about an antislavery panorama, and in London *The Overland Route to India* prodded him to act. Brown had eighteen drawings ready by mid-August 1850, and "within the next few weeks six additional drawings" were finished. Printing of the descriptive catalog was underway early in October, and by month's end William Wells Brown was in New-castle upon Tyne exhibiting *Original Panoramic Views of the Scenes in the Life of an American Slave*.[5]

Richard Webb, the Dublin correspondent for the *National Anti-Slavery Standard* of New York, reported on 5 December 1850 that Henry Box Brown had "landed in En-gland with his immortal box," and that there was "a rumor that Wm. and Ellen Crafts are on their way to England too." The Crafts arrived that month. William Wells Brown and the Crafts had lectured together in Massachusetts in 1849, and they joined forces again early in 1851 for a tour of Scotland. The *National Anti-Slavery Standard*'s 6 March 1851 issue reported that William Wells Brown's "lecture was illustrated by panoramic views descriptive of the methods of catching American slaves, which on the whole seemed to excite the highest disgust in the numerous and respectable audience."[6]

William Wells Brown and the Crafts exhibited in Bristol at the beginning of April 1851, but how many times more William Wells Brown showed his panorama is not known. His biographer states that "it is doubtful that Brown's exhibition was remark-ably successful." Brown was primarily a lecturer—he had delivered more than 400 lec-tures in Britain and "addressed not fewer than 200,000 persons," he said at Bristol—and he intended the panorama as a way to illustrate his talks. Traveling with it was proba-bly more troublesome and expensive than he desired. No later reports of performances of William Wells Brown's panorama have been located.[7]

The first antislavery panorama to be exhibited in Britain was produced by a white American, the Reverend W. H. Irwin, who took his *Panoramic Exhibition of American Slavery* with him from the United States. On the voyage he met a fugitive slave named Charles, who had escaped from Virginia and was working as an assistant to the ship's cook. An actual fugitive slave would make his exhibition more interesting to audiences, and Irwin convinced the man to join him. They arrived in London and gave their first exhibition privately to an audience of abolitionists, probably to elicit endorsements. One of those present, a Reverend J. Sherman, proposed that because by landing in England Charles had become a freeman, he should take the name Charles Freeman, "a suggestion which was adopted by acclamation."[8]

Irwin's panorama played to the public at Royal Victoria Hall, at Leicester Square, London's central entertainment district, in the spring of 1850. The *London Anti-Slavery Reporter* gave the show a positive notice. "We earnestly invite those unacquainted with its details, or anxious to have their feelings of detestation deepened against the horrid institution, to an inspection" of the panorama. The *British Friend* of London also endorsed this "pictorial mode of information . . . now exhibited, by a generous and enterprising American, named Irwin."[9]

Irwin's panorama followed a narrative line with some similarities to Henry Box Brown's *Mirror of Slavery*. "The panorama opens with a scene on the African coast," explained the *Anti-Slavery Reporter*, "and then follow a series of paintings embracing the great outlines of slavery in the United States, and the escape of slaves into Canada." Irwin professed to have gained his expertise on slavery through a residence of twelve years in the slave states. "He accompanies the panorama with illustrative remarks, hav-ing himself personally witnessed the events each department of the panorama is intended to represent, with the exception only of the African scene."[10]

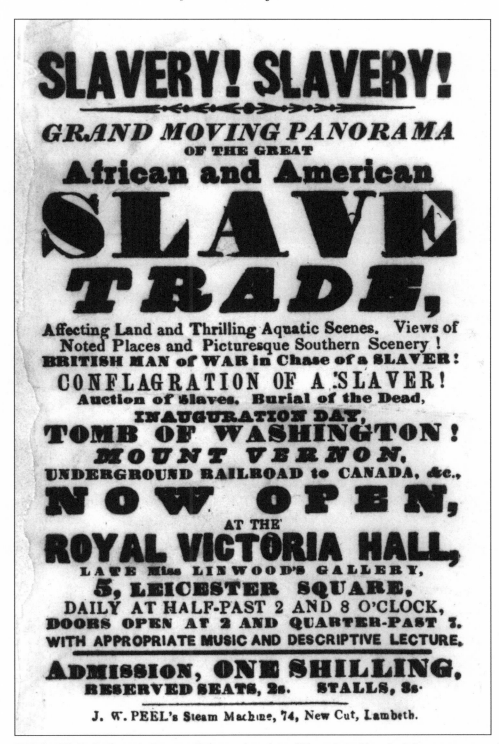

Handbill for W. H. Irwin at Leicester Square, London. Although neither Irwin's name nor a date appear, the venue and description of the panorama match the Reverend Irwin's spring 1850 London exhibition, and the scrapbook that contains the handbill dates it to April 1850.

As such, Irwin became a character in the panorama, apparently as an antislavery missionary operating within the slave South. The *British Friend* described a scene "in a cane brake, to avoid the notice of the master," in which Irwin met with a slave who had been punished with heavy irons on his legs for attempting to escape. The irons "had eaten into the flesh, and he was dying of the sores." Irwin's sympathy and prayers "strengthened his sinking spirits to meet his end in a few days afterwards." In another scene a husband and wife strive to reach Canada, "their land of promise; but, exhausted by fatigue, exposure, and hunger, the woman lies down to die."[11]

"Notwithstanding the flattering prospects" with which they began, reported Charles Freeman, "the expenses necessarily incurred in starting it, and placing it fairly before the public" forced Irwin to mortgage the panorama. The London engagement "proved a failure," and they "resolved to try its chance in some of the provincial towns." The exhibition did fairly well in Colchester, and in Ipswich "we were more successful than we had ever been." They were about to move on to Norwich, when the noteholder "came down from London and seized the picture." According to Freeman, this action left Irwin "with wife and child almost destitute."[12]

In time the Reverend W. H. Irwin managed to reclaim his panorama. In his narrative, *The Escaped Slave*, published in 1853, Charles Freeman recounted Irwin's travails. An undated account describes the Reverend Irwin's presentation of a "narrative panorama" on slavery at the Cosmorama Rooms with Charles Freeman. Copies of Freeman's narrative were on sale for two pence, which places the date of this exhibition at 1853 or later. Nothing further has been learned of Irwin or Freeman in England.[13]

It is not known whether Henry Box Brown was aware of these other antislavery panoramas. Though neither William Wells Brown nor W. H. Irwin had great success as exhibitors, their paths suggest the different ways that Box Brown might present *Mirror of Slavery* in Great Britain. William Wells Brown was well known in abolitionist circles, and local organizations facilitated his exhibitions. He did not rely solely on revenue from the panorama to carry on his public appearances. The Reverend Irwin operated his panorama independently as a paying business, putting him in the competitive entertainment world. Though the antislavery press noticed him favorably, without sponsorship Irwin suffered financial problems.

Irwin's difficulties illustrated the advantages of maintaining support from organized antislavery. Such help came with certain standards to be met. One of William Wells Brown's hosts, Dr. John Bishop Estlin, of Bristol, told an American correspondent in May 1851 that "we have been endeavouring to improve the tone of Brown and Crafts Exhibition altering their too *showman like* hand bills." In another letter he elaborated, writing that "they had kind, but not judicious, (& some vulgar) advisers in the North of England. . . . Some of their hand-bills have been headed 'Arrival of 3 Fugitive Slaves from America'!!! as if 3 monkeys had been imported, and their public appearance has been too often of the *exhibitive* kind." Estlin surely would have disapproved of the handbill for W. H. Irwin's London exhibition. The handbill promised an exciting show without indicating any opinion about slavery. Like commercial panoramas about foreign places, the lure was the exotic subject.[14]

In Liverpool Henry Box Brown had assistance from antislavery activists, yet like Irwin he needed the revenue of admission fees. For his first English foray into exhibition with James C. A. Smith, Brown followed a middle course between the paths of William Wells Brown and W. H. Irwin. Hewing to the standards of the antislavery friends would prove a challenge, however, not the least of which was to avoid becoming "too showman like."

"Witnessed by large numbers"

Not only did antislavery friends contribute to redeem Henry Box Brown's panorama, they also helped by acting as his advocates. A few days after *Mirror of Slavery* closed in Liverpool, on 10 December 1850, the *Liverpool Mercury* published a letter about Brown signed "A Hater of Slavery." The writer stated that Brown, "from his own modesty," had not told "the Liverpool public" that "his family are still in bondage." When he "undertakes to entertain us with his performances, which have given such universal satisfaction and delight," explained the writer, Brown seeks "to enable himself to purchase the redemption of his children." His three children "are valued by their master at $500 each," and "to raise this 1500 dollars, then, is Mr. Brown's aim in his visit to England." The writer exhorted English fathers to "sympathise with him in the exertion which he is making," and warned that despite "all the interest which the people of Liverpool have felt and shown . . . unless they feel more in the right place, his children will live and die in slavery."[15]

Such a public endorsement carried much weight. "A black abolitionist hoping for a successful visit had to have his or her antislavery credentials certified," writes the historian C. Peter Ripley. "Completing the certification process and collecting British testimonials were the first requirements for a good tour." By describing the exhibition as a means to rescue Brown's children, the Liverpool letter cast *Mirror of Slavery* as a charitable rather than as a commercial enterprise. With local antislavery activists thus assured that their assistance served a higher purpose, Brown would more readily gain their help.[16]

From Liverpool Henry Box Brown and James C. A. Smith went to Manchester, thirty-five miles inland. Manchester was England's third-largest city and a factory town where cotton mills reigned. In 1844, four years before he co-authored *The Communist Manifesto*, Friedrich Engels called Manchester "the masterpiece of the Industrial Revolution." A dozen years later the American novelist Nathaniel Hawthorne wrote that it was "a dingy and heavy town" and not "particularly worth visiting, unless for the sake of its factories."[17]

On Saturday, 14 December 1850, "The New and Original Panorama Or Mirror Of American Slavery" opened in Manchester at the Mechanic's Institution. It ran at that venue for a week. The *Manchester Guardian* gave it a notice on 18 December: "Brown describes the views, and he and his friend, James Smith, a man of colour, who packed him in the box and accompanied it to Philadelphia, introduce several plantation melodies, &c." The report stated that "it is probable that the panorama will not remain in Manchester beyond tomorrow," and encouraged "those friends of the anti-slavery movement and others who desire to see it and its exhibition" to "lose no time."[18]

Enough of them attended that the show stayed on in the city. For the following week, beginning on 21 December, the panorama could be seen at "Newall's Buildings, Market-st." Local advisors may have felt that the name *Mirror of Slavery* was not sufficiently descriptive for the English public, for Brown retitled the panorama twice in Manchester, first as "Panorama or Mirror of American Slavery" and next as "The Great American Moving Tableaux." If a change of titles might attract more patrons, Brown and Smith were evidently ready to adapt.[19]

They offered additional shows "on Christmas and New Year's Day, for the convenience of strangers . . . at ten and twelve in the morning, and two and four in the afternoon; six and eight in the evening." Also advertising special holiday shows was *The Grand Moving Panorama of the Overland Route to California across the Rocky*

Mountains. The *Manchester Guardian* commented that this panorama was "one of the most interesting of the exhibitions in the town destined to tempt young folk during the approaching Christmas holidays." Brown and Smith probably extended their run in Manchester to catch the holiday traffic because the exhibitions on 1 January 1851 were the last advertised there.[20]

Manchester was a center for English reform activism, and most of the people known to have helped Henry Box Brown during his first months in England came from around that city. Among them were sisters Hannah and Rebecca Walton, shoe dealers who helped a number of fugitive slaves. James C. A. Smith reported later that he and Brown "commence the Exhibitions by the assistance of some of the friends—and we got a long pretty well and after we begian to make a little money and some of the friends to the Anti-Slavery Cause thought it best to save what we could." If they understood that the panorama's purpose was to raise money to rescue Brown's children, it seems reasonable that their friends would help them not only to accumulate funds but also to secure them. "There fore," Smith wrote, "we lef[t] what we could do without with a friend in Manchester—whos[e] name is Walton." Another friend that Smith mentioned was one James Bryce, who lived in a town adjacent to Manchester. As a coachman, Bryce may have assisted Brown and Smith in the transportation of the panorama.[21]

Another helper was the Reverend Thomas Gardiner Lee, a reformer on several fronts and pastor of the New Windsor Independent Chapel in Salford, which borders Manchester. Slavery was not as overwhelming an issue in Great Britain as in the United States, and for most British activists it was but one of a number of causes that engaged their attention. Many of these social reformers, like Lee, came out of the non-conformist, or dissenting, churches, the Protestant denominations outside the established Church of England. The historian Douglas A. Lorimer explains that the antislavery movement was "part of a broader moral crusade" that included "free trade, temperance, peace, parliamentary reform, foreign and home missions, anti-church establishment, and women's rights." Lee's church, for instance, sponsored a "Total Abstinence Society," and Lee himself had published a paper on "the means of Elevating the Working Classes."[22]

For Henry Box Brown and James C. A. Smith, who had managed in the United States to stay clear of the arguments that divided abolitionists, the ideological milieu of English reform presented a different set of potential pitfalls. One friend, Dr. Frederick Richard Lees, was a lifelong campaigner for temperance, as a lecturer, author, and editor. Another, Thomas Holliday Barker, an accountant and commission agent in Manchester, was so ardent an advocate of temperance that "he refused fermented wine in the sacrament as administered by the Wesleyans." Barker was an active lecturer and wrote pamphlets attacking the liquor trade and promoting vegetarianism. Lees's and Barker's experiences as advocates would have made them valuable advisors to Brown and Smith on conducting their own tour with the panorama. On the other hand, the Americans, no matter how pure their antislavery credentials, risked alienating their friends if their behavior did not meet the reformers' standards.[23]

With the help of their new antislavery friends, Brown and Smith set out on their first English tour. They began in the smaller cities and towns in the manufacturing district of southern Lancashire. The extended exhibitions at Liverpool and Manchester gave way to shorter runs and more travel.

On 8 January 1851 Brown and Smith opened at the Theater Royal in Blackburn, a mill town twenty-four miles northwest of Manchester. The advertisement in the *Blackburn Standard* announced, "For Four Days Only! Just Arrived In England!" A short article in the newspaper also called attention to the show. An endorsement in Brown's

1851 *Narrative* indicates that he and Smith did not limit their performances to theatrical venues: "We, the Teachers of St. John's Sunday School, Blackburn, having seen the exhibition in our School-room, called the 'Panorama of American Slavery,' feel it our duty to call upon all our christian brethren, who may have an opportunity, to go and witness this great mirror of slavery for themselves."[24]

After Blackburn, Brown and Smith took the panorama five miles south to the town of Darwen. Beginning on 16 January they exhibited at the "school-room" on William Street "to numerous and respectable audiences." One who attended commented in the *Manchester Examiner and Times* that "the painting is elegant, and could not fail in giving satisfaction to all." The performers continued south another eight miles to Bolton, a manufacturing town with more than sixty cotton factories, where Nathaniel Hawthorne noticed that "the tall brick chimneys rise numerously in the neighborhood." They were there for only a few days but "exhibited in Bolton with much success."[25]

Such short runs were viable in part because Lancashire was one of the few places in the world in 1851 where a tour could be conducted by train. The county had an extensive railroad network, a reflection of its industrialization, and Brown and Smith likely took advantage of it. The railroad was the most efficient and probably the most economical way for them to get about with the bulky panorama.

By Friday, 24 January, "The Great American Moving Tableaux; or Panorama of American Slavery" had opened in Preston, another cotton-manufacturing center, located nineteen miles northwest of Bolton. The exhibit was at the Corn Exchange each evening through Saturday, 1 February, with matinees on Tuesday, Thursday, and Saturday. The advertisements offered admission to "schools at reduced prices."[26]

Local newspapers praised the exhibition. The *Preston Chronicle and Lancashire Advertiser* called the panorama "a brilliant piece of art" and stated that "a vast number of individuals, including a great number of school children, have visited the exhibition, all of whom have been gratified by their visit." The *Preston Pilot and County Advertiser*'s account agreed that the panorama was "beautifully executed" and that Brown delivered "a most interesting series of lectures on American slavery." It also reported that at the matinee on 24 January, "the Rev. H. R. Smith made some very apposite remarks on the usefulness of exhibitions of this nature." Similarly, after the evening performance the same day, "the Rev. J. Kitton . . . addressed the audience, and spoke in very warm tones of the lecturer."

The endorsements of the clergymen were a stamp of approval. John Kitton recalled a few years later that Brown "behaved very well & excited considerable sympathy." Kitton wrote that he had "then lived in Preston & was able to promote [Brown's] interests & did so all I could." He remembered that Brown "dined once or twice with me," and that James C. A. Smith "once visited me too." Kitton also provided Brown with a letter of endorsement. Dated 7 February 1851, the letter stated that Kitton had "three times seen your exhibition." As "to its faithfulness as a mirror of the horrors of the African slave trade, and of American slavery," he wrote, "I am able to testify" that, if anything, Brown's panorama "under-states the dreadful horrors of American slavery *as it is* even now."[27]

Kitton's endorsement expressed the hope that Brown would "soon accomplish the desire of your heart, viz., to realize funds sufficient to enable you to purchase the freedom of your children." Similarly the *Preston Chronicle* explained that Brown's exhibition had the dual purpose of "enlightening the English mind with respect to slavery, and also to raise money by which he can purchase the manumission of his wife and three children, who are still held in bondage by the slave-owner from whom he escaped."[28]

Although friends and the press certainly associated this aim with the exhibition, Brown's role in promoting it is not clear. In Liverpool, according to the letter from "Hater of Slavery," Brown "from his own modesty" did not raise the subject of redeeming his family, and there are no other reports that Brown brought up the topic. This purpose for the exhibition may have best evoked sympathy if Brown did not present it directly. Perhaps James C. A. Smith talked up the redemption of Brown's family. The subject could have become effectively self-sustaining once it was featured in Brown's press coverage. Performers usually kept a folder, often a well-made showpiece bound in leather or the like, that contained accumulated testimonial letters and clippings, to be presented at newspaper offices in hope of favorable coverage, and also shared with friends such as Kitton.[29]

Brown and Smith returned to the Bolton area by 9 February 1851 for an engagement at Temperance Hall in Little Bolton from the tenth through the fifteenth. The *Bolton Chronicle* gave the exhibition strong support, and it was held over through 22 February. The newspaper printed John Kitton's endorsement and encouraged "the people of Bolton" to see the "series of paintings . . . exhibited by Mr. Henry Box Brown, portraying in striking but true colours slavery's horrors." The show would enable those attending "to form a just estimate of American slavery," and would also make them "more capable of appreciating the blessings of English freedom." The newspaper especially recommended the paintings to "religious persons and to Sunday scholars."[30]

The *Bolton Chronicle* promoted the second week of Brown's "painfully interesting panorama" with another enthusiastic article. The panorama, it declared, "conveyed through the eyes to the senses" such "ideas of horror and suffering" as "it would be impossible to receive from the perusal of a printed history." The article closed with an exhortation about a "circumstance we would strongly impress upon our readers: the main object of the proprietor in exhibiting the panorama is to enable him to realize funds sufficient to *purchase* the freedom of his *own children*."[31]

While Brown and Smith were exhibiting in Bolton, Richard Webb sent word to the *National Anti-Slavery Standard* in New York that he had been told "by some Abolitionists in Manchester, that Henry Box Brown is doing well." He reported that Brown had "his famous box along with him." Webb hoped that Brown would "meet a worthy reception in England," and that "he, and all like him, who come to this country, may do credit to their race and to the cause they are identified with."[32]

From the show's close in Bolton on 22 February until the beginning of April, no exhibition notices have been found. There may have been other appearances, but it seems probable that for at least a part of this period Brown and Smith stopped exhibiting so that Brown could prepare a new edition of his *Narrative*. Brown knew from his American experience that touring was an effective way to sell books. Indeed he had "the book all ready" a year before. It is likely that he brought the "ready" manuscript to England. With the funds generated by the successful exhibitions, Brown was now able to publish it. He probably returned to the Manchester area to work on the book. Brown and Smith had left their possessions, presumably including the manuscript, there, and the only name to appear in the credits for this edition of the *Narrative* besides Brown's is that of Thomas Gardiner Lee, the clergyman from Salford, who provided the book's introduction. Salford is next to Manchester, where the book was printed.[33]

Lee's introduction was dated 8 April 1851. By then, Brown and Smith had resumed touring. They opened on 1 April for five days at Burnley, thirty-six miles north of Manchester. The *Manchester Examiner and Times* reported that they performed at "the Church of England Literary Institution; the attendance was numerous, and seemed much pleased with the lectures." By mid-April they were in Yorkshire, the county to the east of Lancashire, for "well attended" exhibitions at the "Wesleyan School-room" in Skipton. "We earnestly recommend all those who wish to form correct opinions of the abominations of American slavery, to patronize Mr. B's panorama," declared the Skipton correspondent for the *Leeds Mercury*. "The young especially should not neglect the opportunity, as they may derive more information from the impressive scenery than they can do from the perusal of many works written on the subject."[34]

On 3 May, a correspondent told Samuel May Jr., the Boston abolitionist, that "Box Brown I believe is now in Yorkshire . . . I saw in the papers he had advertised exhibiting his panorama of slavery. I am afraid he will not find it [a success] as W. W. Brown has one also exhibiting, which I hear is much better." That same day the *Leeds Mercury* reported that Henry Box Brown had met "with extraordinary success" in Bingley, a town between Skipton and Leeds. For three nights "the large room at the Odd Fellows' Hall has been crowded to suffocation," and on the last night Brown had arranged a second performance "at ten o'clock" to accommodate the crowds. One night "a gentleman called out when the performance was half done, 'Mr. Brown, we have seen sufficient; not that we are tired, but you show too much for so little a charge.'" Two local clergymen also addressed the audiences and passed "high praise on Mr. Brown's brilliant scenery and instructive lectures."[35]

Brown and Smith next went to Bradford, a manufacturing city of 103,000 five miles southeast of Bingley. "The theater of the Mechanics' Institute has been crowded every night during this week and last," the *Bradford Observer* reported on 8 May, "to witness the panorama of Mr. Henry Box Brown, depicting, in a striking and painful manner, the abominations and horrors of slavery, as it exists in the so-called liberty-loving states of America." At the close of the Friday exhibition three clergymen spoke and "manifested in good set terms" the "just indignation and horror of true Englishmen," according to the newspaper, which also noted that the facts of Brown's escape were "well known to all readers of newspapers."[36]

The next venue was Leeds, a city of 172,000 only a few miles from Bradford and a center of woolen manufacturing. The engagement at Leeds would prove a key event in Brown's career. It came two weeks after Bradford, and during the interim Brown must have obtained a supply of the new edition of his *Narrative*. At Leeds, "there was an active demand for the autobiography of Mr. Brown."[37]

Likely because he had books to sell, Brown planned a theatrical stunt to herald his Leeds appearance. A considerable amount of advance work went into this event. Handbills announced it, and advertisements appeared on 17 May in three Leeds newspapers. Two of them printed short articles calling attention to the ads.[38]

In a dramatic reenactment, Henry Box Brown would arrive at Leeds conveyed by railroad inside the "identical box" in which he had escaped from slavery. The *Leeds Mercury* reported that on 22 May 1851, "he was packed up in the box at Bradford" and "forwarded to Leeds" on the 6 P.M. train. "On arriving at the Wellington station, the box was placed in a coach and, preceded by a band of music and banners, representing the stars and stripes of America, paraded through the principal

GREAT ATTRACTION CAUSED in ENGLAND by Mr. HENRY BOX BROWN, a fugitive slave, that has made his escape from Richmond, in Virginia, to Philadelphia, a distance of 350 miles, locked up in a box, 3 feet 1 inch long, 2 feet wide, and 2 feet 6 inches high, will leave Bradford for Leeds, on Thursday next, May Twenty-second, at six o'clock P.M., accompanied by a band of music, packed up in the identical box, arriving in Leeds at half-past six, then forming a procession through the town to the Music-Hall, Albion-street, where Mr. Brown will be released from the box before the audience, and then will give the particulars of his escape from slavery, also the song of his escape. He will then show the great Panorama of American Slavery, which has been exhibited in this country to thousands, and patronized by the Nobility and Clergy.
Doors open at seven o'clock, to commence at eight precisely.
Admission—Front seats, 2s.; second seats, 1s. 6d.; gallery, 1s.
For further particulars see hand bills.
Tickets to be had at the Newspaper offices.

Leeds Mercury, 17 May 1851

streets of the town." The newspaper recorded that "the procession was attended by an immense concourse of spectators." James C. A. Smith "rode in the coach with the box, and afterwards opened it at the Music Hall."[39]

The "last 'resurrection' (as he calls it)" took place at 8:15 P.M. at the hall on Albion Street. One of the clergymen who had spoken at his Bradford exhibition, the Reverend Andrew Lynn, introduced him. Lynn, a Methodist New Connexion nonconformist, declared that "personal interviews with Mr. Brown, and other information" convinced him that Brown's "object was to enlighten the people of this country as to the horrors of American slavery." The *Leeds Times* reported that "the entertainment then commenced, and gave great satisfaction to an audience which was by no means so numerous as the merits of Mr. Brown and his panorama deserve."[40]

Brown's journey confined him in the box for two and three-quarter hours. The circumstances were of course far different than those of his escape. This time he was in control of events and would not be put on his head. He could speak to Smith and listen to the fanfare, and he might have had a few peepholes in the box. Nonetheless the choice of this method was telling. If it was publicity that Henry Box Brown sought, there were ways to get it without the carnival atmosphere. For British abolitionists such as John Bishop Estlin, who had complained that the handbills for William Wells Brown and Ellen and William Craft were "too showman like," Brown's staged arrival at Leeds would have been beyond the pale. After the train ride and parade, Brown did retain a veneer of respectability when a minister introduced him at the theater. He had not moved entirely out of the orbit of proper reform. But certainly more than one abolitionist read accounts of this event with dismay.

Following the reports of the celebrated opening there was nothing further in the press about the Leeds run. Perhaps the initial publicity carried the show, or perhaps Brown relied on handbills to promote the exhibition. Admission prices were two shillings for "Front seats," one shilling and six pence for the "second seats," and one shilling for the gallery. After a disappointing first night, the *Leeds Mercury* noted that "Mr. Brown, on Thursday evening, announced a reduction of his charges for admission; and stated that the scholars and teachers in Sunday schools would be admitted by special arrangement." With a publication to sell, admission fees were not his only source of income, but to move his books Brown needed audiences.[41]

In its coverage the *Leeds Mercury* mentioned that Henry Brown "was held a slave by Mr. William Barrett, tobacco merchant, who is now visiting the Great Exhibition in London." The exhibition, best remembered today for its centerpiece, the Crystal Palace, attracted many foreign visitors. Special newspaper supplements published lists of passengers arriving in England to attend. Because Brown's new *Narrative* gave his master's name, an alert reader of the book and of the visitor lists might have made the connection.

British readers doubtless found Brown's new narrative an easier go than did American readers of the 1849 *Narrative*. The "First English Edition" of the *Narrative of the Life of Henry Box Brown* was published in Manchester, probably early in May 1851. The book opens with a short preface in the author's voice justifying the narrative's publication. The Reverend Thomas Gardiner Lee's six-page introduction follows, incorporating a number of testimonials from others about Henry Box Brown. The narrative proper fills the next sixty-one pages. It includes the lyrics to his arrival hymn and concludes with the lyrics to the song "Escape from Slavery of Henry Box Brown." An eight-page appendix gives Brown's version of the story of "the Shovel and the Hoe" and "a few specimens of the laws of a slave-holding people." The single illustration is the frontispiece, an engraving based on the 1850 Boston *Resurrection* lithograph. There are numerous typographical errors throughout the book, suggesting a production that for cost-saving was hurried rather than careful.[42]

The 1851 *Narrative* contains much material not found in the 1849 *Narrative*. It gives the names of Brown's siblings, of John Barret and William Barret, and of the factory's overseers before John F. Allen. It tells more about the First African Baptist Church and details Brown's encounters with Nancy Brown's masters. James C. A. Smith, who was not named in the 1849 *Narrative* because he was still in Richmond, is prominent in the 1851 *Narrative*. He is referred to as "Dr. Smith," which is a little confusing because his service as a dentist, the source of his honorific, is not mentioned. Samuel A. Smith, still held in the Virginia penitentiary and therefore yet at risk, is identified only as the "storekeeper." The new volume also omits the names of Brown's parents, whom he said by then had gained their freedom, and the name of the minister who bought his wife and children.

The title page states that the book was "Written by Himself." Although the 1851 *Narrative* is more directly Brown's expression than the 1849 *Narrative*, Brown did not put the words on paper. Compared to Charles Stearns's elaborations in the 1849 *Narrative*, the work of the writer for the 1851 *Narrative* is more transparent. The new edition stays closer to the story, and it is clearer that Brown was the original source. Only he would have known the many new names presented. For example, when detailing the division of the estate among John Barret's sons, which included Brown and his mother and siblings, the 1851 *Narrative* gives the names of Barret's sons, including one identified as "Stronn." That is undoubtedly the amanuensis's rendering of Brown's spoken pronunciation of Strachan, the maiden name of John Barret's wife and the middle name of two of Barret's sons.[43]

Like that of the 1849 *Narrative*, the basic account of the 1851 *Narrative* seems authentic. Its telling is unreliable at times, as when it presents stilted dialogue that could hardly have been remembered in any case. In addition, the new narrative still suffers from a surplus of rhetorical flights. It is hardly plausible that when Brown spoke of the pain he felt when his wife and children were sold away, his exact words

Title Page from *Narrative of the Life of Henry Box Brown* (Manchester, England, 1851). The verse is likely of English origin.

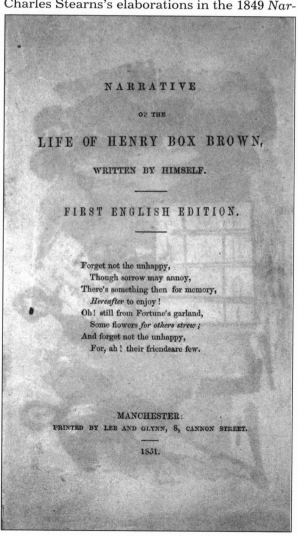

NARRATIVE

OF THE

LIFE OF HENRY BOX BROWN,

WRITTEN BY HIMSELF.

FIRST ENGLISH EDITION.

Forget not the unhappy,
Though sorrow may annoy,
There's something then for memory,
Hereafter to enjoy!
Oh! still from Fortune's garland,
Some flowers *for others strew;*
And forget not the unhappy,
For, ah! their friends are few.

MANCHESTER:
PRINTED BY LEE AND GLYNN, 8, CANNON STREET.

1851.

in singing for the purpose of obtaining money to assist those who were buying and selling their fellow-men. He thought at that moment he felt reproved by Almighty God for lending his aid to the cause of slave-holding religion; and it was under this impression he closed his book and formed the resolution which he still acts upon, of never singing again or taking part in the services of a pro-slavery church. He is now in New England publicly advocating the cause of emancipation.

After we had sung several other pieces we commenced the anthem, which run thus—

> Vital spark of heavenly flame,
> Quit, O! quit the mortal frame,—

these words awakened in me feelings in which the sting of former sufferings was still sticking fast, and stimulated by the example of Dr. Smith, whose feelings I read so correctly, I too made up my mind that I would be no longer guilty of assisting those bloody dealers in the bodies and souls of men ; and ever since that time I have steadfastly kept my resolution.

I now began to get weary of my bonds ; and earnestly panted after liberty. I felt convinced that I should be acting in accordance with the will of God, if I could snap in sunder those bonds by which I was held body and soul as the property of a fellow man. I looked forward to the good time which every day I more and more firmly believed would yet come, when I should walk the face of the earth in full possession of all that freedom which the finger of God had so clearly written

Page from *Narrative of the Life of Henry Box Brown* (Manchester, England, 1851). Page 49 contains text probably written in the United States.

130

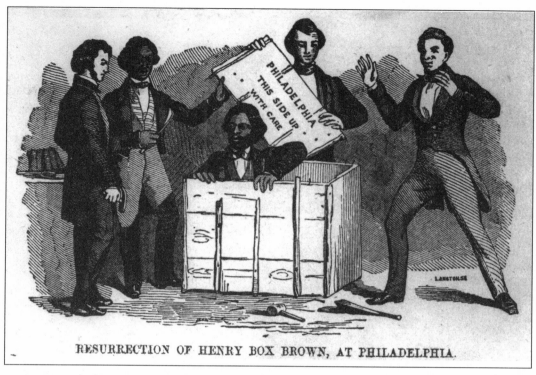

RESURRECTION OF HENRY BOX BROWN, AT PHILADELPHIA.

Above: *Resurrection of Henry Box Brown,* 1851. An engraver named Langton was engaged by Brown for the 1851 *Narrative,* published in Manchester, England, and based the frontispiece illustration on the 1850 Boston lithograph, **below.**

THE RESURRECTION OF HENRY BOX BROWN AT PHILADELPHIA.
Who escaped from Richmond Va in a Box 3 feet long 2½ ft deep and 2 ft wide

were "those internal pangs which are felt by the soul when the hand of the merciless tyrant plucks from one's bosom the object of one's ripened affections." This passage, in fact, has the ring of the overwrought prose of Charles Stearns, and it is not beyond possibility that Stearns had a hand in the 1851 *Narrative*.[44]

There is every reason to conclude that the main text for the "First English Edition" was actually produced in Massachusetts in the spring of 1850. There is no dated material in the 1851 *Narrative* subsequent to April 1850, except in the Reverend Lee's Introduction. In telling of the Christmas 1848 choir performance at First African Baptist Church, and of the moment that James C. A. Smith stopped singing, the 1851 *Narrative* states that Smith "is now in New England publicly advocating the cause of emancipation." That description of Smith's activities was accurate early in 1850 but not when the new book appeared. If the Reverend Lee or some other friend read the manuscript and perhaps did some editing, this statement still slipped through into the 1851 *Narrative*.[45]

The writer of the 1851 *Narrative* remains unidentified. The author reinterviewed Brown so it would have been someone present in the Boston area in early 1850. The production of the panorama helped Brown to open doors, and he might have found a writer through, for example, Josiah Wolcott's connections with post–Brook Farm literary circles. It is also possible that Charles Stearns restrained himself and rewrote Brown's narrative or that he collaborated with another person. Whoever wrote it, compared to the 1849 *Narrative*, Henry Box Brown's story in the 1851 *Narrative* stands more nearly on its own, and of the two the 1851 *Narrative of the Life of Henry Box Brown* is the superior edition.[46]

"Nothing good to write about"

Henry Box Brown and James C. A. Smith did well with their exhibition in the first five months of 1851. Unfortunately, that success bred conflict. James C. A. Smith's letters that summer to American abolitionists describe how their friendship came apart.

The pair had left their accrued earnings for safekeeping with Hannah Walton, one of the sisters who were shoe dealers in Manchester. According to Smith, without his knowledge Brown went to Walton and "took nearly all the money." The incident sparked a dispute that became an unreconcilable breach.[47]

Henry Box Brown's chance to appropriate the money likely came between the end of the Bradford exhibition about 8 May and his boxed entrance into Leeds on 22 May. Brown probably traveled to Manchester then to pick up copies of his new *Narrative* from the printer. The exhibition at Leeds continued until about the end of May, and it was probably shortly thereafter, at the beginning of June 1851, that Smith learned what Brown had done.[48]

The discovery upset Smith, for he believed the money was equally his. "From the time of our going togeather before the Panorama was <u>completed</u> to the present time," he wrote, "I never have received any thing from the consurn.—only our expences being <u>paid</u> therefrom—and our a greements was that we would save what we could after expeces paid . . . as we intended saving Our moneys to geather as we were partners in the Business." Having followed their Manchester friends' advice to have someone trustworthy keep the funds, said Smith, "when the amount reached to near a hundred Pounds in English money—Brown gets nearly all of it within ten Pounds."[49]

The money that Brown took was a significant sum. The Reform Bill of 1832 defined voters as men paying at least ten pounds per year in rent, a requirement that excluded much of the English working class. A weekly income of five or six pounds supported a family at a middle-class standard.

After Smith found out the money was gone he confronted Brown. Brown "at length said I did not have any part in the Consurne at all," wrote Smith, and denied him "any right or title to any Part of the <u>Panorama</u>." Brown and Smith had apparently returned to Manchester by then, for Smith discovered that Brown "had picked the lock of my trunk and had taken therefrom all papers that whould sure what right I had in the Consurn." Brown had depended on Smith to conduct their correspondence in the past, consequently Smith may have held some of their letters and other important papers. If Brown were determined to assert his ownership of the enterprise, taking possession of these documents would have hindered Smith's claims to the contrary. Others soon became aware of the dispute, and, Smith wrote, Brown stated to them "that he did not in tend to give me a cent."[50]

On 13 June 1851 Brown gave Smith a notice of discharge. "I here by give you notice that I have nofuther acassion for your services and that in future I shall not supply you with meat, clothes, and other necessaries as I formerly have done as payment for your services." As transcribed by Smith, the discharge note was signed "H. Box. <u>Brown</u>."[51]

"Now sir could you have thought such a thing," asked Smith, surprised and hurt by the discharge. "To prevent an exposure and for the Sake of the Cause," antislavery friends "went and talk to Brown to see if they could get him to terams without making it any more Public than what it was." Though "they give him his own words," Brown resisted their mediation, continued Smith, until "after two or 3 weeks bother he mad an acknowledgement that we were equal <u>Partners</u>—but the money was all made away so that I could not get it."[52]

The chronology of Smith's account suggests that Brown's admission of partnership, if such it was, occurred about the beginning of July 1851. On 12 July Smith wrote to William Lloyd Garrison: "I am sorry to say that Henry Box Brown is not doing any good to the Cause." Smith was severe in his assessment of Brown. "When we first arrived in Liverpool—we made some progress in the anti-Slavery Cause but since then I am afread to say that [not] much good has been done by the Slave who escaped in the Box—but however I can not say much at this time."[53]

The rift became permanent. On 29 July 1851 the *London Gazette* published a legal notice, also printed in the *Manchester Guardian* on 9 August, officially ending the partnership. About a week later on 6 August, at the urging of English friends, James C. A. Smith wrote long letters of similar content to Syracuse abolitionist Gerrit Smith and to William Lloyd Garrison about the partnership's dissolution and "the mean acts of the man . . . whom I have done much for." To Gerrit Smith, James Smith regretted "that I have nothing good to write about." Almost two months after Brown had dismissed him, Smith was still upset. "You can see from the manner in which he tryed to put me of

with out a penny—that he must be a bad one," wrote Smith to Garrison. "I think he is worst then the tyrant himself," he continued in language that turned rhetorical, "for he is more like the proude pauper—<u>aristocrat</u> which grinds out of existance the manliness

NOTICE is hereby given, that the partnership heretofore subsisting between the undersigned HENRY BOX BROWN and JAMES CÆSAR ANTHONY SMITH, in the business or profession of exhibitors of a moving tableau or panorama, carried on by them in different parts of England, under the firm of "Brown and Smith," has been this day dissolved by mutual consent. The business in future will be carried on by Henry Box Brown alone, who will receive and pay all debts and sums of money respectively due to or owing by the late firm.—As witness the hands of the parties this twenty-fifth day of July, 1851.

H. B. BROWN.
J. C. A. SMITH.

Manchester Guardian, 9 August 1851

of its toiling victims and bathes itself in the blood and sweat of the slaughtered children of God."[54]

Smith explained to the American abolitionists what he believed to be the real reason behind Brown's actions. "You may wonder how such a change could have taken place with Brown," wrote Smith. "He is after geting a wife in this Country—one of the English fair sex." According to Smith, Henry Box Brown had been "telling the peopele that his wife could not be purched—but stated that he could by his children for the sume of fifteen hundred dollars." This statement is consistent with the message that "Hater of Slavery" sent to the *Liverpool Mercury*. In fact, James C. A. Smith said, in response to the letter that he had sent from Boston to Nancy Brown's owner, "the master of his wife said he would take $1500 for her and her children if Henry Box. Brown would promise to treat them kindly." Smith alluded to their further discussions on the topic. "I used to be teling him that he ought to try and get his wife and children which was in slavery before he thought of any thing else."[55]

By Smith's account, Brown's untruthful statements that his wife could not be redeemed were at the heart of their conflict. "A number of persons do not belive no tale like that," Smith said, and some of them asked Smith "whither Brown could get his wife or not if he had the money—I did not wish to do any harm—but I could not tell a lie and know it—therefore I said—that in accordance with what the man wrote to us who owned them—I said she could be purchesed." Because "I told the truth," Smith concluded, "I think that has given so much offence to him and made him try to do me this harm."[56]

In his letter to Garrison, Smith stated that when they were first in England and "we were not doing very well," Brown "appeared to be quite easey but after we began to do pretty well—it seems that he is not the same man." Smith wrote to Gerrit Smith that "I must tell the truth tho it may be Bad—Brown has be heaved very bad sence he have been here—and in deed his Character is that bad I am ashamed to tell it, for he drinks smoke, gamble, sware and do many other things too Bad—to think off."[57]

These were serious charges, and Smith, perhaps with second thoughts about what he had written, modified them in a postscript. He explained that he did not mean that Brown was "with those that is generally found in the Rum and Brandy vaults," and clarified by listing particulars. Brown indulged "in all such habits as drinking—what is Calld. Rasbury wine, pop, pepermint, Sampson, Jinny Lind, soabrity, gingerrote, ginger Beer, gingerade, Blackbeer, and many other things of that nature." Brown also used tobacco—"smoking pipe, segars and chewing tobacco takin snuff"—and, wrote Smith, Brown gambled, "playing doman noes—dice, drafts, and Begertels—& such as I do not remember the names." To Garrison, he wrote, "you can understand from this that I did not mean he was a regler drunkerd."[58]

Intemperance was not much tolerated in the English moral reform movement. If Brown had strayed from the path of disciplined behavior that many of their antislavery friends expected and to which Smith adhered, Smith's specifics indicate that only by the strictest standards was Brown a libertine. Smith, whose return address was that of Thomas Holliday Barker, the Manchester temperance campaigner, stated that "the friends see the corse that Brown i[s] persuing is not to do the cause of humanity any good."[59]

Once their conflict played out to the official dissolution of their partnership, the two former comrades parted ways. No record of any further contact between them has been found. Smith wrote that all involved worked to keep the affair no "more Public than it was," and it seems to have remained a private matter. The Reverend John Kitton, the Preston clergyman who had provided an endorsement letter for Brown,

10/ for Browns wife and Children —
and the Master of his wife said he
would take $1500 for her and her
children if Henry Box Brown
would promies to treat them kindy
this Brown has never acknowledge to
any person — and I used to ask him
why did he not tell when he was asked
the name of the Man that Own his
wife and where she lived he said
be cause the abolitionist would fret
the Man so much that he would
refuse to sell his wife — I believe that
until I knew better he have told the
people that the man who own is wife
wrote him word that he would not
sell the woman — but said he will sell
the three small children for fifteen
hundred dollars and all belong to the same
person — and a member of persons don't
belive no tale like that — and be cause I
told the truth. this is the reason he
have thus treated me cruel — I have
the Copy of the letter the mans name &
place any time you wish to have it —
for it ought to be published — — I am
yours Oft   James C. A. Boxer, Smith

Tenth of Eleven Pages of Letter. J. C. A. Boxer Smith to Gerrit Smith, 6 August 1851.

stated later that the pair toured "no longer as partners, but as opponents." Yet he did not assign blame for the breakup and remained willing to help Brown. The fact of the separation, announced in the press, circulated more widely than the reasons for it.[60]

The only accounts of the split, beyond the published notices of separation, are James C. A. Smith's letters to the American abolitionists. Smith felt wronged but was also scrupulously honest, and there are no reasons to doubt that his representation of what happened was fairly accurate. Even so, Henry Box Brown was hardly as bad as Smith painted him.

The 1851 *Narrative* tells how overseer Wilson Gregory had encouraged young Brown to use tobacco that he might better judge the factory's products. In Richmond, too, Brown probably gambled. Smith's accounting of the beverages that Brown consumed seems to include only beer and wine. The variety of flavors that Smith listed— raspberry, peppermint, ginger—suggests that Brown was literally tasting the fruits of liberty. Slavery was a condition of deprivation, and what Brown before had been denied he now sampled. A dispute that began over money escalated to encompass the differences between the sober Smith and the gregarious Brown. Smith voiced his disapproval of actions that, although illustrative of Brown's character, did not define it.[61]

More fundamental was Smith's charge that Brown had falsely told English friends that Nancy Brown could not be redeemed from slavery. Smith recalled that Brown's prevarication on the matter dated to Smith's arrival in Boston, when Brown had said his wife's master "would not answer any letters." Smith asked him "why did he not tell when he was asked the name of the man that own his wife and where she lived." Brown replied that "the abolitionist would fret the man so much that he would refuse to sell his wife," wrote Smith. "I believe that un till I knew <u>better</u>." In England, the pattern continued, for "Brown have been telling the peopele that his wife could not be purched," a story of convenience, Smith concluded, because he sought a new wife.[62]

Henry Box Brown's side in the dispute is unrecorded, except indirectly in Smith's letters. He obviously saw things differently than Smith. By May 1851 almost three years had passed since Brown had lost his wife and children. By his own account he mourned deeply, and then, the tears shed, he became resolute and struck out anew. He was "resurrected" and since had moved a long way from his former life as a slave in Virginia.

In Boston, according to Smith, Brown was already deflecting the notion of purchasing his family. Perhaps Brown's vision for his new life resisted the idea that the past he had escaped should take so large a place in it.[63] Nevertheless, the goal of redeeming his family became prominently associated with the exhibition in Great Britain. Brown may have neither initiated nor emphasized that objective, and his illiteracy may have prevented him from fully realizing how importantly it featured in newspaper coverage of the exhibition. Yet he does seem to have traded on a declared purpose that was not his actual intention. In the glow of full halls and some celebrity, Brown apparently came to believe that he could play one role on stage and a different one in private.[64]

Public figures routinely practice such deceptions, but James C. A. Smith objected and would not lie for Brown. Smith's letters suggest that his revelations to their English friends angered Brown. If Brown had said his wife could not be purchased, and this story had gained circulation, his comrade's contradiction was damaging to his reputation. Brown likely perceived Smith's honesty as a breech of trust or even as a betrayal. Brown apparently believed that his partner's loyalty was no longer to him first, and, with the justification that it was his fame that attracted audiences to the exhibitions, he asserted his right to the savings.

Smith wrote Garrison that "Box Brown have told the friends here that none of the abolitionist in the United States did not give him any thing nor never done any thing for him." Although Brown may have spoken in the heat of argument, his words conveyed an attitude that rejected dependence. He would not have his freedom of action limited by obligations to antislavery friends. With the success of the exhibition, Brown may have felt that he was ready to take his chances outside the antislavery camp. The tour selling his first *Narrative* had been remunerative; the new edition offered a similar opportunity.[65]

Brown was certainly thinking as a showman when he planned his well-advertised box trip to Leeds. Imagine the scenario: After setting that scheme in motion, he traveled to Manchester. There he took the saved funds and lifted the papers from Smith's trunk. If his action was out of retribution he was also practical, for he needed the business papers and the working capital to become independent. Brown found a new place of deposit, picked up the books, and returned to Bradford to stage his publicity event.

An unsuspecting James C. A. Smith accompanied the box on the train from Bradford and then sat next to it on the coach for the parade through the streets of Leeds, amid crowds attracted by the band, banners, and box. With Brown hidden, Smith was at the center of attention. All along, Brown, inside the box, knew what he had done in Manchester. Smith, outside the box, was in the dark, little knowing that this would be his last exhibition with Brown. Much as his resurrection from the box at Philadelphia came to be a symbol of transformation, Henry Box Brown's second resurrection from the box at the Music Hall in Leeds marks another stage of his self-liberation.

Brown's independence came at a high personal price and by blunt means. Brown may have found fault with Smith, but even so he cast off a brave and steadfast friend whose gravest sin against him was to tell the truth. For "all my time and labor," lamented Smith, he received little if any money and no gratitude. The split pushed Brown outside of organized antislavery activism. Smith told Gerrit Smith that the English friends thought the American abolitionists "ought to know those that are not worthy to be numbered with your <u>rank</u>." Correspondents who had previously mentioned Brown's progress ceased doing so. In subsequent years there were a number of gatherings of fugitive slaves in Great Britain, under the aegis of various antislavery societies, but there is no record of Henry Box Brown's attending any of them.[66]

At least in part, however, Brown was out of touch with organized abolitionism in Britain by choice. If he exercised his freedom in a manner that Smith and the English antislavery friends disapproved, if he sought to marry again and indulged his tastes, those decisions were Brown's to make. He had escaped the walls of slavery. If organized antislavery proved to have barriers to freedom, he would escape again.

Chapter Eight

African Prince

On the Circuit

After the dissolution of the partnership Henry Box Brown took full possession of the panorama. Whether James C. A. Smith received anything from the enterprise is unknown. In return for the accoutrements to the exhibition, Brown may have paid Smith a sum to settle their accounts.

Before he could exhibit again, Brown had to regroup. He and Smith had operated the show as a team, and he would not find the same dedication in any new partner. Essential to replace were Smith's writing skills. John Kitton reported that Brown was "very illiterate—could read but not write," and an exhibition required advertising, contracts, and other written documents. In addition Brown would miss the assistance of antislavery friends. Smith's letters named a number of friends who had helped previously and doubtless sided with Smith in the conflict. Although Brown may have retained some allies, his prospects depended on finding his way outside of antislavery circles.

Although probably with not a little scrambling, Henry Box Brown did prove resourceful. Sometime in the latter part of 1851 he went back on the road. The new tour took the exhibition through Cheshire, the county to the south and west of Lancashire, and Staffordshire, the county south of Cheshire. One account reports that Brown visited the group of towns that were called the Staffordshire Potteries for their manufacturing of chinaware. In March 1852 Brown reached Wolverhampton in southern Staffordshire.[1]

As Brown's staged arrival in his box at Leeds had signaled, his conduct of the exhibition was becoming more "showman like." By its nature Brown's panorama always had more of the popular show about it than the usual forms of antislavery advocacy, and Brown's publicity now played like the brassiest of entertainments. His advertisement in the *Wolverhampton and Staffordshire Herald* promised an "Unrivalled Treat!" In the *Wolverhampton Chronicle* he was equated with the Hungarian revolutionary hero as "The American Kossuth!!!" Not only had the panorama been "exhibited to three hundred and sixty-five thousand persons since its arrival in this country," but it had official imprimatur: "Mr. Henry Box Brown is traveling under the patronage of the Ministers, Superintendents, and Magisterial authorities of Lancashire, Yorkshire, Cheshire, and Staffordshire."

As for the exhibition itself, there was an opening act by "the celebrated Italian Minstrels," singing selections from opera, and the scenes were "accompanied by the celebrated Italian Harpists." (Likely a change of costume enabled some of the same performers, who were possibly not of Italian descent, to man both groups.) "At the conclusion of the Exhibition," stated the advertisement in the *Herald*, "Mr. Brown will sing a Song descriptive of his escape, and several other Plantation Melodies, and exhibit the identical box in which he made his escape."[2]

If he was spicing up the packaging, Brown was not forsaking the cause. At the center of Brown's exhibition there remained an antislavery moving panorama. But Brown's immediate priority was to gain the measure of independence that derived from a profitable business. Adding an opening act and marketing the show as entertainment were steps to attracting the good attendance that he needed. Brown probably continued to lecture under religious or reform auspices when the opportunity arose. By not depending on such sponsors, however, he remained unencumbered. His key to success was to establish his show on the circuit.

The historian Richard Altick observes that during this period "no English trait was more widespread throughout the entire social structure than the relish for exhibitions." For English entertainment in the 1850s, London was unmatched in breadth and scale. There, among so many grand offerings, Brown's exhibition would not have stood out. Beyond London, on the circuit, *Mirror of Slavery* had strong selling points: the powerful subject of slavery, a vivid yet morally instructive moving panorama, authentic music, and Henry Box Brown himself.[3]

The more typical antislavery format then was the lecture, of which there were many, including not a few given by African Americans. In Staffordshire at the same time as Brown, for example, "Mr. A. Benson, a gentleman of colour, of New York," lectured at Litchfield on the "Evils and Present Aspect of American Slavery, and the way in which the British public may assist in Abolishing Slavery in the United States." John Brown, a fugitive slave from Georgia, spoke on "American Slavery" at Stourbridge to a room "crowded to excess," and then lectured at Kinver on "Cotton Cultivation in the West Indies by Free Negroes."[4]

The black abolitionists on the circuit represented only a small fraction of the multitude of lecturers on many topics speaking in every English city and town. Madame Mario spoke on "Italy and Garibaldi" and the Reverend Spence offered one of the many series of "Lectures to the Working Class." Dr. F. R. Lees, one of the abolitionist friends mentioned in James C. A. Smith's letters, presented "A course of Three Lectures, demonstrating the Scientific and Scriptural basis of Tee totalism." There were numerous "Astronomical Lectures," including that of a Mr. Holden "with all the new discoveries, illustrated by his beautiful transparent ORRERY, 24 feet in diameter."[5]

Musical performers were also numerous on the circuit. George Buckland presented "his Grand Musical Entertainment, entitled 'The Market Town'"; Miss Lizzy Stuart gave a musical show called the "Ploughman Poet"; and Miss Clara Seyton performed "The Omnibus," in which she "introduced a variety of characters in costume, and after each character a song." A standard format was the variety show: one at Wigan Theater, for instance, included Edward Bulwer Lytton's "'Lady of Lyons' followed by a parlour entertainment by Mr. Dewhurst and his family"; next "That licks me," a comic song by Mr. B. Ware; then dancing by Mr. McCarthy and Mademoiselle Camille; and finally "the laughable farce of 'Box and Cox.'"[6]

The roster of touring performers offered a wide variety of talents. The versatile "Mr. Gallaher, the celebrated Solo-dramatic Ventriloquist," presented at one venue "Family Perplexities" in three acts; at another "Paddy's Knapsack, an illustration of Irish life"; and at a third venue "the Burlesque Character of Miss Josephine Jumbleton, in Full Bloomer Costume." Professor Chadwick lectured "to crowded audiences on Electro-Biology," and "Jacobs, the Wizard, Ventriloquist, and Improvisore," advertised his performance as "Comic Entertainment." Professor Wohlgermuth "gave a capital display of his magical art," and so it appears did Signor Blize, "the necromancer and celebrated plate dancer." Also there were circuses: Boorne's hippodrome circus, Quaglieni's Sardinian Circus, and the Great United States Circus, which advertised itself as the "Largest and most complete equestrian Establishment in the world, numbering 200 men and horses."[7]

Moving panoramas such as "Groves' Diorama of the Holy Land" maintained an educational cachet that could attract proper audiences. "The Great Moving Panorama of South Africa, Cape Colony, and the Kaffir War," and the "Panorama of Australia, by a Returned Emigrant" played to the nationalist spirit of Empire. A moving panorama "graphically portraying the ills of intemperance" carried a reform message. Mr. Davies's diorama "exhibited his complete view of curiosities in optical illusions; astronomical diagrams, the solar system, the earth's annual motion, a collection of wild beasts, and other amusing curiosities, including the female ghost." These panoramas were always narrated, and a number of them enhanced the performance in other ways. Advertisements noted that "Music Accompanies" the display of "Clare's Microscopic & Dioramic Exhibition." John Gadsby's "Illustrations of Biblical and Oriental Life" combined "a diorama consisting of twenty-three Oriental views" with "a large number of persons . . . attired in Eastern costume."[8]

Special oil paintings might constitute an exhibition by themselves, such as "Wellington Revisiting the Field at Waterloo," or "Selous's Two Grand Sacred Paintings" of Jerusalem. A new way to present views was the magic lantern, which used gaslight to project images painted on glass slides. Mr. Petrice exhibited "a series of dioramic views by means of a powerful magic lantern," and the Reverend Lewis illustrated his lecture on *The Pilgrim's Progress* "with the oxy-hydrogen lime light." After the development of the photographic glass-plate negative in the mid-1850s, Mr. Gregson was able to use a magic lantern to exhibit "his photographic dissolving views in the Odd Fellow's Hall."[9]

Blackface minstrels had sustained popularity in England beginning in the mid-1840s. The Ohio Minstrels "gave their delineations of negro life in the Lecture Hall . . . in a manner that elicited warm applause." The Christy Minstrels appeared so often that many different groups must have used the name. Indeed, one report stated that "The Chrystie Minstrels" performed so far below the "moderate" expectations of the audience that they were "several times hissed, and on leaving the rooms were assailed by the not inappropriate terms of 'duffers.'" The descriptive term Henry Box Brown used in his own advertisement, "Plantation Melodies," was one that audiences would have associated with the minstrels.[10]

The success of the blackface minstrels disseminated their misrepresentations of black character throughout Britain. Certainly many of those who attended Henry Box Brown's performances perceived him by way of the minstrel stereotypes, including well-meaning people who supported the antislavery cause. Although minstrels often played venues that proper persons did not patronize, "minstrel shows which appeared outside the music-halls appealed to a distinct audience of their own." In fact, states the historian J. S. Bratton, "the dissenting lower middle classes, the ministers, shop keepers, and respectable ladies"—prime audiences for Henry Box Brown's appeal—"who were in some ways the most deprived and repressed cultural group in the land, found it possible to go to minstrel shows." Partly because these shows served as "the only access the *respectable* popular audience had to certain liberating elements of popular entertainment," Bratton contends that many were susceptible to "the transfer of antislavery sympathy to black-face performers." In Britain as in America, abolitionist leanings did not preclude muddled conceptions of race.[11]

In spreading prejudice, the minstrels were not alone. During this period a number of written works of racialist thinking appeared in Britain, including in 1850 *The Races of Man* by Robert Knox, a pseudoscientific system of classification of the sort that George R. Gliddon promoted in the United States. The historian Nancy Stepan calls *The Races of Man* "a racial fantasy in which Saxons, Celts, gypsies, Jews, and the dark races of the world played out their biological destinies." Popular entertainments borrowed from such sources. Dr. Kahn's Grand Anatomical Museum offered a "Gallery of

All Nations," which included "upwards of sixty models, showing the various races of men on the earth, from the fair faced Caucasian to the most abject and degenerate specimen of the negro tribe." In England, states the historian Douglas Lorimer, "popular and literary sources were just as significant as scientific ones in the formation of the 'nigger' stereotype."[12]

Henry Box Brown, then, contended at two levels. His rivals in drawing an audience were the wide variety of entertainments on the English circuit. That challenge faced all touring performers. For Brown there was also opposition to his panorama's message, derived partly from politics and class and largely from prejudice. This was a more difficult foe to counter.

Brown was well able to compete at the level where his own efforts brought results. To publicize a show, advertisements in local newspapers were a standard means but not always sufficient. A newspaper advertisement for Banvard's panorama of the Mississippi after it left London to tour the circuit recommended that "for further Particulars see Small Bills, circulars, and descriptive Pamphlets." Another newspaper article described what was likely a common practice when it reported that "one of the unauthorized bill posters of the town . . . was engaged by the master of an itinerant equestrian corps to post his placards." To advertise his lectures on "American Slavery," with "illustrations presented by means of a Powerful Magic Lantern," Ebenezer F. Quant in 1854 employed what he called a circular—a single sheet printed on both sides and then folded to make four pages. The front page billed the show and the inner pages carried endorsements and quotations from positive reviews. A space on the first page remained blank so that Quant could add the location and time for specific appearances.[13]

Such prepared publicity materials reduced the showman's dependence on the newspapers for publicity. Editorial policies varied. Many towns had only one newspaper, and some did not carry advertisements for shows. Where one newspaper might supplement an advertisement with a favorable article, the

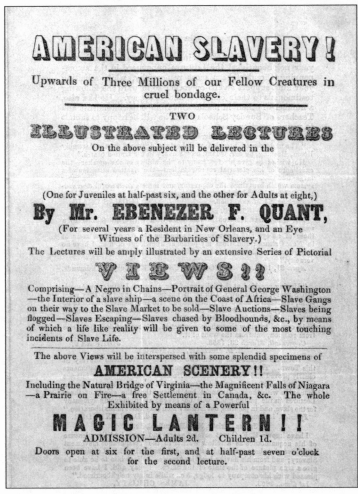

Ebenezer F. Quant Circular, 1854. Front page.

next might refuse the advertisement or give the show negative coverage.

Henry Box Brown encountered an unfriendly newspaper editor in March 1852 when he presented his panorama in Wolverhampton, Staffordshire, a town near the major manufacturing city of Birmingham. The open pit coalfields that caused the region to be known as the Black Country adjoined Wolverhampton. A few years later, Nathaniel Hawthorne wrote that the town reminded him "of Boston, though dingier." The exhibition began on Monday, 15 March, at the Corn Exchange, with performances scheduled through the next Saturday.[14]

The run began well, with several hundred in attendance opening night. Among those present was T. H. Brindley, the editor of the *Wolverhampton and Staffordshire Herald*.

> **CORN EXCHANGE, WOLVERHAMPTON.**
> **UNRIVALLED TREAT!**
> Under the distinguished Patronage of the Ministers, Superintendents, and Sabbath-School Teachers of Lancashire, Yorkshire, Cheshire, and Staffordsh re.
>
> MR. HENRY BOX BROWN, the celebrated American FUGITIVE SLAVE, who escaped from Slavery, packed as Luggage, in a box, 3ft. 1in. long, 2ft. wide, and 2ft. 6in. high, travelling a distance of 350 Miles!—from Richmond, Virginia, to Philadelphia, Pennsylvania, the journey occupying 27 hours, will exhibit his unrivalled American
>
> **PANORAMA OF SLAVERY,**
> On the Evenings of Monday, Tuesday, Wednesday, Thursday, Friday, and Saturday, March 15, 16, 17, 18, 19, and 20.
> The Scenes will be described by Mr. Henry Box Brown.
> Signor Antonio Abecco, Signor Michelangelo di Lonardo, and Vincent Abecco, the celebrated ITALIAN MINSTRELS, will introduce several splendid pieces from the Italian Opera of "Sonnambula," "Puritani," "Romeo o Giulietta," &c., &c. Duetto from the Opera of "Il Matrimonio Segreto," by Simarosa. Duet, "Suoni La Tromba," Bellini.
> At the conclusion of the Exhibition Mr. Brown will sing a Song descriptive of his escape, and several other Plantation Melodies, and exhibit the identical box in which he made his escape.
> This Exhibition has been visited by 365,000 persons since its arrival in this country.
> Admission.—Front Seats, 1s.; Second Seats, 6d.; Gallery, 4d.
> Doors will be open at Seven; Panorama commence moving at Eight precisely.
> 5:77

"Unrivalled Treat!" Advertisement from *Wolverhampton and Staffordshire Herald,* 10 March 1852

There is reason to believe that Brindley came to Brown's exhibition predisposed to scoff. The previous month he had published a critical account of a lecture on slavery in Dudley "by an itinerant Negro, to a select audience, numbering something less than a dozen persons." After the lecture, "which was of the ordinary character, detailing the usual amount of horrors &c.," the article said that "the lecturer retired to a public house" and passed the evening "in the exciting game of 'Knock-'em-down,' varied by an occasional throw of the dice, a little fighting, much swearing, and some excellent songs."[15]

At Brown's exhibition on opening night, a local schoolmaster named William Yateman sat near Brindley and the editor's companion, an American named Hobbs. As Brown displayed the panorama and described the scenes, Hobbs and Brindley grew vocal in expressing their opinions. Yateman admonished them two or three times, but the pair continued their ever-louder commentary. Early in the second half of the panorama, as Brown explained the scene "View of the Lake of the Dismal Swamp," Brindley asked Yateman, "Is it right the audience should be gulled in this way?" The schoolmaster responded, "If you are a man speak out like a man, it's a public lecture, and the lecturer will reply." Brindley then called out to Brown and asked him where the Dismal Swamp was. Brown replied correctly that it was in Virginia. Brindley persisted, "Is it not in North and South Carolina?" Brown said, "The swamp I am exhibiting is in Virginia." Hobbs, the American, jumped in, "It is evident he knows nothing about it; it is evident he was never there." Brown then asked that the gentleman wait until the close of the lecture when he would answer any further questions. "Shortly after, and indeed as each successive view passed," Yateman recalled, "Mr. Hobbs said they nearly all were incorrect, and both Brindley and Hobbs were ridiculing them."[16]

Undoubtedly Brown had experienced disruptions during previous performances and had developed ways of handling hecklers. Theatrical audiences of the era were not reluctant to speak out during performances. Although most comments were likely respectful, some were bound to have been rude, whether for reasons of racism or political opposition or from antagonism born of inebriation.

Editor Brindley was no mere heckler, however. In the next issue of his newspaper, he attacked in print. "Mr. Henry Box Brown's panorama," he began, "like his oral representation of slavery, is a gross and palpable exaggeration." Compared to "the best and most authentic descriptions of American slavery," which he specified as the "pictorial illustrations of the southern states" in the panoramas of Banvard, John R. Smith, and others, "the evidence of travellers in the slave States," and "the statements of even former slaves themselves," Brown's exhibition was "a jumbled mass of contradictions and absurdities, assertions without proof, geography without boundary, and horrors without parallel."[17]

As much as the panorama's supposed inaccuracies, Brindley also found Henry Box Brown himself offensive. The editor expressed wonderment that "clergymen and other respectable individuals, and even portions of the press" could endorse the "foppery, conceit, vanity, and egotistical stupidity of the Box Brown school." He stated that testimonials were read to the audience at the exhibition, "and they are full of fulsome compliment to the bejewelled 'darkey' whose portly figure and overdressed appearance bespeak the gullibility of our most credulous age and nation."

As the public exchange about the location of Dismal Swamp indicated, Brindley knew less about the South than he thought he did. Brown was being damned not by faint praise, but rather by false paint. The editor cited, as one proof of the inaccuracy of *Mirror of Slavery*, the pictures in Banvard's *Mississippi*, the panorama William Wells Brown had criticized for its "mild representation" of slavery. Brindley's language included "darkey," a word from the minstrel show, and he wrote that Brown's stories were "related in the richest nigger style," a descriptive phrase borrowed from the advertising copy for the Virginia Minstrels or Ethiopian Serenaders. It is notable that in his critique of Brown's exhibition Brindley appealed to the authority of other creative representations of slavery on the circuit.

The *Herald* article had an immediate impact on Brown's attendance. On Tuesday evening the audience was again several hundred, but by Friday night there were only thirty or forty in the audience. In a second article, entitled "The Nigger Panorama" and published on 24 March 1852, Brindley crowed. "It is gratifying to hear," he wrote, "that the nightly attendance has been meagre in the extreme" to see "the celebrated Box Brown" and "the terrible wonders of this sea-serpent-surpassing and fire-and-brimstone-smacking exhibition." The article again aimed at Brown personally, referring to him as "ludicrous and semi-baboonish," calling him "the bejewelled and oily negro," and stating that his "obese and comfortable figure and easy *nonchalance* remind one of various good things and sumptious living."[18]

Where Brown "had previously been in the habit of receiving from 50£. to 70£. a week," after the article "his receipts began to fall away immediately." A traveling show would rarely be extended credit and thus faced most of its expenses at the beginning of an engagement, with payments due for transportation, rental of the hall, advertising, and lodging. Box office receipts paid for daily living and replenished the kitty for the next engagement. The final shows, if the run was successful, produced the profit. Brindley's attack made the Wolverhampton engagement a financial disaster.[19]

Brown may have feared that the articles would diminish his audiences anywhere near Wolverhampton. He pulled out of Staffordshire and returned north to Lancashire, where the exhibition played Tyldsley and Leigh, both a few miles northwest of Manchester, and other towns that he had missed on the first tour. At some point in the spring or early summer of 1852 Brown took the exhibition to the far northwest of England, where it "did well" at Carlisle.

Brown did not let Brindley's articles pass, however. Great Britain's laws regarding libel were considerably more beneficial to a plaintiff than those of the United States, and Brown had suffered demonstrable financial damage. He obtained legal counsel and sued the *Wolverhampton and Staffordshire Herald* for libel. The case was heard on 28

July 1852, at Warwick, on the Midland Circuit, before a judge and "Common Jury." The proprietor of the *Herald*, a man named Smith, was the defendant. Brown's lawyers, Macaulay and Field, cited both of Brindley's articles as libels. Henry Box Brown appeared as a witness, and the *Times* (London) reported that "though his dress was rather fine, and he displayed some jewellery about his person, his manner of giving his evidence was quiet and creditable; and his pronunciation altogether correct." Yateman, the schoolmaster who had taken exception to Brindley's behavior at the Monday evening performance, testified that he "had visited and admired the plaintiff's panorama," and that Brown "did not speak in the ridiculous manner imputed to him" by Brindley.[20]

The *Herald*'s advocate told the jury that criticism of public performances was a part of the press's duty to protect the public from "such exaggerated, preposterous, and, to a certain extent, indecent exhibitions, as this panorama evidently was." In his summary the judge told the jurors "not to scan too nicely the language used with regard to the panorama itself," for criticism of such works should "not be fettered or restricted," but "observations made upon personal character" must be weighed "with more rigour." The jury found for Henry Box Brown and awarded him damages of one hundred pounds.[21]

It may have been a Pyrrhic victory. The *Times* (London) report on the proceeding also reprinted Brindley's two articles about Brown in their entirety. Thus the attacks were read far more widely than if Brown had not sued for libel. The *London Anti-Slavery Reporter* reprinted the account of the trial from the *Times* and declared that the result "affords a convincing proof that in this country, at least, the character and feelings of a coloured man cannot be outraged with immunity." Even persons sympathetic to Henry Box Brown, however, might have read Brindley's attack on Brown and his exhibition and accepted some part of it as warranted. The *Anti-Slavery Reporter* never again carried a story about Brown's performances.[22]

The historian R. J. M. Blackett observes that "what is interesting is that not one of the prominent blacks in Britain came to Brown's defense." He speculates that they may have decided that "to involve themselves in a debate on British racism would have been to run the risk of alienating potential support[ers]" of the antislavery cause. Their silence may have also represented further fallout from Brown's dispute with James C. A. Smith and from the subsequent negative assessment of Brown by English anti-slavery activists.[23]

"You have no doubt read the account of a suit brought by Box Brown against an editor for damages, in which he got a verdict for £100," wrote William Wells Brown from London to Wendell Phillips on 1 September 1852. In the letter Wells Brown expressed his disapproval of Box Brown's taste in fashion, and by implication his choice of lifestyle. "The editor was certainly to blame, yet Brown is a very foolish fellow, to say the least. I saw him some time since, and he had a gold ring on nearly every finger on each hand, and more gold and brass round his neck than would take to hang the bigest Alderman in London. And as to ruffles about the shirts, he had enough to supply any old maid with cap stuff, for half a century. He had on a green dress coat and white hat, and his whole appearance was that of a well dressed monkey." William Wells Brown clearly did not fathom such showiness; apparently he was either unfamiliar or unsympathetic with the custom, as among Richmond blacks, of dressing fancily for occasions like Sunday promenades. "Poor fellow," William Wells Brown concluded, "he is indeed to be pitied."[24]

If the attention was not all favorable, the libel case did bring Henry Box Brown publicity, that lifeblood of the showman. With his court-won award he moved forward. During 1852 he reprinted his narrative. The "Second English Edition" of the *Narrative of the Life of Henry Box Brown, written by Himself* is identical to the "First English Edition" except for the title page. It was a "Stereotyped Edition, Printed by Samuel Webb, Bilston." The size of the press run is unknown, but surviving copies are rare, suggesting that it was not large. Bilston is a town very near Wolverhampton. The proximity invites the speculation that Brown may have used some of his award to pay for the new printing.[25]

Tales of Slavery

We need not say here how "UNCLE TOM'S CABIN" has found its way into every home—how, on both sides of the Atlantic, it has created a sensation unknown in the history of literature.[26]

In March 1852, the same month that the *Wolverhampton and Staffordshire Herald* attacked Henry Box Brown, Harriet Beecher Stowe's *Uncle Tom's Cabin; or, Life Among the Lowly* was published in Boston. The novel quickly became the most widely known story about American slavery. The impact of *Uncle Tom's Cabin* in the United States and Great Britain grew ever larger when the book was adapted for theatrical presentation. A variety of new shows soon joined Henry Box Brown's panorama on the circuit.

Uncle Tom's Cabin had been serialized in the *National Era*, a Washington, D.C., newspaper, and the book appeared in print shortly before the last newspaper installment on 1 April 1852. In a few days 10,000 copies were sold, and within a year sales in the United States reached 300,000 copies, "then an unprecedented number for any book, except the Bible, in so short a period of time," the historian Thomas F. Gossett notes. The numbers were even larger in Great Britain. Because Stowe's work was not protected by copyright, her own "Author's Edition" competed with numerous pirated British editions. Gossett estimates that altogether nearly a million copies were sold there.[27]

Several London reviews of *Uncle Tom's Cabin* made reference to Henry Box Brown, an indication that the 30 July 1852 article in the *Times* (London) about his libel case had gained him some notoriety. In a review for the *London Daily News* on 4 August, the writer contrasted the measured approach of Harriet Beecher Stowe to "the exaggerations of Box Brown panoramas." Stowe "selects no hideous exceptional crimes of individual slaveholders," said the reviewer, implying that Brown did, and she "rejects everything that could disgust needlessly or offend unjustly." So far as is known, Brown had yet to perform in or near London. The reviewer's impression of the panorama must have been based on Brindley's hostile articles, as reprinted in the *Times*.[28]

The reviewer for the *London Morning Post* a month later drew a different lesson from Brown's case, which Stowe's book "brought forcibly to our recollection." By comparing the story of *Uncle Tom's Cabin* to the court's decision for Brown, "the contrast between English liberty and American liberty could not be better illustrated," declared the reviewer. "The black man, the fugitive slave, who had been hunted from the shores of America, recovered damages from the newspaper editor who had exceeded the fair bounds of criticism."[29]

It is unknown whether Henry Box Brown learned about these reviews, but there can be no doubt that he became aware of the "Tom-mania," as the *London Spectator* termed it, sweeping across Britain. A wide range of *Uncle Tom's Cabin* merchandise was soon available in stores. The advance of Tom-mania in the town of Preston, Lancashire, was likely typical. "The Author's Edition" was available there by September 1852, and pirated editions followed. Advertisements began in mid-October for a version of the novel to appear in thirteen weekly parts, with each installment to include two engravings "printed separately on the finest Plate Paper" by the celebrated illustrator George Cruikshank. Also in October, Preston readers were offered *The Uncle Tom's Cabin Almanack or Abolitionist Memento for 1853*. The *Almanack* borrowed the name of Stowe's novel but not its text. It featured an almanac page for each month, a variety of articles on antislavery topics, and twenty illustrations. Although the *Almanack* included stories of escapes from slavery and profiles of eight black abolitionists, and Brown could hardly have been unknown to the book's compilers, neither he nor his famous escape were mentioned, an exclusion that perhaps reflected the bad reputation of Henry Box Brown in certain abolitionist circles.[30]

A Preston advertisement in November 1852 pointed toward the adaptations of the novel for the stage, offering the book, S*ongs, Duets, &c from* UNCLE TOM'S CABIN. In December, "Messrs. Saqui & Miranda" gave a musical entertainment of *Uncle Tom's Cabin* in Preston, performed "by a party of vocalists from the Liverpool and Manchester concerts," with "the songs composed and arranged to give a vivid description of American slavery." By then, English theatrical adaptations were plentiful, with six dif-

ferent versions of *Uncle Tom's Cabin* on the London stage, and across the country eleven additional shows plus four pantomimes.[31]

The *Uncle Tom's Cabin* concerts were not the first theatrical adaptation in Preston. Presented for two weeks in November–December 1852 was the *Panorama of Uncle Tom's Cabin*, with "Mr. E. Woods, lecturer." The *Preston Chronicle and Lancashire Advertiser* reported that "audiences have been large, owing chiefly to the attendance of scholars from Sunday and day schools, who testified their approbation of the exhibition by loud plaudits." Enhancing the show was "the singing and piano-forte accompaniment of several pieces on the subject of American slavery." A Preston correspondent reported later that James C. A.

EXCHANGE ROOMS, PRESTON.
THIS EVENING,
AND EVERY EVENING DURING THE NEXT WEEK, THE
GRAND PANORAMA
OF
UNCLE TOM'S CABIN :
OR, THE HORRORS OF AMERICAN SLAVERY,
By *Harriet Beecher Stowe*,

PAINTED ON TEN THOUSAND FEET of CANVASS, by two celebrated Artists, and accompanied with MUSICAL MELODIES illustrating the subject.

Superintendents of Sabbath Schools are respectfully informed that Scholars will be admitted at Half Price.

There will be Exhibitions on the afternoons of Monday, Tuesday, Wednesday, Thursday, and Friday, at three o'clock, for the benefit of Boarding and Day Schools.

Doors open for Evening Exhibitions at seven o'clock, to commence at eight precisely.

An early visit is requested, as its stay is limited.

Reserved Seats, 1s. ; Second do., 6d. ; Back do., 3d.

Programmes of Scenes to be had at the doors each evening.

Preston Pilot, 4 December 1852

POSITIVELY FOR SIX NIGHTS ONLY.
IN THE EXCHANGE ROOMS, LUNE-STREET.
MR. HENRY BOX BROWN
WILL open, on Monday next, February 28th, his great AMERICAN PANORAMA OF SLAVERY, being his farewell exhibitions previous to retiring.

Prices of Admission:—Front Seats, 1s.; Second Seats, 6d.; Back Seats, 3d.

Remember—Saturday, March 5th will positively be the last night.

Doors open at Seven, to commence at Eight.

Preston Chronicle, 26 February 1853

Smith, Henry Box Brown's erstwhile partner, had been there in this period "with a panorama purporting to illustrate *Uncle Tom's Cabin*." It is possible that Smith was associated with Woods's panorama and had been one of the performers of the songs about slavery.[32]

For Henry Box Brown, the adaptations of *Uncle Tom's Cabin* to the stage and especially to the moving panorama represented a new kind of competition. Few of the numerous antislavery lecturers on the pre–*Uncle Tom* circuit had offered a theatrical presentation comparable to Brown's. The new shows lessened to some extent the singularity of Brown's exhibition. Of course, when *Uncle Tom's Cabin* brought the subject of American slavery to the fore in Britain, that attention had the potential to be a benefit beyond any loss of audience to the new shows.

At the end of February 1853, about three months after Woods's *Panorama of Uncle Tom's Cabin* played there, Henry Box Brown arrived in Preston with his exhibition. "During the present week," the *Preston Chronicle* reported, "Mr. Henry Box Brown has been exhibiting his painting of scenes in the life of the American slave, in the Exchange

OPENING OF THE MYSTERIOUS BOX IN PHILADELPHIA.

A Leeds Woodcut. Antislavery activists in Leeds perceived the "want of a cheap variety of well-written, judiciously-selected, and popular Anti-Slavery Tracts," intended "for distribution after public meetings, lectures, and on all suitable occasions." So they published a series of eighty-two tracts, from one to twenty-eight pages each, with a total printing of a half-million copies. The tracts were collected in a volume entitled *Five Hundred Thousand Strokes For Freedom,* noted by the *Anti-Slavery Watchman* in December 1853: "We have before us the first eighty-two, bound in a neat wrapper, price 2s."

Number 35 in the series was entitled "Singular Escapes From Slavery." In eight pages it featured the stories of Henry Box Brown and William and Ellen Craft, and presented this illustration, one of the "woodcuts, expressly executed" for the series. The tract is noteworthy as the only other piece of British antislavery literature found to feature Brown, besides the two editions of his narrative.

Rooms." The relatively recent run of the *Panorama of Uncle Tom's Cabin* had not quenched the public's appetite, for the newspaper stated that "Mr. Brown intends to prolong his visit," a sign that his audiences had been satisfactory.[33]

Brown's advertisement announced that these were "his farewell exhibitions previous to retiring." The meaning of this statement is uncertain. Perhaps Brown was temporarily tired of life on the road or had doubts about his future success in the midst of the craze for shows related to *Uncle Tom's Cabin*, then at its most fervent. Possibly it was a showman's artifice to entice audiences in Preston who had seen *Mirror of Slavery* when Brown and James C. A. Smith first showed there two years before. Though he may have stopped performing for a time, Brown carried on and outlasted the fad for *Uncle Tom's Cabin* panoramas.

In mid-May 1853, some three months after Brown's visit, yet another panorama of *Uncle Tom's Cabin* played Preston. When this exhibition later received attention in the press, at least one reader thought of Henry Box Brown. Two black men operated the show. One, named Charles Hill, claimed to be a fugitive slave, and the other, according to a Preston resident, "comes from London, and has travelled about a good deal in this neighbourhood and in Scotland" with his panorama. "He professes to be earnestly engaged in the temperance cause," and "gains favour with simple, kind-hearted people, who afterwards have reason to regret their acquaintanceship with him." The men's partnership ended in Glasgow in December 1853 when the pair fell out over the division of their profits.[34]

In January 1854 the man known in Preston as Charles Hill called at the office of the British and Foreign Anti-Slavery Society in London. Now using the name Andrew Baker, he claimed to be a fugitive slave who had escaped to Liverpool from Charleston, South Carolina, by hiding on the ship *Summers*. Louis Alexis Chamerovzow, the society's secretary and editor of the *London Anti-Slavery Reporter*, assisted Baker but also made inquiries in Liverpool about the *Summers*. No ship of that name had entered the port, he was told.[35]

Chamerovzow refused further help to Baker, who then convinced another anti-slavery newspaper, the *Bond of Brotherhood*, to publish a letter for him, supposedly directed to his former mistress in Baltimore. A man in Belfast saw Baker's letter and wrote to Chamerovzow that a similar letter had been published in that city in December 1853, dictated by a fugitive slave named Reuben Nixon, who had then "absconded suddenly with a guitar." Based on that report Chamerovzow concluded that Andrew Baker and Reuben Nixon were "different names for the same individual."

Meanwhile the man Baker had departed from London to lecture against slavery, traveling to Cambridge, Huntingdon, and Biggleswade. His "apparent piety" and "touching tale," along with "ready tears and excellent acting," created "a very great sensation." At Offord Darcy, however, Baker claimed he was appearing under the patronage of the British and Foreign Anti-Slavery Society and was authorized to solicit donations. Chamerovzow investigated and then confronted the man on his return to London.

The man admitted the deception and told his story. His true name was Reuben Nixon, he said, and he had never been a slave. He had been born free in Albany, New York. After a stint with a circus and time in Sing Sing prison, Nixon began "passing himself off as a fugitive" to collect funds along the Underground Railroad. His impostures were eventually discovered, and the United States became "an inconvenient abode." Early in 1853 he left for Great Britain and there "fell in with *a coloured man, who had a panorama illustrating Uncle Tom's Cabin*, and in company with this man he travelled." After their quarrel in December 1853 in Glasgow, Nixon had gone to Belfast.[36]

Unconvinced by Nixon's glib promises to go straight—for his parents had taught him to be "a liar," he said, "so that he *could* not now speak truth"—Chamerovzow published a warning entitled "Coloured Lecturers.—Caution" in the 1 March 1854 issue of the *Anti-Slavery Reporter*. He told his readers to beware of "certain coloured men who are now going through the country, with and without a panorama or dissolving views, delivering lectures on American Slavery, Temperance, and other subjects." They "calculate upon the sympathy of the public," especially of persons opposed to slavery, with "a skilfully-invented and well-told tale of woe, and suffering, and hair-breadth escapes."[37]

Chamerovzow's vague warning against "coloured lecturers" provoked James C. A. Smith to respond from Ashton-under-Lyne, Lancashire, a town not far from Manchester. Henry Box Brown's former partner expressed distress that Chamerovzow had issued the warning yet withheld "the names of the parties alluded." His letter appeared in the next issue of the *Anti-Slavery Reporter*. "Sir I am a *coloured* man, and have a *Panorama*, and some times lecture on the horrors of *Slavery*," Smith remonstrated. "I shall at once be suspected as one of the culprits alluded to in your able columns." Not only might the warning injure those working "to overthrow the cruel system of Slavery," Smith said, but he also thought it unfair to him personally. "I can say that my conduct, since my arrival in England, will bear the strictest investigation."[38]

Little is known of Smith's life after 1851. In 1852 Smith had written to the First African Baptist Church in Richmond to transfer his membership to a church in Lancashire. Smith's 1854 letter, almost three years after the split with Brown, is evidence that he continued to reside in England and remained active in antislavery and in the exhibition of a moving panorama. His defense of his good name is the last word discovered from James C. A. Smith.[39]

Chamerovzow conceded Smith's point and, with Smith's letter, he published an article in the *Anti-Slavery Reporter* that identified Reuben Nixon. The black abolitionist Samuel Ringgold Ward was in London at the time and saw Smith's letter. Ward wrote to the *Reporter* that he knew James C. A. Smith and recalled giving him the nickname "Boxer" at the Syracuse convention of January 1850. "I am happy to say that if Mr. Smith is an impostor, he must have become such since he came to England," declared Ward. "I believe him to be a true man."[40]

The publication of Smith's letter and the warning about Nixon also attracted the attention of the Reverend John Kitton. When Brown and Smith had appeared in Preston in 1851 he assisted them and provided an endorsement. Kitton wrote to Chamerovzow inquiring about "the Negro calling himself Henry <u>Box</u> Brown, & passing himself off as the slave who escaped from Richmond, Va. to Philadelphia in a box or chest." Kitton had "not seen Brown since . . . but have always intended again aiding Brown if in my power. I should just like to know whether he is or is not an imposter."[41]

Chamerovzow's reply to Kitton is unknown. Although Brown was certainly no imposter, if Chamerovzow remembered the allegations against Brown from 1851 he might still have lumped him with the wayward Nixon. Their cases, however, differed not only in degree but also in kind. Nixon was a charlatan who made a career of multiple deceptions that took advantage of the generosity of the friends of the slave. Brown was an authentic hero who, on the 1851 tour of Lancashire and Yorkshire, was untruthful about his intention to purchase his wife and seems to have learned a lesson from the result. There is no evidence that he ever profited afterward by dishonest presentations of himself. Brown's advertisements exaggerated as a matter of course, but they did not misrepresent the content of his show or his motive for exhibiting it.

The warnings against Reuben Nixon notwithstanding, new reports of Nixon's schemes appeared at intervals in the antislavery press through 1857. Nixon's continued activities suggest that the "Tom-mania" that swept Great Britain made ready ears for his false words. For Henry Box Brown, even though the *Uncle Tom's Cabin* phenomenon brought new competition on the circuit, the more important development proved the enlargement of the audience for performances related to American slavery. Rather than retiring, as his advertisements at Preston had hinted, Brown stayed his independent course as a showman with a message.

New Panoramas

Henry Box Brown continued to tour throughout the 1850s. Early in 1855 a report of Brown's exhibition appeared in the *Empire*, a weekly published in London. Calling Brown "a celebrated fugitive slave from America," who had been subjected to "some of the horrible cruelties so faithfully depicted in his panorama," the article declared that "such a man is worth both seeing and hearing." Brown "gives a vivid and genuine description of each passing scene, and, occasionally," it stated, "intersperses some 'nigger' songs." The exhibition was "a most effectual mode of instructing," the article continued, and "deserves, nay more, it demands, the support and encouragement of all Christians and every lover of freedom."[42]

In 1859 the *Windsor and Eton Express* asked, "Who is there that has not heard of Box Brown, as he is familiarly termed?" The *Buckinghamshire Advertiser* said that Brown "appears to have gone the circuit of almost the whole Kingdom," and the *West London Observer* noted that "in many of the principal towns of Yorkshire and Lancashire he has paid his second and third visits with equal success and satisfaction." The endorsements he had accrued impressed the *Windsor and Eton Express*. "Mr. Brown's exhibition seems to ensure support wherever he goes," it observed, "as by the programme it would appear that he has met with very distinguished patronage."[43]

The 1855 article in the *Empire* especially recommended Brown's panorama to "our younger friends." Numerous reports indicate that children made up a substantial part of Brown's audiences. One of those children was Samuel Fielden, of Todmorden, in Yorkshire. In his autobiography Fielden wrote that black antislavery lecturers "had a very great effect on my mind, and I could hardly divest myself of their impressions, and I used to frequently find myself among my playmates dilating much upon the horrors of slavery." He went to see them "sometimes with my father, and at other times with my sister." Fielden particularly remembered Henry Box Brown and his panorama. Brown "was a very good speaker and his entertainment was very interesting," recalled Fielden. "He used to march through the streets in front of a brass band, clad in a highly-colored and fantastic garb, with an immense drawn sword in his hand."[44]

Such a procession served to advertise and stimulate interest in the exhibition. How regularly Brown paraded is unknown. It was at least a recurring feature and might have become his standard practice at certain types of venues. As for Brown's "highly-colored and fantastic garb," several sources were more specific. One referred to Brown "attired in his dress of an African Prince," and another told of him "presenting himself in the streets in the character of an African King, richly dressed, and accompanied by a footman." In a later handbill Brown called himself "the African Prince."[45]

Brown's character of the African prince probably derived partly from the imagery in *Mirror of Slavery,* in particular from the scenes of Africa and of the Nubian family, to which he was quite attentive. By 1852 he had revised the billing of the exhibition to *Panorama of African and American Slavery,* and when he created two new songs for the performance of the panorama, both songs were about the Nubian family. Although "African" added a dash of the exotic to his show package, that small commercial advantage was hardly reason enough to explain his emphasis of it. Brown's role of African prince reflected not only his theatrical flamboyance but also his consciousness of African connections.[46]

To claim Henry Box Brown as a precursor to twentieth-century Pan-Africanism goes beyond the evidence. Nevertheless, at a time when the most widely played African American persona in British popular culture was either the minstrels' Jim Crow or Stowe's Uncle Tom, Brown presented the African prince. Whatever else an African prince might have signified to English audiences, he was neither a comical figure of derisive fun nor a stoic victim of oppression.

Early in 1859 Brown returned to the London area with a new panorama. He had married again, and his wife accompanied him as a performer in the exhibition. She was almost certainly English, but of her, and of their marriage, there is no information except from reports of the shows. Because advertisements and articles identify her only as "Mrs. H. Box Brown," not even her given name is known. Several accounts describe her performances as accomplished, an indication that she probably had a background in show business prior to their marriage.[47]

Brown and his wife traveled with two panoramas, offering two exhibitions at each venue. They presented *Mirror of Slavery*, now called the *Grand Original Panorama of African and American Slavery*, with a new final segment: "some dioramic views from the Holy Land, which are excellently painted, and ably described by Mrs. H. B. Brown." The Holy Land had become a staple subject of panoramic exhibition. Whether these added scenes were linked to the original narrative line of *Mirror of Slavery* is unknown.[48]

The subject of the second panorama testified to Henry Box Brown's commitment to popular entertainment. "Since the sad Revolt in our Eastern Empire has occurred," the *West London Observer* reported, "Mr. Brown has had a panorama of the great Indian Mutiny painted, which he now exhibits alternately with his great American panorama, either of which affords a most excellent evening's entertainment." As a veteran showman attuned to the English public's interests, Brown would have seen an opportunity in the recent uprising against British colonial rule in India. In addition, by 1859 he was often revisiting venues that he had played before, and a new panorama might attract people who had already seen his antislavery panorama.

The Indian mutiny occurred in 1857. Through the quasi-governmental East India Company, Great Britain had colonial dominion over a large part of the Indian subcontinent. Maintaining control was an army composed for the most part of British officers who commanded Indian soldiers called sepoys. Rumors spread that a new kind of rifle cartridge had been lubricated with animal fat, which would have caused the sepoys to violate Hindu and Muslim religious practices in handling it. Despite British denials, anti-British sentiment seized on the rumors and precipitated the mutiny.[49]

Incidents of disobedience began early in 1857, and open mutiny erupted in Meerut, a town near Delhi, on 10 May 1857. Rebellion spread quickly to Delhi and across India. In June Indian troops revolted at Cawnpore. Eight hundred Europeans there surrendered after a siege of several weeks. As they began to board boats that would take them away, they were attacked and slaughtered, except for about one hundred and twenty-five women and children. British troops recaptured Cawnpore in mid-July 1857 and discovered that the captured women and children had been executed. The "Massacre at Cawnpore" became in England the most notorious event of the mutiny and its bloody suppression. British forces took Delhi in September, and by the end of 1857 the military aspect of the mutiny was over.

British newspapers carried extensive reports of these distant events, but few readers knew much about the places that had now assumed significance. Thus, even before

"The Muhurrum Festival.—The Procession of the Tazzies." *Illustrated London News,* 17 October 1857. Using stock images, in July 1857 the *Illustrated London News* first reported "The Mutiny in India," which had started in May. Drawings newly made in India began to appear late in August and increased in number during September and October 1857.

the mutiny had been quelled, in September 1857 a 360-degree panorama of Delhi opened in London. A magazine article stated that the painting was "lectured on daily by one of those smooth-tongued expositors, with a white wand, that moves like a clock-hand over the surface of the picture."[50]

By the end of the 1850s the moving panorama, supplanted by new pictorial mediums, was in decline as a format for exhibition. Richard Altick writes that the Indian Mutiny was the last event to inspire a flowering of panoramas. Of Henry Box Brown's mutiny panorama little is known but it was probably not dissimilar to its competitors. Gompertz's *Diorama of the Indian Mutiny* opened in London in May 1858. It contained about fifteen scenes, "each one covering 500 square feet of canvas." Among the scenes were views of the city and fortifications of Delhi; the encampment of the British relief army outside Delhi, featuring the commander, Lieutenant General Henry William Barnard; the "bloodstained Assembly Rooms at Cawnpore;" the slaughter of English women and children, which a reviewer called "sickening;" the March from Lucknow; and "The Fall of Delhi." The performance included "a sax-tuba band" that played "between the change of scenes."[51]

Undated handbills describe two other panoramas of the Indian Mutiny. One at Mr. Wyld's Great Globe, a Leicester Square attraction, contained "40 Immense Tableaux, illustrative of the Manners and Customs of the Inhabitants, Embracing the Cities of Lucknow, Delhi, Calcutta, Madras, Cawnpoor, Muttra, Meerut, Agra, the Himalaya Mountains, &c. &c. &c." The second was a double feature, pairing a "New & Magnificent" Daguerrean-format "Diorama of the Cities of Lucknow & Delhi, their Palaces, Temples, Mosques, and Tombs," with "a moving diorama of The Seat of War in Upper

India, In 42 tableaux of the principle Cities, Palaces, Mountains, and Rivers, including Calcutta, Benares, Allahabad, &c &c."[52]

Henry Box Brown's panorama of the Indian mutiny probably did not stray far from these themes. It was "descriptive of the war in India, and contains many interesting views of this recent fearful struggle," said a report in the *Windsor and Eton Express*. "The last scene, a very brilliant one, represents the 'Mahommedan festival of the Mohurrin,'" the article continued. "Appropriate music is performed during the exhibition."[53]

Undoubtedly Brown's panorama presented the British side of the Indian Mutiny, for it would have been commercial suicide to exhibit in England from any other perspective. To a degree such a point of view put his two panoramas at odds. Where the panorama of slavery spoke to the aspirations for freedom of an oppressed people, the panorama of the mutiny would have celebrated the restoration of imperial dominion. It is possible that Brown's version of the mutiny was sensitive to such issues, for it did not close with a scene of military victory. Instead, the final scene of the panorama depicted a festival during Muharram, the first month of the Islamic year. At any rate, if there were contradictions in Brown's stance, many Britons shared them. His panorama on the Indian Mutiny perhaps measures how fully Brown himself had come to identify with, as reported in the *Windsor and Eton Express*, "that 'great, glorious, and free country,' as he calls England."[54]

Beginning on Wednesday, 2 March 1859, Brown and his wife exhibited "at the Town Hall, Brentford, to crowds of spectators." A correspondent of the *Windsor and Eton Express* declared that "Mr. Brown's entertainment is unquestionably one of the most popular that ever visited this town," and the run continued into the next week. On Monday and Tuesday the Independent Order of Odd Fellows and the Ancient Order of Foresters were patrons of the exhibition. "The commodious room at the Town Hall was literally crammed," reported the *West London Observer*. Because "hundreds were unable to gain admission" on Tuesday and thus missed Mrs. Brown's "vivid and able manner" of describing the panorama of the Indian mutiny, on Wednesday "Mrs. Brown appeared again with the panorama of the Indian war, in which, as on previous occasions, she was listened to with breathless interest, and loudly applauded."[55]

At Brentford, Henry Box Brown unveiled a new interest. "With Professor Chadwick (who was engaged expressly for the occasion)," reported the *West London Observer*, Brown concluded one of the shows with "several experiments in mesmerism, human magnetism, and electro-biology." These were his "first experiments in public" with "mesmerism and biology," and proved "excellent and very successful." The stage science of Brown and Chadwick "afforded the crowded audience much pleasure and amusement."[56]

The panorama exhibition moved to Temperance Hall in Hammersmith, another town just west of London, on 14 March. The newspaper account of the run there suggests how the Browns used flexible scheduling and the alternation of the panoramas to build audiences and encourage return attendance. On both Monday and Tuesday Brown "delivered his illustrative and telling lecture on African and American Slavery," followed by the "dioramic views from the Holy Land" narrated by Mrs. Brown. The response was "so unmistakable" that two more performances were scheduled for Wednesday. On Thursday Mrs. Brown presented the panorama of the Indian mutiny. Her descriptions were "very well written," reported the newspaper, and her delivery "very charming to her audience." The hall was "overflowing," with many turned away. At the two mutiny performances on Friday "the hall was equally crowded, and everyone appeared gratified with the entertainment."[57]

TEMPERANCE HALL,

Black's Road, Bridge Road, Hammersmith.

POSITIVELY FOR FIVE NIGHTS ONLY.

COMMENCING on Monday, March 14, 1859, Mr. H. BOX BROWN, The Celebrated American Fugitive Slave, begs most respectfully to inform the Nobility, Gentry, and Inhabitants generally, that he will make his first Visit to this Town, and exhibit his Grand, Original Panorama of African and American Slavery. Followed by Dioramic Views from the Holy Land.

PART I. The Nubian Family.—Seizure of Slaves.—Religious Sacrifice.—March to the Coast.—Cape of Good Hope.—Slave Feluca.—Interior of a Slave Ship.—Spanish Slaver at Havannah.—Landing Slaves.—Nubian Family at Auction.—Grand Fourth of July Celebration.—Grand Auction Block.—Virginia Chain Gangs.—Brand and Scourge.—Interior of Charleston Workhouse.

PART II. Sunday among the Slaves.—Sugar Plantations.—Cotton Plantation Slaves at Work.—The Dismal Swamp.—Nubians Escaping by Night.—Ellen Craft's Escaping.—Distant View of Richmond, Virginia.—HENRY BOX BROWN, escaping.—The Natural Bridge, and Jefferson's Rock.—City of Washington.—Tomb of General Washington.—HENRY BOX BROWN released at Philadelphia.—Burning Alive.—Promise of Freedom.—Universal Emancipation, and t her Views too numerous to insert.

N.B.—The Public at large are respectfully invited to observe that the Proprietor of this Entertainment was himself born a Slave at Richmond, Virginia, and to escape from that accursed System was, on March 29, 1849, packed in a small box, 3 feet, 1 inch long, and conveyed 350 miles to obtain his liberty. But not being able to breathe the pure air of Freedom in the so-called Free States of America, he was compelled to seek the shores of Great Britain, where he has for the last seven years travelled with his Entertainment of African and American Slavery, with the utmost success, picturing Slavery in its true colours, and advocating the sufferings of four millions and a half of Slaves who are now held in cruel Bondage.

MRS. H. BOX BROWN will appear with "The War in India" on Thursday and Friday evenings.

Appropriate Music will be in attendance.

Reserved Seats, 1s.   Back Seats, 6d.

Doors open at half-past Seven—Commence at Eight.

MR. BROWN will open his Entertainment at Uxbridge Town Hall, on Monday, March 21, and at the Windsor Theatre, on the 28th.

West London Observer, 12 March 1859. The illustration, no doubt commissioned by Brown for his publicity kit, drew its image from the 1850 Boston lithograph of the scene (page 82).

After the Wednesday evening exhibition at Hammersmith, Brown paid a social call. Nearly five hundred members of the Ancient Order of Foresters had gathered in Hammersmith to celebrate the opening of a new court, as the lodges of the group were called. The Ancient Order of Foresters had evolved from its origins as a provider of burial insurance into a popular fraternal organization attractive to both small merchants and skilled tradesmen. Brown's presentation of the panorama that evening had caused him to miss a parade that featured the "entire band of the Royal West Middlesex Militia in full uniform" and other Foresters "in full costume on horseback." When he arrived at the hall, he found that the first round of toasts and the "imposing ceremony of opening a new Court" had already taken place.[58]

"Mr. Box Brown, who is a member of the order," stated a newspaper reporter, "here entered the room, attired in his dress of an African Prince, and excited great attention." Called to speak, Brown evidently had stood before in such a forum and was ready with appropriate words. He said that "he observed with great pleasure the blessing that shines upon the Order, and congratulated them on the opening of a New Court. 'He hoped they might meet annually every fortnight,'" the newspaper story quoted Brown—a line he likely used more than this once— "and after reference to his having worked sixteen hours a day for six years, and expressing his gladness at being a Member of the Order, he concluded by saying, 'May God smile upon it, and may we do our duty to support it.'"

As a Forester, Brown was a brother to this large gathering of strangers. Two weeks previously in Brentford the Foresters and the Odd Fellows had been sponsors for his shows.

Both had lodges throughout the country. Through such patronage Brown's fraternal membership might well have benefited his attendance in many locales.

The next week, on 21 March 1859, the exhibition opened in Uxbridge. Brown "obtained good audiences," in contrast to the "frequent rejection" afforded "real and genuine native talent," the local newspaper complained. "Whether it be the novelty of the thing, or the superior style and getting up of the exhibition, or the fact that the performer is a negro and a fugitive slave, is a problem which we cannot solve."[59]

The following week Brown exhibited the antislavery panorama in Windsor, where it was again successful enough to carry over for a second week. At the Wednesday matinee, "the theatre was crowded with 900 children from the various schools," and on Friday evening "about 500 juveniles attended." At the Saturday performance "the officers of the 2nd Life Guards" were present, and the patrons for the next Tuesday's show were "his Worship the Mayor and the Masonic Order." The final Friday matinee "was devoted to the amusement of a number of the pupils of Eton College."[60]

The show moved westward to Maidenhead, where, in the correspondent's words, "it did not seem to take in this town, as things of that kind usually do, the attendance not being large." By the second week of May the Browns had moved farther west to Wallingford, a town near Oxford. There "the audience on each occasion was smaller than anticipated," said the *Reading Mercury*. "We fear that Mr. Brown must have been a loser by the week's engagement," reported the *Berkshire Chronicle*. A certainty on the circuit was unpredictability: one week the show "met with great support," and the next "it did not seem to take."[61]

The next-known newspaper notice of Henry Box Brown comes from January 1862. Civil war gripped the United States by then, and, alert to public's shifting interest, Brown changed his exhibition accordingly. His advertisement in Leigh, a town in southern Lancashire, announced that Brown's "Original Mirror of Africa and America" would be accompanied by "his Grand Moving Mirror of the American War, which has been the theme of admiration in most of the principal cities and towns in England." A panorama on the war that had already toured "most" of England less than a year after the hostilities began must have been created quickly. The advertisement promised that "an Efficient Band" would play and that "Valuable Presents" would be given away "at each entertainment." Brown gave four shows in Leigh "to delightful audiences" and the following week exhibited in the nearby town of Atherton. By March 1862 he had moved on to Yorkshire, where he exhibited at Brighouse, a town near Halifax, to meager audiences.[62]

Brown's success with his *Grand Moving Mirror of the American War* was likely short-lived. In contrast to his firsthand knowledge of the subject of slavery, after eleven years in Britain Brown knew no more about the American Civil War than many in his audiences. Other lecturers were more current, such as a young man named Archibald MacKenzie, another former Richmonder newly arrived in Britain. MacKenzie appeared in several towns in the same part of Yorkshire when Brown was there, speaking on the "Origin and Objects of the present struggle in America," and on the evils of slavery.[63]

Whereas Brown's panorama of the Indian mutiny might have played for two years and more after that conflict ended, his *Mirror of the American War* was much sooner outdated. New inventions were making the news more immediate. For example, Major Robert Anderson, the Union commander of Fort Sumter, sat for a photographic portrait in February 1861, and carte de visite copies were offered for sale in New York even before the Confederate siege of the fort began in April 1861. Via steamship such visual reportage could be in the hands of a publisher in England not months but weeks later.

The painted imagery in Brown's panorama was overtaken by events in the war. Henry Box Brown had been successful as an exhibitor of moving panoramas, and stuck with what he knew, but the prime era of the moving panorama was closing.[64]

"King of all Mesmerisers"

The last days of December 1863 found Henry Box Brown in Aberdare, Wales. At his show there, "notwithstanding the bait of 'presents,'" reported the *Bristol Daily Post*, "the attendance was by no means large." More notable than Brown's draw at this venue was his new exhibition. His 1859 performance at Brentford of "mesmerism, human magnetism, and electro-biology" proved more than a one-time experiment. At Aberdare, Brown had been "lecturing at the Temperance-hall, for two or three nights past on electro-biology."[65]

"Electro-biology" was mesmerism on stage. Mesmerism itself was derived from the work of Franz Anton Mesmer, a Vienna-trained physician. Mesmer developed theories of magnetic and gravitational influences to explain human ills, which he laid out in 1766 in an essay on "The Influence of the Planets on the Human Body." He believed that one person might have influence over another by application of "animal magnetism." During residences in Vienna and then Paris, Mesmer earned the disapproval of the scientific establishment, but his ideas survived his death in 1815. The word *mesmerism* came to be associated primarily with one aspect of Mesmer's method, the introduction of a trance in the patient.[66]

In England, mesmerism branched into the realms of medicine and mysticism. The physician James Braid set the scientific course. In his 1842 "Practical Essay on the Curative Agency of Neuro-Hypnotism," he showed that hypnotism, a word that he introduced, involved suggestion, not animal magnetism. On the mystical side, circles of experimenters in animal magnetism also took up other pursuits like spiritualism. A journal on such subjects called the *Zoist* was published from 1843 to 1856.[67]

The most visible practitioners of mesmeric art in England borrowed their stage language from the dabblers in mysticism, but in their performances used suggestion, as described by Braid and others, to induce hypnotic trances. One early historian of the phenomenon states that mesmerism as a public entertainment began in Britain about 1850. It was introduced from the United States through exhibitions "by a couple of itinerant Americans," whose method utilized "a little disk of zinc or copper held in the hand of the 'subject' and steadily gazed on by him." The Americans "styled themselves 'professors' of a new art which they termed *Electro-Biology*." When Henry Box Brown first appeared in England, at Liverpool in November 1850, he alternated nights at the theater with the American G. W. Stone, who presented "Electro-Biology, or the Electrical Science of Life." Another of the Americans was Sheldon Chadwick, who exhibited as "Professor Chadwick." During the 1850s, the tours of Brown and of Chadwick took them through many of the same towns on the circuit, so they may have crossed paths prior to 1859. Based on their joint performance at Brentford, Brown probably learned at least some of the mesmerist's techniques from Chadwick.[68]

A report on Chadwick's exhibition in Uxbridge on 12 March 1859 stated that "the large room of the Chequers Inn was crowded every night during the last week with persons of almost all classes." It was during this run that Chadwick appeared on stage with Brown; it seems likely that Brown's later performances were similar to Chadwick's. "Mr. Chadwick," the account said, "seemed to possess a most wonderful influence of all who submitted themselves to his operation: he sent them to sleep, awoke them, made them jump about transfixed to their chairs; at his command they were rivitted to the platform, from which they could not move, unless commanded to do so by the operator; they jumped, they danced, they rang imaginary bells, rolled about, held one leg in the air, as long as the mesmeriser chose, and then they were all sent to sleep again; in fact, Mr. Chadwick seemed to possess absolute control over their powers both mental and physical."[69]

As the apparent possessor of superior powers, the mesmerist played a role that was strong, yet offered a benign and trustworthy presence. While notions of "electro-biology" and "animal magnetism" helped to create the proper atmosphere for a performance, the driving force was the personality of the operator. When he set his subjects to harmless antics, fashioning fun from human behavior, the electro-biologist was an entertainer whose amusement hinted at deeper forces.

Henry Box Brown went on from Aberdare to Tredegar and Merthyr Tydfil, two other industrial towns in southern Wales. Coal mines and ironworks marked the hill-and-vale landscape of the region. The lure of jobs had made Merthyr Tydfil the largest town in southern Wales. A notice of Brown's performance there late in February 1864 appeared in the *Cardiff Times*: "Box Brown, the African Biologist, gave a grand entertainment at the Temperance-hall on Saturday, first presenting himself in the streets in the character of an African King, richly dressed, and accompanied by a footman."[70]

Shortly thereafter, on 10 March 1864, Brown placed an advertisement in the *Merthyr Star*. After two months of "giving Lectures and Experiments in Mesmerism and Electro Biology at Aberdare, Tredegar, and Merthyr, to the largest audiences ever known to assemble on such occasions," the advertisement stated, Brown had delivered his last lecture on those subjects in Merthyr on 29 February "to the largest assemblage ever witnessed there." Now, it announced, "for a short time only," Brown would exhibit "his great original PANORAMA OF AFRICAN AND AMERICAN SLAVERY."[71]

The enthusiastic tone of Brown's advertisement was in contrast to newspaper reports from this period of small turnouts for Brown's exhibitions. Brown was accustomed to the ups and downs of show life, and his advertisement, a rare sample of his voice, struck a confident and even ebullient note. With showman's panache, it proclaimed him "the King of all Mesmerisers."[72]

Reports have been found for one other exhibition by Brown in southern Wales, for six nights at Pontypridd in August 1864. "The mystery and fun of mesmerism are being exhibited at the old Temperance Hall by Mr. Box Brown, a dark gentleman, who has evidently had much practice in the art," stated the *Bristol Daily Post*. The *Cardiff and Merthyr Guardian* referred to Brown as "the king (?) of all mesmerisers," an indication that he had again used the appellation on his handbills. "This mesmeric wonder has taken his departure," the *Cardiff Times* reported on 12 August 1864. "Mr. Brown has not been so much patronised as might have been expected."[73]

MR. H. BOX BROWN,

THE

King of all Mesmerisers,

AFTER having been for the last two months giving Lectures and Experiments in Mesmerism and Electro Biology at Aberdare, Tredegar, and Merthyr, to the largest audiences ever known to assemble on such occasions, gave his last lecture in Merthyr, on Monday, February 29th, at the Temperance Hall, to the largest assemblage ever witnessed there.

Mr. B. now exhibits at the above Hall, his great original PANORAMA of AFRICAN and AMERICAN SLAVERY, for a short time only.

For particulars, see hand-bills.

Merthyr Star, 10 March 1864

Though perhaps not at Pontypridd, Henry Box Brown met with success enough to sustain him on the British circuit for another decade. A later handbill stated that he had conducted "a lengthened tour of 25 years in England." From his first shows at Liverpool in 1850, Brown exhibited in Great Britain until 1875, when he was about sixty years old. Like other now-long-forgotten entertainers, in his day the name H. Box Brown was probably known to some millions of people.[74]

Over the years, Henry Box Brown evolved away from performance with a political content. He did not disavow antislavery, for he was still exhibiting *Mirror of Slavery* in 1864, although its political purpose had been overtaken by events. Rather he had moved on in pursuit of his chosen career in show. By the time of the Emancipation Proclamation, Brown had emancipated himself, in a sense, from his personal history of enslavement. When he presented electro-biology, it did not matter that he had been a slave, for mesmerism was an act with no particular connection to slavery. Brown's status as a fugitive slave was no longer his primary identity. He had become H. Box Brown, a professional performer with a variety of talents. He was the African prince. He was the King of all Mesmerizers. He was who he had made himself to be.

~Chapter Nine~

American Reprise

Stateside Traces

In the United States of 1875, Henry Box Brown's moment had long come and gone. Lacking the literary skills of a William Wells Brown or a Samuel Ringgold Ward, Box Brown was unable to keep American readers informed of his progress in Great Britain. Items about Brown did appear at first in the American press, mostly in anti-slavery newspapers, but even that trickle of information dried up after the 1851 split with James C. A. Smith and the British abolitionists. Brown had made a celebrated entrance onto the American stage in 1849. His chance for a second act with the panorama in 1850 ended with his abrupt exit to England. In his native land, Henry Box Brown was remembered only for his escape.[1]

Reminders of the escape appeared from time to time in the American press. Samuel A. Smith, his co-conspirator, was the subject early in 1854 of what the *Richmond Whig* called "the tempest over the case of the 'Red Boot man.'" From the time that he entered the Virginia State Penitentiary in 1849, Smith had been a model prisoner. He was serving as the head measurer and cutter in the prison shoe shop when troubles arose among the inmate shoemakers. In April 1853, another prisoner assaulted Smith, stabbing him repeatedly with a shoe knife, with nearly fatal results. The penitentiary superintendent, Colonel Charles S. Morgan, believed that Smith had been injured carrying out Morgan's policies and subsequently sought a pardon for him. This humanitarian gesture led to a public investigation of Morgan by proslavery hardliners in the Virginia legislature. They accused Morgan of exhibiting "marked clemency" towards "Red Boot" Smith, "a man guilty of an offense that the people of the state were more sensitive upon than any other question whatever." The matter burned brightly in Richmond newspapers for a few weeks until Morgan was cleared in February 1854.[2]

Samuel A. Smith recovered from his wounds and, needless to say, served his full sentence. He was released on 18 June 1856 and immediately set out to the North, arriving in Philadelphia on 21 June. The *New York Tribune* reported on the public meeting held by "the colored citizens of Philadelphia" to honor Smith "as a martyr to the cause of Freedom." The article, probably written by William Still, made the first public identification of Smith as the one "who boxed up Henry Box Brown in Richmond, Va." It also reported that Samuel Smith was married in Philadelphia "to a lady who had remained faithful to him through all his sore trials and sufferings." Smith "took his departure for Western New York," and no more is known of him.[3]

Henry Box Brown's story made an impression on many people, including several from Maine. The Maine artist Harrison Bird Brown (1831–1915), before becoming well known in Portland under his own name, went to California early in the 1850s, where he signed his landscape paintings and drawings as "Henry Box Brown." In July 1855 the *Portland (Maine) Inquirer*, reporting on a speech by William Wells Brown there, said that "Mr. Brown—otherwise called 'Box Brown,' from his having escaped from slavery in a box,—is now in this city." The *Liberator* reprinted the item but corrected the identification, stating that the real Henry Box Brown "is now in England."[4]

If Brown's name was recalled, the man himself perhaps was not. In May 1854, slave hunters in Boston seized a fugitive from Richmond named Anthony Burns. His extradition to Virginia was strongly resisted and became a famous instance of opposition to the Fugitive Slave Act. A portrait of Burns must not have been available in 1854 when *The Boston Slave Riot, and Trial of Anthony Burns* was published in Boston. The same portrait of Henry Box Brown that had been the frontispiece of his 1849 *Narrative,* with a few minor changes, graced the cover of this pamphlet.[5]

No further notices of Henry Box Brown in American newspapers have been found until after the Civil War. On 9 June 1870, Richmonders read about Brown's escape in a wire-service article in the *Richmond Dispatch* entitled "Henry Box Brown." Two days later, the *Petersburg Courier* carried the same story with the heading "The Underground Railroad." A local Petersburg editor who remembered the case added a subhead: "Red Boot Smith and Henry Box Brown." The article contained the text of an address by William Still "at a recent celebration in Philadelphia of the ratification of the fifteenth amendment." In his speech, Still told the story of Brown's 1849 escape and described his arrival at Philadelphia.[6]

William Still's account of Henry Brown's escape reappeared in 1872 in *The Underground Rail Road*, one of the most important of the antislavery memoirs published after the Civil War. Still's book collected documents and stories of the many fugitive slaves whom he had aided as they passed through Philadelphia to liberty. The reviewer for the *New York Times* wrote in April 1872 that it was "a highly interesting volume, filled with incidents that might form themes for a number of novels like *Uncle Tom's Cabin*." Finding a ready audience, the first edition of Still's new work ran to 10,000 copies that were sold by private subscription, and it was reprinted several times in the next few years.[7]

Still's account of "Henry Brown, Arrived by Adams' Express," picked up the story in Philadelphia where Brown's telling in his *Narrative* had ended. In a volume of many tales of bravery and ingenuity, Brown's escape stood out as one of the most amazing. More than any other source, William Still's book made Henry Box Brown's escape part of the lore of the Underground Railroad.[8]

"Prof. H. Box Brown"

Across the Atlantic William Still had brought new attention to the story of Henry Box Brown's escape. If Brown learned of Still's book in Great Britain it might have influenced his course of action. In 1875, accompanied by his wife and daughter Annie, Brown returned to the United States.

The three Browns came to America to present "a first-class European Entertainment." At age sixty, Henry Box Brown now performed as a conjurer. Brown had adapted to mesmerism when moving panoramas became outmoded, and for him electro-biology had run its course as well. Theatrical magic had emerged by the 1870s as a staple of British popular theater, and its leading practitioners were among the best-known entertainers. The Brown family had probably developed their exhibition of magic tricks on tour in Great Britain. From his previous shows Brown carried over to conjuring his character as the African prince, and he continued to climb into his original box.[9]

On the British circuit Brown would have often seen bills for conjurers, and since it is a truism that showmen are showgoers, he likely had attended performances as well. Just as with mesmerism, Brown was probably familiar with magic acts long before he began presenting one himself. Conjuring was similar to mesmerism in that it could be

THE

BOSTON SLAVE RIOT,

AND

TRIAL

OF

Anthony Burns,

CONTAINING THE

REPORT OF THE FANEUIL HALL MEETING; THE MURDER OF
BACHELDER; THEODORE PARKER'S LESSON FOR THE DAY;
SPEECHES OF COUNSEL ON BOTH SIDES, CORRECTED
BY THEMSELVES; VERBATIM REPORT OF JUDGE
LORING'S DECISION; AND, A DETAILED AC-
COUNT OF THE EMBARKATION.

BOSTON:
FETRIDGE AND COMPANY.
1854.

Borrowed Brown as Burns. A comparison of the portrait on this cover to the frontispiece to Brown's 1849 *Narrative* reveals, even in reproduction, a close enough congruence to conclude that the same engraving plate was used for each.

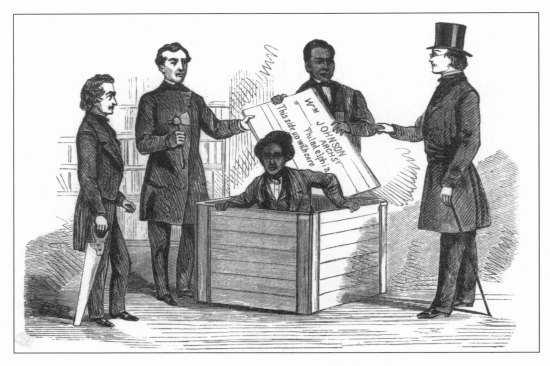

Above, *Resurrection of Henry Box Brown,* from William Still, *The Underground Rail Road* (Philadelphia, 1872). Except for the changes to the box, Still's artist based the engraving on the lithograph, **below,** by Peter Kramer published in Philadelphia probably early in 1851.

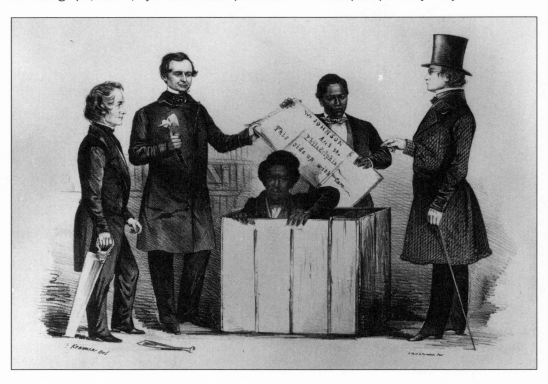

a relatively simple show to take on the road, and in several ways conjuring had advantages over mesmerism. The performance would not have required such intense energy from the aging Brown and he could conduct the exhibition with his family.

As Professor Chadwick had assisted Brown to become a mesmerist, another practitioner may have helped him develop his program of conjuring. Performers of theatrical magic commonly borrowed routines from other exhibitors. The historian Sidney W. Clarke wrote of magic in the 1850s that "copying was then rampant—many a conjuror of even fair ability played the pirate systematically." Some not only adopted another performer's tricks but also another performer's name, a practice that Thomas Frost called "far from infrequent among the fourth-rate entertainers of every class who go the round of the provincial music-halls and assembly-rooms." Another historian of magic, David Price, stated that Henry Box Brown's "program was similar to the programs of other magicians of the time," suggesting that Brown too was a borrower, though only of tricks. He already had a name.[10]

During the middle years of the nineteenth century, according to Geoffrey Lamb, "conjuring developed from a fairground frolic to an acknowledged art." As good a date as any for the beginning of the modern era of magic is 1848, when Jean Robert-Houdin appeared in London for the first time. A French clockmaker who turned his skill to magical mechanisms, Robert-Houdin was active between 1845 and 1856. Often called the father of modern magic, Robert-Houdin popularized many tricks and was probably the most widely copied conjuror of his day. Sidney Clarke contends that Robert-Houdin's main contribution was not in the originality of his tricks but in his understanding of showmanship in conjuring. It is doubtful that Henry Box Brown ever saw Robert-Houdin, but he might have seen the Scots magician John Henry Anderson, "The Great Wizard of the North." One opportunity came when Brown's and Anderson's runs overlapped for two weeks in Liverpool in November 1850, and both went next to Manchester. Active from 1837 to 1866, Anderson was the first magician famous for pulling a rabbit out of a hat, and Clarke judges him "the most eminent of the apparatus school of conjurors." If Brown saw Anderson at London in 1864 he might have noticed that the conjurer was "assisted by his daughters." Anderson was a self-publicist of the first magnitude and has been credited as an originator of the preshow parade as a publicity device.[11]

The rise of the magician was an American phenomenon as well. By the early nineteenth century in the United States, according to Milbourne Christopher, while "in rural areas sleight-of-hand men still entertained at inns," more sophisticated performers "opened the way for conjurers with big shows to play in the same theatres and halls as touring Shakespearean troupes and opera companies." Wyman the Wizard performed six times at the White House for Presidents Martin Van Buren, Millard Fillmore, and Abraham Lincoln. The English-born Robert Heller, who drew much of his initial act from Robert-Houdin, including "Second-Sight," at which Heller was "very sharp," found success in the United States beginning in 1864. Brown could have seen Heller in London in 1868 or during his tour of Britain from 1873 to 1876. The most-successful nineteenth-century magician in the United States was Alexander Herrmann, active from 1869 to 1896. Brown might have seen "The Great Herrmann" when he opened at London's Egyptian Hall in 1869 and played for a "thousand consecutive nights," or during his tour of the principal British cities afterwards.[12]

Henry Box Brown had good reason to begin his American tour in Massachusetts. He knew his way around the state from his book tour in 1849 and his panorama tour in 1850, and even after a quarter century, there would be people in many places who remembered him. He had arrived by 7 November 1875, the date when James N. Buffum, of Lynn, Massachusetts, penned an endorsement that Brown used in his advertisements. Brown probably knew Buffum as a host twenty-five years earlier. The abolitionist Parker Pillsbury recalled that "Mr. Buffum's house was for forty years, not only a safe and well-patronized depot of 'the underground railway,' but a hotel of unlimited, as well as elegant hospitality" for visiting antislavery activists and other reformers.[13]

Other old abolitionists might have also helped Brown. The strong feelings built over years of agitation would not have dissipated even a decade after the end of the Civil War. Although racial prejudice was to be found throughout the North, there was also much sympathy for the struggles of the freedmen. The better sentiments probably contributed to the appeal of black singers on the New England performance circuit of the 1870s. The Jubilee Singers of Fisk University in Nashville first toured New England in February and March 1872 and returned in the period from June 1872 to March 1873. Their performances featured African American spirituals and earned them acclaim and funds for their school. By the end of 1872 the first of numerous imitators appeared. Some, like the Hampton Singers and the Tuskegee Choir, were authentic in their music and purpose, while others capitalized on the Fisk Jubilee Singers' name and reputation.[14]

With the exception of the school ensembles, white promoters operated almost all of the touring black groups. Sheppard's Jubilee Singers, three men and four women, were advertised as "A Genuine Slave Band" who performed "Solemn, Sacred Songs and Old Plantation Melodies." At one venue the troupe played in a performance of *Uncle Tom's Cabin*. The Hyers Sisters, "celebrated colored vocalists," appeared in the musical drama "Out of Bondage." An advertisement for the Estes Jubilee Troupe stated that no others so "perfectly reproduce the real plantation style of voices."[15]

At times white promoters packaged black performers with an eye to the well-proved minstrel model. A "Grand Spectacular Production" of *Uncle Tom's Cabin* in 1878 featured "Two Bands of Jubilee Singers," "Plantation Songs," "The Apotheosis of Eva," and "100 Slaves!" The show also offered "The Four Jolly Coons." Indeed, minstrelsy continued to appeal, with the new wrinkle that some troupes were African American. Blackface acts included Skiff's and Gaylord's Minstrels, Harry Robinson's Minstrels, and Schoolcraft's and Coe's "Ethiopian Entertainment." Haverly was a promoter who put both types of minstrels in the field; whether the Haverly Minstrels with "all the latest Ethiopian novelties," who played Concord, New Hampshire in 1876 were white or black performers is not known.

Thus, Henry Box Brown's position as an African American who managed a show was more unusual than his role as a touring black performer. As for the 1870s New England circuit as a whole, Henry Box Brown probably found the competition for audiences as stiff as in England. There were operas, plays, and lectures. Professor J. O. Hazeley, billed as "The Native African Explorer," lectured on "The Strange Things of Africa."[16] Brown might have noted that Professor Charles E. Sherman billed himself as the "King of Mesmerists." Also on the circuit then were the "veteran phrenologist" Professor O. S. Fowler, Buffalo Bill with Texas Jack, Spaulding's Swiss Bell Ringers, the Kit Carson Star Combination, Aunt Polly Basset and her Yankee Singin Skewl, and variety shows, one featuring a "hindoo juggler" and another a "grotesque dancer and comedian." John H. Murray's "Circus, Pantomime, and Tragedy!" offered leapers, contortionists, and "ascentionists" and promised "positively no side-shows or games of chance." In the category of technological magic, an 1877 advertisement in a Pittsfield, Massachusetts, newspaper was headed "Telephone." It announced "Cornet and Organ Solos, and Vocal Solos and Duets, through the telephone from Westfield." There were also theatrical magicians, including Zera, Crown Prince of Wizards, and Hartz, the King of Wizards, who presented "A Night of Mystery."[17]

In his own exhibition of conjuring, Henry Box Brown was both prince and professor. He billed himself as "Prof. H. Box Brown," and his show was called the "African Prince's Drawing-Room Entertainment." It seems likely that Brown began presenting his show in Massachusetts about the time that he obtained Buffum's endorsement in 1875, but no newspaper reports on his show have been found prior to late 1877. At the end of that year, the Browns were scheduled to appear in Millbury, Massachusetts, a town near Worcester. On 29 December 1877 the *Worcester Evening Gazette* mentioned the upcoming show and said that Brown's escape in a box "will be remembered by many." At the Millbury Town Hall the Brown family would "expose spiritualism and give a miscellaneous exhibition." In addition Brown "will exhibit the box he escaped in and get into it before the audience." The newspaper reported a few days later that the show took place "to a small audience."[18]

On 9 January 1878 the *Worcester Evening Gazette* said that Brown "is in the field as a sleight-of-hand performer." He was to open that day at Worcester's Washburn Hall, and then appear "every evening through the week." The newspaper noted that as an added incentive to attend Brown "gives a present to his lucky patrons." The newspaper also carried an advertisement for "Prof. H. Box Brown" and his "Drawing Room Entertainments." The copy stated that "Prof. Brown will remembered by our oldest inhabitants as a lecturer 28 years ago."[19]

The only other known exhibition was to take place at the town hall in Brookline, Massachusetts, on 2 May 1878. A handbill has survived that announces the performance. No newspaper stories about it have been located, but newspapers tended not to pay much attention to low-budget acts that did not advertise with them. Brown's handbill was likely his primary means of reaching the public. Printed in Worcester, it served for any venue, with a blank space left at the top to fill in the particulars of a local engagement. The printed portion of the handbill contained a brief review

PROF. H. BOX BROWN,

who escaped from Slavery in 1848, in a box 3 feet 1 inch long, will comme os his

DRAWING ROOM ENTERTAINMENTS

in WASHBURN HALL, THIS EVENING, and continue the rest of the week.

Prof. BROWN will be remembered by our oldest inhabitants as a lecturer 28 years ago.

For programme see small bills.

Admission 10 c., Body of the Hall 15 c., Reserved seats 25c.

Worcester Evening Gazette, 9 January 1878

of his escape, a summary of his entertainment career, Buffum's endorsement, and a description of the show. The handbill says nothing about any musical performance, a feature of Brown's earlier career perhaps ceded to the constraints of age.[20]

Professor H. Box Brown could not have matched the magical skills of the top performers, honed from youth and through many years of practice. David Price reports that "his performances have been described as somewhat less than great," but does not say who expressed that opinion. Brown's onstage command was the key to his performance of mesmerism and would have gone a long way toward making his magic work as well. Speaking of conjurers generally, Price emphasizes the importance of stage presence when he explains that "the formula for magic is three parts psychology, one part dexterity, and a dash of mechanics." An effective performance was one that convinced the audience. "Although all one says," wrote Jean Robert-Houdin, in emphasizing the theatricality of magic, "during the course of a performance, is—not to mince the matter—a tissue of falsehoods, the performer must sufficiently enter into the part he plays, to himself believe in the reality of his fictitious statements. This belief on his own part will infallibly carry a like conviction to the minds of the spectators."[21]

Brown's program, as described by his handbill, offered three featured tricks and a series of eleven additional named tricks with handkerchiefs, cards, hats, and boxes. One imagines that Brown interspersed the featured tricks with the sleight-of-hand tricks to give a varied program. The handbill identified Brown as the African prince, which suggests that his attire for the act was a variant on the traditional dress of wizard's robes. Princely flowing robes might also have served purposes of concealment for the magician.

One trick the newspaper mentioned was entitled "Spiritualism Exposed," and the handbill stated that Brown would "expose the Mediumistic Spiritualism, as given by the Davenport brothers." The "notorious Brothers Davenport," Ira and William, were Americans who had toured England from 1864 to 1868. They billed themselves mediums for spiritualism, then much in vogue, and performed as if they were conducting a séance. Volunteers from the audience tied the hands of the Davenports' behind their backs and the brothers then took seats inside a large cabinet where musical instruments hung. With the house lights dimmed, bells rang from inside the cabinet and eerie music emerged, although when the lights were relit the brothers "sat tightly bound."[22]

The Davenports' claims of supernatural effects prompted a pair of English

Handbill, ca. 1875–1878. (Inscription at top cropped.)

magicians, John Nevil Maskelyne and George Cooke, to tour as "Anti-Spiritualists." They "exposed" the Davenports by performing the same tricks without the spiritualist atmospherics. Thomas Frost wrote in 1876 of "those anti-spiritualistic performances which antipathy to humbug has done so much to render popular of late years." Spiritualism remained mysterious and controversial, and thus was a natural subject, whether invoked or exposed, for a showman looking to stir public interest. On the Massachusetts circuit at the same time that Henry Box Brown was exposing spiritualism appeared a show headlined "Everettism!" that promised "the whole Seance of Spiritualism! will take place in Broad Gas Light," including "a Materialized Form."[23]

Brown's handbill stated that "Madame Brown" would introduce the "Mysterious Second-Sight Performance." A routine popularized by Robert-Houdin and presented by Anderson and Heller among others, "second-sight" required two people. One was blindfolded onstage and the other went into the seats and asked an audience member to produce an object. The blindfolded "seer" on stage would then name the object. The handbill copy implied that Mrs. Brown did the speaking, and Brown therefore the "seeing." Typically this trick depended on a verbal code between the two practitioners. The patter of the performer in the audience was on the surface mundane, but, through coded words, it described for the blindfolded seer the unknown object. The more sophisticated the duo's code, the more astounding the effect.

The show concluded with the "Wonderful Sack Feat by Miss Annie Brown." One imagines that this trick was a disappearance. Annie Brown would have stepped into a sack at the center of the stage. Professor Brown then pulled up the sack to cover her and tied the top. After suitable patter, Brown would have revealed the sack to be empty. Suddenly Annie Brown would have appeared at the back of the hall or walked onstage from the side. Perhaps some stage business brought out Mrs. Brown, and Annie slipped offstage under her mother's dress, the empty sack's shape maintained by hidden wires inside it. Her parents advertised that the feat was "such as was never performed before by any child."[24]

A final aspect to the Browns' entertainment derives from the probability that they were an interracial family. It seems most likely that Mrs. Brown was white, and that Annie was biracial. If so, one wonders how audiences in the 1870s responded, and whether adverse social reaction ever impeded the success of the exhibition. No records touch on this subject. Possibly because they were seen in a show business context the matter would have been less remarked. For some viewers, it might have added interest.

How long Henry Box Brown and his family continued to present their magical entertainment is unknown. Indeed, no information about what became of them after 1878 has been found. At age sixty-three Brown could not have spent many more years on the road, but that is where this story must leave him. In the final portion of Henry Box Brown's life there may well have been other twists and turns to his saga. When and where he died is unknown, though doubtless a record will turn up eventually.

"What a weary pilgrimage you had of it in this world," wrote Henry Ridgely Evans of Wyman the Wizard, "wandering up and down, never at rest, traveling thousands of miles by stagecoach, steamboat, and railroad, giving entertainments in little villages and towns . . . and welcomed everywhere by happy children." Henry Box Brown was a showman, a career that even for the most successful performers in that era left little behind but memories. The last of the children who saw Henry Box Brown perform passed away long ago.[25]

Immortality and Beyond

Despite his long career, it is not as a traveling performer that Henry Box Brown is usually remembered. The image that prevails is his moment of resurrection. Depictions of Brown rising in the box have become an icon of slave resistance. Just as his tale of escape astounded and impressed his contemporaries, it retains its power a century and a half later. Each of us can imagine being sealed into a box and trusting to fate.

By the end of his life Henry Box Brown was an obscure figure. His rise as a historical character is fairly recent and has come with increased attention to the Underground Railroad. The primary source for retellings of Brown's journey has remained one of the earliest published accounts, William Still's in *The Underground Rail Road* (1872). A few former abolitionists had direct memories of Brown, such as James Freeman Clarke in *Anti-Slavery Days* (1883), but most accounts, such as Booker T. Washington's in *A New Negro for a New Century* (1900), derived from Still. In his autobiographical *Shadow and Light* (1902), Mifflin W. Gibbs relied both on Still and his own recollection. "Brown, though uneducated," wrote Gibbs, "was imbued with the spirit of liberty, and with much natural ability, with his box he traveled and spoke of his experience in slavery."[26]

In the era suffused with the Lost Cause, Richmond memories of slaves escaping in boxes were stories of crimes. A circa 1896 history of the Richmond police force recounted the antebellum "Dred Scott underground railway case." In this tale, a "northern man" came to Richmond and "represented to the negroes that he was an agent of the underground railway that was carrying slaves to freedom by shipping them in boxes and barrels." With "smooth talk he secured a great deal of money from the negroes, one of whom he killed to get rid of." He attempted a second murder "but his victim jumped out of the window and escaped." A newspaper story from 1903 about "'Red Boot' Smith" and the fugitive slaves found in boxes recalled that Smith's capture "set the whole town agog." It treated Smith as a criminal deserving conviction and referred to the Underground Railroad as "that offensive abolition institution."[27]

In the twentieth century Brown's escape became a part of the standard accounts of the Underground Railroad, serving as an emblem of fugitive ingenuity and determination. Henrietta Buckmaster in 1941 wrote of "the amazing Henry Box Brown whose exploit was a nine-day wonder." The same year Herbert Aptheker described Brown as "peculiar freight" and used his story to argue that slave escapes brought "the truth to the country" about slavery. Benjamin Quarles, in his biography of Frederick Douglass (1948), mentioned both the escape and Brown's appearance at the 1849 New England Anti-Slavery Convention. Larry Gara in *The Liberty Line: The Legend of the Underground Railroad* (1961) drew from Brown's own story of the escape in the 1849 *Narrative* as well as from William Still's account.[28]

Henry Box Brown's escape has today become a well-known episode. Charles L. Blockson wrote of Brown's "inventive transport" in the July 1984 issue of *National Geographic*. In January 2001, The Learning Channel on cable television featured Brown in a program entitled "Great Escapes." The Henry Ford Museum and Greenfield Village, in Michigan, interprets "Living Under Enslavement" at its Web site in part through the story of Henry Box Brown's escape. That the boxed fugitive passed through in transit is a part of the historical pedigree of Baltimore's restored President Street Station, which houses the B&O Railroad Museum. Writer Anthony Cohen personally retraced the route of the Underground Railroad in 1996, including boldly riding inside a box on a train from Philadelphia to New York (though with a phone in his pocket). During Black History Month in February 2000, students at Virginia's Hampton University participated in an Underground Railroad reenactment. The student who portrayed Henry Box Brown said, "I was amazed and in awe when I learned about him."[29]

Brown's story is often represented by the image of his unboxing in Philadelphia. The engraving of it from William Still's book has probably been most widely reproduced. Langston Hughes and Milton Meltzer presented the 1850 Boston lithograph in their volume *A Pictorial History of the Negro in America* (1956), and the same image appeared both in Harnett T. Kane's *Gone Are the Days: An Illustrated History of the Old South* (1960), and Bernard F. Reilly Jr.'s *American Political Prints, 1766–1876* (1991). Others have adapted the scene to different formats. A depiction of Brown in his box occupies a square of a story quilt made by the Ohio Underground Railroad Association.

Brown exhibit, Great Blacks in Wax Museum, Baltimore

Still I Rise: A Cartoon History of African Americans (1997) devotes a page to Brown's escape. The figure of Henry Brown emerges from his box at the Great Blacks in Wax Museum in Baltimore, and by means of a mechanism waves his hand. Measured replicas of the box are on display at the Virginia Historical Society, the Valentine Richmond History Center, and the Uncle Tom's Cabin Historic Site in Dresden, Ontario. At the 2001 dedication of an outdoor box at Richmond's Canal Walk, the city's mayor fitted himself into the metal replica.[30]

Indeed, the box itself has had scholarly appraisal. In 1997 Samira Kawash, writing about the slave narrative as "a meditation on the possibility of freedom itself," addressed the multiple meanings of Brown's box. "Through its various referents," she stated, "the box successively reconstitutes Brown as corpse, as fetus, as first man." Drawing a parallel to the attic where the fugitive Harriet Jacobs hid for seven years, Kawash describes "the space marked out by the box" as an "elsewhere" that was "neither fully within slavery nor fully outside it."[31]

The appeal of Henry Box Brown's tale to children had been recognized as early as 1849 in *Cousin Ann's Stories for Children*. Arthur Huff Fauset included Brown in his work *For Freedom: A Biographical Story of the American Negro* (1927), a history for youth. More recently several authors have presented accounts of Box Brown for young readers. "This Side Up Ship to Philadelphia" appeared in a 1992 collection of "adventure stories" from *Highlights for Children* magazine. Books that tell of Brown include Virginia Hamilton's *Many Thousand Gone: African Americans from Slavery to Freedom* (1993), and Dennis Brindell Fradin's *Bound for the North Star: True Stories of Fugitive Slaves* (2000). In 2001 the magazine *Storyworks* published a short play script by Mack Lewis, "The Daring Escape of Henry 'Box' Brown," for classroom performance. In 2002 a musical about Brown called *Box* was presented at the Learning Corridor theater in Hartford, Connecticut, and the Virginia Opera has created *Oh Freeman!*, an operatic presentation for middle-school students about black civil rights heroes including Brown.[32]

In a 1998 essay about Henry Box Brown, Marcus Wood cites Henry James's observation about *Uncle Tom's Cabin* that "there was for that triumphant work no classified condition." The story swiftly migrated to theater, music, moving panorama, and more, and James thus proposed that it was "much less a book than a state of vision." Referring to the many forms of abolitionist material that Henry Box Brown inspired, Wood states that "this notion of a popular visionary quality superseding or engulfing the text, constantly reinventing it, nicely defines the cultural adoption of Brown's story." Indeed the reinvention of the man of the box continues into the twenty-first century, for, to adopt an expression from theater, Henry Box Brown has proved to have longer legs than *Uncle Tom's Cabin.*[33]

In recent years, artists in a variety of mediums have found material in Brown's story. Patricia Khayyam's nine-minute film entitled "Henry Box Brown" (1990) has been shown at international film festivals. In the opera *Vanqui* by John A. Williams and Leslie Burrs, given its premiere in 1999 by Opera/Columbus in Ohio, the spirits of Vanqui and Prince encounter famous black freedom fighters, one of them Henry Box Brown. The Delaware Humanities Forum commissioned a musical, *Delaware's Railroad to Freedom*, in which Brown is a character; playwright and actor Mike Wiley centers his one-man performance piece, *One Noble Journey*, on Brown's escape; and Tony Kushner, author of the prizewinning drama *Angels in America*, has promised a new play entitled *Henry Box Brown, or, The Mirror of Slavery*. Brown has also inspired poems by Elizabeth Alexander, Lamont Steptoe, and A. Van Jordan. Artist Glenn Ligon's sculptural assemblage *To Disembark* includes marked wooden crates that refer to Henry Box Brown. Regarding her 1987 work, "32 Hours in a Box . . . Still Counting," artist Pat Ward Williams stated, "I think as black people we have to find different solutions to overcome the obstacles that are in our lives politically and also personally. This is a piece about Henry Box Brown and problem solving."[34]

The historian John W. Blassingame remarked in 1977 that Brown's story of escape "sounds incredible but is supported by a wealth of sources." Scholars and publishers have provided access to a number of documentary sources about Brown's life. The 1849 *Narrative* was reprinted in 1969, and William Still's work *The Underground Rail Road* in 1970. Most of James C. A. Smith's known manuscript letters were reproduced by the *Black Abolitionist Papers* project in 1985. The texts of both the 1849 and the 1851 *Narrative* have been made available online. The 1851 *Narrative*, last reprinted in 1852, became available in two 2002 books: in a collection called *Shadowing Slavery: Five African American Autobiographical Narratives*, and by itself in an edition from Oxford University Press, with an introduction by Richard Newman and a foreword by Henry Louis Gates Jr.[35]

Recently scholars have explored aspects of Brown's career after his escape. R. J. M. Blackett placed Brown within the black abolitionist campaign to sway British public opinion in *Building an Antislavery Wall* (1983). Cynthia Griffin Wolff in 1996 wrote that Brown's *Mirror of Slavery* was "an entirely new kind of African American narrative, one that was radically different from the standard slave's story." Wolff states that "the iconoclastic retelling of the slave's story in this panorama" is "Brown's signal achievement." The historian Audrey Fisch has found in contemporary reactions to Brown's performances in England a debate about the propriety of popular entertainments and the tastes of the English audience. H. Box Brown materializes in a book for young readers called *Conjure Times: Black Magicians in America* by James Haskins and Kathleen Benson (2001).[36]

Marcus Wood, a historian of art, in 2000 presented the various images of Brown's unboxing as "perhaps the most potent single metaphor" that the abolitionists possessed "for the displacement of the traditional image of the 'runaway.'" Wood writes that Brown "possessed entrepreneurial flair," became "a star-turn," and was "artistically, the most forward-looking of all abolitionist propagandists." Because Brown "shattered the ceremonial and rhetorical proprieties of the formal lecture hall," he became "out of kilter" with British reformers' expectations and faced the "hostility of the English establishment."[37] In such works the historical Henry Box Brown begins to appear.

Brown Unbound

Plainly there was more to Henry Box Brown than just his escape from slavery. His passage in the box was not a thing apart from the rest of his life but was in keeping with it. The attributes that enabled Brown to succeed as a fugitive he displayed time and again over the years.

As a young boy Henry Brown thought his old master was God. He learned to be more critical of slaveholders, especially after suffering from their disregard for black family life. Although Brown's status stayed humble, signs of his native ability emerged within the constrictions of slavery. He was among the most skillful workers in the tobacco factory and a leading performer in the African Baptist Church choir. He labored to improve his lot until the day his wife and children were sold. At first overwhelmed by their loss, Brown channeled his grief into resolve. He determined to flee, found assistance at the disaffected edge of society, and broke for liberty.

Brown sang a hymn of thanksgiving shortly after his arrival in Philadelphia, and no aspect of his escape better predicted his subsequent career. That he was prepared with an appropriate psalm was surely in itself a key to the accomplishment, for he had visualized success and that vision bore him through grim moments in the box. Even with his inner strength, however, Brown did not control his destiny and depended on fortune. In singing his hymn Brown, with prescient aplomb, both acknowledged the grace of his emancipation and laid claim to being the maker of his own story.

Henry Brown's arrival in the North occured precisely when the abolitionists, and he himself, could use his tale to best effect. At the Boston antislavery convention, two months after his escape, Brown rose to the occasion to perform his arrival hymn and gain a name as a singer. Indeed, through music the freed Brown first showed talent beyond the heroism of his escape. Brown voiced the song of his home community, and his authentic representation stood against minstrelsy's detached rendition and racist trappings. Well before the spiritual was widely heard in the years after the Civil War, Henry Box Brown was introducing a vital American music to audiences in the North and Great Britain.

Brown was not educated and his reading and writing skills probably never exceeded the rudimentary. Even so, he was capable of expressing himself and clearly had a point of view. Not for him were doctrinal disputes, class distinctions, or religiously based proscriptions. Brown found common cause with Benjamin F. Roberts and his independent African American position and ethic of self-effort. If Brown was a different sort of political activist than Roberts, and not as profound a critic of American society as Roberts's uncle Hosea Easton, their examples offered encouragement to Brown to assert his own independence. Brown's actions made it evident that he would captain his own ship, even when his course left behind those once close to him.

Copies survive of the books produced in Henry Box Brown's name and of the numerous prints that depicted him. Lost is *Mirror of Slavery*, his first and most original moving panorama. Before Harriet Beecher Stowe's *Uncle Tom's Cabin*, Brown's artists had designed, and Brown was exhibiting, a narrative about slavery that featured fictional protagonists. In ways novel for its period, *Mirror of Slavery* tapped the expressive potential of montage in theatrical visual art. Brown's panorama was at the forefront in bringing the antislavery message to the theatrical mediums of popular culture, a development that flowered in the 1850s with the many versions of *Uncle Tom's Cabin* and thereby extended the reach of abolitionism immeasurably. Henry Box Brown's *Mirror of Slavery* was an important work of political art that was widely seen at a time when it was wholly relevant.

During 1849 and 1850, when the Fugitive Slave Bill was prepared and then considered in Congress, Henry Box Brown, by exploit if not by name, was probably as famous as any other fugitive slave. Senator Thomas Hart Benton, of Missouri, for example, related an anecdote in 1850 that depended on his listeners' knowledge of Brown's escape for its punch line. Brown's story fed slaveholders' paranoia of abolitionist conspiracy, and his public presence in the North added further irritation. Brown thus contributed to the conditions that brought to passage the Fugitive Slave Bill, the law that forced him into exile.

Once in Great Britain, Henry Box Brown presented his antislavery exhibition to many thousands of people. There was no other antislavery advocate quite like him, with his combination of personal experience of slavery and dramatic escape, a pointed and graphic antislavery exhibition, and longevity on the show circuit. Surely Brown was the only abolitionist to lead a parade through a town dressed as an African prince and brandishing a huge sword. Brown the showman no doubt reached audiences not addressed by more proper lecturers. Unsanctioned by any antislavery organization, Henry Box Brown continued to act in the campaign against slavery throughout the 1850s.

In time Brown disengaged from the realm of the political and became an entertainer for whom the show was the thing. Among the personalities on the circuit, Brown distinguished himself with his persona of the African prince, which he maintained as he progressed from moving panoramas to mesmerism to magic. Just as the stage title "professor" suggested weighty knowledge, or "wizard" mystical powers, Brown's African prince portrayed an entertainer with special qualities. In this public role Brown expressed something of himself personally, for he was assured enough in his African heritage to see it as an asset to be advertised, and his self-anointed title of prince hinted of aristocracy as in fairy tales, in which one born to royalty is, even dressed in rags, always royal and fit to reign.

Henry Box Brown's last-known field of endeavor was conjuring. His reading of the direction of popular entertainment was perceptive. The later nineteenth century was a brilliant era for theatrical magic, when stage conjurors were unsurpassed in offering wonderment. If the Brown family act did not compete with the great conjurors, and in truth seems only to have scratched a living, Brown's foray into magic intrigues for its fact, not its triumph. When his life began in slavery, magic was a destination beyond the horizon. He reached it by a trajectory that in its evolution lends Brown a contemporary aura. Resolute, resourceful, and open to new things, Henry Box Brown embraced his world turned right-side-up with a life of creative transformation.

Endnotes

Introduction

1. This and the next two paragraphs from the *Liberator*, 8 June 1849.

Chapter One: Virginia

1. The most important sources for Henry Brown's early life are Charles Stearns, *Narrative of Henry Box Brown* (Boston, [1849]), cited as 1849 *Narrative*; and *Narrative of the Life of Henry Box Brown, Written by Himself* (Manchester, Eng., 1851), cited as 1851 *Narrative* (quotation on 1). Unless otherwise noted, this chapter is based on the 1849 *Narrative*, 14–37; and the 1851 *Narrative*, 1–17. The 1851 *Narrative* states that Brown was born in 1815 (1), and that he was 15 in 1830 (16). The 1849 *Narrative* says he was born in 1816 (14), and that he was 13 in June 1830 (33) when John Barret gave him to his son William Barret who then sent Brown to Richmond. See also "Brown, Henry Box," *Dictionary of Virginia Biography: Volume Two, Bland–Cannon* (Richmond, 2001), 294–296. The Louisa Road ran northwest from Richmond to a gap in the Blue Ridge Mountains along the path of today's U.S. Highways 22 and 33. The Hermitage is located on today's Virginia Secondary Highway 656. Claudia Anderson Chisholm and Ellen Gray Lillie, *Old Home Places of Louisa County* (Louisa, Va., 1979), 78.

2. 1851 *Narrative*, 17; Virginia Census, Louisa Co., 1820, John Barret household.

3. 1849 *Narrative*, 19; James Silk Buckingham, *The Slave States of America* (London and Paris, [1842]), 2:412; Malcolm H. Harris, *History of Louisa County, Virginia* (Richmond, 1936), 1–2; "List taken of Articles, to be sold for account of Miss Mary Barret, now on her plantation on Little River," 24 Jan. 1832, in Louisa Co. Will Book, 8:337, LVA; Louisa Co. Personal Property Tax Books, 1815–1829, Library of Virginia, Richmond (hereafter cited as LVA). According to the Louisa County Property Tax Books, most of the slaves at the Hermitage actually belonged to John Barret's sister Mary Barret, who never married and lived there her whole life. In 1825, for example, Mary Barret paid taxes on twenty-two slaves, and John Barret paid taxes on five.

4. John Pendleton Kennedy, *Swallow Barn, or, A Sojourn in the Old Dominion*, rev. ed. (New York, 1851), 449–450. "Cymblings" (spelled *cymlings*) are a greenish-white, flower-shaped summer squash also called pattypan.

5. On John Barret, see George Warren Chappelear, *Barret, Volume III, Families of Virginia* (Harrisonburg, Va., 1934), 12, 16, 21–22; Harris, *History of Louisa County*, 287–288. John Barret paid property tax in Richmond for the year 1800, but his name does not appear for 1801 (see Richmond City Personal Property Tax Books, LVA). In 1788 and 1789 Barret served as a witness in a business deal for Patrick Henry, and in 1789 Henry owed Barret £126 (Deed of Dorothea [Dandridge] Henry and Patrick Henry to James Thompson for 214 acres in Henrico Co., 17 Oct. 1788, and verso receipt of 5 Feb. 1789, both witnessed by John Barret, Mss11:2 T3733:1–2, Virginia Historical Society, Richmond; John Barret, Richmond, to Robert Carter, of "Nomony" Hall, Westmoreland Co., 11 Nov. 1789, Carter Family Papers, 1651–1861, Mss1 C2468a 175, Virginia Historical Society, Richmond). At Richmond's new city hall, opened in 1971, the names of the mayors are carved in marble on the wall of the council chamber, and John Barret's name appears three times. The first patents for his father, Charles Barret, are dated 28 Sept. 1730. Nell Marion Nugent, *Cavaliers and Pioneers: Abstracts of Land Patents and Grants, Volume Three, 1695–1732* (Richmond, 1979), 373–374, 375, 383.

6. 1851 *Narrative*, 5; 1849 *Narrative*, 15.

7. 1851 *Narrative*, 3; 1849 *Narrative*, 17.

8. 1849 *Narrative*, 17–18.

9. Ibid, 21 (first quotation), 25 (third quotation); 1851 *Narrative*, 8 (second quotation).

10. 1849 *Narrative*, 25–26; 1851 *Narrative*, 11; Harris, *History of Louisa County*, 4. Brown stated that Ambler's mill was twenty miles away from the Hermitage and Bullock's was ten, but

his numerical estimates are more useful for relative than for absolute values.

In 1820 John Ambler's household included 120 slaves, the largest total in Louisa County, and he remained the largest slaveholder in the county through the next decade. (Virginia Census, Louisa Co., 1820; Louisa Co. Personal Property Tax Books, 1820–1829, LVA). Several men named Bullock appear in the Louisa County Personal Property Tax Books but none who were not slaveholders.

11. 1851 *Narrative*, 14.

12. Ibid. John Barret's eldest son, Charles Barret, lived in Louisa during the 1820s but he never owned more than about a dozen slaves and usually fewer. Though no evidence has been found to prove an emancipation of slaves by Charles Barret, after paying taxes on ten slaves in 1826 Barret paid taxes on only six slaves in 1827. While this reduction might have been a result of slave sales, it could also have come from a small-scale, private emancipation that might have been the basis for the hopes that Henry Brown and other slaves felt when John Barret was on his deathbed. See Chappelear, *Barret*, 28; Louisa Co. Personal Property Tax Books, 1815–1829, LVA; Janice Abercrombie, trans., *Free Blacks of Louisa County, Virginia* (Athens, Ga., 1994).

13. 1849 *Narrative*, 13; 1851 *Narrative*, 14–15. The account in the 1851 *Narrative* states that Barret called for Brown and his mother, not brother, as the 1849 *Narrative* has it. Brother fits the context better, and the 1851 *Narrative* is plagued by many typographical errors. The 1849 *Narrative*'s "brother" seems more probable.

14. Harris, *History of Louisa County*, 288; 1851 *Narrative*, 16. John Barret's date of death is from his tombstone at the Hermitage. Chappelear, *Barret*, 16; WPA Virginia Historical Inventory, The Hermitage, home and graveyard, Louisa Co., survey by Nancy S. Pate, 25 Aug. 1936, VHIR/16/0534, LVA. This latter source does not give the month and year of Barret's death in the report.

15. 1851 *Narrative*, 17, 2. The meaning of "keep Miss" is not clear; there are added connotations to a modern ear. There is a reference to the "keeping room" as a name for a parlor, or "keep" may have derived from "housekeeping." "Keep Miss" does not appear in the several dictionaries of nineteenth-century usage that were consulted.

16. Though its focus is on the 1850s, Gregg Kimball's *American City, Southern Place* gives a comprehensive portrait of antebellum Richmond. Gregg D. Kimball, *American City, Southern Place: A Cultural History of Antebellum Richmond* (Athens, Ga., and London, Eng., 2000), 3–80.

17. J. Miller McKim to Sydney Howard Gay, Philadelphia, 26 Mar. 1849 (as copied by Joseph Ricketson and enclosed with letter to Deborah Weston, 29 Apr. 1849), Weston Papers, Boston Public Library. For another firsthand description of Henry Box Brown, see Anna Thwing Field, in *Hopedale Reminiscences* ([Hopedale, Mass.], 1910).

18. 1851 *Narrative*, 18–19.

19. Joseph Clarke Robert, *The Tobacco Kingdom: Plantation, Market, and Factory in Virginia and North Carolina, 1800–1860* (Durham, N.C., 1938), 161–196.

20. "Barret, William," *Dictionary of Virginia Biography: Volume One, Aaroe–Blanchfield* (Richmond, 1998), 1:353–354; Mutual Assurance Society plats of insured property, 3 Sept. 1817 (Policy No. 2376, vol. 73 [Reel 9]), 15 Dec. 1829 (Policy No. 7073, vol. 90 [Reel 13]), 31 Dec. 1836 (Policy No. 9818, vol. 99 [Reel 15]), 19 Mar. 1844 (Policy No. 12939, vol. 109 [Reel 17]), 22 Apr. 1846 (Policy No. 14257, vol. 114 [Reel 18]), Declarations and Revaluations of Assurance, 1796–1872, microfilm, Mutual Assurance Society of Virginia, Business Records Collection, Acc. 31634, LVA; William Barret will, ca. 1870, in James Nathaniel Dunlop Papers, 1840–1888, Mss1/D9214 a / FA2/Box 8, VHS. William Barret was born in 1786 in Richmond. He escaped the famous 1811 Richmond Theatre fire: he attended the performance but left early before fire destroyed the theater and killed seventy-two people, including the governor and other important citizens. Barret's will contains an entry noting that most of the estate was on account at "J. K. Gilliot & Co., of London." John Kirton Gilliat was the second cousin of William Gilliat, who had taken over the Virginia operations for the family after the death of Thomas Gilliat and the return to England of Thomas's brother John Gilliat (father of John Kirton Gilliat), and one of the partners in the London merchant house J. K. Gilliat & Co. Neil W. W. Gilliat, "John Gilliat 1761–1819," in "About the Gilliat Family," http://gilliat1.50megs.com/custom.html (12 Mar. 2003).

21. 1849 *Narrative*, 37, 53.

22. American Colonization Society, Virginia Branch, Records, 1823–1859, Minute Book, 1823–1828, 17 Jan. 1825, p. 19, Mss3 Am353 a, VHS; Marie Tyler-McGraw, "The American Colonization Society in Virginia, 1816–1832: A Case Study in Southern Liberalism" (Ph.D. diss., George Washington University, 1980), 1; P. J. Staudenraus, *The African Colonization Movement, 1816–1865* (New York, 1961), 23–35.

23. William Barret's name appears in American Colonization Society, Virginia Branch, Minute Book, 1823–1828, 10 Feb. 1824, p. 11; 17 Jan. 1825, p. 22; 16 Jan. 1826, p. 34; 8 Jan. 1827, p. 37; 10 Dec. 1827, p. 43; 10 Dec. 1828, p. 52, VHS. Barret is identified as a manager in *Third Report of the Managers of the Richmond and Manchester Colonization Society* ([Richmond, 1826]), 12, and *Fifth Annual Meeting of the Richmond and Manchester Colonization Society* ([Richmond, 1827]), 2. When the local auxiliary of the American Colonization Society reconstituted itself in Dec. 1828 as the Colonization Society of Virginia, Barret was elected secretary. *Sixth Annual Meeting of the Richmond and Manchester Colonization Society* ([Richmond], 1828), 7–9. Barret is not listed as an officer in the 1832 *Proceedings of the Colonization Society of Virginia, and Report of the Managers* (Richmond, [1832]).

24. 1849 *Narrative*, 40; Henry Irving Tragle, *The Southampton Slave Revolt of 1831: A Compilation of Source Material* (Amherst, Mass., 1971)), esp. xv–xviii, 141–142, 310; William Sidney Drewry, *The Southampton Insurrection* (Washington, D.C., 1900), 33–34.

25. 1851 *Narrative*, 19.

26. American Colonization Society, Virginia Branch, Minute Book, 1823–1828, 15 Nov. 1831, p. 56, VHS; Theodore M. Whitfield, *Slavery Agitation in Virginia, 1829–1832* (Baltimore, 1930; reprint, New York, 1969), 65–94; *Journal of the House of Delegates of . . . Virginia, Begun . . . the Fifth Day of December, One Thousand Eight Hundred and Thirty-One* (Richmond, 1831), 109. See also Alison Goodyear Freehling, *Drift toward Dissolution: The Virginia Slavery Debate of 1831–1832* (Baton Rouge, La., and London, Eng., 1982), esp. chap. 5, "Slavery in Virginia Is an Evil," 122–169.

27. Unsigned letter in *Richmond Enquirer*, 2 Sept. 1831, cited as being from "Veritas" in Whitfield, *Slavery Agitation in Virginia*, 125–126; June Purcell Guild, *Black Laws of Virginia: A Summary of the Legislative Acts of Virginia concerning Negroes from Earliest Times to the Present* (Richmond, 1936), 107; 1851 *Narrative*, 19.

28. Stanley Harrold has recently argued that the debate of 1831–1832 was not determinative in the transition of southern discourse on slavery and that the process had begun earlier. Stanley Harrold, *The Abolitionists and the South, 1831–1861* (Lexington, Ky., 1995).

29. 1851 *Narrative*, 20; Louisa County Deed Book T, 2 June 1832, 468–471, LVA. William Barret paid the personal property tax on seven slaves in 1829; twelve in 1830; eighteen in 1831; twenty-five in 1832; twenty-nine in 1833; and thirty-eight in 1834. Richmond City Personal Property Tax Books, LVA.

30. 1851 *Narrative*, 20–21.

31. Ibid., 21–22.

32. 1849 *Narrative*, 47–48. Hancock Lee lived in Chesterfield County, across the river from Richmond. From 1829 to 1840 Lee's ownership of taxable slaves varied in number from three to eight. Chesterfield County Personal Property Tax Books, LVA. See also William L. Montague, *Montague's Richmond Directory and Business Advertiser, for 1850–1851* ([Richmond, 1850]), 86. In the 1851 *Narrative*, 44, Brown stated that in 1848 he had been with his wife for twelve years. See also 1849 *Narrative*, 54.

33. 1849 *Narrative*, 48; 1851 *Narrative*, 33–34; Virginia Census, Richmond City, 1850. Philip M. Tabb Jr. owned one slave in 1837 and two in 1838; he does not appear in the tax list in 1839. Richmond City Personal Property Books, LVA.

34. Declarations and Revaluations of Assurance, 1796–1872, 31 Dec. 1836 (Policy No. 9818, vol. 99 [Reel 15]), Mutual Assurance Society of Virginia, LVA; Jesse S. Armistead to Joseph C. Cabell, 15 Mar. 1855, Nathaniel Francis Cabell, Collection of Papers Relating to Virginia's Agricultural History, 1771–1879, Acc. 2, Personal Papers Collection, LVA. Brown stated that the factory was "about 300 feet in length", 1849 *Narrative*, 41, but an 1844 plat of William Barret's factory

shows it was not that large. 19 Mar. 1844 (Policy No. 12939, vol. 109 [Reel 17]), Mutual Assurance Society of Virginia, LVA.

35. 1849 *Narrative*, 41–42; 1851 *Narrative*, 22; Robert, *The Tobacco Kingdom*, 201, 211, 214. Robert lists the job titles in tobacco factories of this era as stemmers, dippers, twisters, lump-makers, prizers and screwmen, draymen, hogshead-men, and cooks (197). Brown may have included in his report of very long workdays any time that was allowed for meals, such as a mid-day dinner break.

36. William Cullen Bryant, *Letters of a Traveller; or, Notes of Things Seen in Europe and America* (New York and London, 1850), 73–74; "Elihu Burritt in the South," from the July 1854 issue of the *Bond of Brotherhood*, quoted in the *London Anti-Slavery Reporter*, new series, vol. 2, Oct. 1854, p. 224.

37. 1851 *Narrative*, 25. In the 1849 *Narrative* Brown gave the weekly sum as 75¢ (44). On Richmond tobacco manufacturing and slavery, see John T. O'Brien, "Factory, Church, and Community: Blacks in Antebellum Richmond," *Journal of Southern History* 44 (Nov. 1978): 511–521; and Suzanne Gehring Schnittman, "Slavery in Virginia's Urban Tobacco Industry, 1840–1860" (Ph.D. diss., University of Rochester, 1986). Although not in accordance with the law, many factory slaves eventually hired themselves out, seeking the best situations during the annual hiring period. Only after the slave had found a position was the master informed of the arrangement. See Robert, *The Tobacco Kingdom*, 201.

38. "Elihu Burritt in the South," *London Anti-Slavery Reporter*, Oct. 1854, p. 224; James Miller McKim to "Dear friend," Philadelphia, 28 Mar. 1849, May Anti-Slavery Collection, 1749–1933, Division of Rare and Manuscript Collections, Cornell University Library, Ithaca, N.Y. (hereafter cited as May Anti-Slavery Collection, Cornell).

39. William Chambers, *Things as They Are in America* (London and Edinburgh, 1854), 271–272. The residential hollow that Chambers saw was probably Penitentiary Bottom, located by the penitentiary at the foot of Gamble's Hill.

40. Nannie May Tilley, *The Bright-Tobacco Industry, 1860–1929* (Chapel Hill, 1948), 159 n. 20; Jesse S. Armistead to Joseph C. Cabell, 15 Mar. 1855, Nathaniel Francis Cabell, Collection of Papers, LVA; Richmond City Personal Property and Land Tax Books, LVA; Mary Wingfield Scott, *Old Richmond Neighborhoods* (Richmond, 1950; reprint, Richmond, 1975), 182; "Barret, William," *DVB*, 1:353–354.

41. *Richmond Daily Dispatch*, 24 Aug. 1890; *Richmond Times*, 24 Aug. 1890; 1849 *Narrative*, 42, 44. The Richmond City Personal Property Tax Books, LVA, have entries for "J. F. Allen & Jr." from 1834 to 1840. Beginning in 1841 only "J. F. Allen" appears. See also "Allen, John F.," *DVB*, 1:91–92.

42. 1851 *Narrative*, 23 (first, second, and fourth quotations); 1849 *Narrative*, 43 (second quotation). Property tax records are inconclusive in either proving or disproving Brown's accusations of skimming against John F. Allen. Richmond City Personal Property Tax Books, LVA.

43. 1849 *Narrative*, 45; 1851 *Narrative*, 24–26.

44. 1851 *Narrative*, 26–27; 1849 *Narrative*, 45. John F. Allen opened his own tobacco business before the Civil War as John F. Allen & Co. By the mid-1870s his company began to manufacture cigarettes, one of the earliest to do so. He and Lewis Ginter became partners about 1875 and the company emerged as the most prominent tobacco manufacturer in Richmond. Allen and Ginter exhibited cigarettes at the Philadelphia Exposition in 1876 where they won a bronze medal. Allen sold out and retired about the end of 1880. At his death in 1890 he was noted as an amateur painter and active in the Mozart Association. See "John F. Allen," *DVB*, 1:91–92; *Richmond Dispatch*, 24 Aug. 1890; *Richmond Times*, 24 Aug. 1890; Tilley, *The Bright-Tobacco Industry*, 508.

45. *Richmond Republican*, 30 May 1849; Frederick Law Olmsted, *A Journey in the Seaboard Slave States, with Remarks on Their Economy* (New York, 1856; reprint, New York, 1863), 28. Although slaves were prohibited from assembling without whites present, it seems that in general the authorities acceded to the Sunday socializing.

46. This and the next paragraph from 1849 *Narrative*, 40; 1851 *Narrative*, 30–31. The whites' First Baptist Church, designed in 1841 by the architect Thomas U. Walter, stands today at Eleventh and Broad Streets, and is now used by the Medical College of Virginia of

Virginia Commonwealth University. The original First Baptist Church building from 1802, which the whites sold to the congregation of the First African Baptist Church, was replaced in 1876 by a new building, which stands at Broad and College Streets and is also now part of the Medical College of Virginia. Scott, *Old Richmond Neighborhoods*, 96–98, 110; *The First Century of the First Baptist Church of Richmond, Virginia, 1780–1880* (Richmond, 1880), esp. 68–69, 81, 84–86; Blanche Sydnor White, *First Baptist Church, Richmond, 1780–1955: One Hundred Years of Service to God and Man* (Richmond, [1955]), 14, 19, 29–30, 38, 41–42, 44–45, 51, 54–57, 73, 80–85, 92, 95–99.

47. 1851 *Narrative*, 3, 32; Robert Ryland, "Reminiscences of the First African Baptist Church, Richmond, Va.," *American Baptist Memorial* 14 (Dec. 1855): 354.

48. 1851 *Narrative*, 47; Bryant, *Letters of a Traveller*, 75; Charles Richard Weld, *A Vacation Tour in the United States and Canada* (London, 1855), 294. The First African Baptist choir apparently rehearsed on Sundays after church services, the only day of the week that slave members of the choir would be able to participate: "The Choir asked and obtained the use of the Library one hour every Sunday after morning worship." First African Baptist Church (Richmond, Va.), Minute Books, 1841–1930, Minutes, 1841–1859, Book 1, 6 Apr. 1845, p. 77, Acc. 28255, Church Records Collection, LVA.

49. Eileen Southern, *The Music of Black Americans: A History*, 2d ed. (New York, 1983), 58; Gilbert Chase, *America's Music from the Pilgrims to the Present*, rev. 2d ed., (New York, 1966), 81.

50. Samuel Mordecai, *Richmond in By-Gone Days: Being Reminiscences of an Old Citizen* (Richmond, 1856), 296; O'Brien, "Factory, Church, and Community: Blacks in Antebellum Richmond," 520; Bryant, *Letters of a Traveller*, 74–75.

51. 1851 *Narrative*, 21, 48; James Miller McKim to "Dear friend," Philadelphia, 28 Mar. 1849, May Anti-Slavery Collection, Cornell. Instead of standard musical notation, books of psalmody in this period contained one of several simplified systems of notation.

52. William Wells Brown, *My Southern Home; or, The South and Its People* (Boston, 1880; reprint, Upper Saddle River, N.J., 1968), 144; Ira Berlin, *Slaves without Masters: The Free Negro in the Antebellum South* (New York, 1974).

53. John Kitton, Preston, to L. Chamerovzow, 7 Apr. 1854, Anti-Slavery Papers, MSS Brit Emp S18 C33/35, Bodleian Library of Commonwealth and African Studies at Rhodes House, Oxford University, Oxford, Eng.; *Richmond Examiner*, 28 Sept. 1849; *Richmond Republican*, reprinted in *Baltimore Sun*, 29 Sept. 1849.

54. This and the next paragraph from 1851 *Narrative*, 34–36.

55. This and the next paragraph from ibid., 36–37.

56. Ibid., 37. For the years 1840 to 1844, Joseph H. Colquitt paid property taxes on four slaves; in 1845 he paid on one slave. Samuel S. Cottrell in 1844 paid property tax on a gold watch, but no slaves; in 1845 he paid property taxes on two slaves. It seems likely that Cottrell purchased Nancy Brown in 1844. Richmond City Personal Property Tax Books, LVA.

57. 1851 *Narrative*, 38; 1849 *Narrative*, 50.

58. Alexander MacKay, *The Western World; or, Travels in the United States in 1846–47* (Philadelphia, 1849), 1:251; Kennedy, *Swallow Barn*, 20.

59. Peter P. Hinks, *To Awaken My Afflicted Brethren: David Walker and the Problem of Antebellum Slave Resistance* (University Park, Pa., 1997), 131–137; Virginia Governor (1830–1834: John Floyd), Executive Papers, 1830–1834, Slave and Free Negro Letter Book, 1831, Misc. Items, State Government Records Collection, LVA. The census did not record places of nativity until 1850, when the foreign born comprised nearly 8 percent of the city's population. The total foreign-born population more than doubled during the next decade. See Kimball, *American City, Southern Place*, 31–32.

60. Merton L. Dillon, *The Abolitionists: The Growth of a Dissenting Minority* (De Kalb, Ill., 1974), 88–92; Guild, *Black Laws of Virginia*, 199–200.

61. *Richmond Republican*, 30 May 1849.

62. Guild, *Black Laws of Virginia*, 84.

63. *Richmond Daily Dispatch*, 20 Aug. 1853; *Richmond Republican*, reprinted in *Baltimore*

Sun, 29 Sept. 1849. On the campaign by Richmond authorities against African American–run shops, see Berlin, *Slaves without Masters*, 242–243.

64. *Blevins' Case* (1848) (5 Grattan), *Virginia Reports*, 5:704–706; Virginia Census, Richmond City, 1850; Petition of John A. Blevins to George W. Munford, 5 Aug. 1859, Virginia Governor (1856–1860: Henry A. Wise), Executive Papers, 1856–1859, Pardon Papers, July–Dec. 1859, Sept. 1859, Acc. 36710, State Government Records Collection, LVA (hereafter cited as Wise Executive Papers, Pardon Papers, Sept. 1859).

65. *Richmond Whig*, 30 June 1848; Testimony of Burrell Jenkins, Blevins Depositions, *Commonwealth v. John A. Blevins*, Richmond City Hustings Court, Ended Causes, Sept. Term 1848, Box 182, LVA (hereafter cited as Blevins Depositions, *Commonwealth v. Blevins*); Petition of John A. Blevins to George W. Munford, 5 Aug. 1859, Wise Executive Papers, Pardon Papers, Sept. 1859; Testimony of Thomas B. White, Blevins Depositions, *Commonwealth v. Blevins*.

66. John A. Blevins to George W. Munford, 5 Aug. 1859, Wise Executive Papers, Pardon Papers, Sept. 1859; Testimony of Clement White, Blevins Depositions, *Commonwealth v. Blevins*; *Blevins' Case* (1848) (5 Grattan), *Virginia Reports*, 5:707.

67. *Richmond Semi-weekly Examiner*, 13 Oct. 1848. Blevins was charged on 25 Aug. 1848 with aiding the escape of "John, a slave, the property of John Enders"; on 5 Sept. 1848 with aiding the escape of "John a slave the property of Richard Barton Haxall"; and with aiding the escape of the four slaves in June, the date of the last charge unknown. On 12 Sept. 1848, the Hustings Court sent Blevins's case on to the Circuit Superior Court of Law and Chancery. The trial records were lost in 1865. Blevins unsuccessfully appealed his conviction for the June 1848 escape of four slaves, and the records of that trial are summarized in the appeal record, which noted Blevins had received a sentence of five years. He remained in the penitentiary until 1865. The *Examiner* reported that Blevins "has been, we have heard, from the year 1819 to 1842 in the Penitentiary at different times—if he goes now, we suppose his residence will be permanent." Blevins Depositions, *Commonwealth v. Blevins*; Richmond City Hustings Court, Minute Book 17:592, 594–597, LVA; *Blevins' Case* (1848) (5 Grattan), *Virginia Reports*, 5:703–704; *Richmond Semi-weekly Examiner*, 13 Oct. 1848.

Blevins later claimed that several witnesses had testified falsely in his trial for the June 1848 escape. In a petition for pardon in 1859, Blevins stated that John McAlister and a man named Hoffman "came on two or three different occasions to the jail and secreted themselves" so they would be able to identify Blevins in court; that a witness in the trial, Robert Mayo, had testified that in a previous trial "McAlister was hired to swear to a lie"; and that Hoffman testified he had seen "a man with a white hat on," though Blevins "wore a black hat, invariably, until a few days before my arrest when I purchased a white one." Given that Blevins had not been immediately arrested, it may have been that the state's other evidence was circumstantial and insufficient, and that arrangements were made to ensure his conviction. Petition of John A. Blevins to George W. Munford, 5 Aug. 1859, Wise Executive Papers, Pardon Papers, Sept. 1859.

Soon after the Civil War ended, Laura S. Haviland, an abolitionist and reformer from Michigan, went to Richmond to assist in charitable home-mission work. She wrote that late in 1865, "at a shoe-shop," she met "John Blevins, a noble appearing John Brown sort of man." When "Richmond was taken" in 1865, the penitentiary was opened "and John Blevins, with four hundred other prisoners, walked out free men." Haviland said that he was "sixty years of age, and hard treatment had added ten years to his appearance." Blevins was "teaching a colored school," which he supplemented by working at the shoe shop, "trying to make enough to purchase for himself a suit of clothes." He told her that he planned to return to his home in Philadelphia, and had "just heard from a family that he assisted to their liberty, some of whom had become quite wealthy, and were trying to find him." John Blevins does not appear in Richmond city directories from the period, but a man by that name was recorded there in the 1870 census, aged seventy and living in the home of a shoemaker (Virginia Census, Richmond City, 1870, household of Benjamin Thompson). Haviland wrote that "whenever he went out on the streets he was annoyed by half-grown boys hooting after him, 'Old John Brown, nigger thief.'" Laura S. Haviland, *A Woman's Life Work: Including Thirty Years' Service on the Underground Railroad and in the War*, memorial ed. (Chicago, 1902), 398–399.

68. Richmond City Personal Property Tax Books, LVA; John A. Blevins to George W. Munford, 5 Aug. 1859, Wise Executive Papers, Pardon Papers, Sept. 1859; Testimony of Richard B. Haxall, Robert W. Saunders, Bacon Tait, Alexander Duval, Blevins Depositions, *Commonwealth v. Blevins*. On the motivations of Blevins, see also Nancy Jawish Rives, "'Nurseries of Mischief': Origin and Operations of the Underground Railroad, Richmond, Virginia, 1848–1860" (master's thesis, Virginia Commonwealth University, 1998), 84–88.

69. *Blevins' Case* (1848) (5 Grattan), *Virginia Reports*, 5:706.

70. *Report of the Select Committee Appointed . . . to enquire into the existing Legislation of Congress upon the subject of FUGITIVE SLAVES*, Doc. 50, *Documents of the House of Delegates, 1848–9* (Richmond, 1848), 9–10. "Having shewn the defects existing in the present legislation," the report recommended (18–19) that federal officers be empowered and required to aid the return of fugitive slaves to their owners, which was one of the key provisions in the Fugitive Slave Bill introduced to the U.S. Senate by Senator James Murray Mason, of Virginia, in Jan. 1850; *Congressional Globe*, 31st Cong., 1st sess., 28 Jan. 1850, 21, pt. 1:233–236.

71. This and the next paragraph from 1851 *Narrative*, 38–39. The account of the sale of Brown's wife and children is a synthesis of the accounts in the two *Narratives*, which differ in some of the details.

72. 1851 *Narrative*, 40; 1849 *Narrative*, 51; *Boston Emancipator & Republican*, 7 June 1849. A survey of the *Daily Richmond Enquirer* for advertisements of public auctions of slaves in Aug. 1848 found a woman and three children offered by Nathaniel Boush and Charles B. Hill on 17 Aug. 1848. The only other offering of a woman and three children was on 3 Aug., but the woman was said to be twenty-four years old, probably too young since the Browns had been married about twelve years.

73. 1849 *Narrative*, 52–53.

74. Ibid., 53; 1851 *Narrative*, 42.

75. 1851 *Narrative*, 42–43.

76. 1849 *Narrative*, 53.

77. 1851 *Narrative*, 43.

78. 1849 *Narrative*, 53–54.

79. 1851 *Narrative*, 45. Both *Narratives* state that Nancy Brown and the children were purchased in Richmond by a Methodist preacher. Miller McKim wrote in a letter only a few days after Brown's escape, however, that "Last August his wife & four children who belonged to another man were sold to a trader & carried south. They were purchased from this trader by a Methodist preacher in N.C. The 4th child was not born till the mother reached N. Carolina." The versions in the 1849 and 1851 *Narratives* that have the preacher driving the slave coffle south strain credulity. J. Miller McKim to "Dear friend," 28 Mar. 1849, May Anti-Slavery Collection, Cornell.

80. 1849 *Narrative*, 55; 1851 *Narrative*, 47.

81. 1849 *Narrative*, 56; *Boston Emancipator & Republican*, 7 June 1849; 1851 *Narrative*, 47–48.

82. First African Baptist Church Minutes, 1841–1859, Book 1, 1 Oct. 1848, p. 134, LVA. Church members who were slaves were identified in the minutes by their own names and the names of their masters. Next to Nancy Brown's name in the minute book is "Mr. Colquitt," the name of her former master. A church with several thousand members and much coming and going was unlikely to keep all its records current.

83. 1851 *Narrative*, 47–48.

84. Ibid., 48–49. At the deacons' meeting on 28 Dec. 1848, immediately after the concert would have occurred, "the pastor reported that he had received funds enough to pay the $500. with interest that the church had compromised to pay for the house and lot." First African Baptist Church, Minutes, 1841–1859, Book 1, 28 Dec. 1848, p. 140, LVA. The lyric "Vital spark . . ." is adapted from the poem, "The Dying Christian to his Soul," by Alexander Pope (1688–1744), and appears as the hymn, "Claremont," in William Walker's compilation *The Southern Harmony*, ed. Glenn C. Wilcox (Philadelphia, 1854; reprint, Los Angeles, 1966), 183–186.

85. 1851 *Narrative*, 49; 1849 *Narrative*, 56; *Boston Emancipator & Republican*, 7 June 1849.

86. 1851 *Narrative*, 50. Though Brown's *Narratives* do not identify James C. A. Smith as

the link to Samuel Smith, in a later case (see chap. 3, "Feloniously Advising," 65–68) James C. A. Smith was the conduit for potential escapees to Samuel Smith. The two Smiths may have come into association as neighbors. For a time, James C. A. Smith "kept a cake shop on Broad street, between 3d and 4th streets" (*Richmond Daily Times*, 27 Sept. 1849). By Apr. 1849, and likely for some time prior, Samuel Smith worked at the shoe shop of Stephen Fisher, also located on Broad Street between Third and Fourth Streets. *Richmond Daily Whig*, 15 May 1849; William L. Montague, *The Richmond Directory and Business Advertiser for 1852* (Richmond, 1852), 51.

87. *Richmond Republican*, 9 May 1849. See also *Baltimore Sun*, 16 May 1849.

88. Richmond City Personal Property Tax Books, LVA; 1851 *Narrative*, 50; *Daily Richmond Enquirer*, 8 Sept. 1845.

89. *Richmond Republican*, 10 May 1849, reprinted in *Anti-Slavery Bugle*, 1 June 1849; *Richmond Daily Whig*, 15 May 1849. *Niles' Weekly Register* published on 3 Aug. 1833 the calculation that, if the average 25 percent brokerage fee was added, Americans had spent on lotteries in 1832 a total of about $66,420,000. "That is," the newspaper exclaimed, "five times the sum of the annual expenses of the American government, and . . . nearly three times the whole yearly revenue!" Herbert Asbury, *Sucker's Progress: An Informal History of Gambling in America from the Colonies to Canfield* (New York, 1938), 77–78.

Henry Chafetz, in *Play the Devil: A History of Gambling in the United States from 1492 to 1955* (New York, 1960), 298, explains that policy originated as "side-line lottery betting camouflaged as 'insurance.'" The players wagered that "a particular number would come up" and "higher odds were paid off to the 'insured.'" Vendors of these bets were called "insurance agents," and the bets were called insurance policies.

90. Mordecai, *Richmond in By-Gone Days*, 291–293. Comparing Virginia to the North, a traveler said that "the comparative absence of the excitements of commercial speculation appeared in numerous schemes for lotteries." Russell Lant Carpenter, *Observations on American Slavery, after a Year's Tour in the United States* (London, 1852), 22. In her *Card Sharps, Dream Books, & Bucket Shops: Gambling in 19th-Century America* (Ithaca, N.Y., and London, 1990), Ann Fabian notes: "In the 1840s and 1850s reporters in the northern papers described gambling by African-American men and women. They were particularly struck by their passion for policy" (8).

91. Richmond City Personal Property Tax Books, LVA; Richmond City Hustings Court, Deed Book 48:645 (1 Oct. 1845), LVA.

92. *Daily Richmond Enquirer*, 26 Oct. 1844, 28 June 1845; Richmond City Hustings Court, Deed Book 48:102 (12 Feb. 1845), 155–156 (1 May 1845), 424–425 (18 July 1845), LVA.

93. Richmond City Hustings Court, Deed Book 48:515–516 (12 Aug 1845), 645 (1 Oct. 1845), 656–657 ([n.d.] Oct. 1845), LVA; *Daily Richmond Enquirer*, 22 Sept., 6 Oct. 1845. The *Richmond Examiner* (11 May 1849) was critical of Samuel Smith's "pompous advertisements, first over the signature of the 'Red Boot Man,' and next as lottery vendor." Smith's indenture of 1 Oct. 1845 was in part for a note held by W. M. Newell, of New York City. *Doggett's New York City Directory, for 1849–1850*, 8th ed. (New York, 1849), lists Williard M. Newell & Co., "shoes, &c." (315). The second indenture of Oct. 1845, day not specified, was in part for a bond of $5,000 to Inloes and Brother, a Richmond auction house, and also in part for debts of $3,000 owed to Charles Oat, of Philadelphia. *McElroy's Philadelphia Directory for 1850*, 13th ed. (Philadelphia, 1850), lists Charles C. Oat, merchant (315).

94. *Daily Richmond Enquirer*, 14 Oct., 5 Dec. 1845; Richmond City Hustings Court, Minute Book 16:282 (3 Nov. 1845), 320 (5 Jan. 1846), 352–353 (21 Jan. 1846), 580 (9 Oct. 1846); Minute Book 17:29 (19 Jan. 1847), 151–152 (13 May 1847), 164 (14 June 1847), LVA; Richmond City Personal Property Tax Books, LVA; *Richmond Semi-weekly Examiner*, 11 May 1849. Advertisements for the Eagle Prize Office appeared regularly in the *Daily Richmond Enquirer* beginning 5 Dec. 1845, signed J. Moore & Co. Starting on 6 Feb. 1846, the name of Joseph Chase appeared under the text; the ads ceased after 30 Mar. 1846.

95. *Richmond Daily Whig*, 15 May 1849. See also *Baltimore Sun*, 16 May 1849.

96. *Richmond Semi-weekly Examiner*, 11 May 1849; *Richmond Whig*, 9 May 1849; "Jas Johnson" [Samuel A. Smith] to J. Miller McKim, Richmond, 19 Apr. 1849, May Anti-Slavery Collection, Cornell; *New York Tribune*, 17 July 1856. Testimony in 1848 placed John A. Blevins's residence in

Duval's Addition, located in the section of Richmond now known as Jackson Ward. The lots that Samuel Smith purchased, one of which might have been his residence, were also in Duval's Addition, on Saint James Street and Duval Street. Testimony of Burrell Jenkins, Blevins Depositions, *Commonwealth v. Blevins*; Richmond City Hustings Court, Deed Book 48:102–103 (12 Feb. 1845), 155–156 (1 May 1845), 424–425 (18 July 1845), LVA.

97. Henry Brown's workplace, at Fourteenth and Cary Streets (Montague, *Montague's Richmond Directory and Business Advertiser for 1850–1851*, p. 60), was three blocks from the shoe shop that Samuel Smith operated at Seventeenth and Main (Declarations and Revaluations of Assurance, 1796–1872, 31 Dec. 1844 [Policy No. 12685, vol. 108 (Reel 17)], insuring S. A. Smith's "shoe store and dwelling," Mutual Assurance Society of Virginia, LVA). Brown is known at a later time to have gambled, so it is not unimaginable that he placed policy bets with Smith. A man of integrity, from the point of view of a slave, could have been a policy seller who, rather than refuse to pay or pay only a portion, did pay the proper winnings to a slave who hit a bet. Such a definition of integrity, however, would hardly be suitable for the abolitionist context of Brown's *Narratives*.

Chapter Two: Northbound

1. 1851 *Narrative*, 50.

2. Ibid., 50–51; *Boston Emancipator & Republican*, 7 June 1849. There are conflicting reports of the amount that Henry Brown agreed to pay Samuel Smith to help him escape. Both the 1849 *Narrative*, 58, and the 1851 *Narrative*, 50–51, said Brown had $166 and that the amount agreed on was $86. The *Boston Emancipator & Republican* on 7 June 1849 reported that it was "about $80." A letter that Miller McKim wrote immediately after Brown's arrival in Philadelphia said that "for the service he [Smith] rendered the slave paid him $40." James Miller McKim to Samuel Rhoads, 29 Mar. 1849, Maloney Collection of McKim-Garrison Family Papers, ca. 1814–1940, Papers of James M. McKim, Correspondence 1839–1849, Special Collections, New York Public Library (hereafter cited as Special Collections, New York Public Library).

Brown left the rest of his money with Smith to be forwarded after his arrival. At the time of McKim's letter, the remaining money was still awaited. It never came. The most satisfactory explanation for the differing reports is that the agreed-on price for Smith's assistance was $40, as reported by McKim. When Smith kept the rest of the money, the actual cost to Brown was essentially all his money, $86, which is close to the amount reported in the Boston newspaper. In the *Narratives*, it is possible that his agreement to pay "half" was conflated with what he had actually lost, and thus the total of $166 was obtained by doubling his loss. When his wife was sold in August 1848, Brown had no savings and had to borrow about $20 from James C. A. Smith to regain his furniture. At a rate of $5 per week earned through overwork, from then until Mar. 1849 there was enough time for Brown to have saved $86, even after he repaid the loan from Smith.

3. 1849 *Narrative*, 58–59.

4. Ibid., 59; 1851 *Narrative*, 51.

5. *Richmond Compiler*, 26, 28 Nov. 1842; John B. Mordecai, *A Brief History of the Richmond, Fredericksburg and Potomac Railroad* ([Richmond], Feb. 1940), 18. See also Christopher T. Baer, *Canals and Railroads of the Mid-Atlantic States, 1800–1860* (Wilmington, Del., 1981).

6. *Richmond Republican*, 25 Mar. 1849.

7. Henry Brown was not the first to think of escaping by box. An incident in 1845 suggests the mental and physical cost that his chosen method would require. A box addressed to Louisville, Kentucky, was left at a wharf on the Mississippi River by a free black, who emphasized that it was to be sent on the next boat and handled with care. An hour or two later, a voice called out from the box to "open the door." When opened, a slave emerged "nearly dead with suffocation, and steaming like the escape pipe of a steamboat." The plan was for the box to go to Cincinnati, "whence he was to be conveyed to Canada." The slave stated that "he would have died in a very short time, if he had not been extricated." *Liberator*, 25 July 1845.

8. 1851 *Narrative*, 52.

9. 1849 *Narrative*, 59.

10. *Richmond Daily Times*, 27 Sept. 1849 (also *Richmond Republican*, reprinted in *Baltimore Sun*, 29 Sept. 1849); J. Miller McKim to Sydney Howard Day, 26 Mar. 1849, as copied by Joseph Ricketson and enclosed with letter to Deborah Weston, 29 Apr. 1849, Weston Papers, Boston Public Library; James Miller McKim to Samuel Rhoads, 29 Mar. 1849, Special Collections, New York Public Library. The carpenter Mettauer testified that he "only made one box," and of the boxes used in a later escape attempt, he "was certain neither of them was the one he had made" (*Richmond Daily Times*, 27 Sept. 1849). The *Richmond Republican* (reprinted in the *Baltimore Sun*, 29 Sept. 1849), reported Mettauer "testified that he made a box for (black) Smith, about six months ago."

11. James Miller McKim to "Dear friend," Philadelphia, 28 Mar. 1849, May Anti-Slavery Collection; Lucretia Mott to Joseph and Ruth Dugdale, Philadelphia, 28 Mar. 1849, in *James and Lucretia Mott: Life and Letters*, ed. Anna Davis Hallowell (Boston, 1884), 310.

12. On McKim, see William Still, *The Underground Rail Road* (Philadelphia, 1872; reprint, Chicago, 1970), 679–684; Otelia Cromwell, *Lucretia Mott* (Cambridge, Mass., 1958), 38–39; and Ira V. Brown, "Miller McKim and Pennsylvania Abolitionism," *Pennsylvania History* 30 (Jan. 1963): 56–72.

13. John W. Blassingame, Mae G. Henderson, and Jessica M. Dunn, eds., *Antislavery Newspapers and Periodicals, Volume III (1836–1854)* (Boston, 1981), 61; Larry Gara, *The Liberty Line: The Legend of the Underground Railroad* (Lexington, Ky., 1961), 104–106; William C. Kashatus, "Two Stationmasters on the Underground Railroad: A Tale of Black and White," *Pennsylvania Heritage* 27, no. 4 (fall 2001): 5–11.

14. James Miller McKim to "Dear friend," Philadelphia, 28 Mar. 1849, May Anti-Slavery Collection, Cornell.

15. Samuel A. Smith to James Miller McKim, Richmond, 10 Mar. 1849, May Anti-Slavery Collection, Cornell. There was no bridge as yet across the Susquehanna River on the direct route from Baltimore to Philadelphia. Normally, the railroad cars would be loaded on barges to cross the river. Because of the ice, the barges could not be used, and freight was being loaded off the cars, ferried on smaller boats, and then reloaded on different railroad cars on the other side of the river for the rest of the journey.

16. James Miller McKim to "Dear friend," Philadelphia, 28 Mar. 1849, May Anti-Slavery Collection, Cornell; Pennsylvania Society for Promoting the Abolition of Slavery, Papers, 1748–1979, Minute Book of Pennsylvania Anti-Slavery Society Executive Committee, 1846–1856, Reel 31, Historical Society of Pennsylvania, Philadelphia; Brown, "Miller McKim and Pennsylvania Abolitionism," 72; James Miller McKim to Samuel Rhoads, 29 Mar. 1849, Special Collections, New York Public Library.

17. Samuel A. Smith to James Miller McKim, Richmond, 15 Mar. 1849, May Anti-Slavery Collection, Cornell.

18. James Miller McKim to Samuel A. Smith, Philadelphia, 17 Mar. 1849, May Anti-Slavery Collection, Cornell.

19. James Miller McKim to "Dear friend," Philadelphia, 28 Mar. 1849, May Anti-Slavery Collection, Cornell.

20. Still, *The Underground Rail Road*, 69. Edward M. Davis was the author of *Extracts from the American Slave Code* (Salem, Ohio, and Philadelphia, 1845), a four-page brochure "Compiled from Stoudts Sketch of the Slave Laws, & Statute Books in the Philadelphia Law Library." Edward M. Davis & Co. were "importers" at 27 Church Street. *McElroy's Philadelphia Directory for 1850*, 13th ed. (Philadelphia, 1850), 94.

21. 1849 *Narrative*, 58.

22. Still, *The Underground Rail Road*, 68–69; *Bywater's Philadelphia Business Directory and City Guide, for the Year 1849* (Philadelphia, 1849), 157.

23. James Miller McKim to Samuel Rhoads, 29 Mar. 1849, Special Collections, New York Public Library; Still, *The Underground Rail Road*, 68.

24. James Miller McKim to "Dear friend," Philadelphia, 28 Mar. 1849, May Anti-Slavery Collection, Cornell. McKim apparently did not go to the depot on the night of Thursday evening–early Friday morning; there had been no notification from Richmond, and McKim needed rest.

25. 1849 *Narrative*, 58; 1851 *Narrative*, 53.

26. 1849 *Narrative*, 60; James Miller McKim to S. A. Smith, 17 Mar. 1849; McKim to "Dear friend," Philadelphia, 28 Mar. 1849, May Anti-Slavery Collection, Cornell; Still, *The Underground Rail Road*, 68. Other later versions have the address on the box as "Wm A. Johnson, Arch St., Philadelphia." In particular, several images of the event use "Wm A. Johnson." Samuel Smith used the name James Johnson several times, and it is hard to imagine he would have changed it at the last minute. Possibly his writing was not clear, or people who looked at the box at a later time, after it had been handled and the inscription had become less legible, misread the address.

27. 1851 *Narrative*, 53; John P. Little, *History of Richmond* (Richmond, 1851–1852; reprint, Richmond, 1933), 174–175; William L. Montague, *Montague's Richmond Directory and Business Advertiser, for 1850–1851* ([Richmond, 1850]), 8, 73.

28. 1851 *Narrative*, 53; *National Anti-Slavery Standard*, 7 June 1849. The sort of freight car on which Brown's box was loaded is not certain, for the boxcar was not yet standard. Miller McKim wrote of one of his fruitless visits to the depot that "in opening the crate we were disappointed to find no box." In 1849 the RF&P acquired "two flat cars, each equipped with twelve crates to accommodate freight." McKim's comment implies that the PW&B also utilized freight cars with crates. James Miller McKim to "Dear friend," Philadelphia, 28 Mar. 1849, May Anti-Slavery Collection, Cornell; Mordecai, *A Brief History of the Richmond, Fredericksburg, and Potomac Railroad*, 22.

29. 1849 *Narrative*, 59–60; James Miller McKim to "Dear friend," Philadelphia, 28 Mar. 1849, May Anti-Slavery Collection, Cornell; Mordecai, *A Brief History of the Richmond, Fredericksburg, and Potomac Railroad*, 19. The telegraph connection from Washington reached Richmond in 1847. *Richmond Times*, 27 July 1847.

30. James Miller McKim to Samuel Rhoads, 29 Mar. 1849, Special Collections, New York Public Library; *Cousin Ann's Stories for Children* (Philadelphia, 1849), 25; J. Miller McKim to Sydney Howard Day, 26 Mar. 1849, as copied by Joseph Ricketson and enclosed with letter to Deborah Weston, 29 Apr. 1849, Weston Papers, Boston Public Library. On 21 Oct. 1848, a Goochland County lawyer named John Coles Rutherfoord "left Richmond in the Fredk. cars at 8 A.M.—reached Aquia Creek, 77 miles distant at 12." John Coles Rutherfoord Diary, 21 Oct. 1848–26 Apr. 1851, p. 3, Rutherfoord Family Papers, 1811–1946, Mss1 R9337 b15, section 6, Virginia Historical Society, Richmond.

31. This and the next paragraph from James Miller McKim to "Dear friend," Philadelphia, 28 Mar. 1849, May Anti-Slavery Collection, Cornell; James Miller McKim to Samuel Rhoads, 29 Mar. 1849, Special Collections, New York Public Library. John Coles Rutherfoord wrote of his 21 Oct. 1848 journey that "at Aquia Creek, got in the new steamer Baltimore, a magnificent boat, and arrived at Washington 44 miles from A. C. a quarter before 4 P.M." John Coles Rutherfoord Diary, 21 Oct. 1848–26 Apr. 1851, p. 3, VHS.

32. 1849 *Narrative*, 60–61; James Miller McKim to "Dear friend," Philadelphia, 28 Mar. 1849, May Anti-Slavery Collection, Cornell.

33. 1849 *Narrative*, 61.

34. Baer, *Canals and Railroads of the Mid-Atlantic States, 1800–1860*; 1851 *Narrative*, 55; *National Anti-Slavery Standard*, 7 June 1849.

35. *National Anti-Slavery Standard*, 7 June 1849.

36. Ibid.; James Miller McKim to "Dear friend," Philadelphia, 28 Mar. 1849, May Anti-Slavery Collection, Cornell; 1849 *Narrative*, 62; 1851 *Narrative*, 55–56.

37. 1849 *Narrative*, 62; Baer, *Canals and Railroads of the Mid-Atlantic States, 1800–1860*. James D. Dilts notes that "for a dozen years, off and on, in an uneasy arrangement, [the PW&B] shared the B&O's downtown [Baltimore] depot, bounded by Pratt, Light, Camden, and Charles streets. . . . Until the PW&B opened its new President Street Station in 1850, passengers could transfer from one line to the other by walking across the platform." James D. Dilts, *The Great Road: The Building of the Baltimore and Ohio, The Nation's First Railroad, 1828–1853* (Stanford, Calif., 1993), 421–422 n. 31.

38. 1849 *Narrative* 62; James Miller McKim to Samuel Rhoads, 29 Mar. 1849, Special Collections, New York Public Library; 1851 *Narrative*, 56. John Coles Rutherfoord wrote of a 6 May 1849 journey that he "Left Baltimore yesterday morning at 9 A.M., crossed the Susquehanna at Havre de Grace about 11 A.M., passed through Wilmington between 1 1/2 P.M., arrived in

Philadelphia at 3 P.M." John Coles Rutherfoord Diary, 21 Oct. 1848–26 Apr. 1851, p. 79, VHS.

39. James Miller McKim to "Dear friend," 28 Mar. 1849, May Anti-Slavery Collection, Cornell; Still, *The Underground Rail Road*, 68.

40. 1849 *Narrative*, 62; James Miller McKim to "Dear friend," 28 Mar. 1849, May Anti-Slavery Collection, Cornell; James Miller McKim to Samuel Rhoads, 29 Mar. 1849, Special Collections, New York Public Library; Still, *The Underground Rail Road*, 69.

41. *National Anti-Slavery Standard*, 7 June 1849; James Miller McKim to Samuel Rhoads, 29 Mar. 1849, Special Collections, New York Public Library; James Miller McKim to "Dear friend," 28 Mar. 1849, May Anti-Slavery Collection, Cornell. The sequence of events as described in the *Standard* does not exactly correspond with McKim's sequence, which by virtue of being an eyewitness account is preferred.

42. James Miller McKim to "Dear friend," 28 Mar. 1849, May Anti-Slavery Collection, Cornell. Accounts differ somewhat as to who was present and when. Still's *Underground Rail Road* has all four men (plus Brown) present at the opening of the box, as do most of the images of the event. McKim's account, written a few days after the event, refers to only Still and Thompson, in addition to McKim and Brown. The earliest image of the event, in a volume published by McKim, *Cousin Ann's Stories for Children* (Philadelphia, 1849), shows only two men present (in addition to Brown). The synthesis of these accounts that has been adopted here is that Cleveland was not there at first, per McKim, but came in during, and was a witness, per Still. Lewis Thompson, printer, resided at 31 N. Fifth Street, the address of the Anti-Slavery Society office, and Charles Dexter Cleveland had a "young ladies' school" at 3 Clinton Street. *McElroy's Philadelphia Directory for 1850*, 72, 374. See also "Cleveland, Charles Dexter," *The Twentieth Century Biographical Dictionary of Notable Americans, Volume II, Bro–Cowan*, ed. Rossiter Johnson and John Howard Brown (Boston, 1904; reprint, Detroit, 1968), n.p.

43. James Miller McKim to "Dear friend," 28 Mar. 1849, May Anti-Slavery Collection, Cornell; Lucretia Mott to Joseph and Ruth Dugdale, Philadelphia, 28 Mar. 1849, in Hallowell, *James and Lucretia Mott*, 310; Still, *The Underground Rail Road*, 70. Mott's account, based on secondhand information but written just four days after the event, has Brown's salutation as "Good morning, gentlemen." Still's version, written twenty years later, gives it as "How do you do, gentlemen?" McKim does not mention the salutation in his accounts.

44. Rev. Samuel J. May, quoted in *National Anti-Slavery Standard*, 7 June 1849; James Miller McKim to "Dear friend," 28 Mar. 1849, May Anti-Slavery Collection, Cornell; 1851 *Narrative*, 57.

45. James Miller McKim to "Dear friend," 28 Mar. 1849, May Anti-Slavery Collection, Cornell; 1851 *Narrative*, 57.

46. James Miller McKim to "Dear friend," 28 Mar. 1849, May Anti-Slavery Collection, Cornell; Still, *The Underground Rail Road*, 70; 1849 *Narrative*, ix.

47. James Miller McKim to "Dear friend," 28 Mar. 1849, May Anti-Slavery Collection, Cornell. Among those at McKim's home listening to Brown's performance might have been McKim's young daughter Lucy (1842–1877), later a co-author of the first published collection of spirituals. William Francis Allen, Charles Pickard Ware, and Lucy McKim Garrison, *Slave Songs of the United States* (New York, 1867).

48. Still, *The Underground Rail Road*, 71. William Still had not yet moved to the house in central Philadelphia that is today preserved as a historic landmark.

49. Lucretia Mott to Joseph and Ruth Dugdale, Philadelphia, 28 Mar. 1849, in Hallowell, *James and Lucretia Mott*, 311. McKim also mentioned Dr. Noble's opinion. James Miller McKim to "Dear friend," 28 Mar. 1849, May Anti-Slavery Collection, Cornell. The physician's identity is confirmed in *Bywater's Philadelphia Business Directory and City Guide, for the Year 1849* (Philadelphia, 1849), 103.

50. James Miller McKim to Samuel Rhoads, 29 Mar. 1849, Special Collections, New York Public Library. Brown's assertion of a diminished role for Samuel Smith in his escape is somewhat at odds with his later accounts in the two *Narratives*. Nor do the *Narratives* present James C. A. Smith's contributions as "trifling."

51. J. Miller McKim to Sydney Howard Gay, 26 Mar. 1849, as copied by Joseph Ricketson and enclosed with letter to Deborah Weston, 29 Apr. 1849, Weston Papers, Boston Public Library.

52. 1851 *Narrative*, 59; 1849 *Narrative*, 64; Kathryn Grover, *The Fugitive's Gibraltar: Escaping Slaves and Abolitionism in New Bedford, Massachusetts* (Amherst, Mass., 2001), 202.

53. *Burlington (Vt.) Courier*, ca.12 Apr. 1849, reprinted in *New York Daily Tribune*, 17 Apr. 1849.

54. J. Miller McKim to Samuel A. Smith, 16 Apr. 1849, May Anti-Slavery Collection, Cornell; *New York Daily Tribune*, 17 Apr. 1849.

55. *Pennsylvania Freeman*, 19 Apr. 1849; *Liberator*, 20 Apr. 1849; *National Anti-Slavery Standard*, 26 Apr. 1849.

56. *New York Daily Tribune*, 21 Apr. 1849. The editorial was reprinted in *Pennsylvania Freeman*, 26 Apr. 1849.

57. *National Anti-Slavery Standard*, 26 Apr. 1849.

58. Joseph Ricketson to Deborah Weston, 29 Apr. 1849, Weston Papers, Boston Public Library.

59. Charles Stearns, *Facts in the Life of General Taylor; the Cuba Blood-Hound Importer, the Extensive Slave-Holder, and the Hero of the Mexican War* (Boston, 1848); *Zachary Taylor, Lewis Cass, and Martin Van Buren Compared; or Slavery Extension and Free Soil* (Boston, 1848), 5–6. Stearns's derisive conclusion was that "truly, he is a man eminently fitted to preside over the destinies of this nation!" (6).

60. *Congressional Globe*, 31st Cong., 1st sess., 12 Dec. 1849, 21, pt. 1:1. As recorded on the first day of the House of Representatives session, 12 Dec. 1849, the Democrats held 112 seats, the Whigs 105, and the Free Soilers 13.

61. This and the next two paragraphs from Samuel A. Smith to James Miller McKim, Richmond, 6 Apr. 1849, May Anti-Slavery Collection, Cornell.

62. Ibid. A search through extant Richmond newspapers indicates that William Barret placed no runaway advertisements for Henry Brown, and there is no evidence of any other action by Barret or John F. Allen to retrieve the fugitive. Samuel Smith's emphasis in this letter on "the money in advance to pay the charges" suggests strongly that the freight charges had not been pre-paid when Brown was shipped, leaving McKim's organization to foot the bill. Fortunately, Miller McKim did not honor Samuel Smith's request to burn his letters.

63. James Miller McKim to Samuel A. Smith, "copy in substance," 8 Apr. 1849, May Anti-Slavery Collection, Cornell.

64. Samuel A. Smith to James Miller McKim, 11 Apr. 1849, May Anti-Slavery Collection, Cornell.

65. James Miller McKim to Samuel A. Smith, 12 Apr. 1849, May Anti-Slavery Collection, Cornell.

66. Samuel A. Smith to James Miller McKim, 14 Apr. 1849, May Anti-Slavery Collection, Cornell.

67. This and the next two paragraphs from James Miller McKim to Samuel A. Smith, 16 Apr. 1849, May Anti-Slavery Collection, Cornell.

68. Samuel A. Smith to James Miller McKim, 19 Apr. 1849, May Anti-Slavery Collection, Cornell.

69. "Jas Johnson" [Samuel A. Smith] to James Miller McKim, 19 Apr. 1849, May Anti-Slavery Collection, Cornell.

70. *Richmond Semi-weekly Whig*, page dated 9 May in 11 May 1849 issue (hereafter cited as *Richmond Semi-weekly Whig*, 9 May 1849); *Richmond Daily Whig*, 15 May 1849. The most important sources for the rest of this chapter are Richmond City Hustings Court, Ended Causes, May Term 1849, June Term 1849, Library of Virginia, Richmond; *Richmond Semi-weekly Examiner*, 11, 18, 22, 29 May 1849; *Richmond Enquirer*, 11 May 1849; *Richmond Republican*, 10, 14 May 1849; *Richmond Daily Times*, 27 Sept. 1849; and *Richmond Semi-weekly Whig*, 9, 11, 15, 22 May 1849.

71. Samuel A. Smith to James Miller McKim, 26 Apr. 1849, May Anti-Slavery Collection, Cornell; *Richmond Daily Whig*, 9, 15 May 1849; *McElroy's Philadelphia Directory for 1850*, 451. Passmore Williamson, the addressee, was involved in a famous case in 1855 in which he served 100 days in jail for providing unsatisfactory testimony about an escape. See Still, *The Underground Rail Road*, 73–84. Stephen H. Fisher, owner of the shoe shop where Samuel Smith worked, testified "to having seen a letter in Smith's possession directed to W P Williamson, who Smith had told him was doing a large business in Northern Liberties, Philadelphia, and whom he was going on to see, for the purpose of joining in business." *Richmond Semi-weekly Whig*, 9 May 1849.

72. *Richmond Semi-weekly Whig,* 9 May 1849; *Richmond Republican,* 10 May 1849; *Richmond Daily Times,* 27 Sept. 1849; *Richmond Semi-Weekly Examiner,* 11 May 1849. Sawney was owned by Caroline M. Christian, of New Kent County, and Alfred was the property of Archibald Govan's estate. *Richmond Enquirer,* 9 May 1849.

73. *Richmond Semi-weekly Examiner,* 18 May 1849.

74. *Richmond Daily Times,* 27 Sept. 1849; *Richmond Republican,* 14 May 1849; *Richmond Daily Whig,* 15 May 1849.

75. *Richmond Daily Times,* 27 Sept. 1849; *Richmond Republican,* 14 May 1849; *Richmond Daily Whig,* 15 May 1849.

76. *Richmond Semi-weekly Examiner,* 29 May 1849; *Richmond Daily Whig,* 15 May 1849.

77. *Richmond Daily Times,* 27 Sept. 1849; *Richmond Daily Whig,* 15 May 1849. Although newspaper accounts give the drayman's name as "Sam," documents in the Richmond City Hustings Court, Ended Causes, June Term 1849, LVA, all identify the drayman as David Henderson.

78. *Richmond Semi-weekly Whig,* 9 May 1849; *Richmond Enquirer,* 9 May 1849.

79. *Richmond Semi-weekly Examiner,* 11, 29 May 1849; *Richmond Semi-weekly Whig,* 9 May 1849.

80. *Richmond Daily Whig,* 15 May 1849; *Richmond Republican,* 14 May 1849; *Richmond Enquirer,* 9 May 1849.

81. *Richmond Enquirer,* 11 May 1849.

82. *Richmond Republican,* 14 May 1849; *Richmond Semi-weekly Whig,* 9 May 1849.

83. *Richmond Semi-weekly Whig,* 9 May 1849.

84. *Richmond Enquirer,* 9 May 1849; *Richmond Semi-weekly Whig,* 9 May 1849.

85. *Richmond Semi-weekly Examiner,* 11 May 1849.

86. *Richmond Semi-weekly Whig,* 15 May 1849; *Richmond Republican,* 10 May 1849.

87. *Richmond Republican,* 10 May 1849.

88. Ibid.; *Richmond Semi-weekly Examiner,* 11 May 1849.

89. *Richmond Republican,* 10 May 1849, *Richmond Semi-weekly Whig,* 11 May 1849.

90. *Richmond Semi-weekly Examiner,* 18, 29 May 1849; *Richmond Republican,* 14 May 1849; *New York Daily Tribune,* 17 July 1856, reprinted in Still, *The Underground Rail Road,* 71–73. The prosecution called several witnesses to identify the lettering on the boxes and the drayman's note as Smith's handwriting. Phillip K. White testified: "I have seen Smith's handwriting often, seen him sign several notes—[aside] which he never paid, believe the writing of ticket to be prisoner's" (*Richmond Republican,* 14 May 1849). H. W. Tyler said he was "pretty well acquainted with the marking of the Prisoner," and that he "should take the marking on the lids shown him to be his." Tyler also testified that the writing on the dray ticket, "rather of a running hand," resembled Smith's. John H. Gilmer, Smith's counsel, cross-examined Tyler. "Have you not seen marking like that on the lids, on boxes from Rocketts to Bigger's Corner?" Tyler replied: "Yes, sir—I have seen men, too, very much like Mr. Smith, but never any <u>exactly</u> like him." At that the crowd laughed (*Richmond Daily Whig,* 15 May 1849). The Mayor's Court sent the case on to the Hustings Court. There on 21 May Smith's counsel found a legal technicality that sent the case back to the mayor. At a "called Court of Hustings" on 26 May, with the mayor "acting as Presiding Justice," the case was sent to Superior Court. *Richmond Semi-weekly Examiner,* 22, 29 May 1849; *Richmond Whig,* 22 May 1849.

91. *Richmond Republican,* 10, 14 May 1849; *Richmond Semi-weekly Enquirer,* 25 May 1849. On 12 May the *Richmond Republican* reprinted an article from the *Washington, D.C., National Whig:* "A telegraphic despatch was received in Washington yesterday, addressed to police officers, requesting them to go down to the steamboat, on her arrival at the wharf in this city, and take in charge two large boxes . . . containing live property—slaves." The *National Whig*'s report stated the boxes had been intercepted in Fredericksburg. Who would have sent such a message to Washington is not clear; it was not the Richmond authorities, since they had the boxes in hand and were seeking to take Samuel Smith off the train. Most likely, rumors of what had happened caused some people to become overexcited.

92. *Pennsylvania Freeman,* 17 May 1849. The *Freeman*'s reprint was in turn reprinted in the *Anti-Slavery Bugle,* 1 June 1849. The name of the Adams Express official was E. S. Sanford. *McElroy's Philadelphia Directory for 1849,* 12th ed. (Philadelphia, 1849), 327.

Chapter Three: Among the Abolitionists

1. *New York Herald*, 10, 11 May 1849; *Boston Daily Evening Transcript*, 10 May 1849; *New Hampshire Patriot*, 17 May 1849.

2. *New York Tribune*, 10, 11 May 1849; *Liberator*, 18 May 1849. Rev. Samuel J. May, of Syracuse, wrote that Samuel May Jr., of Leicester, was "my cousin." Samuel J. May, *Some Recollections of Our Antislavery Conflict* (Boston, 1869), 338.

3. *Pennsylvania Freeman*, 17 May 1849; *Liberator*, 18 May 1849; *Anti-Slavery Bugle*, 1 June 1849; *London Anti-Slavery Reporter*, 2 July 1849. The *Liberator*, 18 May 1849, reprinted stories about the arrests from the *Richmond Republican* and *Richmond Whig*; a reprint from the *Richmond Enquirer* appeared in the *North Star* (Rochester, N.Y.), 25 May 1849. A resolution proposed at the 1849 New England Anti-Slavery Convention exemplifies the rhetorical tone of radical abolitionism: "The main pillar of slavery in America," it declared in part, "is the supineness, the guilty supineness, and the truckling, time-serving conduct of her Christian ministers, who do not boldly lift up their voices against those great and crying abominations." *Liberator*, 8 June 1849.

4. William Wells Brown, quoted in *National Anti-Slavery Standard*, 7 June 1849; *Edgefield (S.C.) Advertiser*, reprinted in *National Anti-Slavery Standard*, 14 June 1849. Out of some three million slaves, the historian Larry Gara states that "probably" about two thousand slaves a year escaped from the South. Larry Gara, "Underground Railroad," in *Dictionary of Afro-American Slavery*, ed. Randall M. Miller and John David Smith, rev. ed. (Westport, Conn., 1997), 747–749.

5. *Liberator*, 8 June 1849.

6. 1851 *Narrative*, 59; *Liberator*, 8 June 1849.

7. *Liberator*, 1 June 1849.

8. William and Ellen Craft arrived in Philadelphia in Dec. 1848 and in Jan. and Feb. 1849 toured Massachusetts cities accompanied by William Wells Brown. See advertisement in the *Liberator*, 2 Feb. 1849. On the Crafts, see R. J. M. Blackett, *Beating against the Barriers: Biographical Essays in Nineteenth-Century Afro-American History* (Baton Rouge, La., and London, Eng., 1986), 87–137, esp. 90; "Craft, Ellen," and "Craft, William," *American National Biography*, ed. John A. Garraty and Mark C. Carnes (New York, 1999), 5:647–649. Blackett incorrectly states that William Wells Brown introduced Henry Box Brown at the Jan. 1849 annual meeting of the Massachusetts Anti-Slavery Society (90).

9. *Liberator*, 8 June 1849.

10. Ibid.; *National Anti-Slavery Standard*, 7 June 1849.

11. *National Anti-Slavery Standard*, 7 June 1849; *Eighteenth Annual Report, Presented to the Massachusetts Anti-Slavery Society, by Its Board of Managers, January 23, 1850* (Boston, 1850; reprint, Westport, Conn., 1970), 57 (hereafter cited as *Eighteenth Annual Report, Massachusetts Anti-Slavery Society*). William Still stated that Brown was "christened Henry Box Brown" at the occasion of the opening of the box in Philadelphia (*The Underground Rail Road* [Philadelphia, 1872; reprint, Chicago, 1970], 70). That name first appears in print, however, in the accounts of the New England Anti-Slavery Convention. Still, writing twenty years later, compacted events, perhaps to identify the fugitive from Richmond by his famous name.

12. *Liberator*, 8 June 1849; *National Anti-Slavery Standard*, 7 June 1849. The *Standard* in its article referred to Brown's arrival "two weeks ago," when it was actually two months, a fact known to the editor. This seems to have been a deliberate misstatement for purposes of obfuscation.

13. *Anti-Slavery Bugle*, 21 June 1849; *Liberator*, 8 June 1849.

14. *Anti-Slavery Bugle*, 21 June 1849; *Dover (N.H.) Morning Star*, quoted in the *Liberator*, 22 June 1849.

15. *Liberator*, 8 June 1849; *National Anti-Slavery Standard*, 7 June 1849.

16. This and the next paragraph from *Liberator*, 8 June 1849.

17. Ibid. Daniel Webster and Robert C. Winthrop, Speaker of the House (1842–1850), and Webster's succession as U.S. Senator from Massachusetts, both offended antislavery northerners by their stands on the Fugitive Slave Bill. *Dictionary of American Biography*, s.v. "Webster, Daniel," "Winthrop, Robert Charles."

18. William Lloyd Garrison to Elizabeth Pease, 20 June 1849, in *No Union with Slaveholders, 1841–1849*, vol. 3 of *The Letters of William Lloyd Garrison*, ed. Walter M. Merrill (Cambridge, Mass., 1973), 625.

19. *Boston Emancipator & Republican*, 7 June 1849; *Boston Chronotype*, reprinted in *Boston Emancipator & Republican*, 7 June 1849; *Boston Post*, 31 May 1849; *Worcester Massachusetts Spy*, 6 June 1849; *New York Express*, quoted in *Richmond Republican*, 7 June 1849; *New York Daily Tribune*, 2 June 1849. By "artless," the *Tribune* probably meant "without the art of rhetoric."

20. *Richmond Republican*, 7 June 1849; *Richmond Enquirer*, 12 June 1849.

21. James C. A. Smith wrote that Henry Box Brown was living in Boston in Dec. 1849, the earliest specific reference that he lived there (J. C. A. Smith to William Lloyd Garrison, 6 Aug. 1851, Anti-Slavery Collection, Rare Books and Manuscripts, Boston Public Library). Brown's activities after the 31 May close of the New England Anti-Slavery Society meeting centered on Boston, including the production of two song sheets and his narrative, all of which had appeared by early in Sept. 1849.

22. *Windsor and Eton Express*, 12 Mar. 1859.

23. James Oliver Horton and Lois E. Horton, *Black Bostonians: Family Life and Community Struggle in the Antebellum North* (New York and London, 1979), 2–3; *The Directory of the City of Boston . . . from July 1850, to July 1851* (Boston, 1850), 184; Adelaide M. Cromwell, "The Black Presence in the West End of Boston, 1800–1864: A Demographic Map," in *Courage and Conscience: Black & White Abolitionists in Boston*, ed. Donald M. Jacobs (Bloomington, Ind., 1993), 155–167. See also "Hayden, Lewis" in *American National Biography*, 10:376–377. Hayden's house has been preserved and today has the address 66 Phillips Street. In the late 1850s new numbers were assigned, changing Hayden's from 8 to 66, and in the late 1860s Southac (sometimes spelled Southack) Street was renamed Phillips Street.

24. *Directory of the City of Boston . . . from July 1850, to July 1851*, 101 (Brown is identified as "Brown, Henry Box, lecturer," 161, 177); Horton and Horton, *Black Bostonians*, 47–48; Kathryn Grover, *The Fugitive's Gibraltar: Escaping Slaves and Abolitionism in New Bedford, Massachusetts* (Amherst, Mass., 2001), 189 and 317 nn. 66–67; *Alexandria Gazette and Virginia Advertiser*, 2, 17 Mar. 1840; Roy E. Finkenbine, "Boston's Black Churches: Institutional Centers of the Antislavery Movement," in *Courage and Conscience*, 169–189; George A. Levesque, *Black Boston: African American Life and Culture in Urban America, 1750–1860* (New York and London, 1994), 279–289. esp. 284. Because of the renumbering of the street, it is not clear which building was 41 Southac.

25. Horton and Horton, *Black Bostonians*, 67–70 (quotation on 69).

26. Carleton Mabee, "A Negro Boycott to Integrate Boston Schools," *New England Quarterly* 41 (Sept. 1968): 343–344; Leonard W. Levy and Harlan B. Phillips, "The *Roberts* Case: Source of the 'Separate But Equal' Doctrine," in "Notes and Suggestions," *American Historical Review* 56 (Apr. 1951): 512. The *Liberator*, 10 Aug. 1849, reported on a large "Meeting of Colored Citizens" on 23 July 1849 to protest Boston's separate schools.

27. 1849 *Narrative*, 64; 1851 *Narrative*, iv.

28. *National Anti-Slavery Standard*, 12 July 1849; *Boston Emancipator & Republican*, 12 July 1849; *Eighteenth Annual Report, Massachusetts Anti-Slavery Society*, 58. See also the *Liberator*, 13 July 1849. An announcement of the "Grand Rally of the Friends of Emancipation" stated that expected to be present were William Wells Brown, William Lloyd Garrison, Wendell Phillips, and "Henry B. Brown, THE MAN OF THE BOX." *Liberator*, 22 June 1849.

29. *Anti-Slavery Bugle*, 21 July 1849; *National Anti-Slavery Standard*, 12 July 1849.

30. This and the next paragraph from *Pennsylvania Freeman*, 5 July 1849.

31. Frederick Douglass, *My Bondage and My Freedom* (New York, 1857), 323; *Pennsylvania Freeman*, 5 July 1849.

32. *Worcester Massachusetts Spy*, reprinted in *Boston Emancipator & Republican*, 9 Aug. 1849; *Eighteenth Annual Report, Massachusetts Anti-Slavery Society*, 59.

33. *Worcester Massachusetts Spy*, reprinted in *Boston Emancipator & Republican*, 9 Aug. 1849.

34. William W. Austin, *"Susanna," "Jeanie," and "The Old Folks at Home": The Songs of Stephen C. Foster from His Time to Ours* (New York and London, 1975), 34–37.

35. "Song, Sung by Mr. Brown on being removed from the box" (Boston: Laing's Steam Press, n. d.), copy at Library of Congress. The song sheet was most likely produced shortly after the 1849 New England Anti-Slavery Convention, which ended on the last day of May.

36. 1849 *Narrative*, ix–x. The lyrics published in the 1849 *Narrative* include several more lines than the lyrics published in the 1851 *Narrative* (57–58).

37. Robert C. Toll, *Blacking Up: The Minstrel Show in Nineteenth-Century America* (New York, 1974), 30–31, 65; Hans Nathan, *Dan Emmett and the Rise of Early Negro Minstrelsy* (Norman, Okla., 1962), 113–122, esp. 116, 120.

38. *Boston Daily Evening Transcript*, 1 June 1849; Austin, "*Susanna*," "*Jeanie*," and "*The Old Folks at Home*," 35, 36, 40, 66 (quoting Douglass). Douglass's comments about minstrelsy are examined in context in William J. Mahar, *Behind the Burnt Cork Mask: Early Blackface Minstrelsy and Antebellum Popular Culture* (Urbana and Chicago, 1999), 6–8. See also Carol Brink, *Harps in the Wind: The Story of the Singing Hutchinsons* (New York, 1947), 49, 186.

39. "Escape from Slavery of Henry Box Brown, In a box 3 feet and 1 inch long, 2 feet wide, 2 feet and 6 inches high," American Antiquarian Society, Worcester, Mass.; Stephen C. Foster, "Old Uncle Ned" (New York, 1848), in *Stephen Foster Song Book: Original Sheet Music of 40 Songs*, selected by Richard Jackson (New York, 1974), 105–107; *National Anti-Slavery Standard*, 31 Jan. 1850. A different version appears as "Uncle Ned" in *Christy's Plantation Melodies [No. 1]* (Philadelphia, 1851), 36–37: "Lay down the shovel and the hoe; / Hang up the fiddle and the bow; / Fo' no more work for poor old Ned, / He's gone where the good darkies go."

A contributor to the lyrics for "Escape from Slavery of Henry Box Brown" might have been William Wells Brown. He had included the adaptation of another Stephen Foster number in his song collection; he was familiar with Henry Box Brown, having introduced him at the 1849 New England Convention; he appears to have been the originator of the notion of a box-related nickname for Henry Brown; he was known for his sense of humor; and he was in Boston until his departure for Europe in July.

40. William L. Andrews states that fugitives who were "seasoned veterans of the abolitionist lecture circuit" were "well schooled in the ways that their self-presentation, their modes of address, their idiom, and their tones of voice would affect whites." William L. Andrews, *To Tell a Free Story: The First Century of Afro-American Autobiography, 1760–1865* (Urbana and Chicago, 1986), 100.

41. Though it is not known if Stearns attended the New England Anti-Slavery Convention in May 1849, he may have, for he was present at the Massachusetts Anti-Slavery Society's annual meeting in Boston in Jan. 1849 (*Liberator*, 2 Feb. 1849). Stearns, a lay minister, might have been one of the ministers who assisted Henry Box Brown in the period after the New England convention. It is possible that the genesis of the partnership between Stearns and Brown came as early as June 1849. Stearns as a printer could have facilitated the publication of one or both of Brown's song sheets. The song sheets and the 1849 *Narrative* are typographically linked by the use of the same illustration, entitled "Representation of the Box."

42. Avis Stearns Van Wagenen, *Genealogy and Memoirs of Charles and Nathaniel Stearns, and Their Descendants* (Syracuse, N.Y., 1901; reprint, n.p., [1982]), 142–143; Charles Stearns, *The Black Man of the South, and the Rebels* . . . (New York, 1872; reprint, New York, 1969), 307. In 1846, Mrs. Sarah Stearns, a widow, resided on Gardner Street in Springfield. Boarding there were Miss Rachel W. Stearns, a teacher; William R. Stearns, a jeweler; and Charles B. Stearns, for whom no occupation is given. *The Springfield Almanac, Directory, and Business Advertiser for 1846* (Springfield, Mass., 1846), 120.

43. Charles Stearns to William Lloyd Garrison, *Liberator*, 14 Feb. 1840; Garrison to Stearns, 10 Feb. 1840, in *A House Dividing against Itself, 1836–1840*, vol. 2 of *The Letters of William Lloyd Garrison*, ed. Louis Ruchames (Cambridge, Mass., 1971), 560–563 (see also *Liberator*, 14 Feb. 1840); Stearns to Garrison, *Liberator*, 18 June 1841. Early in 1841 Stearns went west to Detroit where he had the "pleasure" of assisting three fugitives escape to Canada. By Apr. 1841 he was at Oberlin College in Ohio. Oberlin was a center of antislavery activity, but Stearns's unconventional religious beliefs caused him to be "denounced as 'riding a hobby'" and "on the road to ruin," and he moved on. Stearns to Garrison, *Liberator*, 31 Oct. 1845, 18 June 1841. See also Lewis

Perry, *Radical Abolitionism: Anarchy and the Government of God in Antislavery Thought* (Ithaca, N.Y., and London, Eng., 1973), 240–246, 249.

44. Stearns, *The Way to Abolish Slavery* (Boston, 1849), 7; Stearns to Garrison, *Liberator*, 29 Nov. 1844. On the "Great Disappointment," see Alice Felt Tyler, *Freedom's Ferment: Phases of American Social History to 1860* (Minneapolis, Minn., 1944), 74–78. Garrison commented on Stearns's 1844 letter: "As to the Second Advent notions of our worthy friend, we regard them as not only delusive, but irrational and unscriptural." *Liberator*, 29 Nov. 1844.

45. Stearns to Garrison, *Liberator*, 14 Mar., 10 Oct. 1845, 19 Jan. 1849. Aileen S. Kraditor calls the reaction to Stearns's 10 Oct. 1845 letter to the *Liberator* "The Rights of God" controversy. Aileen S. Kraditor, *Means and Ends in American Abolitionism: Garrison and His Critics on Strategy and Tactics, 1834–1850* (New York, 1969), 93.

46. *Liberator*, 2 Feb. 1849; Stearns, *The Way to Abolish Slavery*, 6–7, 10–11. Stearns's pamphlets included *Facts in the Life of General Taylor; the Cuba Blood-Hound Importer, the Extensive Slave-Holder, and the Hero of the Mexican War* (Boston, 1848); *Zachary Taylor, Lewis Cass, and Martin Van Buren Compared; or, Slavery Extension and Free Soil* (Boston, 1848); and *Encroachments of the Slave Power, upon the Rights of the North* (Boston, 1848). The 1849 *Narrative*, iii, carried an advertisement for Stearns's monthly, the *Christian Reformer and Workingmen's Advocate*, which had as its object "to redeem man from all bondage to his fellow men, and from all slavery to wrong doing, and to present him a 'perfect man in Christ Jesus.'" No issues of the *Christian Reformer and Workingmen's Advocate* are known to exist.

47. Stearns, *The Way to Abolish Slavery*, iii.

48. On the slave narratives, see Frances Smith Foster, *Witnessing Slavery: The Development of Ante-Bellum Slave Narratives* (Westport, Conn., and London, Eng., 1979); Charles T. Davis and Henry Louis Gates Jr., *The Slave's Narrative* (New York, 1985); Marion Wilson Starling, *The Slave Narrative: Its Place in American History*, 2d ed. (Washington, D.C., 1988); Andrews, *To Tell a Free Story*; and Robert L. Hall, "Massachusetts Abolitionists Document the Slave Experience," in *Courage and Conscience*, 75–99. The historian C. Duncan Rice explains in *The Scots Abolitionists, 1833–1861* (Baton Rouge, La., and London, Eng., 1981), that in Great Britain "printed slave narratives were all the more eagerly received because they were a genuinely exciting form of literature admissible in dissenting homes normally closed to the novel, which was still widely held to lack redeeming moral value" (176–177).

49. Frederick Douglass, *Narrative of the Life of Frederick Douglass, an American Slave. Written by Himself* (Boston: Published at the Anti-Slavery Office, 1845); William Wells Brown, *Narrative of William W. Brown, a Fugitive Slave. Written by Himself* (Boston: Anti-Slavery Office, 1847); Henry Bibb, *Narrative of the Life and Adventures of Henry Bibb, an American Slave, Written by Himself* . . . (New York: Published by the Author, 1849); Josiah Henson and Samuel Atkins Eliot, *The Life of Josiah Henson, Formerly a Slave, Now an Inhabitant of Canada, as Narrated by Himself* (Boston: Arthur D. Phelps, 1849); *The Fugitive Blacksmith; or, Events in the History of James W. C. Pennington, Pastor of a Presbyterian Church, New York, Formerly a Slave in the State of Maryland, United States*, 2d ed. (London: Charles Gilpin, 1849). See also Starling, *The Slave Narrative*, 35–36, 40–41, 152–153, 342, and annotated bibliography in Andrews, *To Tell a Free Story*, 333–347.

50. *Boston Emancipator & Republican*, 13 Sept. 1849. The review promised, "We shall refer to it again," but no subsequent discussion has been found.

51. *Narrative of Henry Box Brown, Who Escaped from Slavery Enclosed in a Box 3 Feet Long and 2 Wide. Written from a Statement of Facts Made by Himself. With Remarks upon the Remedy for Slavery* (Boston, [1849]); *Liberator*, 14 Sept. 1849.

52. 1849 *Narrative*, 13; James Olney, "'I Was Born': Slave Narratives, Their Status as Autobiography and as Literature," in *The Slave's Narrative*, 161 (second and third quotations), 173 n. 12 (first quotation). Olney speculates "that in preparing the American edition Stearns worked from a ms. copy of what would be published two years later as the first English edition—or from some ur-text lying behind both" (173 n. 12). The text of the 1851 *Narrative*, discussed below, was more likely a revision made in response to the criticisms of Charles Stearns's excesses in the 1849 edition. If there was an "ur-text" for the two editions of Brown's *Narrative*, it was probably

unwritten. The short time that Brown had been in the North, his activity during that time, and his illiteracy preclude a written ur-text from which Stearns could draw for the 1849 *Narrative*. As noted above, Brown began telling his story from the first day he arrived in Philadelphia, and the repetition and practice no doubt made his verbal presentation more consistent and more polished. The ur-text for both *Narratives* was likely Brown's oral account. That is, as the title page has it, both editions of the *Narrative* were written "from a Statement of Facts Made by Himself." 1849 *Narrative*, title page.

53. 1849 *Narrative*, 15, 55; Andrews, *To Tell a Free Story*, 265–291. There is the further matter of the accuracy of Henry Box Brown's "statement of facts." It is possible that he misremembered, especially of times he was under duress, or he may have consciously shaped incidents to cast himself in the best light. To include in the present book those important moments in Brown's life for which there are only accounts based on his telling might be planting approximated or glossed-up stories into what is intended as history. Yet to leave these parts out risks incompleteness.

Brown's handling of numbers is instructive. Consistently, in the 1849 *Narrative*, the 1851 *Narrative*, and in other sources such as advertisements and newspaper articles, Brown used numbers more for their relative, or descriptive, value, than for their absolute value. He was prone to exaggeration. For example, Brown described the tobacco factory where he worked as 300 feet long, but a plat shows it was less than half that length. That Brown's tendency towards number inflation was reflected in the narratives can be taken as an indication that the authors were accurately conveying his telling. At the same time, while Brown's overlarge enumeration may have been partly due to a lack of mathematical training, it is still evidence of imprecision in his reporting.

54. *Liberator*, 14 Sept. 1849; *North Star* (Rochester, N.Y.), 28 Sept. 1849. The review in the *North Star* was signed "J.D.," probably the publisher John Dick.

55. *National Anti-Slavery Standard*, 20 Sept. 1849; *Liberator*, 7, 14, 21 Sept., 12, 19, 26 Oct., 2, 9 Nov. 1849; 1851 *Narrative*, iv. Brown and Stearns returned to Boston in time for Stearns to attend the annual meeting of the New England Non-Resistance Society (*Liberator*, 23 Nov. 1849). Stearns moved to the Kansas Territory in 1854, just as conflict between proslavery and antislavery factions was breaking into warfare, and in 1855 he renounced his radical pacifism (Perry, *Radical Abolitionism*, 240). He corresponded on Kansas with the *National Anti-Slavery Standard* (14 July, 18 Aug. 1855) and the *Liberator* (27 July, 14 Sept. 1855, 4 Jan. 1856). Stearns lived in Colorado during the Civil War and remained dedicated to the abolitionist cause. In 1866 he purchased a plantation in Georgia with the intention of selling it in small tracts to the freedmen, but despite years of labor was unable to make a success of it and retired from the project in 1872. He wrote of the enterprise in *The Black Man of the South, and the Rebels; or, The Characteristics of the Former, and the Recent Outrages of the Latter* (New York and Boston, 1872). Stearns remained active in radical reform efforts and as late as 1902 participated in a conference at Booker T. Washington's Tuskegee Institute in Alabama. Peter Brock, *Pacifism in the United States: From the Colonial Era to the First World War* (Princeton, N.J., 1968), 575, 612, 679–680; James M. McPherson, *The Struggle for Equality: Abolitionists and the Negro in the Civil War and Reconstruction* (Princeton, N.J., 1964), 414–416; McPherson, *The Abolitionist Legacy: From Reconstruction to the NAACP* (Princeton, N.J., 1975), 30, 60–63, 77; and Lewis Perry, *Radical Abolitionism: Anarchy and the Government of God in Antislavery Thought* (Ithaca, N.Y., and London, Eng., 1973), 240–246.

56. *Pennsylvania Freeman*, 25 Oct. 1849.

57. *Cousin Ann's Stories for Children* (Philadelphia, 1849). See also "Preston, Ann" in *Notable American Women, 1607–1950: A Biographical Dictionary*, ed. Edward T. James, Janet Wilson James, and Paul S. Boyer (Cambridge, Mass., 1971), 3:96–97; "McKim, Charles Fallen," and "McKim, James Miller," *DAB*; New Jersey Census, Essex County, West Orange Township, 1870, James M. McKim household, 473B.

58. *Cousin Ann's Stories for Children*, 18, 29 ("Henry Box Brown" appears on 22–26; see esp. 26). In this short account there is one detail of Brown's journey in the box that appears in print nowhere else, that he bored four holes with the gimlet to let in air (25), suggesting that the publisher, Miller McKim, had a role in the preparation of the content.

59. *Richmond Daily Times*, 27 Sept. 1849. A handwritten document headed "Persons in Jail Octo. 8th 1849" lists Samuel A. Smith and James Smith (Richmond, Va., City Sergeant, Papers, 1841–1851, Mss3 R4156 b10, Virginia Historical Society, Richmond). Samuel Smith's summer in the Henrico jail was not without incident. Philip P. Winston, the jailer, later testified that he received a letter from Smith, warning him that several prisoners planned to escape and that Winston's life was in danger. Winston discovered the "man of desperate character" whom Smith had identified as the leader in the plot "with his irons entirely cut off." But for Smith's warning, Winston stated, "I believe I would have been injured, if not murdered." *Report of the Special Committee to Investigate the Conduct of C. S. Morgan*, Doc. 58, *Journal and Documents of the House of Delegates of the State of Virginia for the Session 1853–4* (Richmond, 1853–1854), 23.

60. *Richmond Daily Times*, 27 Sept. 1849. See also *Richmond Republican*, reprinted in *Baltimore Sun*, 29 Sept. 1849. Sawney's testimony indicated that Alfred also knew of James Smith's involvement. The inquisitors recalled Alfred to the stand but he remained guarded in his responses. He admitted that he had visited Smith's cake shop "in company with Sawney, but denied all knowledge of prisoner's aiding and abetting their escape." What happened thereafter to Alfred is unknown, although Alfred was likely caused to suffer for seeking to protect his comrade. Also, it was at this hearing that John Mettauer, a carpenter, testified that he had built a box about six months earlier (by the account of the *Richmond Daily Times* for Samuel Smith, but according to the *Richmond Republican* for "[black] Smith").

61. *Richmond Daily Times*, 27 Sept. 1849; *Richmond Examiner*, 28 Sept. 1849; June Purcell Guild, *Black Laws of Virginia: A Summary of the Legislative Acts of Virginia Concerning Negroes from Earliest Times to the Present* (Richmond, 1936), 168; *Richmond Republican*, 17 Oct. 1849.

62. Richmond City Hustings Court, Minute Book, 18:301, Library of Virginia, Richmond; *National Anti-Slavery Standard*, 31 Jan. 1850; *Richmond Daily Times*, 16 Oct. 1849; *Richmond Examiner*, 16 Oct. 1849; *Richmond Republican*, 17 Oct. 1849. James Smith's lawyers were Thomas Pleasants August, William P. Byrd, and William Hancock. In a moment of candor, the reporter for the proslavery *Examiner* stated that "the ingratitude of Sawney toward Jim Smith is monstrous in the extreme, when the amount of service he was to render is taken in consideration, and whatever opinion may be entertained of Smith, it is certain Sawney is a 'case'" (*Richmond Examiner*, 16 Oct. 1849). Sawney remained in Richmond until 1856, when his owner "Constable Butler" sold him away to Georgia for $580. *Richmond Daily Whig*, 4 June 1856.

63. *Richmond Republican*, 24, 25 Oct. 1849; *Baltimore Sun*, 25 Oct. 1849; Guild, *Black Laws of Virginia*, 117. James C. A. Smith's visit to "Pillsbury" may have been a trip to Philadelphia to inquire for news of Henry Brown.

64. *Smith v. The Commonwealth* (1849) (6 Grattan), *Virginia Reports*, 6:696–699; *Richmond Republican*, 2 Nov. 1849; *Richmond Semi-weekly Whig*, 2, 9, 13 Nov. 1849; *Richmond Examiner*, 9, 13 Nov. 1849; *New York Tribune*, 17 July 1856. Samuel Smith's trial took place in Henrico County Circuit Court, which had jurisdiction over the city of Richmond. A handwritten document in the papers of the Richmond City Sergeant, evidently for the purpose of assembling a jury pool but unused due to postponement, contains Samuel A. Smith's name in an entry repeated 24 times (to be cut apart and distributed), with slightly varying wordings but all to the effect: "attend at State Court house 27th October to try S. A. Smith 1st case." (Richmond, Va., City Sergeant, Papers, 1841–1851, Mss3 R4156 b22, Virginia Historical Society, Richmond). Smith was defended by John Harmer Gilmer and Benjamin Blake Minor. Impaneling the jury proved a long process and not without controversy. By the end of the day only six persons were still in the jury pool. The next day two talesmen—bystanders who had come only to observe the trial—were placed on the jury. Both men admitted they had read about Smith's case in the newspapers and had reached the conclusion that he was guilty, yet both assured the court they were able to give him a fair and impartial trial (*Smith v. The Commonwealth* [1850] [7 Grattan], *Virginia Reports*, 7:593–597). Samuel Smith himself was undoubtedly the source for the *New York Tribune*'s report. Whether or not it is absolutely true, it might be taken as a measure of the hostility of the court and authorities to Smith, whom they were certain they would convict.

65. Herbert Aptheker, *Abolitionism: A Revolutionary Movement* (Boston, 1989), 95, 113; *Liberator*, 23 Nov. 1849.

Chapter Four: The Moving Panorama

1. *Warwick and Warwickshire Advertiser and Leamington Gazette*, 31 July 1852. In the newspaper's story Brown took undue credit for writing the 1849 *Narrative*.

2. A far-from-exhaustive search found only a few antislavery performances before 1849. (In the 1850s after the appearance of *Uncle Tom's Cabin* there were many.) Perhaps the only sustained effort was by the Hutchinson Family, abolitionist singers who performed beginning in 1842. Several instances were inspired by the 1839 revolt of enslaved Africans aboard the ship *Amistad*: a play, *The Black Schooner, or, the Private Slaver Armistad*, presented 2–9 Sept. 1839 at the Bowery Theatre, New York City; and, if not performed at least presented, a collection of "Wax Figures of the Amistad Slaves," exhibited at Peale's Museum, New York, in June 1840, and at Barnum's American Museum in Oct. 1847. George C. D. Odell, *Annals of the New York Stage* (New York, 1927–1949), 4:364, 418, 5:389. In a survey of abolitionist moving panoramas exhibited by African Americans, Allan D. Austin records none that preceded Henry Box Brown's. "More Black Panoramas: An Addendum," *Massachusetts Review* 37 (winter 1996–1997): 636–639.

3. The sketch of the history of the panorama, diorama, and moving panorama draws largely from Richard D. Altick, *The Shows of London* (Cambridge, Mass., and London, Eng., 1978), 128–210. With the aid of a "classical friend," Robert Barker is credited with inventing the word *panorama*, too. Actually his panorama building housed two paintings, one the full ninety feet in diameter and the other, in an upper chamber, somewhat smaller; so the patron for his or her fee got to see two images.

Daguerre's creation of the Diorama is discussed in *L. J. M. Daguerre: The History of the Diorama and the Daguerreotype* (London, 1956), 13–17. Helmut and Alison Gernsheim write of the Diorama: "The great diversity of scenic effect was produced by a combination of translucent and opaque painting, and of transmitted and reflected light by contrivances such as screens and shutters." Daguerre traveled to scenic places, sketching the landscapes as studies for paintings for the Diorama. As an aid in rendering his studies, he used the camera obscura, an optical device with a lens to focus an image on a ground glass. Daguerre fixed on the idea of permanently recording the image on the ground glass of the camera obscura. After much experimentation, and building on the work of others, Daguerre in 1839 announced the Daguerreotype and its method. Helmut and Alison Gernsheim, *L. J. M. Daguerre: The History of the Diorama and the Daguerreotype*, 18 (quotation), 44–45 (in general 13–45), 76–78 (discussion of his photography work, 46–78).

4. Altick, *The Shows of London*, 173. As the numerous panoramas and dioramas enjoyed popular and financial success, more kinds of "-ramas" came into being. The "Cyclorama" featured wax figures on a platform, with a painted scene on a curved-wall backdrop to give an illusion of distance. The "Cosmorama" was a three-dimensional tableaux, which moved across the platform. Other "-ramas" included the Betaniorama, Europorama, Georama, Hydrorama, Kalorama, Kineorama, Nausorama, Neorama, Octorama, Physiorama, Pleorama, Poecilorama, Typorama, Udorama, and Uranorama. Gernsheim and Gernsheim, *L. J. M. Daguerre*, 41.

5. Altick, *The Shows of London*, 198, 203; Odell, *Annals of the New York Stage*, 3:407. Barnum's American Museum exhibited Winchell's panorama "A Trip to Niagara Falls" in 1841, a moving panorama of the "passage of a balloon with three men in 1836, from London to Mayence" in 1846, and a "moving diorama of Napoleon's funeral" in 1847. Another New York venue, the Coliseum on Broadway, offered in 1844 a moving panorama with eclectic views of "North Point, City of Baltimore, Fairy Land, Isle of Cyprus, the City of Lowell, etc." Odell, *Annals of the New York Stage*, 4:584, 5:143, 305, 306.

6. *Description of Banvard's Panorama of the Mississippi River* . . . (Boston, 1847), 20–21; *Scientific American*, 16 Dec. 1848, p. 100; Altick, *The Shows of London*, 205; *Descriptive Pamphlet of Smith's Leviathan Panorama of the Mississippi River!* (Philadelphia, 1848), 3–4; and ads in the *Athenaeum*, no. 1117 (24 Mar. 1859): 303. See also John Francis McDermott, *The Lost Panoramas of the Mississippi* (Chicago, 1958); and "John Banvard's Great Picture—Life on the Mississippi," *Littell's Living Age* 15 (Oct.–Dec. 1847): 511–515. Later tours of mainland Europe by the Mississippi panoramas are said to have influenced many, especially the Germans, to immigrate to the Mississippi Valley.

Wolfgang Born, *American Landscape Painting: An Interpretation* (New Haven, Conn., 1948), 97.

An extant moving panorama is "The Panorama of a Whaling Voyage Round the World," by Benjamin Russell and Caleb Purrington. Held at the Old Dartmouth Historical Society and Whaling Museum, New Bedford, Mass., the canvas is 8 1/2 feet high and 1,275 feet long, about a quarter of a mile in length. Sections of the panorama are effectively illustrated in *American Heritage*, Dec. 1960, pp. 55–62.

7. *Illustrated London News*, 9 Dec. 1848, cited in McDermott, *The Lost Panoramas of the Mississippi*, 43.

8. *Pennsylvania Freeman*, 1 Nov. 1849.

9. Charles Dickens, "Some Account of an Extraordinary Traveller," 20 Apr. 1850, in *Household Words: A Weekly Journal Conducted by Charles Dickens*, no. 4 (London, 1850): 1:73, 77.

10. Ibid., 1:73–74; *Descriptive Pamphlet of Smith's Leviathan Panorama of the Mississippi River!*, 12–13, 23 (quotation).

11. William Wells Brown, *A Description of William Wells Brown's Original Panoramic Views of the Scenes in the Life of an American Slave . . .* (London, 1849), reprinted in *The Black Abolitionist Papers, Volume 1: The British Isles, 1830–1865*, ed. C. Peter Ripley et al. (Chapel Hill and London, 1985), 191 (hereafter cited as Brown, *A Description of William Wells Brown's Original Panoramic Views*).

12. *Saint Louis Weekly Reveille*, 22 Oct. 1849 (date of letter 9 Oct.), cited in McDermott, *The Lost Panoramas of the Mississippi*, 68, 184 n. 1.

13. *Windsor and Eton Express*, 12 Mar. 1859.

14. *Liberator*, 16 Nov. 1849.

15. J[ames] C. A. Smith to William Lloyd Garrison, 6 Aug. 1851, Anti-Slavery Collections, Boston Public Library, and copied in the *Black Abolitionist Papers, 1830–1865*, ed. George E. Carter and C. Peter Ripley (Ann Arbor, Mich., 1993), microfilm edition, 7:0034–0035. The address of Brown's family's master would have become known when Nancy Brown wrote to the First African Baptist Church in Richmond for a letter of dismissal in September 1848. Brown did not have the address with him when he escaped, for Miller McKim asked Samuel Smith about it in a letter dated 16 April 1849. In the 1849 *Narrative* Charles Stearns announced a fund to purchase Brown's family, and it is possible that Stearns had obtained the address. If he had written to the master, it appears that he received no reply. On the other hand, James Smith could have obtained it from the church records before he departed Richmond. First African Baptist Church (Richmond, Va.), Minute Books, 1841–1930, Minutes, 1841–1859, Book 1, 1 Oct. 1848, p. 134, Acc. 28255, Church Records Collection, Library of Virginia, Richmond.

16. At most the proceeds from the 1849 *Narrative* were probably less than half of $1,500, based on rough estimation. At Brown's report of 8,000 copies sold (1851 *Narrative*, iv), and at the cover price of $0.25, maximum revenue from the edition would have been $2,000. It is likely some portion was wholesaled to booksellers. If that portion was 2,000 copies sold at $0.15, total revenue would have been $1,800. If the books were $0.08 each to produce, that $640 subtracted leaves $1,160. Other expenses included at least the book tour and the advertisements in the *Standard*, say $100 leaving $1,060. Even if Stearns took none of the profits, only having his living costs paid for the time he worked on the book at perhaps $50 per month for three months, and Brown's expenses over the same period were similar, that would be $300, leaving $760. This is guesswork accounting but Brown certainly did not have close to $1,500.

17. J[ames] C. A. Boxer Smith to Gerrit Smith, 6 Aug. 1851, Gerrit Smith Papers, Syracuse University, transcribed in Ripley et al., *The Black Abolitionist Papers*, 1:293–301, and copied in the *Black Abolitionist Papers*, microfilm edition, 7:0036–0041; 1851 *Narrative*, 59. Based on the date by which the manuscript for the 1851 *Narrative* was prepared (as will be explained later), Brown's summary of his travels is believed to be for the period prior to Apr. 1850. Thus it would have included the meetings over the summer of 1849, the autumn 1849 book tour with Charles Stearns, and his ventures to raise funds for the panorama from Dec. 1849 through Mar. 1850.

18. *Liverpool Mercury*, 12 Nov. 1850; *Liberator*, 19 Apr. 1850. The *Mercury* account is probably based on Brown and/or Smith's oral testimony, which, allowing for accents, could explain the

misspelling of all three names.

19. *The Directory of the City of Boston* (Boston, 1846–1850/1851); *Witness to America's Past: Two Centuries of Collecting by the Massachusetts Historical Society* (Boston, 1991), 164; Caroline Weston to Anne Weston, Boston, 9 Dec. 1842, Weston Papers, Boston Public Library; Sinclair Hamilton, *Early American Book Illustrators and Wood Engravers, 1670–1870, Volume II, Supplement* (Princeton, N.J., 1968), 152–153.

20. *Witness to America's Past,* 164; Nancy Osgood, "Josiah Wolcott: Artist and Associationist," *Old-Time New England* 76 (spring/summer 1998): 5–34, esp. 9–15; Marianne Dwight to Anna Parsons, 19 Oct. 1845, cited in *Autobiography of Brook Farm*, ed. Henry W. Sams (Englewood Cliffs, N.J., 1958), 146. It is possible that Charles Stearns knew Josiah Wolcott as a neighbor, for in the 1849 Boston directory, Stearns lived at 30 Charles Street; in the next directory Wolcott lived at 29 Charles; and there may have been overlap in their tenures.

21. Charles Knowles Bolton, "Workers with Line and Color in New England, 1620–1870: Biographical Notices of Artists and Art Craftsmen Born before 1845," Mss. L377, Boston Athenaeum; Malcolm Johnson, *David Claypool Johnston: American Graphic Humorist, 1798–1865* (Lunenburg, Vt., 1970), 5–14. There is, in addition, the corroborating fact that Samuel Worcester Rowse and David Claypool Johnston were both associated with Josiah Wolcott a year later, in 1851, as illustrators for the *Carpet-Bag.* Hamilton, *Early American Book Illustrators and Wood Engravers,* 2:152–153.

22. Copy of contract between J. W. E. Hutchings and E. R. Smilie, for sale of *Hutchings' Pictorial Map and Chart or, Grand Classical Panorama of the Sea and Shores of the Mediterranean,* 20 Mar. 1848, in J. W. E. Hutchings Scrapbook, Boston Public Library.

23. Brown, *A Description of William Wells Brown's Original Panoramic Views,* 1:191–192. The parallels with cinema are useful for descriptive purposes, but are far from exact, and in addition are anachronistic. Terminology for the panorama, therefore, will avoid cinematic language.

24. Sources for images could have been abolitionist broadsides, plates in slave narratives, periodicals such as the *Illustrated London News,* and prints like the one sought early in 1849 by a Worcester abolitionist who wrote that he was "trying to ascertain where the remaining engraving of the five of the scenes on the coast of Africa could be found" (Thomas Earle, Worcester, to Anne Warren Weston, 30 Apr. 1849, Weston Papers, Boston Public Library). Because scenes in the panorama could be painted singly and sewn together at the end, there were a number of ways the process might have proceeded, for a scene not included originally in the plan could have been dropped in, but it does seem likely that an overall concept of the sequence would have been worked out before the painting got underway.

While there is no direct evidence that Charles Stearns had any involvement in Brown's panorama, he had worked very closely with Brown immediately before the panorama project began, and it seems likely enough that the two would have maintained their relationship. Stearns knew the antislavery argument and could have contributed in the formative stages of the panorama. There is an intriguing straw in some similarity of word usage. In Stearns's 1849 pamphlet, *The Way to Abolish Slavery,* appears: "'Husband, where are you going?' plaintively enquires the sorrow-stricken wife, as he is knocked off upon the auction block to the highest bidder." In a later article about the panorama there is a description of a scene with "'Heartless Knock-'em-off' officiating as auctioneer." The use of the same, uncommon expression by both Stearns and a writer of the panorama is at least suggestive. Charles Stearns, *The Way to Abolish Slavery* (Boston, 1849), 10; *Leeds Mercury,* 24 May 1851.

In a 1996 essay about *Mirror of Slavery,* Cynthia Griffin Wolff has Brown himself "concocting the specific sequence of 'scenes' that comprised his 'MIRROR OF SLAVERY'" (31). Wolff is more on the mark elsewhere in the essay in calling Brown the "impresario" (30). Cynthia Griffin Wolff, "Passing Beyond the Middle Passage: Henry 'Box' Brown's Translations of Slavery," *Massachusetts Review* 37 (spring 1996): 30–31.

25. George R. Gliddon, *The Nile . . .: Its Ancient Monuments, Its Modern Scenery, and the Varied Characteristics of Its People, on the River, Alluvium, and Deserts, Exhibited in a Grand Panoramic Picture, Explained in Oral Lectures, & Illustrated by a Gallery of Egyptian Antiquities, Mummies, &c.* (London, 1849), [vii], 13.

Henry Box Brown's panorama had 49 scenes. If there was a title scene, making 50, and each frame was 8 feet high by 12 feet wide, there would have been 4,800 square feet of area to be painted, and the panorama would have been in the neighborhood of 600 feet long.

26. There is no evidence, but it is possible that William Craft, Brown's fellow fugitive, who had set up shop as a furniture maker, could have provided carpentry. Craft resided at Lewis Hayden's house, just down the block from Brown's residence. *Boston Directory . . . from July, 1849, to July, 1850* (Boston, 1849), 126, 184; *Directory of the City of Boston . . . from July 1850, to July 1851* (Boston, 1850), 101.

27. Charles C. Green, *The Nubian Slave* (Boston, 1845); John Lewis Burckhardt, *Travels in Nubia*, 2d ed. (London, 1822; reprint, Farnborough, Eng., 1968), 278. A copy of *The Nubian Slave* is at the Library of Virginia. The prints were by Lane and Scott, lithographers, Boston, and the printer was Bela Marsh.

28. On the Egyptian revival, see Erik Iversen, *The Myth of Egypt and Its Hieroglyphs in European Tradition* (Copenhagen, 1961; paperback, Princeton, N.J., 1993), and John A. Wilson, *Signs & Wonders upon Pharaoh: A History of American Egyptology* (Chicago and London, 1964). Even Martin Bernal admits that "the conventional view of a period of Egyptomania does contain an element of truth." Martin Bernal, *Black Athena: The Afroasiatic Roots of Classical Civilization* (New Brunswick, N.J., 1987), 1:267.

29. Edgar A. Poe, "Some Words with a Mummy," *American Review* 1 (Apr. 1845): 363; William Stanton, *The Leopard's Spots: Scientific Attitudes toward Race in America, 1815–59* (Chicago, 1960), 45–49; Lemuel Shattuck, *Report to the Committee of the City Council Appointed to Obtain the Census of Boston for the Year 1845* (Boston, 1846), 75; Gliddon, *The Nile*, 21. Gliddon's lectures were contained in George R. Gliddon, *Ancient Egypt: Her Monuments, Hieroglyphics, History and Archaeology, and Other Subjects Connected with Hieroglyphical Literature* (New York, 1843).

30. *Boston Daily Evening Transcript*, 1 Nov. 1843. Gliddon later presented his theories in a volume significant in the history of pseudoscientific racism: Josiah C. Nott and George R. Gliddon, *Types of Mankind; or, Ethnological Researches, Based upon the Ancient Monuments, Paintings, Sculptures, and Crania of Races, and upon Their Natural, Geographical, Philological, and Biblical History* (Philadelphia, 1854).

31. *Boston Daily Evening Transcript*, 4 Nov. 1843.

32. *Liberator*, 14 Mar. 1845 (and weekly until 30 May 1845), 30 May 1845. About Charles C. Green, nothing has been uncovered, though the search was not exhaustive; whether he had attended Gliddon's lectures is not known. It is unlikely that the author used a pseudonym, for Charles C. Green, "artist," appeared in the 1844 Boston city directory, although the name does not appear in the next year's directory. *Stimpson's Boston Directory* (Boston, 1844), 253.

A Boston precedent to *The Nubian Slave* as antislavery romantic poetry appeared in the *Star of Emancipation* (Boston, 1841), published "for the Fair of the Massachusetts Female Emancipation Society." In the collection is a play in meter entitled *The Fugitives*, set on "A Carolinian Plantation" (37–68). A mother and her sons escape with their sister to prevent their master from violating the girl. They are chased but reach Canada: "it is sweet / To feel no terror creeping o'er our souls" (66).

33. *Liberator*, 14 Mar. 1845; Green, *The Nubian Slave*, [3], 4, 5. In Green's lines—"His shadowy pathway led beside / Those lofty piles by Pharaohs reared, / He saw them now in ruins vast, / Pillar, and sphynx, and architrave, / Huge relics of the mighty past"—there is something of the spirit of Shelley's 1815 *Alastor*: "Among the ruined temples there, / Stupendous columns, and wild images / Of more than man, where marble daemons watch." *The Complete Works of Percy Bysshe Shelley: Poems*, ed. Roger Ingpen and Walter E. Peck (New York, 1965), 1:177–178.

34. Green, *The Nubian Slave*, [2], 7, 8.

35. *Liberator*, 14 Mar. 1845. The evidence of the debt to Green's poem is found in the titles of the scenes in Brown's panorama, as will be delineated in chapter five.

36. James Buchanan to Nimrod Strickland, 24 Dec. 1849, at New-York Historical Society, quoted in Holman Hamilton, *Prologue to Conflict: The Crisis and Compromise of 1850* (Lexington, Ky., 1964), 44–45.

37. *Congressional Globe*, 31st Cong., 1st sess., 31, pt. 1:99, 103, 171.

38. Ibid., 244, 451, 476.

39. *The Resurrection of Henry Box Brown at Philadelphia*, Boston, Jan. 1850, PGA—Brown—Resurrection (B size), Prints and Photographs Division, Library of Congress.

40. *National Anti-Slavery Standard*, 24 Jan. 1850; Frederick J. Blue, *The Free Soilers: Third Party Politics, 1848–54* (Urbana, Ill., Chicago, Ill., and London, Eng., 1973), 1–15, esp. 3. See also Alan M. Kraut, "Partisanship and Principles: The Liberty Party in Antebellum Political Culture," in *Crusaders and Compromisers: Essays on the Relationship of the Antislavery Struggle to the Antebellum Party System*, ed. Alan M. Kraut (Westport, Conn., and London, Eng., 1983), 71–99. The wing of the Liberty Party that remained abolitionist at first called itself the Liberty League. Its most prominent member, and candidate for president in 1848, was Gerrit Smith, of Syracuse. In July 1849, the Liberty League "adopted the name of 'Liberty Party,' instead of that it has heretofore worn; the former having no claimant since the 'translation' of its late owner into the Free Soil party—a fate, by the way, more like Jonah's than Enoch's." *Pennsylvania Freeman*, 26 July 1849.

41. *Non-Slaveholder* (Philadelphia) 5, no. 3 (Mar. 1850): 54; *Syracuse Impartial Citizen*, 23 Jan. 1850.

42. *National Anti-Slavery Standard*, 31 Jan. 1850; James C. A. Smith to *London Anti-Slavery Reporter*, 13 Mar. 1854, printed in 1 Apr. 1854 issue (also reprinted in Ripley et al., *The Black Abolitionist Papers*, 1:383–384); Samuel Ringgold Ward to Louis Chamerovzow, 1 Apr. 1854, printed in *London Anti-Slavery Reporter*, 1 May 1854 (reprinted in Ripley et al., *The Black Abolitionist Papers*, 1:387). James Smith stated, in reference to being a conductor of the Underground Railroad, that "I was so called by the Slaveholders as had been reported in several of the papers." None of these newspaper reports have been located.

43. *National Anti-Slavery Standard*, 31 Jan. 1850; *Syracuse Impartial Citizen*, 23 Jan. 1850. The two sources are possibly divergent. The *Standard* has Brown singing "Escape from Slavery of Henry Box Brown" at the morning session of the third day, and simply "song by Brown" to open the afternoon session. The *Impartial Citizen* has it that Brown and Smith together sang "Escape" to open the afternoon session. Between the two accounts the *Standard's*, prepared by a reporter, is probably more precise than the *Impartial Citizen's*, written by Samuel Ringgold Ward who was a participant in the meeting. Either the *Impartial Citizen* put the performance of "Escape" at the wrong session, or, as is quite possible, Brown sang "Escape" to open both sessions.

44. *Non-Slaveholder* 5, no. 3 (Mar. 1850): 54.

45. Henry Box Brown [and James C. A. Smith] to Gerrit Smith, Boston, 1 Feb. 1850, in the *Black Abolitionist Papers, 1830–1865*, microfilm edition, 6:0376. The letter was signed "Henry Box Brown," and a postscript added, "Brother James Boxer Smith sends his love to you all so."

46. Henry Box Brown to J. Miller McKim, Boston, 3 Apr. 1850, May Anti-Slavery Collection, Cornell; J. Miller McKim to Henry Box Brown, 8 Apr. 1850, in 1851 *Narrative*, iii–iv; Samuel J. May to Henry Box Brown, 26 Apr. 1850, in 1851 *Narrative*, v–vi.

47. Benjamin F. Roberts to Rev. A. A. Phelps, Boston, 19 June 1838, Anti-Slavery Collection, Boston Public Library. Also in Ripley et al., *The Black Abolitionist Papers*, 3:269–271.

48. B. F. Roberts, "Our Progress in the Old Bay State," *Washington New Era*, 31 Mar. 1870; Amos A. Phelps to Benjamin F. Roberts, Boston, 16 May 1838, Anti-Slavery Collection, Boston Public Library; George Washington Forbes, "William Cooper Nell," section 3, p. 3, typescript, Boston Public Library; *Liberator*, 4 May, 12 Oct. 1838; Benjamin F. Roberts to Rev. A. A. Phelps, Boston, 19 June 1838, Anti-Slavery Collection, Boston Public Library. No copies of Roberts's newspaper, the *Anti-Slavery Herald*, are known to exist.

49. James Oliver Horton and Lois E. Horton, *Black Bostonians: Family Life and Community Struggle in the Antebellum North* (New York and London, 1979), 76; R. B. Lewis, *Light and Truth; Collected from the Bible and Ancient and Modern History, Containing the Universal History of the Colored and the Indian Race, from the Creation of the World to the Present Time* (Boston, 1844). The 1849 printing of *Light and Truth* is cataloged at the University of Rochester Library with the 1836 and 1844 editions. A second edition appeared in 1851, published in Boston by M. M. Taylor. On Robert Benjamin Lewis, see Earl E. Thorpe, *Black Historians: A Critique (A Revision of Negro*

Historians in the United States) (New York, 1971), 33–35.

50. Martin Robison Delany, *The Condition, Elevation, Emigration, and Destiny of the Colored People of the United States. Politically Considered* (Philadelphia, 1852), 128–129.

51. Lewis, *Light and Truth*, 329–330; George R. Price and James Brewer Stewart, eds., *To Heal the Scourge of Prejudice: The Life and Writings of Hosea Easton* (Amherst, Mass., 1999), 3–6; Peter P. Hinks, *To Awaken My Afflicted Brethren: David Walker and the Problem of Antebellum Slave Resistance* (University Park, Pa. 1997), 63–90, esp. 86–87; Roberts, "Our Progress in the Old Bay State."

52. Price and Stewart, *To Heal the Scourge of Prejudice*, 21; Rev. H. Easton, *A Treatise on the Intellectual Character, and Civil and Political Condition of the Colored People of the U. States; and the Prejudice Exercised Towards Them: with a Sermon on the Duty of the Church to Them* (Boston, 1837), original 56 pp., reprinted in Price and Stewart, *To Heal the Scourge of Prejudice*, 63–123. The printer Isaac Knapp was William Lloyd Garrison's original co-publisher and the printer for the *Liberator*. The sermon alluded to in the title was not included in the book; a note said it would be printed in a forthcoming volume, but Hosea Easton died soon after the *Treatise* appeared.

53. Easton, *A Treatise*, in Price and Stewart, *To Heal the Scourge of Prejudice*, 67 (fifth quotation), 76, 81 (first quotation), 83 (fourth quotation), 84, 85 (second quotation), 87 (third quotation), 91. It is possible that Easton's *Treatise* influenced Charles C. Green eight years later in making *The Nubian Slave*. Green's feeling for his subject might well have led him to read Easton's book. There are thematic parallels, such as the links to ancient Egyptian culture and the emphasis on the merit of African life, and especially in both that the tragedy began in Africa.

54. Price and Stewart, *To Heal the Scourge of Prejudice*, 6; Horton and Horton, *Black Bostonians*, 82–83; Roberts, "Our Progress in the Old Bay State"; Carleton Mabee, "A Negro Boycott to Integrate Boston Schools," *New England Quarterly* 41 (Sept. 1968): 350–351; *Liberator*, 28 Dec. 1849; Moorfield Storey, *Charles Sumner* (Boston and New York, 1900), 60. Roberts's lawyer Charles Sumner argued in the appeal that the blacks-only Smith School, to which young Sarah Roberts had been assigned though there were other schools closer to her home, could not be considered an "equivalent" to the other schools. It was inconvenient, stated Sumner, but more important it treated black children like a different class of people. The Boston School Board "cannot brand a whole race with the stigma of inferiority and degradation, constituting them into a *caste*." In doing so the school board had violated the fundamental right of all citizens to "*equality . . . before the law*." *Argument of Charles Sumner, Esq. against the Constitutionality of Separate Colored Schools, in the Case of Sarah C. Roberts* vs. *the City of Boston* (Boston, 1849), 21, 31, cited in Leonard W. Levy and Harlan B. Phillips, "The *Roberts* Case: Source of the 'Separate But Equal' Doctrine," in "Notes and Suggestions," *American Historical Review* 56 (Apr. 1951): 513–514.

55. *Liberator*, 5 Apr. 1850.

56. *Boston Atlas*, 4, 10 Apr. 1850; *Boston Daily Evening Transcript*, 12 Apr. 1850; *Washington Daily Union*, 25 Mar. 1849. Gliddon's exhibition continued through 29 Apr. The *Panorama of the Nile* was an English production that, before Gliddon acquired it, had been exhibited in London in July 1849 at Egyptian Hall, Piccadilly. The panorama covered "1720 miles of Egypt and Nubia." The first section, "Ascent of the Nile," had twenty-eight scenes, and the second section, "Descent of the Nile," had twenty-two scenes. Scenes of Nubia included, among others, the twenty-fourth, "A Nubian Weaver, his primitive Loom and simple Apparatus"; the thirty-third, "Nubian Village, Manners and Customs: lady in full dress"; and the thirty-fourth, "Group of *Baràbera, Abábde*, and *Bishárri*, of Nubia; with a *Hàwee, Saádeh*, or Serpent-charmer: dancing *cobra*, &c." *Boston Daily Evening Transcript*, 12 Apr. 1850; Gliddon, *The Nile*, 7–8.

57. *Liberator*, 19 Apr. 1850.

58. *Boston Herald*, 23, 30 Apr. 1850.

59. *Boston Daily Evening Traveller*, 29 Apr. 1850; *Boston Herald*, 1 May 1850. An advertisement for *Mirror of Slavery* ran in the *Boston Herald* from 23 Apr. through 8 May 1850.

60. *Worcester Massachusetts Spy*, 8, 15 May 1850.

61. *Liberator*, 31 May 1850.

62. Ibid.

63. Ibid., 26 Apr. 1850. Chief Justice Lemuel Shaw was Herman Melville's father-in-law. *Roberts* v. *City of Boston* was cited as precedent in the 1896 U.S. Supreme Court decision, *Plessy* v. *Ferguson*, which established "separate but equal" as constitutional, until overturned in the 1954 *Brown* v. *Board of Education* case. Levy and Phillips, "The *Roberts* Case," 516.

64. *Liberator*, 14 June 1850. Leon F. Litwack states that following the court decision "Boston Negroes turned to legislative appeals and formed the Equal School Rights Committee." Litwack cites *Report of the Colored People of the City of Boston on the Subject of Exclusive Schools. Submitted by Benjamin F. Roberts, to the Boston Equal School Rights Committee* (Boston, 1850). The campaign finally succeeded when Boston schools were integrated by an act of the state legislature in 1855. Leon F. Litwack, *North of Slavery: The Negro in the Free States, 1790–1860* (Chicago, 1961), 149 n. 90.

65. *National Anti-Slavery Standard*, 16 May 1850.

66. Ibid.

67. *Springfield Republican*, 22 May 1850.

68. *Boston Herald*, 1 May 1850; 1851 *Narrative*, v. A Dover viewer noted, "I have attended the exhibition of H. B. Brown's Panorama, in this village, with very deep interest." Even if Brown's presence in Boston at the end of May 1850 cannot be confirmed, copies of Brown's *Narrative* were there. A newspaper satirist, writing about the "Anti-Slavery Convention at the Melodeon," described a vendor "narrowly watching a small stock of books such as Parker's Sermon, William Box Brown's narrative, &c, evidently laboring under the insane idea that some deluded mortal under the influence of the eloquent speakers, should rush to his stand and purchase a full, true and particular account of the ground and loftly tumbling executed by an escaped slave in a box during his travels from the south to the north, or some other work of like character." *Boston Herald*, 28 May 1850.

69. 1851 *Narrative*, iv–v.

70. *North Star* (Rochester, N.Y.), 1 Mar. 1850; *Worcester Massachusetts Spy*, 30 Oct. 1850. Similar accounts about Swift appeared in the *Worcester National Aegis*, 30 Oct. 1850, and in the *New York Daily Tribune*, 26 Oct. 1850, in "The Fugitive Case at Worcester" that reported "he has confessed himself as an impostor, and asserts that it was the intention of himself and another to travel through the country, and raise all the funds they could by exciting the sympathies of the abolitionists."

Chapter Five: Mirror of Slavery

1. Rev. Justin Spaulding, letter, 12 July 1850, transcribed in 1851 *Narrative*, iv–v; *Worcester Massachusetts Spy*, 15 May 1850.

2. *Narrative of the Life and Adventures of Henry Bibb, an American Slave, Written by Himself* (New York, 1849). Even if the panorama artists adapted rather than simply copied the source images, those images are still a guide to the content of the panorama scenes.

3. Richard D. Altick, *The Shows of London* (Cambridge, Mass., and London, Eng., 1978), 203–210; Walter M. Bayne, *Description of Bayne's Gigantic Panorama of a Voyage to Europe* (Boston, 1848), 2.

4. Rev. S. H. Chase, *A Short History of J. Insco Williams' Panorama of the Bible*, 2d. ed. (Boston, 1850), 2. The *Panorama of the Bible* was destroyed by fire in Mar. 1851 at Independence Hall, Philadelphia. Williams exhibited a second version from 1856 to 1871. (George C. Groce and David H. Wallace, *The New-York Historical Society's Dictionary of Artists in America, 1564–1860* [New Haven and London, 1957], 689). That the scenes of a panorama might be arranged "in historical order" seems a simple concept, yet from all indications it was not common and most of the examples (as judged from titles) came in the later wave of moving panoramas in the mid-1850s.

5. *Liberator*, 19 Apr. 1850; Ralph Waldo Emerson, "Life and Letters in New England," in *The Complete Writings of Ralph Waldo Emerson* (New York, 1929), 1050; Albert Brisbane, *Social Destiny of Man; or, Association and Reorganization of Industry* (Philadelphia, 1840; reprint, New York, 1968). Friedrich Engels included Fourier in the category of Utopian Socialists. Fourier envisioned a highly organized community of 1,620 to 1,800 people, called a Phalanx, on land about three

miles square, planted in fields, orchards, and gardens. At the center is the Phalanstery, a three-story communal building in which all live, eat, and have leisure. The Phalanstery has a center and two wings; a separate building, housing granaries and stable, forms the fourth side of a central parade ground. The inhabitants associate in Groups, organized into Series, and the Series constitute the Phalanx. Groups and Series are specialized work units, and members can move from one to another to vary their work. The least desirable work receives the highest pay. See Mark Holloway, *Heavens on Earth: Utopian Communities in America, 1680–1880* (London, 1951), 133–158. The description above is from 134–136.

6. Nancy Osgood, "Josiah Wolcott: Artist and Associationist," *Old-Time New England* 76 (spring/summer 1998): 5–34, esp. 9–14; *Witness to America's Past: Two Centuries of Collecting by the Massachusetts Historical Society* (Boston, 1991), 162–164. Brook Farm was not Fourierist at its founding in 1841, but was converted in 1844. Beginning in July 1844 the resources of Brook Farm went into building a Fourierist central building called the Phalanstery. When the almost-completed Phalanstery burned in Mar. 1846, the community could not weather the resulting financial blow, and Brook Farm disbanded in 1847.

Josiah Wolcott painted his first view of Brook Farm in 1843, and in Dec. 1843 signed the call for a Boston convention on Fourier. The New England Fourier Society was formed in Jan. 1844 and Wolcott served on its executive committee for two years. The Brook Farm ledger from Nov. 1844 to Oct. 1846 records Wolcott as a shareholder who received interest. Wolcott joined the Brook Farm committee on religion in Oct. 1845. For the Boston Union of Associationists, formed in Nov. 1846, Wolcott served as the treasurer and as a director. He was a charter member of the Boston Religious Union of Associationists, formed in Jan. 1847, and participated in activities of the group through Dec. 1847. Osgood, "Josiah Wolcott: Artist and Associationist," 9–14.

7. Brisbane, *Social Destiny of Man*, 97–98; Carl J. Guarneri, *The Utopian Alternative: Fourierism in Nineteenth-Century America* (Ithaca, N.Y., and London, Eng., 1991), 79; Philip S. Foner, *American Socialism and Black Americans: From the Age of Jackson to World War II* (Westport, Conn., and London, Eng., 1977), 8–13.

8. *Boston Daily Evening Traveller*, 29 Apr. 1850.

9. **The African Slave Trade** was an abolitionist topic in 1850 not merely as a historical legacy but also because the trade was still active. The United States had banned further imports of slaves in 1808, the legal slave trade to the Spanish colonies ended in 1817, and that to Brazil in 1831, but "down to 1850 both Cuba and Brazil imported large numbers of slaves, regardless of international agreements; there was certainly some involvement in this trade by North American, British and French traders." As many as a million slaves were imported to the Americas between 1830 and 1850. In 1850, too, there were allegations that slaves were being smuggled into the United States from Cuba and other points, and voices in the South were calling to reopen the slave trade with Africa. Robin Blackburn, *The Overthrow of Colonial Slavery, 1776–1848* (London and New York, 1988), 546; Kwame Anthony Appiah and Henry Louis Gates Jr., *Africana: The Encyclopedia of the African and African American Experience* (New York, 1999), 303, 535.

Although *The Nubian Slave* depicted the slave hunters as Europeans, "almost all slaves had lost their freedom long before they first came into contact with the transatlantic trader and the slave ship." Many were seized in war by other Africans who first enslaved them. Whether the panorama showed the slave hunters as Europeans or Africans is unknown. David Eltis, *Economic Growth and the Ending of the Transatlantic Slave Trade* (New York and Oxford, 1987), 13.

10. Green, *The Nubian Slave* (Boston, 1845), 4. In the scene **Religious Sacrifice**, something akin to Olaudah Equiano's analogy, in his 1789 account of life in Africa, of "the Israelites in their primitive state" may have been intended: "They have many offerings, particularly at full moons; generally two, at harvest, before the fruits are taken out of the ground; and when any young animals are killed, sometimes they offer up part of them as a sacrifice," Equiano wrote. "Like the Israelites in their primitive state," he continued, "we had also our sacrifices and burnt-offerings, our washings and purifications." Olaudah Equiano, *The Interesting Narrative of the Life of Olaudah Equiano*, ed. Robert J. Allison (1789; reprint, Boston and New York, 1995), 41, 44–45.

Regarding the scene **Beautiful Lake and Mountain Scenery in Africa**, a note of confusion derives from a reviewer in the *Liverpool Mercury*, 15 Nov. 1850, who described the scene as "the

Nubian, in the enjoyment of his freedom midst his own beautiful lake and mountain scenery." If the reviewer correctly placed the Nubian in this scene, then the assumption that the previous scene, **Seizure of Slaves**, implied or illustrated the capture of the Nubians would be misplaced. The next scene after **Scenery** seems to imply that the Nubians were enslaved, thus the presence of the Nubian still free in **Scenery**, after **Seizure**, would have made the panorama plot disjointed. (It seems too modern a construction for **Scenery** to have been a flashback, imagined by the enslaved Nubian.) The most plausible explanation is that the reviewer, after attending a performance, composed the review, perhaps on deadline, with a program or advertisement listing the scene titles at hand—for how else would he have gotten the title exactly—and conflated the image of the second scene, **The Nubian Family in Freedom**, with the title of this scene.

11. Dating from the late seventeenth century, the felucca was a "low-sided ship with two masts slightly inclined toward the bow, and rigged with lateen sails," and was "common throughout the Mediterranean" (Enzo Angelucci and Attilio Cucari, *Ships* [New York, 1977], 110). That Boston in 1850 was a seafaring town may have been a factor in the nautical emphasis. With the particular attention the panorama pays to the intra-African slave trade, and the specific designation of the felucca, it seems likely that a firsthand source was available. Perhaps someone spending "two years before the mast" had brought back sketches. Alternately, the imagery may have derived from a source such as the series of prints circulating in Boston abolitionist circles.

12. By the 1840s, a number of nations had made a commitment to stop the transatlantic slave trade. In the mid-1840s, an average of nearly 66 naval ships patrolled the West African coast, about half British and also French, U.S., and Portuguese-Angolan. British patrols made more than 85 percent of captures, which in the period 1846–1850 totaled 68 ships with slaves aboard detained, 329 ships without slaves aboard detained, and almost 25,000 slaves disembarked. (Eltis, *Economic Growth and the Ending of the Transatlantic Slave Trade*, 87, 94–95, 97–99). In contrast, the U.S. squadron on antislavery trade duty from 1843 to 1861 varied from 3 to 8 ships, and Blackburn describes a "lack of zeal in Washington for prosecuting slave traders." *The Overthrow of Colonial Slavery*, 547.

13. Abolitionists in 1850 took seriously proposals of radical southerners to admit Cuba as a new slave state to balance the new free state of California. The *Boston Emancipator & Republican*, 11 Apr. 1850, reported that "the long talked of rumors concerning a plot to invade Cuba, are acquiring some consistency. . . . should the Executive withdraw opposition to the scheme, it would be successfully carried out within six months." In May 1850 a small, independent army actually invaded Cuba. Neither the Cuban people nor the "Southern slaveholding" population supported the invasion, which failed, and Cuba remained Spanish. See Robert E. May, *The Southern Dream of a Caribbean Empire, 1854–1861* (Baton Rouge, La., 1973), esp. 22–29.

After a campaign of many years by antislavery activists, in 1834 the British government had legislated the gradual emancipation of the slaves working on the plantations in the British West Indies. (Appiah and Gates, *Africana*, 863–864). The process began on 1 Aug. 1834, an event celebrated annually by abolitionists. Henry Box Brown had attended such an event in 1849. The West Indian emancipation was a close-at-hand example that a government that had the will could implement emancipation.

14. *Leeds Mercury*, 24 May 1851. The *Mercury* review describes one of the auction scenes as including "notices in large letters, such as 'Great sale of slaves of foreign and domestic production, in Liberty-square, near the Free Church.'" The scene entitled **Grand Slave Auction** was later listed as "Grand Auction Block." *West London Observer*, 12 Mar. 1859.

15. David J. McCord, ed., *The Statutes at Large of South Carolina* (Columbia, S.C., 1840), 7:90–92, records a 1768 legislative act "for appropriating the present Work House for a place of Correction."

According to a European visitor to Charleston, "There are two tread-wheels in operation. Each employs twelve prisoners, who work a mill for grinding corn. . . . Six tread at once upon each wheel, while six rest upon a bench placed behind the wheel. Every half minute the left hand man steps off the tread-wheel, while the five others move to the left to fill up the vacant space; at the same time the right hand man sitting on the bench, steps onto the wheel, and begins his movement, while the rest, sitting on the bench, uniformly recede. Thus, even three minutes sitting, allows the unhappy being no repose. The signal for changing is given by a small bell attached to the wheel. The prisoners are compelled to labour eight hours a day in this manner. Order is preserved by a person, who, armed with a cow-hide, stands by the wheel. Both sexes tread promiscuously upon the wheel." Karl Bernhard, duke of Saxe-Weimar-Eisenach, *Travels through North America, during the Years 1825 and 1826* (Philadelphia, 1828), 2:9.

16. *West London Observer*, 12 Mar. 1859. Both of the Brown's panoramas could have used as a source for the images of slaves working on a sugar plantation published in the *Illustrated London News*, 9 June 1849, pp. 388–389. William Wells Brown's panorama included the scene, "A Sugar Plantation, with Slaves Cutting Cane—Steam Sugar Mill." *A Description of William Wells Brown's Original Panoramic Views of the Scenes in the Life of an American Slave, from His Birth in Slavery to His Death or His Escape to His First Home of Freedom on British Soil* (London, 1849), reprinted in *The Black Abolitionist Papers, Volume 1: The British Isles, 1830–1865*, ed. C. Peter Ripley et al. (Chapel Hill and London, 1985), 201.

Women at Work is the scene that most directly addresses issues concerning women, a theme found throughout the panorama. About twenty scenes include women in some way. Many radical abolitionists were conscious of issues concerning the rights of women. The kind of work depicted in **Women at Work** may have been agricultural or domestic or a tableaux of several occupations.

In 1850, the image of slaves picking cotton had not yet become the seminal image of slavery that it became later. William Wells Brown described his similar scene: "The 'picking season,' as it is called, is the hardest time for slaves on a cotton plantation. As the cotton must be picked at a certain stage of ripeness, the slaves are usually worked, during this season of the year, from fourteen to sixteen hours out of the twenty-four. . . . During the task time, if a slave fails to accomplish his task, he receives five cuts with the cat-o'-nine-tails, or the negro whip, for every pound of cotton that is wanting to make up the requisite number. In the distance you observe a woman being whipped at the whipping-post, near which are the scales for weighing the cotton." Ripley et al., *The Black Abolitionist Papers*, 1:200.

17. *Liberator*, 5 Jan. 1849. Josiah Wolcott or one or another of the other workers on the panorama may have known Henry Wadsworth Longfellow's 1842 poem, "The Slave in the Dismal Swamp," which begins "In dark fens of the Dismal Swamp / The hunted Negro lay" (*Henry Wadsworth Longfellow: Poetical Works* [Boston and New York, 1904], 1:105; originally published in Longfellow, *Poems on Slavery*, 2d ed. [Cambridge, Mass., 1842]). Located in southeastern Virginia and northeastern North Carolina, the Dismal Swamp originally covered as much as 2,000 square miles. Lake Drummond, the lake in the scene title, is in Virginia, "with a swampy heavily forested shoreline of twenty miles." In the swamp interior was a community of free blacks and fugitive slaves, known as Maroons, estimated by Hugo Prosper Leaming to have numbered as many as 2,000. On the edges of the swamp lived free blacks who were a link between the Maroons and the outside world. The origins of the Maroon community in the Dismal Swamp went back as far as the early eighteenth century. Hugo Prosper Leaming, "Hidden Americans: Maroons of Virginia and the Carolinas" (Ph. D. diss., University of Illinois at Chicago Circle, 1979), 403, and, in general, 324–577.

William and Ellen Craft appeared with Henry Box Brown at the 1849 New England Anti-Slavery Convention. Because Ellen Craft was in Boston, the artists could have sketched her from life and had her description of the scene firsthand. For the escape Ellen Craft's difficult role required her to sit with the white travelers. She said as little as possible. On the steamer, she recalled, "the gentlemen then turned the conversation upon the three great topics of discussion in first-class circles in Georgia, namely, Niggers, Cotton, and the Abolitionists." Her railroad seatmates from Petersburg to Richmond were a threat because they were so friendly. In Baltimore, the last slave town, an officer at first would not allow William to proceed without papers showing that he belonged to his "master," Ellen, but this too was resolved, and the Crafts arrived in Philadelphia on Christmas Day in 1848. William and Ellen Craft, *Running a Thousand Miles for Freedom; or, The Escape of William and Ellen Craft from Slavery* (London, 1860), reprinted in *Slave Narratives*, ed. William L. Andrews and Henry Louis Gates Jr. (New York, 2000), 677–742 (quotation on 706).

18. Testimony of William Yateman, *Wolverhampton & Staffordshire Herald*, 4 Aug. 1852.

19. The *Manchester Examiner and Times*, 5 April 1851, noted that "Mr. Brown entered at length into the history of his own escape, and how he was conveyed in a small box to Philadelphia, labeled—'This side up, with care.'"

20. The *Leeds Mercury*, 24 May 1851. The Natural Bridge, located well west of Brown's route of escape, was identified with Thomas Jefferson, who owned it from 1774 until his death in 1826. Abolitionists sought to enlist the Founders, through their writings and actions, for the antislavery cause. Though modern scholarship emphasizes Jefferson's acute ambivalence on slavery and effective support of the system, in the nineteenth century he was seen by many as being antislavery.

It is possible to imagine that the personification of General Taylor stemmed from the influence of Charles Stearns, the author of *Facts in the Life of General Taylor; the Cuba Blood-hound Importer, the Extensive Slave-Holder, and the Hero of the Mexican War* (Boston, 1848). President Taylor's death in July 1850, soon after the panorama came out, would not have greatly changed the meaning.

By 1850 a movement had begun to purchase and restore Mount Vernon, including Washington's gravesite, and many visitors to Washington made the pilgrimage down the Potomac. An 1862 abolitionist tract stated: "Though, by inheritance and other circumstances entirely beyond his control, Washington found himself a slave-holder, yet he never defended the institution of slavery, or desired its perpetuity.... Through his whole life, his desire to clear himself and his country from the foul blot was sincere and constant." George Livermore, *An Historical Research Respecting the Opinions of the Founders of the Republic on Negroes As Slaves, As Citizens, and As Soldiers*, 3d ed. (Boston, 1863), 28.

21. The Fairmount Water Works was also depicted in other moving panoramas: "Fairmount Water Works, near Philadelphia, on the Schuykill River ... furnishes one of the most beautiful and useful combinations of nature and art to be seen in the whole country.... Fairmount is a great place of resort. The views of the Schuykill and the surrounding country, from the top of the reservoir ... the beauty of the numerous fanciful fountains ... the interest and immense utility of these vast arrangements when viewed as a magnificent work of art—all combined, serve to render this a place of great attention." *A Description of the Mammoth Cave of Kentucky, the Niagara River and Falls, and the Falls in Summer and Winter; the Prairies, or Life in the West; The Fairmount Water Works and Scenes on the Schuykill, &c. &c. to Illustrate Brewer's Panorama* (Boston, 1850), 5–6.

22. William Wells Brown also had a scene in his panorama of Henry Bibb's escape. See Ripley et al., *The Black Abolitionist Papers*, 1:204.

23. A North Carolina case from 1842 could have inspired **Tarring and Feathering in S. Carolina**. Lunsford Lane was a free black from Raleigh, who traveled north and then returned to Raleigh. He was arrested and charged with "*delivering abolition lectures in the State of Massachusetts.*" At a "call court" no guilt was found, but a mob had formed. He was taken to jail for safety, but trying to sneak out that night, Lane was seized by the mob: "Then a bucket was brought, and set down by my side.... in a moment, one of the number came forward with a pillow.... They commenced stripping me, until every rag of clothes was removed. Then the bucket was brought near, and I felt relieved when I found it contained tar. One man whom I knew ... was the first to dip his hands into the tar, ... he, with three other 'chivalrous gentlemen' ... gave me ... a complete coat of tar, sparing only my face. Then ripping open the pillow at one end, they held it over my head and commenced applying its contents to the tarred portions of my body.... A fine escape, thought I, from hanging, provided they do not set fire to the feathers. I had some fear they would." Rev. William G. Hawkins, *Lunsford Lane; or, Another Helper from North Carolina* (Boston, 1863), 146, 147, 155–156.

An account of an actual **Burning Alive**, which occurred 28 Apr. 1836 in Saint Louis, appeared in the 1840 *American Anti-Slavery Almanac*: "A black man named McIntosh, who had stabbed an officer, that had arrested him, was seized by the multitude, and fastened to a tree *in the midst of the city*, in the open day, and in the presence of an immense throng of citizens, was burnt to death." The details of the murder are dreadful. The "Hon. Luke E. Lawless,

Judge of the Circuit Court of Missouri, at its session, in St. Louis, some months after, decided that since the burning of McIntosh was the act, directly or by countenance, of a *majority* of citizens, it is a 'case which transcends the jurisdiction,' of the Grand Jury!" *The American Anti-Slavery Almanac, for 1840: . . . Calculated for Boston; Adapted to the New England States* (New York and Boston, 1839), 23.

In the sequence, the first and third scenes, **Tarring and Feathering** and **Burning Alive**, are about horrors. If the second scene, **The Slaveholder's Dream**, was a straightforward representation of the idealized hopes of slaveholders, then it was a dream tarnished by the repression necessary to achieve it, as shown in the surrounding scenes. *Mirror of Slavery* here may have had its effect by a sort of panoramic montage.

24. In her *Right Way The Safe Way, Proved by Emancipation in the British West Indies, and Elsewhere* (New York, 1862; reprint, New York, 1969), 12–13, L. Maria Child captured the abolitionists' feeling for the **West India Emancipation**: "When the clock *began* to strike twelve, on the 31st of July, 1834, there were nearly 30,000 slaves on the island of Antigua; when it *ceased* to strike, they were all freemen! . . . Scarcely had the *last* tone sounded, when lightening flashed vividly, and a loud peal of thunder rolled through the sky. . . . It was followed by a moment of profound silence. Then came the outburst! . . . They clapped their hands, they leaped up, they fell down, they clasped each other in their free arms, they cried, they laughed, they went to and fro, throwing upward their unfettered hands. High above all, a mighty sound ever and anon swelled up."

25. *Liberator*, 19 Apr. 1850; George R. Price and James Brewer Stewart, eds., *To Heal the Scourge of Prejudice: The Life and Writings of Hosea Easton* (Amherst, Mass., 1999), 119. For all the visual imagery generated by the antislavery crusade, there were few representations of emancipation made prior to 1863. Representative of general practice was William Wells Brown's 1850 panorama, which concluded with a scene of the fugitive reaching Canada, entitled "The Fugitive's Home—A Welcome to the Slave—True Freedom" (Ripley et al., *The Black Abolitionist Papers*, 1:213). Images that treated emancipation not symbolically but concretely, that is, showing freed people as yeoman farmers or as families in liberty, almost all date from the 1860s. A conspicuous exception would have been the masthead of the *Liberator*. **Grand Industrial Palace**, a depiction of the fruition of emancipation represented in a complex, integrated social setting, seems to have been an image without contemporary parallel.

26. Brown exhibited *Mirror of Slavery* continuously for about ten years; the latest notice located of its exhibition comes from 1864 (*Merthyr Star*, 10 Mar. 1864). If over that time he toured forty weeks a year, and averaged 5 shows per week (and several weeks are documented in which he gave 8 shows), he would have presented 200 shows per year.

27. *Liberator*, 31 May 1850; *Bradford Observer*, 8 May 1851; *Bolton Chronicle and South Lancashire Advertiser*, 8 Feb. 1851; *Wolverhampton & Staffordshire Herald*, 24 Mar. 1852, reprinted in the *Times* (London), 30 July 1852; *Leeds Mercury*, 3, 24 May 1851; *Liverpool Mercury*, 12 Nov. 1850.

28. *Wolverhampton & Staffordshire Herald*, 24 Mar. 1852; *Liverpool Mercury*, 15 Nov. 1850; *Times* (London), 30 July 1852; *Bolton Chronicle and South Lancashire Advertiser*, 8 Feb.1851.

29. *Liberator*, 31 May 1850; *Springfield Republican*, 22 May 1850; *Liverpool Mercury*, 12 Nov. 1850; *Leigh Chronicle*, 11 Jan. 1862.

30. *London Empire*, reprinted in *National Anti-Slavery Standard*, 3 Mar. 1855; J[ohn] Kitton, Preston, to L. Chamerovzow, 7 Apr. 1854, Anti-Slavery Papers, MSS Brit Emp S18 C33/35, Bodleian Library of Commonwealth and African Studies at Rhodes House, Oxford University, Oxford, Eng.

31. *Wolverhampton & Staffordshire Herald*, 24 Mar. 1852, reprinted in the *Times* (London), 30 July 1852. Brown never stated in his two *Narratives* that his master, William Barret, preached to the slaves but did say that his overseer John F. Allen held a Sunday school. 1849 *Narrative*, 45–46; 1851 *Narrative*, 27–28.

32. The earliest-located newspaper report of this method of presenting "Escape from Slavery of Henry Box Brown" was in the *Wolverhampton & Staffordshire Herald*, 24 Mar. 1852; two years into the exhibition, but the story also appears in the 1851 *Narrative*. Elsewhere in this volume it is argued that the text of the 1851 *Narrative* was actually prepared by Apr. 1850, before the

premiere of *Mirror of Slavery* (83–84, 132). If this dating of the text is correct, then Brown was presumably telling the story of "the shovel and the hoe" to set up his song at appearances even before he began exhibiting the panorama. According to the *Wolverhampton & Staffordshire Herald* it was at the scene "Sunday Among the Slave Population" that Brown told the story of "the shovel and the hoe."

33. 1851 *Narrative*, 62–63.

34. William Stanton, *The Leopard's Spots: Scientific Attitudes toward Race in America, 1815–59* (Chicago, 1960), 62.

Chapter Six: Expatriation

1. *Washington, D.C., National Era* (n.d.), reprinted in *National Anti-Slavery Standard*, 17 Oct. 1850.

2. This and the next paragraph from Holman Hamilton, *Prologue to Conflict: The Crisis and Compromise of 1850* (Lexington, Ky., 1964), 84–146, esp. 107; Stanley W. Campbell, *The Slave Catchers: Enforcement of the Fugitive Slave Law, 1850–1860* (Chapel Hill, 1970), 3–25.

3. *Providence Republican Herald*, 28 Aug. 1850; *Providence Post*, 2 Sept. 1850.

4. This and the next paragraph from *Providence Post*, 2, Sept. 1850. One account says that Brown was "severely beaten," but there are no subsequent mentions of any lingering physical disabilities or of time spent recuperating from the attack. Kelton, who according to court testimony was intoxicated at the time of the attacks, had also brought charges against Henry Brown, but these were dismissed. The *Providence Post* (3 Sept. 1850) reported that Kelton's "fine and costs were paid, when an idea struck the counsel for the defendant and an appeal taken. It was probably understood that Mr. Brown's business would not admit of his remaining in the city until the next session of the Court of Common Pleas."

5. *Providence Post*, 2 Sept. 1850; *Boston Emancipator & Republican*, 5 Sept. 1850; *Pennsylvania Freeman*, 12 Sept. 1850.

6. *National Anti-Slavery Standard*, 19 Sept. 1850.

7. Campbell, *The Slave Catchers*, 23.

8. Henry Brown and James Smith to Gerrit Smith, 15 Sept. 1850, Gerrit Smith Papers, Syracuse University, Syracuse, N.Y., in the *Black Abolitionist Papers, 1830–1865*, ed. George E. Carter and C. Peter Ripley (Ann Arbor, Mich., 1993), microfilm edition, 6:0578.

9. Ibid. In writing this letter, James Smith used a large close-parenthesis in lieu of other punctuation. Smith wrote in Brown's name; and the blend of "I" and "we," sometimes mixed in the same sentence, shows how closely the two were working. James Smith later wrote to Gerrit Smith: "I wrote to you for a letter when we was about to leave New York which was received—and I must also thank you for your kindness." J. C. A. Smith to Gerrit Smith, 6 Aug. 1851, in *The Black Abolitionist Papers, Volume 1: The British Isles, 1830–1865*, ed. C. Peter Ripley et al. (Chapel Hill and London, 1985), 293.

10. Thomas G. Lee, "Introduction," 1851 *Narrative*, vi.

11. Advertisement in the *Boston Impartial Citizen*, 14 Sept. 1850; *Burlington (Vt.) Courier*, 12 Apr. 1849, reprinted in *New York Daily Tribune*, 17 Apr. 1849; "Henry Box Brown," *The Liberty Almanac for 1851* (New York, 1850), 15.

12. *Anti-Slavery Bugle*, 8 Mar. 1851. The Philadelphia version, though it is in the collections of the Library Company of Philadelphia and not in the collections of the Library of Congress, is noted in Bernard F. Reilly Jr., *American Political Prints, 1766–1876: A Catalog of the Collections in the Library of Congress* (Boston, 1991), 332–333.

13. Francis Jackson, "Account of expenses in sending Wm & Ellen Craft to England by Steamship via Halifax Nov. 1850," Boston Public Library. Brown and Smith probably paid less than $130 each, which was the New York to Liverpool fare on the steamer *Atlantic* of the Collins line. *New York Tribune*, 8 Oct. 1850.

14. *Liverpool Mercury*, 5 Nov. 1850; Samuel Ringgold Ward, *Autobiography of a Fugitive Negro* (London, 1855; reprint, New York, 1968), 235–236; *Liverpool Mercury*, 5 Nov. 1850. The *Anti-Slavery Bugle* (21 Dec. 1850) gives the date of 30 Oct. 1850 for Brown's arrival in Liverpool. No ship

from New York is listed in the *Liverpool Mercury* as arriving that day.

15. Ward, *Autobiography of a Fugitive Negro*, 241; William Wells Brown quoted in Howard Temperley, *British Antislavery, 1833–1870* (Columbia, S.C., 1972), 223.

16. *Liverpool Mercury*, 5 Nov. 1850. One friend of the slave in Liverpool who might have helped Brown and Smith was Francis Bishop, a Unitarian missionary to the poor. He boarded fugitives at his mission, which, after the increasing arrivals caused by the Fugitive Slave Act, became an "English terminus for escaped slaves." Douglas Charles Stange, *British Unitarians against American Slavery, 1833–65* (Rutherford, N. J., 1984), 117.

17. Richard D. Webb to "My dear Friend" (Mrs. Maria [Weston] Chapman), 12 Nov. 1850, Anti-Slavery Collection, Rare Books and Manuscripts, Boston Public Library.

18. Dr. John Bishop Estlin to "Miss Weston," 14 Nov. 1850, Anti-Slavery Collection, Boston Public Library; James C. A. Smith to William Lloyd Garrison, 6 Aug. 1851, Anti-Slavery Collection, Boston Public Library, and *Black Abolitionist Papers*, microfilm edition, 7:0034–0035.

19. *Liverpool Mercury*, 12 Nov. 1850.

20. Smith to Garrison, 6 Aug. 1851, *Black Abolitionist Papers*, microfilm edition, 7:0034–0035; *Manchester Examiner & Times*, 14 Dec. 1850.

21. *Liverpool Mercury*, 15 Nov. 1850.

22. Ibid., 19, 22, 26, 29 Nov., 3 Dec. 1850. A later report stated that Brown "arrived in Liverpool in 1850, and exhibited his panorama there with success." *Times* (London), 30 July 1852. One account states that they also raised money by sales of copies of a lithograph. Ripley et al., *The Black Abolitionist Papers*, 1:298.

Chapter Seven: English Freedom

1. J. B. Harley, "England *circa* 1850," in *A New Historical Geography of England,* ed. H. C. Darby (Cambridge, Eng., 1973), 560, 588.

2. Frederick Douglass, "An Appeal to the British People, reception speech at Finsbury Chapel, Moorfields, England, May 12, 1846," in *The Life and Writings of Frederick Douglass: Early Years, 1817–1849,* ed. Philip S. Foner (New York, 1950), 163, 164. For African American abolitionist activities in Great Britain, see R. J. M. Blackett, *Building an Antislavery Wall: Black Americans in the Atlantic Abolitionist Movement, 1830–1860* (Baton Rouge, La., and London, Eng., 1983).

3. Blackett, *Building an Antislavery Wall,* 146.

4. John Francis McDermott, *The Lost Panoramas of the Mississippi* (Chicago, 1958), 18–67; *Illustrated London News,* 30 Mar. 1850, quoted in Richard D. Altick, *The Shows of London* (Cambridge, Mass., and London, Eng., 1978), 206–207; *Times* (London), 7 Jan. 1851.

5. William Wells Brown, *A Description of William Wells Brown's Original Panoramic Views of the Scenes in the Life of an American Slave, from His Birth in Slavery to His Death or His Escape to His First Home of Freedom on British Soil* (London, 1849), reprinted in *The Black Abolitionist Papers, Volume I: The British Isles, 1830–1865,* ed. C. Peter Ripley et al. (Chapel Hill and London, 1985), 191–224; William Edward Farrison, *William Wells Brown: Author & Reformer* (Chicago and London, 1969), 174, 176. Mary Ann Estlin, referring to the *Description,* noted on 4 Oct. 1850 that "to-day W. B. sent us a proof, for some additional names to be inserted" (Estlin to Anne Warren Weston, 4 Oct. 1850, Anti-Slavery Collection, Rare Books and Manuscripts, Boston Public Library). Farrison reports that William Wells Brown's panorama was kept in London for five or six weeks, but whether it was exhibited during that period is not clear (176).

6. *National Anti-Slavery Standard,* 26 Dec. 1850, 6 Mar. 1851; Blackett, *Building an Antislavery Wall,* 124. At Glasgow William Wells Brown's panorama was shown for four days at the Trades' Hall. At Aberdeen, the local newspaper reported, "In the morning school children came to see the panorama and listen to the fugitives; in the afternoon and evening large crowds came to hear them speak." Quoted in Blackett, 124–125.

7. Farrison, *William Wells Brown,* 176, 185, 244; *Special Report of the Bristol and Clifton Ladies' Anti-slavery Society during Eighteen Months, from January, 1851, to June, 1852 . . .* (London, 1852), 10 n.

8. *The Escaped Slave: An Autobiography of Charles Freeman. With a Preface by the Rev. J. Whitby, Ipswich* (London, 1853), 77–79, 82–83.

9. *London Anti-Slavery Reporter*, 1 May 1850, p. 73; *British Friend* (London), July 1850, p. 179.

10. *London Anti-Slavery Reporter,* 1 May 1850, p. 73.

11. *British Friend*, July 1850, p. 179.

12. *The Escaped Slave*, 83.

13. Altick, *Shows of London*, 283. In *Some Recollections of Our Antislavery Conflict* (Boston, 1869), Samuel J. May mentioned a visit from a Dr. W. H. Irwin who had been "living in Georgia in 1834" and who, at the time May was writing, had recently left Louisiana, where he had been "one of many Union men who have been stripped of their property and driven out of the State by President Johnson's and Mayor Monroe's partisans" (134).

14. Farrison, *William Wells Brown*, 186; Clare Taylor, comp., *British and American Abolitionists: An Episode in Transatlantic Understanding* (Edinburgh, 1974), 377–378.

15. *Liverpool Mercury*, 10 Dec. 1850.

16. Ripley et al., *The Black Abolitionist Papers*, 1:11, 13.

17. Friedrich Engels, *The Condition of the Working Class in England in 1844*, trans. and ed. W. O. Henderson and W. H. Chaloner (New York, 1958), 50; Randall Stewart, ed., *The English Notebooks by Nathaniel Hawthorne* (New York, 1962), 350. "Of the steam power available to British industry at mid-century, the most important regional concentration was driving nearly a quarter of a million power looms in the cotton industry," writes J. B. Harley in "England *circa* 1850" in *A New Historical Geography of England*, 560. Distances between English cities in this and following instances are derived from the maps in H. A. Piehler, *England for Everyman* (New York, 1961), 1–32.

18. *Manchester Examiner & Times*, 14 Dec. 1850; *Manchester Guardian*, 18 Dec. 1850. The *Guardian* stated that James C. A. Smith had accompanied the box to Philadelphia. Whether this untruth was a mistaken impression of the reporter or promulgated by Brown or Smith is not known. Perhaps Brown dressed up the story to enlarge Smith's role in the escape.

19. *Manchester Examiner & Times,* 14, 21 Dec. 1850.

20. Ibid., 21 Dec. 1850; *Manchester Guardian*, 14 Dec. 1850.

21. J. C. A. Smith to Gerrit Smith, 6 Aug. 1851, in Ripley et al., *The Black Abolitionist Papers*, 1:295, 299 n. 3. James Bryce lived in Chorlton-on-Medlock according to *Slater's Classified Commercial Directory of the Towns and Villages in the Extensive Manufacturing District round Manchester* (Manchester, Eng., 1851).

22. Douglas A. Lorimer, *Colour, Class, and the Victorians: English Attitudes to the Negro in the Mid-Nineteenth Century* (Leicester, Eng., and New York, 1978), 115. An important focus for Rev. Thomas Gardiner Lee's activism was "the English Operatives." His essay, *A Plea For the English Operatives: Being a Competing Essay for the Prize Offered by John Cassell, Esq.: In Which the Means of Elevating the Working Classes Are Humbly Suggested* (London, 1850), described the harsh conditions the working class faced but maintained a respectable tone while presenting the radical ideas of the workers movement. His position was not extreme: "There can be no analogy between the operatives in this country and the slaves in the colonies." Yet he did report a common belief, which he did not personally endorse, that "religion was nothing but an engine employed by the rich, through the medium of hirelings, to keep men under restraint while some selfish projects were being carried to completion." Lee's opinion was that taxes were too high on the poor, and that land—controlled by the aristocracy—was not taxed enough. "If there were half the want of honour among thieves and robbers, as exists in circles calling themselves respectable, not to say religious, then the whole system of dishonesty would be with the greatest ease subverted and destroyed" (12 [third quotation], 21 [second quotation], 86 [third quotation]).

23. Ripley et al., *The Black Abolitionist Papers*, 1:295, 299 nn. 4 and 5; Frederic Boase, *Modern English Biography . . ., Volume VI—L to Z, Supplement to Volume III* (Truro, Eng., 1921; reprint, London, 1965), 33; *Slater's Manchester & Country Directory*, 1851; Boase, *Modern English Biography . . ., Volume IV—A to C, Supplement to Volume I* (Truro, Eng., 1908; reprint, London, 1965), 267.

24. *Blackburn Standard*, 8 Jan. 1851; 1851 *Narrative*, vi.

25. *Manchester Examiner & Times*, 25 Jan. 1851; Harley, "England *circa* 1850," 585; Stewart, *The English Notebooks by Nathaniel Hawthorne*, 193; *Bolton Chronicle & South Lancashire Advertiser*, 8 Feb. 1851 (stating that Brown and Smith had exhibited there "a few weeks ago").

26. This and the next paragraph from *Preston Chronicle and Lancashire Advertiser*, 25 Jan. 1851; *Preston Pilot and County Advertiser*, 25 Jan. 1851.

27. John Kitton to Louis Chamerovzow, 7 Apr. 1854, Anti-Slavery Papers, MSS Brit Emp S18 C33/35, Bodleian Library of Commonwealth and African Studies at Rhodes House, Oxford University, Oxford, Eng.; *Bolton Chronicle and South Lancashire Advertiser*, 15 Feb. 1851.

28. *Bolton Chronicle and South Lancashire Advertiser*, 15 Feb. 1851; *Preston Chronicle & Lancashire Advertiser*, 25 Jan. 1851. The *Preston Chronicle* inaccurately reported that Brown's former master had owned his family.

29. *Liverpool Mercury*, 20 Dec. 1850.

30. *Bolton Chronicle and South Lancashire Advertiser*, 8, 15 Feb. 1851.

31. Ibid., 15 Feb. 1851.

32. *National Anti-Slavery Standard*, 20 Mar. 1851. When Webb's letter, dated 20 Feb. 1851, appeared in the *Standard*, it read, "Henry Box Brown is doing well in Bristol," a city in the southwest of England. Perhaps Webb wrote "Bolton," and his poor penmanship (it was egregious) caused the *Standard*'s editor to misread what he wrote. Abolitionists in Manchester would readily know of events in Bolton, close by, but not as readily of news from Bristol, much farther away. No evidence of an appearance by Henry Box Brown in Bristol in this period has been found.

33. Ripley et al., *The Black Abolitionist Papers*, 1:293, has it that Brown and Smith exhibited at the Staffordshire Potteries before the summer of 1851. Because Brown was in that area in the latter part of 1851, the statement probably misplaced the Staffordshire appearance in time. A series of china and earthenware factory towns, which later combined to form modern Stoke-on-Trent, the Staffordshire Potteries were quite distant from any other known venue found for this period. If an exhibit did take place there before the summer of 1851, the only period when it could have happened, taking into account time for travel, was the 22 Feb. to 1 Apr. period for which no documentation of exhibitions has been found. The only English letter of endorsement quoted in the Introduction, which was dated 8 Apr. 1851, to the 1851 *Narrative*, vi, came from Blackburn, where Brown and Smith opened on 8 Jan. 1851. This 8 Jan.–8 Apr. window for Lee's Introduction supports the theory that Brown prepared the book between late Feb. and late Mar. 1851.

34. *Manchester Examiner & Times*, 5 Apr. 1851; *Leeds Mercury*, 19 Apr. 1851.

35. Joseph Lupton to Rev. Sam. May Jr., 3 May 1851, Anti-Slavery Collection, Rare Books and Manuscripts, Boston Public Library; *Leeds Mercury*, 3 May 1851.

36. *Bradford Observer*, 8 May 1851.

37. Harley, "England *circa* 1850," 578; *Leeds Times*, 24 May 1851.

38. *Leeds Times,* 17 May 1851; *Leeds Intelligencer*, 17 May 1851; *Leeds Mercury*, 17 May 1851. The article in the *Intelligencer* stated: "'HEY, JOHN BROWN THE BLACK MAN.'—Reader, start not! we are not about to give you any more of a song once very popular amongst the lower classes. We simply wish to call your attention to an announcement in our advertising columns."

39. *Leeds Mercury*, 24 May 1851.

40. Ibid.; *Leeds Times*, 24 May 1851. The Methodist New Connexion was an off-shoot of the Wesleyan Methodist Church.

41. This and the next paragraph from *Leeds Mercury*, 17, 24 May 1851.

42. *Narrative of the Life of Henry Box Brown, Written by Himself. First English Edition* (Manchester, 1851).

43. 1851 *Narrative*, 16.

44. Ibid., ii.

45. Ibid., 49.

46. Henry Box Brown and Charles Stearns had worked together very closely when touring to sell the first book. William Lloyd Garrison's hard critique of the first edition—that it was written in a "loose and declamatory" style—would have been particularly meaningful for Stearns, a longtime admirer. Perhaps feeling an obligation, after his first flawed effort, to do better by Brown,

Stearns might have been willing to assist on an improved edition. Flights of rhetoric reminiscent of Stearns's style in the 1849 *Narrative* appear at points in the 1851 *Narrative*, especially in the preface and the appendix. A possibility is that Stearns had a collaborator, who interviewed Brown and provided the text to the new narrative, with Stearns providing the bracketing material. He might have recruited his sister, Rachel W. Stearns, a teacher who lived in Springfield with their mother. Rachel Stearns was a significant contributor to a later book he wrote, and one could imagine that she would have been a more patient listener to Brown than her brother. See her contributions to Charles Stearns, *The Black Man of the South, and the Rebels; The Characteristics of the Former, and the Recent Outrages of the Latter* (New York, 1872), 165–169, 187–188, 196–199, 239–240, 256–257, 262–264, 306–309. See also "Journals of Rachel Willard Stearns, 1834–1837," at Schlesinger Library, Radcliffe College, Cambridge, Mass. (microfilm: Research Publications, 1976); and Candy Gunther, "The Spiritual Pilgrimage of Rachel Stearns, 1834–1837: Reinterpreting Women's Religious and Social Experiences in the Methodist Revivals of Nineteenth-Century America," *Church History* 65 (Dec. 1996): 577–595.

47. J[ames] C. A. Boxer Smith to Gerrit Smith, 6 Aug. 1851, Gerrit Smith Papers, Syracuse University, transcribed in Ripley et al., *The Black Abolitionist Papers*, 1:293–301, and copied in the *Black Abolitionist Papers*, ed. George E. Carter and C. Peter Ripley (Ann Arbor, Mich., 1993), microfilm edition, 7:0036–0041 (hereafter cited as : J. C. A. Smith to G. Smith, 6 Aug. 1851).

48. Smith stated that Brown had taken the money "last may." J. C. A. Smith to G. Smith, 6 Aug. 1851.

49. J[ames] C. A. Smith to [William Lloyd] Garrison, 6 Aug. 1851, Anti-Slavery Collection, Rare Books and Manuscripts, Boston Public Library, and copied in *The Black Abolitionist Papers*, microfilm edition, 7:0034–0035 (hereafter cited as J. C. A. Smith to Garrison, 6 Aug. 1851).

50. J. C. A. Smith to G. Smith, 6 Aug. 1851; J. C. A. Smith to Garrison, 6 Aug. 1851.

51. J. C. A. Smith to G. Smith, 6 Aug. 1851.

52. J. C. A. Smith to Garrison, 6 Aug. 1851; J. C. A. Smith to G. Smith, 6 Aug. 1851.

53. J. C. A. Smith to [William Lloyd] Garrison, 12 July 1851, Anti-Slavery Collection, Boston Public Library, and copied in the *Black Abolitionist Papers*, microfilm edition, 7:0001–0002.

54. *Manchester Guardian*, 9 Aug. 1851; J. C. A. Smith to G. Smith, 6 Aug. 1851; J. C. A. Smith to Garrison, 6 Aug. 1851. The dissolution agreement is dated 25 July 1851. See also Ripley et al., *The Black Abolitionist Papers*, 1:299 n. 6. For several reasons, it seems that the letter to Gerrit Smith was written before the letter to Garrison. The letter to Smith is written on a stationary with small pages, as if James Smith did not think the letter would be so long, and the appearance of the text has a feeling of starts and stops, as if it were being composed. Though the letter was dated 6 Aug., in the text Smith said he was enclosing the issue of the *Manchester Guardian* with the notice of dissolution of the partnership, which appeared on 9 Aug., and following that were three postscripts. The letter to Garrison is on a larger page, and its penmanship is smoother, as if the writer knew what and how much he would say.

55. J. C. A. Smith to G. Smith, 6 Aug. 1851 (first, fourth, and fifth quotations); J. C. A. Smith to Garrison, 6 Aug. 1851 (second and third quotations); *Liverpool Mercury*, 20 Dec. 1850.

56. J. C. A. Smith to G. Smith, 6 Aug. 1851 (first and third quotations); J. C. A. Smith to Garrison, 6 Aug. 1851 (second and fourth quotations).

57. J. C. A. Smith to Garrison, 6 Aug. 1851; J. C. A. Smith to G. Smith, 6 Aug. 1851.

58. J. C. A. Smith to G. Smith, 6 Aug. 1851; J. C. A. Smith to Garrison, 6 Aug. 1851.

59. J. C. A. Smith to G. Smith, 6 Aug. 1851. The historians Jane H. Pease and William H. Pease, in *They Who Would Be Free: Blacks' Search for Freedom, 1830–1861* (New York, 1974), observe that "those Negroes who took the advice of their British hosts and conformed to their wishes had a much easier time" (65). Similarly, and in reference to Henry Box Brown among others, Douglas Lorimer writes: "The experience of fugitive slaves who came to England without the education and preparation in North American abolitionist circles, without experience in the arts of gracious living, and without the necessary introductions to influential Englishmen, contrasted sharply with that of their more favoured brethren." *Colour, Class, and the Victorians*, 53.

60. John Kitton to Louis Chamerovzow, 7 Apr. 1854, Anti-Slavery Papers, Bodleian Library of Commonwealth and African Studies at Rhodes House, Oxford University.

61. J. C. A. Smith to Garrison, 6 Aug. 1851.

62. Ibid. (first and fifth quotations); J. C. A. Smith to G. Smith, 6 Aug. 1851 (second, third, and fourth quotations). When the owner of Nancy Brown and the children replied to Smith in Boston and stipulated not only a price but that Brown must also "promies to treat them kindly," such pious posturing would have been received with contempt. Yet Smith, no friend of slaveholders, quoted this condition in his letters and in the letter to Gerrit Smith emphasized it with underlining. Was the slaveholder's condition an indication that Henry Brown as husband had not treated his wife kindly? If indeed Brown's marriage was troubled, a situation worsened by the conditions of slavery, Brown would not have volunteered the information in the *Narratives*. Such a marital situation, however, might help account for Brown's reluctance even in Boston to advance the redemption of his wife. On the other hand, James C. A. Smith knew enough of Brown's Richmond life to have been aware of hidden marital problems and perhaps in the heat of his dispute with Brown brought it forward. His underlining of the phrase raises a possibility only. It should be noted that members of Richmond's First African Baptist Church who abused a spouse or committed adultery could be brought before the church's deacons for discipline, and Brown's name never appears in those records.

63. The project of purchasing Brown's family may have always been pushed harder by those around him. Charles Stearns solicited funds for the purpose in a footnote to the 1849 *Narrative*, 54, and James C. A. Smith took the initiative to write the family's owner. Brown went along with their efforts but perhaps not wholeheartedly.

64. If the advertisements for the panorama are a measure, Brown did have the showman's tendency to stretch the truth. Exaggerations appeared in several advertisements for the panorama, including those published after Smith's departure, which one assumes Brown composed. An advertisement in the *Bolton Chronicle and South Lancashire Advertiser*, 8 Feb. 1851, declared that "the Scenic Representations consist of about 100 Splendid Paintings, exhibiting *Slavery as it is*." There were actually 49 scenes. If each scene were 10 feet high by 20 feet wide—it is hard to imagine them larger—the panorama would have had 9,800 square feet of canvas. A handbill for J. R. Smith's "Tour of Europe" claimed it to be "The Largest in the World! Containing Upwards of 30,000 Square Feet of Canvas," and further "The Views are 40 Feet across" (Handbill, St. Martin's Scrapbook, Leicester Square, vol. 1, no. 182, Victoria Library, Westminster Libraries and Archives, London, Eng.). "Four-mile" Smith was not one to minimize his wares. Yet an advertisement in the *Manchester Examiner & Times*, 21 Dec. 1850, stated that Brown's panorama was "Painted on 50,000 feet of canvas!"

65. J. C. A. Smith to Garrison, 6 Aug. 1851.

66. Ibid.; J. C. A. Smith to G. Smith, 6 Aug. 1851.

Chapter Eight: African Prince

1. In *The Black Abolitionist Papers, Volume I: The British Isles, 1830–1865*, ed. C. Peter Ripley et al. (Chapel Hill and London, 1985), 293, it is stated that Brown played the Staffordshire potteries during the tour of winter–spring 1851. As outlined in chap. 7 n. 33, that tour is possible, although it seems more likely that Brown's visit came during the second tour, without James C. A. Smith.

2. *Wolverhampton Chronicle*, Mar. 1852, at http://www.wolverhamptonarchives.dial.pipex.com/local_migration_18th.htm (25 Feb. 2003); *Wolverhampton & Staffordshire Herald*, 10 Mar. 1852.

3. Richard D. Altick, *The Shows of London* (Cambridge, Mass., and London, Eng., 1978), 3.

4. *Wolverhampton & Staffordshire Herald*, 28 Jan., 4 Feb., 3 Mar. 1852.

5. *Huddersfield Examiner*, 15 Feb.1862; *Preston Chronicle & Lancashire Advertiser*, 3 Apr., 20 Mar., 9 Oct. 1852.

6. *Staffordshire Advertiser*, 17 Jan. 1852; *Reading Mercury*, 21 May 1859; *Windsor and Eton Express*, 19 Feb. 1859; *Preston Chronicle & Lancashire Advertiser*, 14 Feb. 1852.

7. *Staffordshire Advertiser*, 22 Nov. 1851, 10, 17 Jan. 1852; *Macclesfield Courier and Herald*, 25 Oct. 1851; *Preston Chronicle & Lancashire Advertiser*, 14 Feb., 11 Sept. 1852; *Windsor and Eton Express*, 12 Feb. 1859; *Cardiff Times*, 1, 15 July 1864; *Berkshire Chronicle*, 30 Apr. 1859.

8. *Staffordshire Advertiser*, 20 Sept., 18 Oct. 1851, 24 Jan. 1852; *Aris's Birmingham Gazette*, 12

Jan. 1852; *Cardiff Times*, 21 Oct. 1864; *Preston Chronicle & Lancashire Advertiser*, 10 Apr. 1852; *Reading Mercury*, 16 Apr. 1859. As Richard Altick puts it: "Aware as the showmen were of the value the English temper placed upon knowledge, if only by way of lip service, at no time did their publicity wholly lack some promise of instruction" (*The Shows of London*, 3). Another combination was presented when "Dr. Wm. Child, of the Leeds Institution, gave his scientific amusements in electricity, accompanied with a splendid diorama of his four years' travels in America amongst the savage tribes of Indians. During the lecture a medical galvanizing machine was at work, for the benefit of all to prove its powers." *Preston Chronicle & Lancashire Advertiser*, 23 Oct. 1852.

9. *Preston Chronicle & Lancashire Advertiser*, 24 Apr., 2 Oct. 1852; *Bradford Observer*, 8 May 1862; *Windsor and Eton Express*, 26 Feb. 1859; *Halifax Courier*, 15 Mar. 1862. A report describes a lecture at which "the magic lantern did not act satisfactorily, no doubt owing to the impurity of the air, there being so many in the place." *Windsor and Eton Express*, 19 Mar. 1859.

10. *Bradford Observer*, 13 Mar. 1862; *Windsor and Eton Express*, 7 May 1859.

11. Harry Reynolds, *Minstrel Memories: The Story of Burnt Cork Minstrelsy in Great Britain from 1836 to 1927* (London, [1928]), 103–104; J. S. Bratton, "English Ethiopians: British Audiences and Black-Face Acts, 1835–1865," *The Yearbook of English Studies: Literature and Its Audience* II Special Number (1981): 128, 133, 139.

12. Nancy Stepan, *The Idea of Race in Science: Great Britain, 1800–1960* (Hamden, Conn., 1982), 41(on the development of new racial attitudes in Britain in the 1850s, see 20–46); Douglas A. Lorimer, *Colour, Class, and the Victorians: English Attitudes to the Negro in the Mid-Nineteenth Century* (Leicester, Eng., and New York, 1978), 160; *Preston Chronicle & Lancashire Advertiser*, 15, 22 May 1852.

13. *Carlisle Journal*, 13 Feb. 1852; E. L. Quant to Chamerovzow, Leeds, 10 Aug. 1854, Anti-Slavery Papers, MSS Brit Emp S22 G85, Bodleian Library of Commonwealth and African Studies at Rhodes House, Oxford University, Oxford, Eng. "From a glance at the enclosed circular I think it probable that you will have some recollection of me," Quant wrote.

14. Nathaniel Hawthorne, 29 June 1856, in *The English Notebooks of Nathaniel Hawthorne*, ed. Randall Stewart (New York, 1962), 367; *Wolverhampton & Staffordshire Herald*, 10 Mar. 1852.

15. *Wolverhampton & Staffordshire Herald*, 25 Feb., 4 Aug. 1852. It is within the possibility of time and place that the lecturer in this story was Brown, but it seems unlikely because his lecture was not ordinary.

16. As Brindley and Hobbs continued to speak during the performance, Yateman reproved them, to which Brindley replied, "If you insult me I'll bonnet you," and put his hand up to his hat. Yateman answered, "If you bonnet me you and I will meet again." It seems, however, that no physical altercation came about.*Wolverhampton & Staffordshire Herald*, 4 Aug. 1852; *Times* (London), 30 July 1852.

17. This and the next paragraph from *Wolverhampton & Staffordshire Herald*, 17 Mar. 1852.

18. Ibid., 24 Mar. 1852.

19. *Times* (London), 30 July 1852.

20. Ibid.

21. Ibid.

22. *London Anti-Slavery Reporter*, 2 Aug. 1852.

23. Blackett, *Building an Antislavery Wall*, 159. Douglas Lorimer, *Colour, Class and the Victorians* (53–54), interprets this episode as an example of the "ridicule and abuse" to which African American abolitionist lecturers were subject, as does Blackett (158–159). More recently, Audrey A. Fisch, *American Slaves in Victorian England: Abolitionist Politics in Popular Literature and Culture* (Cambridge, Eng., 2000), 73–83, interprets editor Brindley's articles as more an intervention to save the English public from its own bad taste than merely abuse of Brown. As some contemporary readers of newspaper accounts of the libel trial probably did, she also seems to take Brindley's characterization of Brown's showmanship to heart, suggesting that Brown's exhibitions "reveal a kind of callous complacency about any larger purpose for his work and expose the financial motivations which may have undergirded all his activities in England, even his momentary rebellion in the English courts" (81).

24. William Wells Brown to Wendell Phillips, 1 Sept. 1852, *Black Abolitionist Papers, 1830–1865,* ed. George C. Carter and C. Peter Ripley (Ann Arbor, Mich., 1993), microfilm edition, 7:0720–0721.

25. *Narrative of the Life of Henry Box Brown, Written by Himself. Second English Edition* (Bilston, Eng., 1852). The only copy of this edition that has been located is in the collections of New York Public Library. It is also cited in Samira Kawash, *Dislocating the Color Line: Identity, Hybridity, and Singularity in African-American Narrative* (Stanford, Calif., 1997), 67.

26. *The Uncle Tom's Cabin Almanack or Abolitionist Memento for 1853* (London, 1853), 4.

27. Thomas F. Gossett, *Uncle Tom's Cabin and American Culture* (Dallas, Tex., 1985), 164, 239.

28. *London Daily News,* 4 Aug. 1852, quoted in Fisch, *American Slaves in Victorian England,* 78, 130. The *Daily News* reviewer, for instance, characterized Brown's panorama as an "exaggeration," a word used both by Brindley and by the lawyer who defended him. Fisch contrasts Henry Box Brown's "buffoonery" to the "cultured" Sarah Remond (72), but her characterization of Brown's performances is based largely on Brindley's libelous articles in the *Wolverhampton & Staffordshire Herald* and the review in the *London Daily News* that probably also relied on Brindley's articles.

29. *London Morning Post,* 10 Sept. 1852, quoted in Fisch, *American Slaves in Victorian England,* 80, 130.

30. *Preston Chronicle & Lancashire Advertiser,* 11 Sept., 16 Oct., 13, 20 Nov. 1852. *The Uncle Tom's Cabin Almanack,* 72, carried an advertisement for the serially published edition of the book with Cruikshank's illustrations. An advertisement in the *Preston Chronicle & Lancashire Advertiser* on 13 Nov. 1852 claimed that *The Uncle Tom's Cabin Almanack* had already sold 20,000 copies and another on 24 Dec. proclaimed 40,000 copies sold.

31. *Preston Chronicle & Lancashire Advertiser,* 20 Nov., 11 Dec. 1852. Gossett states that "*Uncle Tom's Cabin* as a play was almost as great a popular success in many foreign countries as it had been as a novel." *Uncle Tom's Cabin and American Culture,* 281; see also 260–283, 367–387.

32. *Preston Chronicle & Lancashire Advertiser,* 27 Nov., 11 Dec. 1852; John Kitton to Louis A. Chamerovzow, 7 Apr. 1854, Anti-Slavery Papers, MSS Brit Emp S18 C33/35, Bodleian Library of Commonwealth and African Studies at Rhodes House, Oxford University.

33. This and next two paragraphs from *Preston Chronicle & Lancashire Advertiser,* 26 Feb. 1853; *Preston Pilot and County Advertiser,* 26 Feb. 1853.

34. James Stephenson, Preston, to *London Anti-Slavery Advocate,* June 1854, p. 165; *London Anti-Slavery Reporter,* 1 Apr. 1854, p. 95; 1 July 1854, p. 165. The saga of Reuben Nixon may be followed through articles in the *London Anti-Slavery Reporter,* 1 Mar., 1 Apr., 1 May, 1 July, 1 Aug., 1 Sept. 1854, 1 Aug. 1855, 2 Mar. 1857; and *London Anti-Slavery Advocate,* Aug. 1853, May, June 1854.

35. This and next two paragraphs from *London Anti-Slavery Reporter,* 1 Apr. 1854, pp. 94–96.

36. Ibid.; *London Anti-Slavery Advocate,* May 1854. Nixon's account to Chamerovzow is an interesting concoction. Although it is hard to give credence to a man who said he was incapable of speaking the truth, there is additional evidence for some parts of the tale. One writer stated, "I have no doubt he was at Sing-Sing prison, as he is able to tell many particulars which could only be known from experience" (*Anti-Slavery Reporter* 1 July 1854, p. 164.) When Henry Box Brown and James C. A. Smith were touring the northeastern United States in the summer of 1850, there were a series of frauds reported. The *North Star* had exposed an imposter in Mar. 1850 by the name of William Johnson (*North Star,* [Rochester, N.Y.], 1 Mar. 1850.) The "colored man known as Charles W. Swift," who was making appearances in the Worcester, Mass., area in Oct. 1850 turned out to be the same person as John Allen, who had been "in the eastern part of this state, and in the northerly part of this county, last June, and July." The perpetrator in these American incidents seems to have acted just as Nixon said he did in the United States, and as Nixon did do in England: a number of aliases, believable stories well-told to gullible abolitionists. Very similar to Chamerovzow's account was a report from Worcester: the man known as Swift or Allen "acknowledges the attempt to deceive, attributes it to bad advice; and promises reformation" (*Worcester Massachusetts Spy,* 30 Oct. 1850). It is not unreasonable to speculate that William Johnson, Charles W. Swift, and John Allen were different names for the same individual, Reuben Nixon, alias Andrew Baker or Charles Hill.

Nixon's story of touring with a partner exhibiting a panorama was corroborated by two letters from a correspondent in Preston, James Stephenson, who stated that he called himself Charles Hill (*London Anti-Slavery Advocate*, Aug. 1853, June 1854). Stephenson was presumably the unnamed correspondent in an article in the *Anti-Slavery Reporter* who stated that "Hill was first introduced to the Preston folks at Whitsuntide last year." *London Anti-Slavery Reporter*, July 1854, p. 165.

As for Reuben Nixon, after having in Feb. 1854 "made a clean breast of it" to Chamerovzow, he asked for help, which was provided. Nevertheless, within a few days Nixon had "robbed a coloured messmate of clothes, &c." and absconded. A scheme in Brighton was discovered, and Nixon was convicted in Mar. 1854 to three months' hard labor for being a rogue and a vagabond (*London Anti-Slavery Reporter*, 1 Apr., p. 96, 1 May 1854, pp. 108–109; *London Anti-Slavery Advocate*, May 1854, pp. 157–159). The jail term did not change his ways. A jailer named Nash wrote Chamerovzow, who was no longer forgiving and had helped prosecute Nixon: "The man of colour whom you brought to the Reformatory left of his own accord yesterday/Sunday . . . going to church—He certainly is the most consummate liar I ever met with" (Nash to Chamerovzow, 31 July 1854, Anti-Slavery Papers, MSS Brit Emp S18 C34/112, Bodleian Library of Commonwealth and African Studies at Rhodes House, Oxford University.) Articles in the antislavery papers indicate that new deceptions by Nixon plagued the antislavery movement regularly up to 1857 (*London Anti-Slavery Reporter*, 1 Aug. 1855, 2 Mar. 1857). In the epilogue to *American Slaves in Victorian England*, 95–98, Fisch recounts episodes from Nixon's continuing frauds in 1857.

37. *London Anti-Slavery Reporter*, 1 Mar. 1854, p. 60; 1 Apr., p. 95. See also Ripley et al., *The Black Abolitionist Papers*, 1:383.

38. *London Anti-Slavery Reporter*, 1 Apr. 1854, pp. 93–94. See also Ripley et al., *The Black Abolitionist Papers*, 1:383–384.

39. First African Baptist Church (Richmond, Va.), Minute Books, 1841–1930, Minutes, 1841–1859, Book 1, 16 May 1852, p. 200, Acc. 28255, Church Records Collection, Library of Virginia, Richmond. The entry reads: "May 16, 1852. Dismissed by letter J. C. A. Smith to Preston England (postage paid 24 cents)."

40. *London Anti-Slavery Reporter*, 1 May 1854, pp. 107–108; Ripley et al., *The Black Abolitionist Papers*, 1:387.

41. Kitton to L. Chamerovzow, 7 Apr. 1854, Anti-Slavery Papers, MSS Brit Emp S18 C33/35, Bodleian Library of Commonwealth and African Studies at Rhodes House, Oxford University.

42. *London Empire*, undated notice reprinted in *National Anti-Slavery Standard*, 3 Mar. 1855.

43. *Buckinghamshire Advertiser and Uxbridge Journal*, 26 Mar. 1859; *Windsor and Eton Express*, 12 Mar. 1859; *West London Observer*, 12 Mar. 1859; *Windsor and Eton* Express, 26 Mar. 1859. On the northeast coast of England, the *Newcastle Chronicle* recorded interest in the "life-like delineation of scenes of which happily in this free country we could otherwise form but a faint idea." Fisch, *American Slaves in Victorian England*, 119 n. 6.

44. *National Anti-Slavery Standard*, 3 Mar. 1855; "Autobiography of Samuel Fielden," in *The Autobiographies of the Haymarket Martyrs*, ed. Philip S. Foner (New York, 1969), 142. Other observers reported Henry Box Brown's popularity with children. The *Preston Chronicle & Lancashire Advertiser*, 25 Jan. 1851, for example, noted that "a vast number of individuals, including a great number of school children, have visited the exhibition." The *Wolverhampton & Staffordshire Herald*, 24 Mar. 1852, reprinted in the *Times* (London), 30 July 1852, referred to "the juvenile ragamuffins, who for the most part make up the . . . audiences."

Fielden's description of Henry Box Brown dates from the years between 1855, when he was eight years old, and 1860. Fielden immigrated to the United States in 1868. On 4 May 1886 he was the last speaker at a labor meeting at Haymarket Square in Chicago. There were about 200 listeners still left from a crowd of more than 1,000, when 180 policemen marched onto the scene. Fielden announced "We are peaceable." Without warning, a bomb was thrown among the policemen, killing 1, fatally wounding 6 others, and injuring about 70. The police opened fire on the audience, killing and wounding an unknown number, in what became infamous as the Haymarket Massacre. Fielden was arrested with other labor leaders, who, because they were found guilty of the bomb attack without any evidence except for their radical ideas, became known as the

Haymarket Martyrs. At first condemned to hang, Fielden's sentence was commuted to life imprisonment, and he was pardoned in 1893. Foner, *Autobiographies of the Haymarket Martyrs*, 5–10, 137, 147.

45. *West London Observer*, 19 Mar. 1859; *Cardiff Times*, 11 Mar. 1864.

46. *Wolverhampton Chronicle*, Mar. 1852, at www.wolverhamptonarchives.dial.pipex.com/local_migration_18th.htm (25 Feb. 2003).

47. *West London Observer*, 12, 19, March 1859; *Windsor and Eton Express*, 2 April 1859; *Berkshire Chronicle*, 14 May 1859.

48. This and the next paragraph from *West London Observer*, 12 Mar. 1859. The advertisement for Brown's exhibit listed the scenes of *Grand Original Panorama of African and American Slavery*. It follows the story line of the original panorama, as advertised in the *Springfield (Mass.) Republican* on its first public performances, but the following scenes from the original panorama are not listed by name: "The African Slave Trade," "Beautiful Lake and Mountain Scenery in Africa," "Chase of a Slaver by an English Steam Frigate," "Interior of a Slave Mart," "Gorgeous Scenery of the West India Islands," "View of Charleston, South Carolina," "Separation after Sale of Slaves," "Modes of Confinement and Punishment," "Women at Work," "Whipping Post and Gallows at Richmond, Va.," "Slave Prisons at Washington," "Fairmount Water Works," "Distant View of the City of Philadelphia," "Henry Bibb Escaping," "Nubian Slaves Retaken," "Tarring and Feathering in S. Carolina," "The Slaveholder's Dream," "West India Emancipation," and "Grand Industrial Palace." Because the advertisement promised "other Views too numerous to insert," the unlisted scenes may have continued to be part of Brown's panorama. On the other hand, their omission from the advertisement might also suggest that Brown had condensed the panorama to focus on his own experiences.

49. The sepoys had to bite off the end of the cartridge to load a rifle. By taking into their mouths what they believed was animal fat, the Hindu and Muslim soldiers feared that they would violate religious prescriptions and render themselves unclean, thereby losing caste and becoming subject to banishment from their communities. Christopher Hibbert, *The Great Mutiny: India, 1857* (New York, 1978), esp. 75–78.

50. *Athenaeum*, 26 Sept. 1857, p. 1213.

51. Altick, *The Shows of London*, 481; *Illustrated London News*, 8 May 1858, p. 462.

52. St. Martin's Scrapbook, Leicester Square, vol. 1, no. 181, items 192d and 192i, Victoria Library, Westminster Libraries and Archives, London, Eng.

53. *Windsor and Eton Express*, 12 Mar. 1859.

54. Ibid. The Muslim commemoration of the martyrdom of the grandson of the Prophet Mohammed takes place during Muharram, the first month of the Islamic year, and in parts of India is still observed with colorful processions. David Pinault, *Horse of Karbala: Muslim Devotional Life in India* (New York, 2001), esp. 11–21.

55. *Windsor and Eton Express*, 12 Mar. 1859; *West London Observer*, 12 Mar. 1859.

56. *West London Observer*, 12 Mar. 1859.

57. Ibid., 19 Mar. 1859.

58. This and the next paragraph from ibid., 19 Mar. 1859. The newspaper stated that the procession "presented a scene that, with the exception of the Trades' memorials to the late lamented Queen Caroline, was never before witnessed in Hammersmith."

59. *Buckinghamshire Advertiser and Uxbridge Journal*, 26 Mar. 1859.

60. *Windsor and Eton Express*, 2, 9 Apr. 1859.

61. *Reading Mercury*, 23 Apr., 14 May 1859; *Berkshire Chronicle*, 14 May 1859.

62. *Leigh Chronicle*, 11, 18 Jan. 1862; *Halifax Courier*, 8 Mar. 1862; *Buckinghamshire Advertiser and Uxbridge Journal*, 26 Mar. 1859. None of the reports about Brown from the 1860s that have been located mention Mrs. Brown, and it is unknown if she accompanied him on the road. Perhaps their daughter Annie was too young to travel during the early 1860s, and Mrs. Brown stayed home with her.

63. *Huddersfield Examiner*, 1, 8 Mar., 5 Apr. 1862. See also *Halifax Courier*, 15 Mar. 1862. MacKenzie, said to have been about 18 years old, appeared at Huddersfield, Holmfirth, Lockwood, and Slaithwaite. "The lecturer stated that the present internecine war in the United States

was in reality, if not avowedly, a war of slavery," reported the *Huddersfield Examiner*, 8 Mar. 1862, and "that the black was as capable of appreciating liberty as well as his whiter complexioned fellow being."

64. A. Lawrence Kocher and Howard Dearstyne, *Shadows in Silver: A Record of Virginia, 1850–1900, in Contemporary Photographs Taken by George and Huestis Cook with Additions from the Cook Collection* (New York, 1954), 7–8.

65. *Bristol Daily Post*, 1 Jan. 1864. The newspaper identified Brown as "a coloured person, in whom, doubtless many readers will recognize an individual who travelled the country some years ago with a panorama of Uncle Tom's Cabin, stating himself to be a freed slave or runaway."

66. On Franz Anton Mesmer, see Vincent Buranelli, *The Wizard from Vienna* (New York, 1975), esp. 13–37; Alan Gauld, *A History of Hypnotism* (Cambridge, Eng., 1992), 1–22; John C. Hughes and Andrew E. Rothovius, *The World's Greatest Hypnotists* (Lanham, Md., New York, and London, Eng., 1996), 13–60; and Maurice M. Tinterow, *Foundations of Hypnosis: From Mesmer to Freud* (Springfield, Ill., 1970), 31–57.

67. James Braid's lecture, "Practical Essay on the Curative Agency of Neuro-Hypnotism" (1842), was incorporated into his 1843 book, *Neurypnology; or, the Rationale of Nervous Sleep Considered in Relation with Animal Magnetism* (London, 1843). Excerpts appear in Tinterow, *Foundations of Hypnosis*, 269–316. Braid's contributions are also discussed in Gauld, *History of Hypnotism*, 279–287, and Hughes and Rothovius, *World's Greatest Hypnotists*, 133–141. On the *Zoist*, see Frank Podmore, *Mesmerism and Christian Science: A Short History of Mental Healing* (London, 1909), 143. Podmore states that the English mystical mesmerists, beginning in 1853 with the introduction from the United States of "table-turning and spirit-rapping," evolved into Spiritualists. Later evolutions included theosophy and Christian Science (150).

68. William B. Carpenter, *Mesmerism, Spiritualism, &c.: Historically & Scientifically Considered . . .* (New York, 1889), 35–36. See also Podmore, *Mesmerism and Christian Science*, 148–149, and Hughes and Rothovius, *World's Greatest Hypnotists*, 160–162. At the "Concert Hall, Lord Nelson-Street," Liverpool, G. W. Stone played 8 and 11 Nov. 1850; Brown played from 12 Nov. through 29 Nov. 1850; Stone played 2 Dec.; Brown 3 Dec.; Stone 4 Dec.; Brown 5 and 6 Dec. 1850 (*Liverpool Mercury*, 8, 12, 15, 19, 22, 26 Nov., 3 Dec. 1850). Professor Chadwick appeared in Wolverhampton in Feb. 1852, only a month before Brown's marked exhibition there, and was in Preston in Jan. 1853, a month before Brown's second Preston exhibition. In 1859 Chadwick and Brown were in West London at the same time. See *Wolverhampton & Staffordshire Herald*, 25 Feb. 1852; *Preston Chronicle & Lancashire Advertiser*, 29 Jan. 1853; *Windsor and Eton Express*, 29 Jan., 5, 12 Feb., 12 Mar. 1859.

69. *Windsor and Eton Express*, 12 Mar. 1859.

70. *Cardiff Times*, 11 Mar. 1864. On southern Wales during that period, see David Williams, *A History of Modern Wales* (London, 1950), 213–228.

71. *Merthyr Star*, 10 Mar. 1864.

72. Ibid.

73. *Bristol Daily Post*, 5 Aug. 1864; *Cardiff and Merthyr Guardian*, 12 Aug. 1864; *Cardiff Times*, 12 Aug. 1864.

74. Handbill, "PROF. H. B. BROWN," ca. 1875–1878, reproduced in David Price, *Magic: A Pictorial History of Conjurers in the Theater* (New York, London, and Toronto, 1985), 58. The text of the handbill lists "various entertainments" that Brown had presented in England: "the Panorama of American Slavery, the Holy Land, the great Indian Mutiny, the great war between the North and South, Mesmeric Entertainments."

Chapter Nine: American Reprise

1. Readers of antislavery newspapers knew that Brown and James C. A. Smith had arrived at Liverpool, as reported by the *Anti-Slavery Bugle*, 21 Dec. 1850, and the *National Anti-Slavery Standard*, 26 Dec. 1850. Mention of their exhibitions appeared on 20 Mar. 1851 in the *Standard*. A brief report of the May 1851 Bradford-to-Leeds box trip appeared in the *National Anti-Slavery Standard*, 19 June 1851, and the *Liberator*, 11 July 1851. The *Standard* article was apparently

based on the 24 May 1851 article in the *Leeds Mercury*, while the *Liberator*'s article drew from the *Standard*.

No public mention has been found of James C. A. Smith's summer 1851 letters to Gerrit Smith and William Lloyd Garrison, describing the split of the partnership. An account of Brown's libel suit against the *Wolverhampton & Staffordshire Herald* appeared in the *New York Times*, 13 Aug. 1852, based on the *Times* (London), 30 July 1852. The *New York Times* article noted, with an exclamation point, "In the course of the hearing it came out that Brown was making from £50 to £70 per week!" The final report on Brown found in the American press was a reprint of an undated article from the *London Empire* in the *National Anti-Slavery Standard*, 3 Mar. 1855.

2. *Richmond Whig*, 20 Feb. 1854; *Report of the Special Committee to Investigate the Conduct of C. S. Morgan*, Doc. 58, *Journal and Documents of the House of Delegates of the State of Virginia for the Session 1853–4* (Richmond, 1853–1854), 33, 36. In Apr. 1853 a miscreant named Jack Norvall was called to the front of the Virginia State Penitentiary shoe shop to be punished. As the prisoner walked forward he took "a sharp pointed shoe knife in his hand, concealed under his apron." When the Norvall passed the cutting board where Samuel Smith "stood unarmed," he seized Smith "with one hand, and commenced cutting him with the knife in the other." Before Norvall could be stopped Smith was "wounded in five or six places," one blow scraping a rib and barely missing his heart. Colonel Charles S. Morgan, the superintendent of the penitentiary, personally tended his wounds. With no system for parole, pardons were commonly given. Morgan prepared a petition for pardon, had it circulated, and advocated the pardon before the board that forwarded recommendations to the governor. *Report of the Special Committee*, 33.

Morgan's efforts to obtain a pardon for Smith became an issue in the Virginia legislature when Morgan was renominated for superintendent. A delegate defended him by stating "he was not prepared to believe that [Col. Morgan] had any sympathy with the Abolitionists." (*Richmond Whig*, 11 Feb. 1854.) Morgan was from western Virginia and thought the charge "was intended to affect other gentlemen like myself, whose nativity is beyond the blue mountains." The governor's comment was said to be "I can't, and I won't pardon him!" (*New York Tribune*, 17 July 1856, reprinted in William Still, *The Underground Rail Road* (Philadelphia, 1872; reprint, Chicago, 1970), 71–73) The House of Delegates appointed a "Special Committee to Investigate the Conduct of C. S. Morgan," which held three days of hearings. The committee's *Report* (3) rebuked Morgan for seeking the pardon of Smith but cleared him of the more serious allegations. "Mere industry and orderly behavior" or even "a crime on his person" were not sufficient to pardon because "the highest considerations of public policy require the utmost vigilance in detecting and strictness in punishing crimes of this class." The *Richmond Whig*, 20 Feb. 1854, reported that the matter had "entirely subsided," and Morgan was "quietly" reelected as superintendent.

In his own testimony to the committee, Morgan rejected "the charge of abolition" brought "because I have had the temerity to do an act of simple justice to a prisoner, who had periled his life in obedience to my orders." He concluded in direct and dramatic fashion: "Here is the knife with which the carotid artery of one of my officers was separated by a free negro, and from which he died in a few minutes. . . . I also present the knife with which Norvall attempted to assassinate Smith in April last, from which you will be able to appreciate the true dangers of rebellions and attempts at assassination in prison; and you can judge for yourselves of my responsibility and duty in reference to them." *Report of the Special Committee*, 35.

3. *New York Tribune*, 17 July 1856. Sawney, one of the two slaves Samuel Smith had attempted to ship, and the one who had cooperated with the authorities, afterward became the property of one Constable Butler. On 3 June 1856, with Samuel A. Smith's release from prison imminent, Butler sold Sawney south. The *Richmond Whig* identified Sawney as "one of those whom 'Red Boot' Smith boxed up some years ago," and reported that Sawney "goes to Atlanta, Ga." (*Richmond Whig*, 4 June 1856). The timing of the sale of Sawney might have been coincidental, or it might have been a measure of the deep unease that a Samuel Smith caused slaveholders, as if, once released, he would have proved an irresistible Pied Piper.

As for the lady who had "remained faithful" to Smith, at a hearing after his arrest in 1849 a woman identified as "Miss Catharine Dolbow" testified "that she had been living with Mr. Smith about six months. She was not his wife." She said that on the morning of the failed escape she had eaten "breakfast with Smith upstairs." *Richmond Semi-weekly Whig*, 9 May 1849.

4. Robert V. Hine, "An Artist Draws the Line," *American Heritage* 19 (Feb. 1968): 29–35, 102–103. esp. 102; *Liberator*, 27 July 1855. John Russell Bartlett was appointed U.S. commissioner to survey the borderline with Mexico. Bartlett also made drawings of the border, and in Mar. 1852 hired two San Francisco artists, one of them the so-called Henry Box Brown, "to render some of his field sketches into finished water colors, and further commissioned Brown to go into the upper Sacramento Valley to draw scenes of Indian life there." Brown's sketches are at the University of California at Berkeley. Hine, "An Artist Draws the Line" (102).

5. *The Boston Slave Riot, and Trial of Anthony Burns* (Boston, 1854). A truer-to-life portrait of Anthony Burns, "drawn by Barry from a daguereotype [*sic*] by Whipple and Black," appears on a Boston broad sheet of 1855 held at the Library of Congress and reproduced in Bernard F. Reilly Jr., *American Political Prints, 1766–1876: A Catalog of the Collections in the Library of Congress* (Boston, 1991), 389. An organized mob assaulted the federal courthouse in Boston to free Anthony Burns, though in vain, and at his trial distinguished lawyers argued Burns's unsuccessful defense. When he was to be transferred from the courthouse to the southbound ship in the harbor, a huge crowd gathered and the way had to be cleared by troops: "Twenty-two companies, including two of cavalry, and not less than a thousand soldiers" (Charles Emery Stevens, *Anthony Burns: A History* [Boston, 1856; reprint New York, 1969], 134). In addition to their shared portrait and that both escaped from Richmond, Anthony Burns was linked to Brown in another way. After Burns was returned to Richmond, sympathizers in Massachusetts learned of his whereabouts and purchased his freedom. In Aug. 1858 Anthony Burns wrote to William Lloyd Garrison that he was "now in Maine, making preparations to travel with a panorama, styled the Grand Moving Mirror—scenes of real life, startling and thrilling incidents, degradation and horrors of American slavery—for the purpose of selling my book, a narrative." A letter to the *Liberator* three weeks later reported that "Mr. Burns is now travelling with the 'Moving Mirror of American Slavery,'— an exhibition giving truthful representations of slavery, by one of the best artists in America." The letter stated that "Mr. B. is engaged evenings in describing these panoramic scenes to large audiences," and that "Mr. B. will travel with the Exhibition in New Hampshire and Massachusetts during the coming fall and winter," but there is no information on his success (*Liberator*, 13 Aug., 3 Sept. 1858). See also "Burns, Anthony," *Dictionary of Virginia Biography: Volume Two, Bland–Cannon* (Richmond, 2001), 417–418.

Other moving panoramas presented by African Americans are discussed by Allan D. Austin in a letter to the *Massachusetts Review* 37 (winter 1996–1997): 636–639. For one example, in a May 1855 advertisement in *Frederick Douglass' Paper*, J. N. Still, of Brooklyn, Long Island, sought venues for the "Diorama of Uncle Tom's Cabin." The paintings were by "an eminent French artist, and show as large as life." In seeking venues, Still proposed a fifty-fifty split with any church or society "who will provide a place, secure an audience, and defray the expences." Still was likely William Still's brother John N. Still. On 31 May 1855, the *Diorama of Uncle Tom's Cabin* was presented at the African Methodist Episcopal Church on Bridge Street in Brooklyn. On 5 June it was shown at Dr. Pennington's Church on Prince Street in New York City. The extent and success of Still's tour with the panorama is not known. *Frederick Douglass' Paper*, 25 May 1855; George C. D. Odell, *Annals of the New York Stage* (New York, 1931), 6:422, 412.

6. *Richmond Dispatch*, 9 June 1870; *Petersburg Daily Courier*, 11 June 1870. The name "Red Boot Smith" was a mocking one and was used to refer to Samuel Smith only in Richmond and Virginia.

7. Still, *The Underground Rail Road*; *New York Times*, 18 Apr. 1872. The *Times* reviewer criticized Still for the "error of making too large a book." Lurey Khan, *One Day, Levin . . . He Be Free: William Still and the Underground Railroad* (New York, 1972), 216. Khan's book is the kind that provides invented dialogue. Still became a successful businessman, operating a coal yard on Washington Avenue in Philadelphia. At the 1876 Philadelphia Centennial Exhibition, Still displayed *The Underground Rail Road* "in various styles of binding" in a glass case (212, 224).

In 1856 Still mentioned "the noted Henry Box Brown" in a letter published by the *National Anti-Slavery Standard*, 2 Feb. 1856, and by the *London Anti-Slavery Reporter*, 1 May 1856.

8. Still, *The Underground Rail Road*, 67–73. The book's account is mostly a word-for-word rendition of William Still's speech text of 1870, but also folds in new material about Miller McKim and Samuel Smith. It seems likely that between his 1870 speech and the final preparation of *The Underground Rail Road*, Still had a conversation with McKim. In the speech, Still had himself going to the railroad station to look for a box, while in the book it was, as was accurate, McKim. Also, with the passage of more than twenty years since "the marvellous resurrection of Brown," Still in his account confused a few elements of the story. At one point he referred to "James A. Smith, a shoe dealer," when it was Samuel A. Smith who was the shoe dealer, not James C. A. Smith. Still also said that during the second failed attempt the two boxes containing the "heroic young fugitives" were "some distance on the road" when they were captured. In reality they never left the station. Overall, Still's account fits well with Miller McKim's closer-to-the-event reports of Brown's arrival (70, 68, 71).

9. Handbill, "PROF. H. B. BROWN," ca. 1875–1878, reproduced in David Price, *Magic: A Pictorial History of Conjurers in the Theater* (New York, London, and Toronto, 1985), 58.

10. Sidney W. Clarke, *The Annals of Conjuring* (London, 1924–1928), 15:86, published serially in the *Magic Wand and Magical Review*, vols. 13–17, 1924–1928, a bound compilation in the Manus-Young Collection, Rare Book and Special Collections, Library of Congress; Thomas Frost, *The Lives of the Conjurers*, new ed. (London, 1881; reprint, Ann Arbor, Mich., 1971), 261–262; Price, *Magic*, 58. A good overview of the history of theatrical magic is Steven S. Tigner, "Magic and Magicians," in *Handbook of American Popular Culture*, ed. M. Thomas Inge, 2d ed., rev. and enl. (Westport, Conn., 1989), 671–720.

11. Geoffrey Lamb, *Victorian Magic* (London, 1976), xi; Clarke, *The Annals of Conjuring*, 15:125; Frost, *The Lives of the Conjurers*, 259; *Liverpool Mercury*, 8, 15, 19, 22, 26 Nov. 1850. See also Milbourne Christopher, *The Illustrated History of Magic* (New York, 1973), 131–154, for Robert-Houdin, and 111–130 for Anderson. Robert-Houdin did have a second run in London in 1853, but the odds of Brown's having seen him are much less than for the performers who played Britain more extensively. Brown may have never seen any of the magicians here mentioned, and drawn instead from less well known performers; it was the nature of the field, however, that those magicians had probably seen and borrowed from the top names. Directly or indirectly, the premier conjurers influenced all.

A third magician who played London in 1848 (presenting an act "pirated" from Robert-Houdin) was the German Carl Herrmann. In time, Herrmann's model was important for modern magic when he came to rely less on sets and props and more on a presentation of unadorned sleight-of-hand, the more amazing for the lack of gadgetry. He also performed in evening dress rather than the traditional wizard's robes. Brown could have seen Herrmann when he appeared in England in 1863 and 1872. Christopher, *The Illustrated History of Magic*, 181–190.

12. Christopher, *The Illustrated History of Magic*, 68, 190–196; Tigner, "Magic and Magicians," 675; Clarke, *The Annals of Conjuring*, 15:198–199; Henry Ridgely Evans, *The Old and the New Magic*, 2d ed., rev. and enl. (Chicago, 1909), 188–200. Alexander Herrmann was the younger brother of Carl Herrmann.

13. Handbill, "PROF. H. B. BROWN," ca. 1875–1878, in Price, *Magic*, 58; Parker Pillsbury, *Acts of the Anti-Slavery Apostles* (Boston, 1884), 485.

14. Andrew Ward, *Dark Midnight When I Rise: The Story of the Jubilee Singers Who Introduced the World to the Music of Black America* (New York, 2000), 159–168, 188–200, esp. 198–199.

15. *Pittsfield Sun*, 29 Nov. 1875, 14 June 1876; *Concord (N.H.) Daily Monitor*, 1 Feb. 1876; *Providence Evening Press*, 17, 20 Mar. 1876. An advertisement for Sheppard's Jubilee Singers (*Pittsfield Sun*, 29 Nov. 1875) stated, "These singers make no pretentions to musical abilities, they being unable to read or write."

16. *Worcester Daily Spy*, 15 Mar., 15 Jan., 21 Mar. 1878; *Pittsfield Sun*, 14 Feb., 3 May 1877; *Providence Journal*, 15 Jan. 1876; *Concord (N.H.) Daily Monitor*, 15 Feb. 1876.

17. *Pittsfield Sun*, 3 Nov., 22 Dec. 1875, 12 Apr., 23 Aug. 1876, 28 Feb., 7 Mar., 9 May 1877; *Springfield Republican*, 16, 23 Nov. 1875, 1, 6 Jan. 1876.

18. Handbill, "PROF. H. B. BROWN," ca. 1875–1878, in Price, *Magic*, 58; *Worcester Evening Gazette*, 29 Dec. 1877, 1, 2 Jan. 1878.

19. *Worcester Evening Gazette*, 9 Jan. 1878.

20. Handbill, "PROF. H. B. BROWN," ca. 1875–1878, in Price, *Magic*, 58. For the Browns' operation, advertising in a newspaper might have been an occasional luxury. A survey of Boston newspapers for items about conjurers, researched and written by H. J. Moulton for Harry Houdini, *Houdini's History of Magic in Boston, 1792–1915* (Glenwood, Ill., 1983), contains no reference to Henry Box Brown.

21. Price, *Magic*, 11 (second quotation), 58 (first quotation); Jean Robert-Houdin cited in Henry Ridgely Evans, *Magic and Its Professors* (New York, 1902), 37.

22. Handbill, "PROF. H. B. BROWN," ca. 1875–1878, in Price, *Magic*, 58; Frost, *The Lives of the Conjurers*, 332–333; Christopher, *The Illustrated History of Magic*, 155–156.

23. Christopher, *The Illustrated History of Magic*, 155–156; Frost, *The Lives of the Conjurers*, 352 (the first edition of the book was published in 1876); *Worcester Evening Gazette*, 24 Jan. 1878.

24. Handbill, "PROF. H. B. BROWN," ca. 1875–1878, in Price, *Magic*, 58.

25. Evans, *The Old and the New Magic*, 201–202 (the first edition was published in 1906).

26. James Freeman Clarke, *Anti-Slavery Days: A Sketch of the Struggle Which Ended in the Abolition of Slavery in the United States* (New York, 1883; reprint, Westport, Conn., 1970), 94; Booker T. Washington, N. B. Wood, and Fannie Barrier Williams, *A New Negro for a New Century* (Chicago, [1900]; reprint, New York, 1969), 193–194; Mifflin Wistar Gibbs, *Shadow and Light: An Autobiography with Reminiscences of the Last and Present Century* (Washington, D.C., 1902; reprint, Lincoln, Neb., and London, Eng., 1995), 13–14. Gibbs remembered Brown as "William Box Brown."

Other early accounts of Brown drawn from William Still's memoir *The Underground Rail Road* include H. F. Kletzing and W. H. Crogman, *Progress of a Race; or, The Remarkable Advancement of the Afro-American* (Atlanta, 1897; reprint, New York, 1969), 108–111, and J. W. Gibson and W. H. Crogman, *The Colored American from Slavery to Honorable Citizenship* (Atlanta, 1903), 98–101.

27. *Illustrated Richmond Police and Fire Department Directory* (Richmond, [1896]), 21; "How 'Red Boot' Smith Finally Was Unmasked," *Richmond News Leader*, 20 Nov. 1903. Much of the story in the *Directory* came from an 1855 murder case involving a man named Francis Auburn (see *Richmond Daily Enquirer*, 15 Oct. 1855, and *Richmond Daily Dispatch*, 15 Oct. 1855). The story grafted the supposed shipment of slaves "in boxes and barrels" to the Auburn case. *Illustrated Richmond Police Directory*, 21.

A century later, the Richmond press has been more positive. "Remembering a Hero: Henry 'Box' Brown," appeared in the *Richmond Free Press*, 24–26 Feb. 1994, and the *Richmond Times-Dispatch* published a profile on 17 Feb. 1998 by Stacy Hawkins Adams, "Henry 'Box' Brown." Included in the development of the "Canal Walk" on the Richmond river front is the commemoration of Brown and the Underground Railroad through "a bronze re-creation" of his box near Dock and Fifteenth Streets, where a bronze medallion on the walk quotes Brown on what he would do to be free: "Buoyed up by the prospect of freedom . . . I was willing to dare even death itself." http://www.richmondriverfront.com/historical_exhibits.shtml (19 Feb. 2003).

28. Henrietta Buckmaster, *Let My People Go: The Story of the Underground Railroad and the Growth of the Abolition Movement* (New York and London, 1941), 164–165; Herbert Aptheker, *The Negro in the Abolitionist Movement* (New York, 1941), 16–18; Benjamin Quarles, *Frederick Douglass* (Washington, D.C., 1948), 113–114; Larry Gara, *The Liberty Line: The Legend of the Underground Railroad* (Lexington, Ky., 1961), 49–50.

29. Charles L. Blockson, "Escape From Slavery: The Underground Railroad," *National Geographic* 166, no. 1 (July 1984): 10–11 (quotation 11); "Great Escapes: Henry 'Box' Brown," http://tlc.discovery.com/convergence/escape/stories/stories_2.html (20 Feb. 2003); Henry Ford Museum and Greenfield Village, "Living under Enslavement: African Americans on Hermitage Plantation," http://www.hfmgv.org/education/smartfun/hermitage/house/box.html (20 Feb. 2003); B&O Railroad Museum, Baltimore, http://www.borail.org/slide12.asp (2/20/03); Donovan Webster, "Traveling the Long Road to Freedom, One Step at a Time," *Smithsonian* 27, no. 7 (Oct. 1996): 48–60; Alison Freehling, "Underground Railroad: Student Actors Relive the Flight of Slaves," *Richmond Times-Dispatch*, 25 Feb. 2000, originally published in the *Newport News Daily*

Press, 23 Feb. 2000, as "HU Students Remember Dangerous Run to Freedom."

30. Langston Hughes and Milton Meltzer, *A Pictorial History of the Negro in America* (New York, 1956), 131; Harnett T. Kane, *Gone Are the Days: An Illustrated History of the Old South* (New York, 1960), 269; Bernard F. Reilly Jr., *American Political Prints, 1766–1876: A Catalog of the Collections in the Library of Congress* (Boston, 1991), 332–333; Barbara Payne, "Underground Railroad Story Quilt," Friends of Freedom Society, Ohio Underground Railroad Association, http://www.fofs-oura.org/story.htm (19 Feb. 2003); Roland Owen Laird Jr. and Taneshia Nash Laird, *Still I Rise: A Cartoon History of African Americans* (New York and London, 1997), 88; Christopher Corbett, "In Search of Baltimore's African-American Roots," *Washington Post*, 25 Feb. 1996.

Great Blacks in Wax Museum, http://www.roadsideamerica.com/map/md.html (19 Feb. 2003) showing Brown in the box; Paul Reyes, "Strange Fruit: The Dream of Elmer Martin," *Oxford American* 41 (fall 2001): 62–70, esp. 64, 65; Sara B. Bearss, *The Story of Virginia: An American Experience* (Richmond, 1995), 30; Mark St. John Erickson, "Interpreting the War: Three Exhibits Add Historical Meaning to Civil War Artifacts," *Newport News Daily Press*, 4 July 1993; http://www.valentinemuseum.com/index.html (24 Mar. 2003); Uncle Tom's Cabin Historic Site, "Follow the North Star," http://www.uncletomscabin.org/follow.htm (19 Feb. 2003); "Mayor Finds Himself in a Tight Spot," in "Street Talk," *Style Weekly*, 16 Oct. 2001, p. 8. See also Jeremy M. Lazarus, "Sunday Will Mark 154th Anniversary of His Amazing Escape to Freedom: 'Box' Brown," in "Cityscape," *Richmond Free Press*, 20–22 Mar. 2003, A2.

31. Samira Kawash, *Dislocating the Color Line: Identity, Hybridity, and Singularity in African-American Narrative* (Stanford, Calif., 1997), 23, 65–66, 68. Kawash explains Brown "as first man" as derived from his carrier, "Adam's Express" (229 n. 90).

32. Arthur Huff Fauset, *For Freedom: A Biographical Story of the American Negro* (Philadelphia, 1927), 60–61; Fran Pelham and Bernadette Balcer, "This Side Up Ship to Philadelphia," in *In the Shadow of an Eagle, and Other Adventure Stories*, compiled by the Editors of *Highlights for Children* (Honesdale, Penn., 1992), 27–31; Virginia Hamilton, *Many Thousand Gone: African Americans from Slavery to Freedom* (New York, 1993, 92–95); Dennis Brindell Fradin, *Bound for the North Star: True Stories of Fugitive Slaves* (New York, 2000); Mack Lewis, "The Daring Escape of Henry 'Box' Brown," *Storyworks* 8, no. 5 (Feb. 2001): 26; "Greater Hartford Academy of the Arts presents a staged reading of "Box" . . . in the Black Box Theater on the Learning Corridor campus," 13–14 Dec. 2002, http://www.thevoicenews.com/News/2002/1213/Entertainment_Directory/ (24 Mar. 2003); Veni Fields, " 'Oh Freedom!' Educates in an Entertaining Style: Virginia Opera Sings Praises of America's Often Unsung Black Civil Rights Heroes," *Norfolk Virginian-Pilot*, 2 Mar. 2001.

33. Marcus Wood, " 'All Right!': The Narrative of Henry Box Brown as a Test Case for the Racial Prescription of Rhetoric and Semiotics," *Proceedings of the American Antiquarian Society* 107 (1997): 72, citing Henry James, *A Small Boy and Others* (London, 1913), 167. Benjamin Quarles reviewed the "cultural adoption" (Wood, "'All Right!,'" 72) of Harriet Tubman in his essay, "Harriet Tubman's Unlikely Leadership," in *Black Leaders of the Nineteenth Century*, ed. Leon Litwack and August Meier (Urbanna and Chicago, 1988), 55–57.

34. Patricia Khayyam, "The Power of 'Images,'" *Muslim Journal*, 22 Nov. 1991, p. 5; Charles H. Parsons, "Opera Review: Gary Sheldon—Concert Review, Vanqui and Opera Columbus" *Opera Magazine* (July 1999); Barbara Zuck, "Trio of Dreams about to Come True on Opera Stage," *Columbus Dispatch*, 21 Feb. 1999, http://www.dispatch.com/news/newsfea99/feb99/barb0221.html (26 Feb. 2003); Sue Swyers Moncure, "Original Play Traces 'Delaware's Road to Freedom," *University of Delaware UpDate*, 19 Feb. 1998, http://www.udel.edu/PR/UpDate/98/20/orginal.html# (19 Feb. 2003); Robert W. McDowell, "Manbites Dog Presents an Awe-inspiring *One Noble Journey*," *Spectator Online*, 1 Mar. 2000, http://members.tripod.com/mikewiley/ main_heading_goes_here_subheadin.htm (24 Feb. 2003) and a second review at this site: http://www.indyweek.com/durham/2000-03-01/ae3.html (24 Feb. 2003); see "Tony Kushner," http://www.bedfordstmartins.com/litlinks/drama/kushner.htm (19 Feb. 2003); Peter Marks, "Light Diet, Heavy Plans," in "On Stage, and Off," *New York Times*, 28 June 1996; Elizabeth Alexander, "Passages," in *Body of Life* (Chicago, 1996); Lamont B. Steptoe, "Of Slavery, Exile and Freedom,"

in *In the Kitchens of the Master* (Manasquan, N.J., 1997); A. Van Jordan, "The Journey of Henry Box Brown," in *Rise* (Chicago, 2001); Kimberly Rae Connor, *"To Disembark*: The Slave Narrative Tradition," *African American Review* 30 (spring 1996): 35–57 (Ligon's "To Disembark" premiered at the Hirshhorn Museum and Sculpture Garden in Washington, D.C., 11 Nov. 1993–20 Feb. 1994. "Smart Stuff of One Self," in "On Exhibit," *Washington Post*, 26 Nov. 1993, Weekend Section, 73–74); Moira Roth and Portia Cobb, "An Interview with Pat Ward Williams," *Afterimage* 16 (Jan. 1989): 5–7 (quotation on 7).

35. John W. Blassingame, ed., *Slave Testimony: Two Centuries of Letters, Speeches, Interviews, and Autobiographies* (Baton Rouge, La., 1977), xxxiv; Blassingame, *The Slave Community: Plantation Life in the Antebellum South*, rev. and enl. ed. (New York and Oxford, 1979), 374; Charles Stearns, *Narrative of Henry Box Brown* (Boston, [1849]; reprint, Philadelphia, 1969); William Still, *The Underground Rail Road* (Philadelphia, 1872; reprint, Chicago, 1970); *The Black Abolitionist Papers, Volume I: The British Isles, 1830–1865*, ed. C. Peter Ripley et al. (Chapel Hill and London, 1985); George E. Carter and C. Peter Ripley, comps. and eds., *Black Abolitionist Papers, 1830–1865* (Ann Arbor, Mich., 1993), 17 microfilm reels; *Narrative of Henry Box Brown* (Boston, [1849]) (electronic edition, University of North Carolina at Chapel Hill Libraries), http://docsouth.unc.edu/neh/boxbrown/menu.html [19 Feb. 2003]); *Narrative of the Life of Henry Box Brown* (Manchester, 1851) (electronic edition, University of North Carolina at Chapel Hill Libraries, http://docsouth.unc.edu/brownbox/menu.html (24 Feb. 2003); John Ernest, ed., *Shadowing Slavery: Five African American Autobiographical Narratives* (Acton, Mass., 2002); Richard Newman, ed., *Narrative of the Life of Henry Box Brown* (New York, 2002).

36. R. J. M. Blackett, *Building an Antislavery Wall: Black Americans in the Atlantic Abolitionist Movement, 1830–1860* (Baton Rouge, La., and London, Eng., 1983); Cynthia Griffin Wolff, "Passing Beyond the Middle Passage: Henry 'Box' Brown's Translations of Slavery," *Massachusetts Review* 37 (spring 1996): 23–44 (quotations on 33); Audrey A. Fisch, *American Slaves in Victorian England: Abolitionist Politics in Popular Literature and Culture* (Cambridge, Eng., 2000). Fisch's otherwise valuable work is marred by her conception of Brown's performances as "buffoonery" (9). See also James Haskins and Kathleen Benson, *Conjure Times: Black Magicians in America* (New York, 2001).

37. Marcus Wood, *Blind Memory: Visual Representations of Slavery in England and America, 1780–1865* (Manchester, Eng., and New York, 2000), 103–117 (quotations on 103, 106, 116, and 107); Wood, " 'All Right!': The Narrative of Henry Box Brown as a Test Case," 73. A few of Wood's conclusions suffer from confusion about the Henry Box Brown bibliography. For instance, Wood states that a quotation in *Cousin Ann's Stories For Children* (1849), "appears to be based directly on a reading of the first English edition" of Brown's *Narrative* (116), published two years later in 1851. Wood also subjects the text about Brown in the *Liberty Almanac for 1851* (New York, 1850) to close analysis (112–114) without realizing that it was mostly a reprint of the article in the *Burlington (Vt.) Courier*, 12 Apr. 1849, an account that was likely at best thirdhand.

Index